365 Moments of Grace

Jodi Chapman, Dan Teck

& Over 250 Soulful Contributors

DandiLove Unlimited

This book comes from our hearts and is here to support you in connecting with grace-filled moments in your life. Please know, though, that it is not a replacement for therapy or medical advice. If you are feeling like you could use some extra support, please seek out a professional in your area.

The authors who contributed to this book are from all corners of the world, and we have kept their native English spelling for each of their pieces. For this reason, you will see words like "color" and "colour" or "realized" and "realised" throughout the book – just depending on what part of the world the author is from. We also wanted to find a balance of maintaining consistency throughout the book while still honoring each author's belief system. For this reason, you will see that some words are capitalized in some pieces and not in others. For the most part, we capitalize words relating to God, Source, the Universe, and a Higher Power.

Ordering information available at:
www.365momentsofgrace.com.
For wholesale inquiries, please write to: info@365bookseries.com.

Printed in the United States of America
ISBN: 13-978-0-9893137-9-7
Library of Congress Control Number: 2016932203

www.365bookseries.com

DEDICATION

We would like to dedicate this book to each of the contributing authors who wrote from the heart and, in doing so, opened up all of our hearts to what's possible.

We would also like to dedicate this book to every single person who has experienced a moment of grace and has shared it with someone else. In doing so, you helped another open up to the magic in our amazing world. And we thank you.

Table of Contents

Chapter 2 – Physical Shake-Ups & Near-Death Experiences .. 53

Chapter 6 – Loving Grace **185**

Introduction

Welcome! We're so glad that you're here with us and that you're making time to surround yourself with love, positivity, and most of all...grace! It's our intention that while reading this book you'll feel uplifted with a knowing that there are miracles everywhere and that we live in a truly magical world. It's honestly hard not to believe that this is true after reading story after story on the pages that follow – each filled with goosebump-producing experiences.

One of the things that we most love about this book is the variety of grace-filled moments that are shared. Over 250 co-authors came together to create this book – each of whom is unique. We are spread out all over the world, speak different languages, have different professions, follow different religions, are different races, have unique points of view and experiences...our list of differences goes on and on. Yet we all have one common thread that holds us together: loving grace. Each of us has access to this gift at any time. And, as you'll see throughout this book, each of us has opened ourselves up to this gift and has been forever changed because of it. It's our hope that you, too, either have already experienced loving grace in your own life or will open yourself up to experiencing it moving forward.

Defining Grace

Grace is one of those concepts that is heavenly based, beautifully abstract, and not easily definable. It's one of those words that asks you to sit with it for a little while – to take it into your heart fully and allow it to flow through each part of you so that you can begin to comprehend it – and even then, it holds such mystery.

To us, grace is synonymous with miracles. It's evidence of our connection to our soul and to this magical world that we live in. It's our connection to God/Source. It's the intangible feeling that we aren't ever really alone, mixed with the tangible signs that we experience every single day.

We define grace as presents from the universe that let us know how loved we are, how loving our world is, and how connected we are to all that is. It's a word that's filled with light and love.

Here are just a few examples of what we mean by "moments of grace":

- communicating with and receiving signs from loved ones on the other side – knowing that they are always with you
- feeling with all of your being that someone/something is always near – loving you and wanting the best for you
- surrendering fully to God/the Universe/Source and immediately feeling light and free
- listening to your intuition and later seeing how it saved you from going down a path that wouldn't have felt right
- staring out at the ocean and feeling connected with everything
- finding a feather or a penny exactly when you needed a sign from your loved ones
- looking up at the sky and feeling immense awe and wonder for this vast world that you are part of
- watching a butterfly land on your arm and then fly off onto a flower
- experiencing a miracle that helped you see the world in a different way and feel connected to all that is
- having a near-death experience
- having your prayer answered
- waking up from a dream that felt so real and helped everything make sense again
- looking into a loved one's eyes and feeling completely seen

Grace shows up in so many ways, and it's up to each of us to be open to it and to experience these special moments when they arrive. We know that there's so much happening that we can't see or feel or hear or touch, but we also know that there is much that we can – that we do. And even just witnessing a tiny snippet of the grace-filled miracles that are happening all around us all of the time is enough to wake us up, to invite us to pay attention, and to remind us that we truly are all so, so blessed to be part of this world.

We each experience grace differently, and yet each experience is equally magical. Because of this vastness of possibility, we could never have written this book on our own. The co-authors brought so much richness and variety of life experiences in their pieces, which created a beautiful smorgasbord of grace.

While reading the pieces, we quickly realized that, while grace is synonymous with miracles that bring us joy and love, it's also frequently found through moments of tragedy and sadness – such as losing a loved one or facing a physical illness. While it may seem counterintuitive that something as beautiful as grace could be born from something so painful, we have found this to be true in our own lives and also throughout many of the pieces. Grace often appears after we've been broken open – when our resistance is down. Grace shows up when we're present and can see it – when we've surrendered. And when we're going through something extremely painful, we no longer have the energy to resist – allowing grace to enter.

We were completely inspired by how much of themselves each of the co-authors shared throughout their stories – parts that weren't necessarily easy to share, parts that left them feeling a bit vulnerable and exposed. We are grateful to them for bravely showing up and sharing their oftentimes heart-wrenching moments to show all of us that grace is always available to us. Always. No matter where we are or what we're going through, it's right there next to us – just waiting for us to open up to it and let it in.

Throughout this book, we were honored to witness grace in all of its forms – the happy, the poignant, the miraculous, the tragic, and the everyday experiences as well. Seeing all of these pieces together really drove home for us how grace truly is all around us always.

How to Read This Book

One of our intentions when creating this book was to show that grace can show up where we most expect it and also where we least expect it. We gave each of the co-authors free rein with their pieces and trusted that the book would come together in a cohesive way once we received them all. And that's exactly what happened. The pieces fell into 10 categories, which became our chapter titles:

1. Messages from Our Soul & Beyond
2. Physical Shake-Ups & Near-Death Experiences
3. Everyday Grace
4. Signs of Grace
5. Animals & Nature
6. Loving Grace
7. Earth Angels
8. Divine Interventions & Timing
9. Grace-Filled Transitions
10. Graceful Epiphanies

There are many ways to enjoy this book: you can read each entry in order on the day it appears, or you can flip through at random and let your soul guide you. Perhaps you have a favorite day of the year (such as your birthday or an anniversary) and want to see which piece appears on that day. Or maybe a certain chapter's theme is calling for you to turn to it and flip through and choose a piece that way. For example, if you've recently experienced a loss, you may find it healing to read a piece from the Grace-Filled Transitions chapter. Or if you're feeling a bit disheartened, reading a piece from the Earth Angels chapter will likely uplift you.

There is no right or wrong way to read this book. You can read one piece each morning or night as part of your spiritual practice. Or you can read it in the carpool lane while picking up your kids from school. However and wherever you choose to read it, know that it's a powerful book – one that we believe will help you to feel more grounded, centered, and connected to yourself and to others.

Another suggestion for reading this book is to keep a journal nearby to jot down any grace-filled thoughts and inspirations that enter into your heart as you read the pieces – even if they don't make sense. Chances are, they will when you most need them to. By reading this book, you're consciously inviting grace into your own life – you're letting it know that you're open to receiving it and that you're ready for it to show up. Keeping a journal is a wonderful way to capture your own moments of grace.

You can also read this book with your friends as a way to deepen your relationships and share about your own grace-filled moments together! You can meet (either in person or online) and go through the days, or you can pick and choose them at random and share what you learned about yourself after reading them and taking them into your heart.

Please remember that however you go through this book is perfectly right – just by having it around, you will be opening your heart and letting your soul and the universe know that you're open to receiving grace. (You're receiving it always, but this way you'll be more likely to notice it when it shows up for you.)

We're really excited for you. This is such a special book, and we love that you'll be receiving its energy and experiencing your own grace-filled miracles while reading it.

Giving Back

Because we've both experienced countless moments of grace in nature and around animals, we'll be donating 5% of all profits from sales of this book to the Jane Goodall Institute. (You can learn more about this charity by going to www.janegoodall.org.)

Thank You

Thank you for being part of this grace-filled journey with us. The fact that you're holding this book in your hands means that you're either already living a life filled with grace or you're open to inviting more of it in – both of which are equally exciting and wonderful.

We truly hope that each of the pieces helps you feel more connected to this magical world, and we hope that you'll feel closer to all that is. That's what grace does: it brings you closer to your soul, to Source, and to your truth. We love that so much. We've experienced this loving pull while compiling these pieces, and we're excited for you to experience it as well as you read them all.

Grace is all around us. Always. Sometimes all we have to do to find it is open our hearts and see through the eyes of our soul. We hope this book helps you do exactly that.

Hugs, love, and gratitude,
Jodi and Dan

Chapter 1
Messages from Our Soul & Beyond

G race can show up in many different ways. Sometimes it shows up in ways that are hard to explain – ways that go against logical reasoning. Sometimes it can be hard to believe that it's real and that we aren't just imagining it. What we've come to realize is that so much that happens in our universe goes beyond our minds, and when we experience grace, we feel it in our soul – at the heart of our being. We both believe that no matter how it shows up, grace is a true gift that is meant to be cherished. It is a true miracle.

Throughout this chapter, you'll read pieces that show that the bond between us and our loved ones is eternal. You'll read about loved ones on the other side reaching out to let us know that they are okay and that they are still here. While it's heartbreaking to say goodbye to them here in the physical world, it's comforting to know that our relationships can continue on the other side, if we're open to it.

On the following pages, you'll also read many grace-filled messages from our soul, angels, spirit guides, and God/Source – sharing exactly what we need to know in the perfect moment.

As we compiled these pieces, we found ourselves feeling moved to tears – both through sadness and also through witnessing such pure love. We were left with a sense of awe of our magical world and felt so grateful that we get to live in a place where grace such as this exists. We're all so blessed.

It's our hope that you'll experience goosebumps of your own as you read the following pieces. Grace has so many beautiful ways of showing up and bringing us loving messages, and we can't wait for you to read how it showed up from beyond!

Three Angels and a Tire

By Rani St. Pucchi

"Surrender to Grace. The ocean cares for each wave until it reaches the shore. You are given more help than you will ever know."

- Rumi

One weekend in 1982, I went to Pattaya Beach with my friends and family, including my two-year-old son, Tej. As we walked along the tropical shore, Tej insisted, "Play in water, Mommy." He giggled as I scooped him up in the crook of my arm and carried him to a shallow area. It was such a joy to see him splash in the ocean that I forgot about everything else…including the riptide.

Suddenly, Tej was pulled from my arms. I panicked as he drifted away from me, but miraculously I was able to grab him. Finally, I caught my breath and looked back at the beach. The current had pulled us far out, and we were bobbing in the deep ocean. I screamed and screamed, but my family and friends were too far away, lounging on a remote spot with their backs turned from us.

Just then, out of nowhere, three young girls holding on to a tire surfaced next to us. One said, "Grab the tire. We will get you to shore."

"Oh, thank you, thank you!" I repeated as I held on to the tire with one arm and pulled tiny Tej to my body with the other. A feeling of peace came over me as the girls brought us back to the land.

Reaching the shore, I let go of the tire and struggled through the wet sand with Tej still tucked close. I turned to say thanks, but no one was there. I looked around far and wide, but there was just the two of us and the ocean, spread out as far as the eye could see. No one was even close, nor was there any sign of a tire floating in the surf.

I knew then without a shadow of a doubt that God had sent three angels to save Tej and me. I broke down on the wet sand and, holding my son close, cried tears of joy and gratitude. We had been given a new lease on life that day, and God showed me that I could always trust Him. I was surrounded with His grace.

Legos from Heaven

By Alicia Isaacs Howes

"Clair's Birthday" pinged on my phone, a reminder of my sister and a date I never forget. As I live in the States, I need extra time to send gifts back to England.

That day, the prompt shattered me into shards of grief as I fell to my knees. I couldn't send her a present this year because she had died a few months earlier.

Between sobs, I told Clair I wanted to send a gift to her children instead. But I needed her help because I had no idea what would be appropriate after losing their mum. Plus, she had a knack for choosing just the right present.

I added, "I know you're okay; but I'm missing you here, and today I need a really clear sign that you heard me!"

An hour later I got a text from Regan, one of my students from an Akashic Records class just a few weeks earlier: "Strange question, but do Clair's kids like Legos?"

We weren't close, although she knew about Clair. Of course, I called her straight back.

Regan started with an apology as we didn't know each other well outside of class. However, something life-changing had happened that morning and she couldn't ignore the overwhelming urge to send me that text. She'd been in her Akashic Records but was struggling to believe that she wasn't making up the guidance...until Clair came through in such a powerful way that she realised it couldn't be her imagination.

As the session in her Records ended, she got the impression of Clair walking away then turning to say, "Tell Alicia to give my children Legos Advent Calendars."

That message made me smile from deep inside. Clair was still fabulous at picking the perfect presents, not only for her children, her family, and me, but also for Regan, who could now trust her intuition more deeply. Perhaps the biggest gift for *all* of us, though, was the reminder that when we talk to our lost loved ones, they can still hear us...and we never know when or how we'll hear back!

A Light on the Wall of Crosses

By Mandi Huffhines

While growing up, I had no idea of what I truly believed. I questioned Heaven, God, life, and death. Even as I grew older, I didn't have much faith in other people's beliefs or this being who everyone called "God." What little faith I did have was completely shattered when I lost my baby daughter, Jenna Belle, when she was just four days old.

I so badly wanted to believe and even *tried* to believe, but I was so ANGRY! How can people put their faith in someone who hurts us so badly?

It wasn't until after one of Jenna's Annual Memorial Golf Tournaments that I began to see things differently. As I reflected on the cycle of life and Jenna's place in it, I realized that this child was leaving behind a legacy of helping with sudden infant death syndrome. She had a huge purpose in this life, and I was excited to help her fulfill it.

After the tournament, however, I became ill. This wasn't completely new. Stress from the tournament often caused me to feel down for a few days, and it always took me some time to recover. This time was much more severe, though. I didn't know what was going on with me; I felt out of control. My condition declined rapidly until, in a panicked state, I dialed 911.

When the 911 operator answered, I was staring at a wall of crosses that became covered in light. Through my tears, I told the operator that it was my time to go and I was okay with that. I had made my peace; I was ready. Then, all of a sudden, a voice said, "You are okay. Jenna is okay. It is not your time. Keep doing what you are doing, and you are going to be fine." Then everything became calm, my crying stopped, and the sickness left. I stood and felt like I had never felt before. I felt lighter, like a huge weight had been lifted off my shoulders, like I had been set free. There are no words that could ever possibly describe the sensation except to say that, on that day, I was touched by God.

A Breath of Love

By Ruth Donald

As I plunged into the crystal-clear saltwater pool, I felt the coolness soothe my tired emotions. I breathed out under the water and watched the bubbles rise in glittering clusters towards the sunlight on the surface. I surfaced, turned to take a breath, and began to swim – breathing rhythmically, first to one side and then to the other, the end of the 50-metre pool becoming closer with each gliding stroke.

In my mind, I spoke to my husband and told him that I loved him. I thanked him for always looking after me and for being my friend, my lover, and my companion, and I asked him to show me in some way that I could not miss that he was with me. I turned at the end of the pool and pushed off the wall on my return lap, gaining peace and calm from the warmth of the sun on my shoulders and my back; the mesmeric ascending air bubbles; and the regular, predictable gliding strokes.

When my husband passed without warning the previous week, I started a daily practice of writing to him and talking to him out loud about our love, our life, and our connection. Today more than the ever, I felt as though I was deep in a pool of emotion and that my lifeline was our love and the continuity of our love, despite the change of his absence in the physical world.

Turning again at the pool wall, I began my third lap. Through the rushing of underwater sounds, I heard the words, "I have a message for you." I rolled to one side, breathed, then rolled to the other side and breathed; and the message became present in my mind with a clarity beyond question: *I am the love in every breath you take.*

I felt a current run through my heart. It bumped my breath as tears of love and awe ran down my face. The salt water buoyed me as I suddenly stopped my swim, and the truth of my experience washed over me.

In that moment, I knew with total faith what love is.

Spirit Dreams

By Ty Will

It's been said that spirits come to you in dreams. I know this is true because I have dreamt of a little spirit who indeed came from Heaven.

When I was pregnant with my son, I had an especially vivid dream of a little girl with curly red hair playing in the park. Naturally, I thought I was having a girl, but nine months later I gave birth to a boy – and what a blessing he has been!

Twenty-one years later, my son and his wife were expecting their first child. Unlike many other parents-to-be, they didn't want to know the sex of the child until after their child was born. Two weeks before birth, I once again dreamt of the curly red-haired little girl. One night, she and I played teacups in my dream. The next night, we played hopscotch. After a week of playing with this sweet angel, I called my son and explained to him that he was going to have a little girl with curly red hair and that she and I had been playing all week in my dreams. I waited for another dream that night, but she never came. A week later, my beautiful granddaughter was born with curly red hair.

Years later, my daughter and her husband were trying to have a baby, but they didn't have any luck. For years, I watched their heartbreak. One day, through her tears, my daughter explained to us that she couldn't have babies. That night I had a dream of a black-and-white bus headed to a fair. As I got off the bus, the African-American lady sitting next to me handed me her child and asked me to love her. I cried as I reached out to hold that special gift.

Now I know that one day my daughter and her husband will adopt a little girl. Hopefully, they will name her Grace.

Whispers of Grace

By Mary Lunnen

When I was five years old, I was ill with rheumatic fever. I only remember a little about it: being carried upstairs because I was too weak to walk, the doctor coming to give me injections with a huge needle, being upset at not being allowed outdoors to play with my brother. Oh, and the day our cat jumped through the window above my day bed just as I was eating a bowl of pudding, which went everywhere – making me quite cross and very sticky!

That was all in the daytime. At night, my strongest memory is fear. I expect my mother was often awakened by me crying for her to come to me. She would sing my favourite lullaby, "Little Nut Tree."

There was something else, though, something I didn't remember for years – and then, at first, only partially. In 1994, I was diagnosed with cervical cancer. In the hospital after a major operation, my mother came to me in my dreams, singing the lullaby. This was the first stage of my re-awakening, a whisper of grace.

The experience of having cancer set me on a different path. I learned about visualisation, meditation, Reiki, and other forms of healing. At some point during this time, I remembered hearing a voice in the night when I was that little girl, ill in bed. It was a deep voice, a man's voice, and I remembered the sound of it, the comfort it brought me, even at five years old. But I could not remember the words the voice spoke to me.

I learned to accept that perhaps I would never remember. I felt a sense of loss, while knowing I was so fortunate to at least recall that sense of connection.

As the years passed, my meditation practice deepened, I received help and guidance from many healers, and I became a Reiki healer myself. Then, out of the blue in a meditation, I remembered the words that the deep, reassuring voice whispered to me: "You are safe, my child."

Grace Through Mental Illness

By Catherine M. Laub

In a moment of grace, my angels gave me a mission to speak out about mental illness – including my own. I realize that some people might not consider this a moment of grace. After all, mental illnesses (such as depression, anxiety, and obsessive-compulsive disorder) still carry a stigma and are often ignored. Many of us are afraid to acknowledge them, worried that others will look down on those of us who have them. But if you haven't suffered from these conditions, you can't imagine what we go through.

Like many others who suffer from mental illness, I've had a feeling of being stuck and having no direction in life. For years, I was incapable of doing much physically (or simply lacked the desire to do so), so I mostly watched TV. I was hospitalized twice for suicidal thoughts, and I made an attempt in 2014. I felt like a wall was up, and it wasn't me going through the actions. I knew it was wrong, but I couldn't control myself.

Fortunately, my angels orchestrated the event in a way that helped me get on the right track and receive more help. I'm not ashamed of my experiences. In many ways, they strengthened my spirituality, which helped me through my most difficult times.

Through my experiences with mental illness, I have learned (and have been angelically assigned with sharing) the importance of self-care. I have also learned that, whether or not we experience mental illness, we can help ourselves by following a natural diet, having a fitness routine, getting out in the sun for at least 10 minutes a day, and doing things that interest us. One other thing I learned from the angels was that if someone wears turquoise or uses this color in their daily lives, it will soothe them.

Most importantly, I learned that mental illness is nothing to be ashamed of. It can be an illuminating part of a journey of learning, spiritual development, and grace. I now speak out about mental illness in my campaign, "Brighten Your Day with Turquoise." In doing so, I'm not only changing my own life, but I'm uplifting others as well.

Walking with Angels

By Nadean Ollech

Once, while walking in the Irish countryside, I stopped for lunch at the side of the road. I was wondering what I was doing out there all alone when I suddenly felt a gathering of spiritual beings around me. As I was getting ready to continue walking, I said, "You are welcome to join me." When I picked up my backpack and started walking, I felt a group of angels fall in behind me, walking single file down the road. They were with me until I found a bed and breakfast and called it a day.

Another time, while walking back to a hostel in Bath, England, I was trying to decide if I should go back to Canada. After much debate, I came to the conclusion that, yes, I would go to the east coast (although I had only lived in the west up to that point). I said to the angels, "If this is the right thing, please let me know." As this thought completed, I felt a group of angels fall in line behind me and walk with me until I got back to the hostel and started packing.

After a while in Prince Edward Island (in eastern Canada), I felt that I had to go back to the west again. As I was walking through a park, I said to the angels, "If this is right, I cannot face it alone." Then I felt a group of angels fall into place behind me and walk single file with me for many blocks until I was secure in my decision.

These beautiful experiences, I believe, are the angels' way of making sure that I get the hint that what I am doing or planning to do is the absolute right thing for me at the absolute right time and that they will be there for me through it. What a gift to know that I am not alone. I honestly believe that, whether we feel them or not, we are all walking with angels.

Discovery in Grace Canyon

By Michelle R. Terry

The anticipation of spring's blooms and vegetables keeps me sane enough to live where the winter's air stings the nostrils and makes the gentlest of souls say bad words.

With each seed I plunge into the dirt, I question: *Will it grow?*

I've often wrestled with the intangibility of faith. Every year, I start too many seeds because I lack the certitude to plant only the six I need.

It's also how I have viewed my relationship with God. My mother, my sister, and my daughter can all hear Him. Me? Crickets.

At one point in 2013, I whined to a friend about not having a spiritual connection with God. I thought He had abandoned me. Although my life may have looked perfect, I felt broken on the inside.

After a prayer, my friend told me to close my eyes and tell her what I saw. I giggled, and she prodded until I complied with her request to share my vision.

Canyon walls were on either side of me. The crags were pocked with trees, the earth was in my nose, and I could feel the calm of the river. The sun kissed my face, and I knew something big was about to happen.

What is this place? I wondered. *And what does this have to do with my relationship with God?*

Then I saw my hands, which had been bound in fists, spread open to reveal seeds in each palm. The seeds sprouted the moment they found the sun's rays.

I wept. How could I have missed it? God's unspoken message sent via flowers, tomatoes, and cucumbers. My garden beds spill vibrant life over the sides and display living proof of His grace.

I still plant too many seeds. But I do so with the faith that I'll have my six plants and plenty more to share His promise with others.

The Illusion of Control

By Heather Wiest

As a youth, my home life breathed constant chaos propelled by substance abuse and domestic violence. I battled fear, sleepless nights, depression, and sickness. From as early as age 10, I struggled with disordered eating behaviors and poor body image, especially during times of stress.

Throughout these childhood experiences, I longed to self-protect and isolate. I felt alone in this world and often wondered, *God, are you there?* More than anything, I yearned to be an adult and have control over my circumstances.

During adulthood, however, the struggles continued. At 27, while completing graduate school and working full time as a social worker, I became overwhelmed and increasingly out of control. The combination of going 110% and eating destructively led me to an anorexic state – body, mind, and soul.

While lying on my bed one evening in March 1997, crying alone before God in my dark wilderness, I experienced the most frightening chest pain. Was I having a heart attack? Should I call 911? Was this the end? I entreated the Lord for grace and, seemingly out of nowhere, heard these words:

"Be anxious for nothing. My peace, which surpasses all comprehension, will guard your heart and mind in Christ Jesus. Find Me wholeheartedly."

Immediately, a beautiful light, a glowing embrace, tenderly dissipated the gripping pain. In awe, I rested.

My illusion of control had blocked all healing. Divine love humbled me in the wilderness so I would accept miraculous support. Once I was honest with myself, the inner chambers of my heart – the layers of experiences and emotions needing illumination – gently presented themselves. Each moment gracefully guided me on every level towards restoration and life purpose. Grace-filled rays of love and light supernaturally carried me through the wilderness, mending my inner chambers, allowing me to live wholeheartedly and free!

Becoming Me

By Julia Van Der Sluys

Last year, I began spiritual mentoring as a way to help my panic disorder and evolve my spiritual skills. It's been an amazing journey of discovery, relearning spiritual abilities, connecting with my guides, and meeting my true self, which had been buried under years of ego ruling. While this entire journey has been utterly transforming, it all came to a head when I had a past-life reading with my mentor.

At first, I was a little apprehensive about doing the reading (my ego must have known it was going to be a pivotal event), but I pressed on…and *WOW!* More than just a good reading, it was a soul-defining moment that made all the jigsaw pieces of my life fit together into one giant *a-ha!*

I learned that this is my first-ever human incarnation, so the panic I suffer from finally made sense. I was traversing a human life for the very first time, so *of course* it was scary! Before this lifetime, I had only ever experienced human life vicariously, as an onlooker helping those in my care. As an angel, it was up to me to take on the fear, panic, and overwhelm as one passed or had a traumatic experience, and I was still carrying those feelings into my own human existence. I'm now learning to let go of those old feelings and honour them by living a great human life.

I am here now to experience my own human emotions firsthand. Understanding this, my traumatic childhood and mental prison finally made sense and even began to free me. I realised what an important role I play in bringing this information back to the angelic realm and making a huge difference to others while I am here on Earth.

I always knew I was different, but until now I never realised how much or why. This new understanding marks the beginning of truly becoming *me*.

Surrounded by Angels

By Misty Harding

It had been months since my beautiful bookstore had gone. I was depressed, alone, and feeling like a complete failure.

A few years earlier, I had a good job, house, new car, and a boyfriend. I was also very sick. I had fibromyalgia and was living on pain medication. Then my life fell apart. My boyfriend broke it off. I started to hate my job and to feel like I didn't belong on Earth. I was, by some standards, "successful." So why couldn't I be happy?

Needing to escape, I met a girlfriend in Moab, Utah, where I found a little store and picked up Wayne Dyer's *The Power of Intention* on CD. Listening to it on the way home, I vowed to change my life.

That store had such a profound impact on me that I decided to open one of my own – a place where people could find what they needed to relax, heal, feel better, and feel loved. I found my true calling: being there for others and helping them with messages and healing from the angels.

Then the economy crashed. I spent all my savings and ran up credit cards. I needed to close the store but couldn't because I loved it so much. Down to my last business card, I had been praying about what to do, when I received my answer. A man started a fire in the basement. My beautiful store was gone. It was time to move on. I had failed again. What would I do now?

Months later, I was out walking when I heard a voice saying, "We are here."

I asked, "*Who* is there?" and I heard their names: Analaria (my guardian angel), Archangel Michael, Raphael, Chamuel, Uriel, Zadkiel… on and on…for minutes. I had given up on the angels. I had quit asking for their help. In that moment, when I opened to receive their healing and grace, I knew that I had received something that could never be taken away: my connection to God and the Heavenly Realms, the knowing that I am never alone and that everything would be okay.

Thank you, angels!

Meet Me at the IHOP

By Jody Rentner Doty

Grandma Clara and I had an amazing bond in life. We shared gifts of the spirit, intuition, and our otherworldly "Irish eyes." It didn't surprise me when, two weeks after her passing, I heard her voice ask me to meet her at the IHOP restaurant. As instructed, I slid into a booth and instantly felt Grandma's bubbly spirit across from me. She said, "Jody, please tell your mom for me that she did the best she could and not to worry anymore. *I'm* not worrying!" And with that, Grandma Clara was gone.

I pulled out my cell phone and called Mom to relay Grandma's message. When Mom answered, I could hear her crying on the other end of the line. I noticed Mom's tears stopped immediately and her voice softened when I gave her the message. She thanked me and said this was just what she needed to hear. Mom then explained to me that before she died, Grandma had entrusted the caretaking of her beloved cat to Mom. My mother had been at wit's end with worry because Grandma's cat was not doing well. At the time of my call, Mom had just come home from having the kitty put to sleep. Overcome with guilt and worry, Mom was wondering to herself just what Grandma would have thought. It was a blessing for me to be the messenger. I could feel Mom's stress melt away at the sound of Grandma's comforting words.

It wasn't until a few days later, while I happened to be driving down the same road, that it hit me: Grandma's cat was a three-legged cat named Hoppy. "IHOP." What a perfect way to reach across the universe and relay a message of kindness about her cat, Hoppy. I had to laugh at the cosmic joke. Grandma Clara, after all, had a great sense of humor in life, and it made me smile to know that she hadn't changed a bit in the afterlife.

The Angel in Orange

By Lexi Gaia Verano

I connect people with their angels and have long told my clients that in their times of greatest need, it's best to just let go and let your angels find you. This is the advice that I had to not only give but *live* during one particularly difficult December.

A recent divorce and the overwhelming news that my youngest child had been diagnosed with a disability added to the usual pressures of the holiday season, leaving me feeling depressed, scared, and very alone. So I prayed. I meditated so hard my forehead hurt. And I spoke to the Universe, God, Jesus, Buddha…anyone who might be able to help me.

One night during this time, while walking past a bookstore I had never been to, I felt compelled to step inside. Almost immediately, I was attracted to a book with an orange cover. It was a book about Archangel Gabriel. I had never heard of this angel before but trusted this was the book I needed.

I spent the rest of the night reading. As the book fell from my exhausted hand, my reading transitioned into a dream. A warm orange light announced the arrival of Gabriel. She told me that I was not alone, that she had always been with me. She told me to search my memories for her orange aura.

I remembered birthing my son, how late in the evening a filtered orange light shone across the room, despite the very late hour. Then I recalled an even earlier memory of an emergency surgery when I had been awakened by a warm orange light filling my room and surrounding my hospital bed.

As I woke up from my dream, the book about Gabriel resting by my side, I found it odd that I remembered the smiling, friendly carpet technician who had been here a week earlier. I chuckled as I remembered how he had worn a bright orange shirt.

As I walked into my living room, I saw a piece of paper lying on the floor. It didn't seem like an accident. It seemed placed. I reached down and picked it up. It was my receipt from the carpet cleaners. Then it all made sense. I looked at the bottom of the receipt, and it said: *Your technician today was Gabriel.*

Message in a Candle

By Sharon Halliday

Each week, I get together with a group of women I refer to as my soul tribe. We come from all walks of life, and we each specialise in at least one healing modality. We meditate, talk about our spiritual journeys, and have lunch before returning to our busy lives. Being with these like-minded (and like-hearted) souls brings me joy and comfort.

On one occasion, we witnessed something truly amazing. For my 37th birthday, my tribe surprised me with a beautifully decorated cake. As I was blowing out the candles, I jokingly said, "I can't decide on just one wish," but I chose one and blew out the candles.

Moments later, one of the candles reignited. Someone said, "It looks like you get to make that other wish after all!" So I did, as I blew out the candle. Once more, the extinguished candle lit up. Now there were gasps and whispers coming from my friends and a distinct feeling of excitement in the air. I felt tingles as I prepared to blow out this mysterious candle. I took a deep breath, and as I exhaled, we all anticipated what would happen. The candle came to life…again.

Someone exclaimed, "It's a trick candle!" But I knew differently, and my friend who'd made the cake assured us it was a stock-standard, run-of-the-mill candle.

Vicki, our host, asked each of us for our thoughts. Mum, who had joined us that day, said matter-of-factly, "It's Sharon's Nan." I'd shared a special bond with my grandmother who had passed 13 years earlier.

Vicki confirmed that she'd felt the presence of my Nan, and there was a message from her: "Don't burn out!" Vicki also saw a vision of a cow, which held significance for me.

After the party, while on my way to collect my son from school, I was guided to take a different route. I noticed a car with the license plate: COW. Holy Cow!

That day, I resolved to work less and enjoy life more…and avoid burnout. My life has been forever altered because of my message in a candle.

A Grace Note

By Cindia Carrere

I was always a cautious, "safety-first" kind of kid, following rules to the point of obsession – not someone my parents had to worry about. Although, as a toddler, my first words included messages from the angels, so maybe they worried a little...

An early moment of grace occurred at a church picnic by the river on a warm Sunday afternoon. It was idyllic to my five-year-old self: fried chicken, homemade ice cream, *and* I met my guardian angel!

"Yes, you can play in the water, but stay close to the edge," my parents told me. Of course I would obey; however, no one knew about the sudden drop-off in the river bed. I sank like a stone, and nobody saw. No human, that is.

The angel was so calming ("it" seemed like a *she* to me). Surprised by how easy it was to breathe under water, I stood at the bottom of the river for a long time, content to be with this angel. Suddenly, it felt like my armpits were on fire. Somebody had realized I was missing. Yanked straight up by my wrists, the weight of my body hung entirely from my arm sockets. I remember lying prone on the grass, people fussing over me. The pain in my shoulders would eventually go away, but the sharp contrast between angels and humans would stay with me forever.

This moment of grace is why I keep communication open and have maintained the daily habit of listening to and taking dictation from the angels. Each morning, I jot down this wisdom, which I call *Grace Notes: Angel Intel for Entrepreneurs on Their Soul Path.*

Among the wise messages I've received is this angelic recipe for grace: *Giving and receiving are equally important. Allow yourself to give AND receive that which you want to put into the world (circulate) and experience more of (expand).* The angels even provided an acronym for G.R.A.C.E.: Giving, Receiving, Allowing, Circulating, and Expanding. This idea works in perfect harmony with everything: love, blessings, favor, guidance, forgiveness (of self and others), gratitude, money, or any other area.

What began as a five-year-old's unexpected, underwater introduction to an angel has led to a lifelong connection with angelic wisdom, love, and grace.

Let Me Support You

By Bland Tyree

Recently, during a time when I felt blocked in my efforts to move forward in my life, I said a prayer to the Divine Mother, asking Her to support me. Later that evening while I lay in bed, sleep eluded me as my mind repetitively churned over its litany of worries and things that needed my attention. I took deep breaths to calm myself, but my mind chattered on while my body grew tenser. I did not feel supported.

In the midst of this, I heard a voice say very softly, "Let me support you." I vaguely registered this, but it was quickly drowned out by the stories looping in my mind like a stuck record.

After a few moments, the same voice said again, gently and firmly, "Let me support you." I gradually registered that this was not my mind speaking, and I became more open and curious.

A few moments later, the voice repeated, "Let me support you." I felt a sensation of soft energy cradling the back of my head and neck. My mind stopped. Silence. Spaciousness. My body relaxed. I felt supported. A short time later, I fell asleep.

The following day, I moved through the busiest time of my week feeling a sense of spaciousness and trust. I realized that the Divine Mother had answered my prayer, letting me know that She is always here to support me. Her gentle but insistent invitation to *allow* Her support released me into a space of creative flow and ease. The things that I experienced as obstructions the previous day faded into the background.

Not every day since then has felt equally relaxed and spacious, but the grace of the Divine Mother's presence continues to reverberate, reminding me that I am not separate from Her or from the greater consciousness out of which everything arises.

By remembering to relax and open to this source of love, courage, wisdom, and creativity, grace continues to flow into my life.

On the Wings of an Archangel

By Lori Kilgour Martin

Years ago, while working part time as a sales clerk, I was contemplating a decision to go away with friends for a long weekend. I wanted to go, but I didn't know how I'd be able to afford it. While I sat in my dining room pondering the situation, a comforting voice entered my right ear: "Don't worry about the money; just go."

I trusted this message, which led me out of my rented apartment to join my friends for a wonderful weekend. During the drive back, however, something did not feel right. I opened the door, entered, and noticed the window screens were off. I figured that it must have been the winds, which were very strong that night. I relaxed and went to sleep.

The following morning, I opened my jewelry box and found that pieces were gone. After dialing 911, I was barely able to speak, but I finally managed to explain the situation. When the police arrived, they informed me that I fit the method of operation of a known rapist in the area.

As the days and weeks unfolded, my inner self changed colour. My connection to God became blocked. Sound decision-making and my physical health were compromised. While attempting to accept how fortunate I was, I essentially shut down. My imagination ran wild with "what-if" scenarios, covering me with grey layers of survivor's guilt.

Recently, I was frozen in this energy and called upon Archangel Michael to remove cords of fear and resistance. His royal blue light began appearing often throughout this rough patch. Sensing his presence, I heard his message to me: "You are lovingly wrapped in warmth and protection."

Now, as I look out the window of my current living space, my gaze moves to the snowflakes floating gently down. There is silence. A layer has lifted, the light within is growing stronger, and I am safe. The hand of God flew in on the wings of an archangel. That I was open and receptive to the message was divine intervention. Thank you, snowflakes, Archangel Michael, and God.

I Am You

By Kimberly DuBoise

Late one night, after reading and contemplating a really good book, I experienced a moment of grace.

I was lying down on the floor in my spare bedroom, which I use for an office. I closed the book and looked out the window into the night sky.

Suddenly, I heard the words, "I am you."

It was a voice I recognized somehow. The voice of Spirit.

When I heard the voice, it was as if it knew exactly what I needed to hear at that moment in time. It was confirmation of a spiritual truth I was just beginning to integrate into my life – that of my oneness with the Divine.

One brief and powerful moment, one that touched my heart and stirred my soul, had just occurred. It happened so fast that I almost doubted anything had happened, but I knew I had heard the words clearly: "I am you."

I sat there in the dark in my office, mouthing the words I had just heard. I wanted to prolong the tingling feeling that was still washing over me as I sat with those words. I felt a strange calmness come over me, as well as a strange surge of energy.

Had I really just heard "I am you" spoken to me from above? A message meant for me, coming to me in a moment when I needed it the most?

Yes.

These words reinforced what I had been reading about (unity) and meditating on (oneness). They reinforced within me a spirit of peace. This experience felt like a wave of love washing over me. I had been going through a rough period at the time, emotionally and spiritually. I was questioning my career choice and considering writing a personal memoir that was sure to bring up difficult emotions. I was in search of a sign, in need of reassurance, and it came! It was a gesture of tenderness and indescribable sweetness that I will always remember.

Motherly Love Comforts When It's Needed the Most

By Suzanna Broughton

The time in my life when I have felt most held in the loving arms of grace was after my mother's intentional drug overdose.

I got the news early morning in Australia. Within 12 hours I would be flying to Toronto – the other side of the world. I was distraught and had trouble focusing. I am so grateful to two friends who helped me pack, making sure I had things like socks, a warm jacket, and a toothbrush.

I did, however, remember to bring something to read during the long flight. I felt compelled to grab a book from the top of my full bookcase. I hadn't yet read this book and wasn't even clear why I owned it: *Mary, Queen of Angels* by Doreen Virtue.

Once on the plane, I began to read the book. My heart was soothed by stories of people receiving healing and grace from Mother Mary. Stories of miracles filled my heart and mind as I flew towards what would be the most traumatic few days of my life.

Upon arriving, I got involved in preparations to create a funeral for my mother that honoured her and gave our shocked hearts some peace. While preparing for her funeral, I found out she died with a rosary near her and discovered more about her close affinity with Mother Mary.

The night after her funeral, I lay in bed, exhausted but sleepless, longing for rest. Then I felt it. It was as though someone had their hand lightly cupping the top of my head. The sensation was warm and comforting – like a mother's touch. I wasn't scared. I lay with my eyes closed, enjoying the moment, until I eventually fell asleep.

I don't know if I had just imagined or willed it, if it was Mother Mary or my own mother who comforted me that night. I just know I felt held by much-needed motherly love.

An Apology from Beyond

By Karen Hicks

I had a volatile relationship with my stepfather. I don't remember any single incident that was a catalyst for the friction; it was just always there. As a young girl, I was insecure. From him, I developed a belief that my voice had little value. An alcoholic, he was miserable in his pain (something I understood many years later). I couldn't wait to leave home. At 17, I left for university. At 19, I was "excommunicated" by him because I chose to start a relationship with my birth father, my stepmother, and their two sons (my half-brothers).

A number of years later, my stepfather was diagnosed with terminal cancer. During the year-long period from diagnosis to death, I saw him three times. The first two times, we hardly spoke. The last time, he couldn't speak; he was hours away from passing into his next life and was lost in a morphine haze. My siblings and I were in the hospital room, supporting him in his transition and being there for our mom.

A few months after his death, I went to see a psychic medium. She was someone I had seen several times in the past, and I trusted her gifts. As soon as I sat, she said, "Gerald is here." This was the name for my stepfather that only he and his family used. His message for me was that he waited to die until my siblings and I were all in the room so that we could support my mom when he passed. He also said that at the time of his death, he saw all the wrong he did and that he was sorry.

These words were such a powerful, healing, liberating gift for me. In that moment, I felt more connected to him than I ever had before. I could breathe easily, and forgiveness came automatically.

The Healing Power of the Love Within

By Qatana Samanen

My very first imagery session with my Chakra Guides was quite wonderful. Each one shared insights and guidance that I found fascinating, helpful, and deeply moving.

At the start of my second session, however, I find that nothing is happening. Suddenly, I feel a sharp pain in my right temple. Steve, the person guiding me, suggests I journey through imagery to the first time I felt that pain. I find myself instantly transported to the kitchen in my childhood home.

The little girl who spilled the milk stands by the open refrigerator door. I watch in horror as the white puddle slowly spreads from the shards of broken glass. She is terrified about what she has done. She doesn't know what's going to happen now, but she knows it will be bad. After all, spilling the milk is a *very* bad thing.

Steve suggests I tell the little girl (my former self) that, even though she spilled the milk, she's still lovable. He encourages me to take her in my arms and tell her I love her.

I am appalled at what she's done. I can't possibly do that. The little girl has spilled the milk, and in our house growing up, you did *not* spill the milk!

I recognize how preposterous this is. I have been a psychologist for many years. I've told countless people who've done things a whole lot worse than spilling the milk that they're worthy of love, regardless of the mistakes they've made. Yet I cannot bring myself to tell this to the little girl. I stand there completely paralyzed, unable to act, yet longing to.

Suddenly, completely unbidden, Eagle (the guide of my heart) emerges and wraps its enormous wings around the little girl. Eagle tells her that she is loveable and that Eagle loves her.

I am overwhelmed with the healing power of this unconditional love that I've longed for all my life. I am astonished to discover it's here, deep within me. This is the moment I embark on my path of transformation through imagery, my path of personal transformation, as well as the centerpiece of my life's work.

Someday You're Going to Laugh About This

By Melissa McHenry Beahm

I drove through the Rio Grande Valley of Texas, enjoying the bright sunshine, light traffic, and music from the radio. I had nothing dramatic happening in my life at the time. Each day was sort of like the next: looking for work, helping others promote our shows by providing posters and flyers to display and invite. I was traveling to four or five parks that day to share the news that we'd be performing in a nearby resort.

Suddenly, an image appeared in my van, sitting in the passenger seat. It seemed to be a man (of sorts), but the vision was just pixelated white, gray, and black boxes forming the shape of a person. The image did not glow angelically white or flame devilish red. It did not stir in me any feelings of apprehension. It just sat there, like the screen of an old black-and-white TV late at night when the broadcast had ended.

I remember a feeling of surprise and puzzlement at the sight of him. And then, he spoke. "Someday you're going to laugh about this."

I responded, "Really?"

He said, "Yes," and then disappeared.

Whaaaat?

I continued to drive. The radio continued to play. *Someday I'm going to laugh about this? Laugh about what?* I wondered. *What is this "this" about which I will laugh? And who was that guy? Where did he come from? And where did he go? Was he my spirit guide? Was he an angel?*

My thoughts have swirled around this moment ever since, searching for the answers. Nothing like this had ever happened to me before, and nothing like it has happened since.

While I still ponder the metaphysical and spiritual aspects of this visit, I can see that this vision was a moment of grace. Not only did it open my mind to all sorts of wonderment, the message itself gives release to worries about the future. I can breathe a sigh of relief now because someday we will be laughing about this!

The Lady of the Lake

By Vicki Talvi-Cole

What a challenging day! I felt run down with murky, toxic, emotional energies and thoughts running amok within me. Closing my eyes, allowing my tears to fall (precious gems to heal and expand my golden heart), I began to breathe – opening, embracing, and stilling myself within the moment. Then, within my heart, there appeared a crystal-clear lake, inviting me to dive in.

Intrigued, I stepped in, welcoming the coolness that encompassed my feet. As I gazed into the clear water, I became aware that I was standing on smooth, soft crystals.

I continued farther in – up to my waist, and then, as I felt my breath quickening, I noticed the water was at my chest. Taking a deep breath, holding it – I plunged in, diving down, deeper and deeper.

As I swam under the water, a voice came singing through me: "Breathe!"

Wait! What? Who said that? I thought. *And how can I breathe in water? I'm not a fish!*

The singing voice responded: "The water is alive – Living Crystal Waters. Breathe!"

Trusting, I began to breathe, slowly at first, then more fully. Life Energy refreshed and filled every nook and cranny of my being, cleansing, reconnecting, and reigniting my inner beauty, lifting me up. I felt freer and calmer, with crystal-clear awareness gliding through me.

Soon, I discovered I was at the other end of this magical lake. My feet touched the bottom, and I slowly emerged onto the soft, firm shore. The sun warmed me, illuminating the droplets of water dripping down from my body, glistening like liquid honey. Just as the sun rises anew each day, I felt new – transformed.

Renewed with the beauty of life's love and joy bursting within me, I began expanding this inner beauty outward. Like a lighthouse with a focused beam turning slowly, shining my light, I realized I had become one with the Living Crystal Waters, emerging as "The Lady of the Lake" – empowered, beautiful, grateful, moving with elegance, soul-filled with mystery and grace.

Start with a Blank Piece of Paper

By Susan Parker Rosen

I am a 65-year-old woman who has recently received numerous blessings, but my situation was very different just five short years ago.

At that time, I became quite ill and could not walk without severe pain. Therefore, I lost my job and a deep depression crept in, which prevented me from being able to solve my problems logically. Consequently, my bank account soon emptied.

One night, I dreamt that I was having a conversation with one of my favorite aunts who had recently passed. In that dream, I asked her for advice on my predicament. She said, as clear as day, "Just start with a blank piece of paper." Then she hugged me, and the dream abruptly ended.

I had done significant ancestry research on that side of my family and had thought about writing a book about the mysteries surrounding my findings but never followed through. That day, however, was different. I was obsessed with writing, and I felt a spirit guiding me as I put my initial thoughts on paper.

Day after day, I found myself at my word-processing program, filling my time with various characters and plots. I started to amuse myself at the tight situations my quirky characters would find themselves in. Three years later, I self-published that work.

By taking my aunt's suggestion to start with a blank piece of paper, I experienced the power of grace and discovered how incredibly strong I am. I also realized that I could write not only a mediocre book but one that has obtained a 4+ rating on Amazon. Most of all, I found how much I was able to accomplish...at any age.

A Journey of Grace

By Ioana Adriana Terec

My journey of Grace began before I was even born. My mother was taking birth-control pills in an attempt to not remain pregnant, but Grace had a different plan. In the fourth month of me growing in her womb while she was still taking the pills, Grace said to her: "Let her come, because I want her to." She stopped taking the pills, and I was born on October 6, 1979, in Romania.

Living under the communist system was hard, and my heart dreamed of something greater. In October 2000, the voice of Grace spoke again, this time coming to me in a dream. She said: "I will send you to America because I have work to do there; through you, I will touch many lives."

I thought it was just a dream. It's so hard to get a visa in my country, but I've learned that with God's Grace everything is possible. At 11 a.m. on June 26, 2002, I became one of only 10 people out of 300 applicants to receive a visa! I also found out that my plane to Los Angeles was taking off at 11 p.m. on that very day!

I arrived in the L.A. airport only to find out that the family that was supposed to come and help me would not be coming after all. Also, because everything happened so fast, the only money I had was Romanian lei, which I wasn't able to use in America. I sat down on my suitcase and cried as I contemplated my situation: I was 22 years old, newly arrived in a foreign country with no money, no family or friends, and unable to speak English.

But I still had God's Grace and my dream.

Once again, Grace made the impossible possible! In the airport, I met five Romanians who were going to the exact location where I was supposed to go for work!

With the money from my first paycheck, I bought a Bible and taught myself English from it – reminded by every word of the voice of Grace, my journey of faith, and how it had led me to wonderful places.

Make Space for Grace

By Susan Mullen

It was heavenly as I sat alone on my own secluded Caribbean beach. All I could hear were the soft sounds of waves as they met the shoreline. All I could feel was the sun and a light breeze. To the right, I saw my endless, white-powder beach. There wasn't another soul in sight. It was at this moment that I realized I could finally *breathe*.

Welcome to my sanctuary.

Meditation is where I go to connect, find peace, or receive universal guidance. Every visit is different. I have learned to enter *expecting nothing*. My only requirement is to just *show up and make space* to receive or experience whatever is trying to reach me. Sometimes it is the respite of solitude. And sometimes I am cracked wide open.

On this particular visit, I was feeling discontent. I had been questioning why I was being pulled in a different, uncharted intuitive direction with my clients. So the nothingness of *just being* was bliss.

After several quiet minutes, a white dove caught my eye. I remember thinking, *How beautiful to see a dove in my sanctuary.* Then I realized that he was coming toward me. He landed gently, resting against me.

We both just sat in silence, looking ahead. I soaked up the sun and the unspoken love that his soul was infusing into mine.

Then he suddenly flew up to become face to face with me. He told me his name: Michael. I was immediately given the knowledge that it was Archangel Michael. He looked me in the eye and said, "You are here to experience so that you can help others with their experiences."

I was innately aware of how these words landed in my soul. They changed everything. He came to encourage me to stop resisting an important piece of myself and my life's purpose.

Then he took off in flight, back over the celestial sea. My deeply grateful eyes followed until he was out of sight.

A Beautiful Spirit Being's Message

By Mathew Hart

When I was 23 years old (and an agnostic), a Beautiful Spirit Being materialized before my eyes in the full light of day, forever changing the way I perceived my life. Without uttering a single word, the Beautiful Being communicated to me that God was real, that a dimension of spirit existed, and that prayer was a worthy and powerful practice (not just for me, but for the Beautiful Being as well).

Five seconds later, the Beautiful Being disappeared just as suddenly as he had arrived, but not before the following additional knowledge was silently yet indelibly impressed upon my young heart and mind: *You are loved. You are cared for. You are respected. You are forgiven. You are important. You are special.*

Unfortunately, it would take me another 23 years before I was finally ready to share this message. You see, although I felt that it was intended for more hearts and minds than my own, it would end up taking me many years before I unequivocally knew, without a hint of reservation or doubt, that I fully understood the true meaning of the message. Now, I am finally ready to share the Beautiful Being's wisdom:

God is real. A dimension of spirit exists. Prayer is a worthy and powerful practice. And, unconditionally and without exception: We are all loved. We are all cared for. We are all respected. We are all forgiven. We are all important. We are all special.

And one more thing: The Beautiful Being appeared in a simple white robe with shoulder-length brown hair, a fully bearded face, and the most calming, compassionate eyes I had ever seen. Although I was born to non-practicing Jewish parents and was never educated in religion, I immediately knew in my heart that the Beautiful Being was Jesus. To this day, that was the only time that Jesus materialized before me, but that was one amazing moment of grace.

A Divine Gift from Heaven

By Isabella Rose

My cell phone rang early in the morning on July 12, 2013. I didn't get up to answer it, but I knew by the ring tone that it was my mom. Immediately afterwards, the house phone rang. I knew something was wrong, so I called her back. What I learned would forever change my life.

"Your aunt is dead."

"What? No? It must be a mistake," I replied.

"No, Isabella, it's not. She was shot in her driveway shortly after midnight."

I was shocked, confused, and in utter disbelief. I couldn't fathom it. My aunt was an intelligent, good, kind-hearted woman who naturally helped others. Who would do this to her? And why?

Just over four months later, she came to me during a Reiki healing I was receiving. She spoke through the practitioner, answering my questions and calming my fears and concerns. I could tell by the way she spoke that it sounded like my aunt, but it wasn't until she talked about the last day I saw her that I knew for certain that it really was her. As I listened to her words, tears streamed down my face.

Over the next two years, I continued communication with my aunt through a medium and through my own internal senses. Through each contact, I witnessed the progression of her soul – from expecting justice, to understanding it was all part of a soul contract, to forgiveness and love.

During one direct channeling through a medium, she shared the knowledge that she and my other ancestors had reviewed the Family Book. I was to write a happy chapter for our family, ending the cycle of trauma. Three days before the New Moon, following the conclusion of the trial, I took the opportunity to do this. I lit a blessing candle for our family and asked for guidance. I got in my car and quickly realized that I was driving by the murder scene and releasing all discordant energy left behind into the universe for healing and transmutation.

What had begun as a waking nightmare led me to this Divine Gift from Heaven.

Grace of Our Divine Mother

By Sally Pullinger

I have been a trance medium for 40 years, so I am used to spirit beings coming through me – especially my own beloved guide, Chung Fu. I am so grateful for this work, I feel so blessed in my life, and I feel my family is held in the great loving embrace of many Beings of Light.

Over the years, all of this had become quite "normal" to me, but then something extraordinary happened: I was going into trance to receive Chung Fu – relaxing, letting go, breathing deeply – but he didn't come in. Instead, I felt a deeper and deeper silence and a sensation of falling, falling, down and down. My body felt strange and heavy. I really did not know what was happening. I was so used to Chung Fu arriving with a little chuckle, some slightly heavier breathing, and that deep tone of his voice that is so comforting. I asked him inside, "Where are you? What is going on?"

In response, I heard, "Relax, Beloved, all is well. Let go."

Then I heard very long, impossibly high, bird-like sounds and realised they were coming out of my body. My arms lifted up to become wings, my whole body was arching, and my neck was stretched forward like a bird. The high sounds became incomprehensible utterances in some strange alien tongue. The presence was so powerful. Overwhelming love filled my heart. Inside, I recognised this Feminine Being from a higher dimension.

After about 10 minutes, the presence left me. It was an overwhelming *feeling of loss. My heart was burst wide open. I just wanted to stay with* Her forever.

When Chung Fu came into me shortly afterwards, he said that our temple had been visited and blessed by Isa Isa (pronounced "Eessa Eessa"), who is the Goddess Isis. Ever since then, She comes in daily to bless our humble temple. I am so grateful for Her presence in our lives, and now She speaks in English, too!

Divine Mother, you are grace, love, inspiration, beauty, peace, and so much more!

Grace at a Funeral

By Carolyn McGee

My friend lost her mother after a long illness, and what made it even harder was that her mom was so afraid of dying. Her mom wanted to believe that her spirit would continue; but she was fearful, which really distressed my friend.

While attending the funeral, I closed my eyes to pray for my friend's mom. I have a close spiritual relationship with Jesus and felt him standing behind me with his hand on my right shoulder. Then, in my mind's eye, I saw Jesus leave my side and walk up the center aisle to stand by the casket. I was so shocked that I opened my eyes!

I quickly closed them to regain the vision. Jesus looked me in my eyes to make sure I understood that he was with my friend's mom, he had always been by her side, and he would continue to be with her. He was there to take her home. As I continued to watch, his energy merged into the casket with her. It was so powerful and clear that she was now and forevermore with Christ and God. My heart filled with joy and the grace of God. I cried tears of gratitude for the confirmation that we are all connected and valued children of God.

I felt so blessed to be able to provide this message of hope and everlasting love to my friend. She and her family gained incredible peace and grace from this vision. It brought them serenity to know that their mom was not alone and that her spirit was carried home in loving arms.

You Are Never Alone

By Jeanette St. Germain

It had been months of screaming fights, slamming doors, and toiletries thrown down the hall. My brother and I listened from our shared bedroom, our toddler innocence shaken by the venom in the air. We didn't understand the almost-constant anger, the yelling mixed with cutting silence. Our parents were little more than children themselves, struggling to make sense of marital expectations and family responsibilities.

Then one night, my dad stopped coming home. I was only three years old, but I remember the frazzled look in my mother's eyes, the indignant, blaming madness that sparked every time she looked at me. She would mutter under her breath about "that other woman" and spin long-winded tales about how he had abandoned us, not wanting a family or his children. I missed him terribly and, even worse, thought it was my fault he was gone.

My heart cried out to the universe, begging for release from the space of confusion and rejection at my core. There were many nights I would sit by the window, watching cars drive by, praying one of them would bring my dad home. I knew that if my mother saw me cry, she would perceive me as weak or disconnected from reality; so, alone, my tears flowed. My love was hidden, expressed as rattled sobs no louder than a whisper.

One evening, as I rocked beneath the window sill, the air around me suddenly started to thicken. There was a tangible buzz, like an electric wave building to its peak. The hairs on my arms stood up, as if graced by an invisible hand, and I felt a gentle, calming warmth spread through me.

I looked up and noticed a golden glow emanating from some unknown source in front of me. My eyes widened as a male figure materialized, with luminous blue eyes, pearlescent wings, and sunlit-auburn hair. His smile reached to my center and expanded, creating a cocoon of purest love. He was the breath of God, a peaceful blanket wrapped around my heart. As if in response to my thoughts, I heard the words, "We hear you; you are never alone."

Rest High, Sweet Friend

By Shannon Leigh Brokaw

"Oh, how we cried the day you left us..." sang Vince Gill from my car radio as I slowly made my way out of the cemetery.

Twenty-three years young, a man full of life, potential, and a silent personal struggle that no one could ever understand. I had just spoken to your parents as we tried to make sense of your untimely passing and figure out the who, what, why – but it was too nonsensical for my comprehension.

I wracked myself with a hidden and painful guilt, not knowing how I could have missed the signs. I had heard the talk, yet I brushed it off. I pushed you away your last year of life, not wanting to tarnish a lineage with your darkness.

How I had hoped and believed that when you phoned me out of the blue one month prior to your passing that you were on the mend and getting your life back together. You loved your family and had a beautiful girlfriend who meant the world to you. You wanted to live, you told me.

I lectured you about the importance of being clean. "The next time you have an overdose, you won't wake up. Please think of the heartache you'll cause your parents and brother, as well as Joy." I will never forget that conversation – the last one we ever had.

When the phone call came through that you, my sweet friend, were no longer on this earth, a piece of me died. I spent years wondering how I could ever be a good friend to someone if I couldn't even help you.

Then one quiet evening, as I sat in silence, you came to me. I could not mistake the wind coming through the back door for anything other than you; I could smell and feel you go through me. "It is way past time to let this guilt go," you whispered. You were home, where you belonged, and I finally found my grace at peace with your passing.

In memoriam of Eric A. Alberts

A Child's Grace

By Marva Collins-Bush

I felt abandoned by my parents because neither of them had been in my life for a long time. I was raised by my maternal great aunt who I always referred to as my grandmother and called Momma. As young as seven years old, I was carrying a heavy burden that should not have been mine to carry. Before that, I was a fairly carefree and fun-loving kid. I remember that day as if it were right now. I had been at school all day and came bounding into the house with the energy of a seven-year-old. Momma said, "Marva, sit down. I want to talk to you." At the end of our talk, she said, "You can't tell anybody."

I found myself singing a song I'd heard Paul Robeson sing, one that really touched me: "Sometimes I Feel Like a Motherless Child." Somehow that song gave me comfort. When Momma heard me quietly singing that song, she said, "Why Marva, I am going to tell your mother." I stopped singing. My words and my songs were gone.

I went out to the front yard, lay on my back, and watched the cloud formations. That somehow comforted my seven-year-old mind. I'd heard my aunt talk about forever and ever – eternity. I could not wrap my brain around these concepts. I just didn't get it.

I was thinking about those concepts when I saw myself rise from my body. As I rose, an angel took my hand and we continued to rise. When we reached a high place we walked to the precipice. He talked to me for a while, then gestured with his hand and showed me forever and ever. I could scarcely take it in at first. Then I found my place in it and settled in. I was part of forever and ever. I found the place where I was not alone.

The Moment I Discovered My Soul

By Simone Wiedenhöft

I was getting ready to do some office work when I felt a strange feeling coming up, like a strong force pushing against my inner door from somewhere deep inside.

I had never experienced something like that before. To make things more confusing, a question popped up in my mind, again and again: *What am I?* I had no idea how to respond.

So I did what I normally do when faced with big questions: I lay down on my bed, closed my eyes, and tuned in to my inside world. "Dear Universe, please let me know what is important for me to know," I prayed. And then I asked, "What am I?"

The next moment, it was like something huge exploded right inside of me. I suddenly saw, with my physical eyes still closed, all kinds of whirling colors and shapes, and I felt connected to a strong and powerful pulsing energy. Feeling this connection filled me with peace, joy, and pure amazement.

It took me a while to realize that what I was experiencing in that moment was my actual ME. That pulsing energy was my very own essence. This experience was my first introduction to the infinite soul I truly am. I could hardly believe it. What a blessing to feel my truth!

After a while, I started seeing souls in people I worked with. Some were pulsing fields of flowing energy. Some seemed to have a more solid shape, with energies moving inside these shapes. Some even looked organic, like large fields of flowers waving in the wind. I saw all different kinds of colors, and some were changing their colors constantly.

But no matter which particular form or color they had, each was beautiful and powerful. Getting in touch with every single one filled me with peace, joy, and divine wonder.

What I've learned through my encounters with all these souls – beginning with my own – is that we are all infinite energetic beings, unique in our personal expression, huge beyond our own imagination. Even if we can't feel it right now, there is no doubt that we are all beautiful souls.

Visits from Mom

By Felicia D'Haiti

About a week after my fourth child was born, I was hospitalized for having an infected hematoma (a swelling of clotted blood) in my abdomen. It took doctors nearly two weeks to determine why I was experiencing such extreme pain that I could no longer sit up, get out of bed, or walk unassisted. I truly felt helpless as I lay in a hospital bed and watched my husband come back and forth to the hospital with our newborn and three older children.

Once I got home, my mobility had not improved much. I found myself needing help and praying often for healing. There were many times that my husband had to work the night shift after I returned home but was still recovering. He would make sure the baby was asleep and I was set up in our recliner for the night because I still could not get in and out of bed unassisted.

It was during these nights that I noticed, out of the corner of my eye, a shadow passing my door in the hall going in and out of my son's room. I often thought I was dreaming or seeing things. When I would go to check on him, he was comfortable and sleeping well. Sometimes, when his crying woke me up, I saw the shadow for a split second as I was getting up. By the time I was able to get up and go into his room, he was no longer crying but lying in his crib, awake and waiting for some milk or to be changed.

Still wondering if I was seeing things, I asked my other children if they had seen anything. My oldest son talked about Grandma coming at night to read stories to him and make sure he was all right. I then began to reflect on the possibility that my mom, who had died suddenly four years prior, was still with me. I felt even more blessed, protected, loved, and safe. I realized then that I would never be alone.

Named by Grace

By Pami Woodruff

"It's a girl," I said upon awakening after one of those incredibly vivid dreams that are common when you're expecting. "And her name is…"

My then-husband and I had been trying to conceive for several years, so we were excited when the pregnancy was confirmed. We had asked the ultrasound tech not to tell us the gender because we wanted to be surprised, which meant coming up with two sets of names.

"James Nicholas? Maybe Rebecca Lynn?" I'd ask.

"My niece is Rebecca," he'd counter. "What about Carla?"

We'd tossed names about like hacky sacks all spring and summer. By mid-July, I'd gotten to the uncomfortable stage of my pregnancy, and we still didn't have a name.

Then, the dream. A voice – I had labeled it God – told me, as clear as day, "Her name is Virginia Suzanne."

Not "will be." "Is."

"…Virginia Suzanne," I told him. "Virginia after your late mom, and Suzanne is a variation on my middle name. It's perfect!"

And she was. Pretty, happy, outgoing, and with the smooth, gliding movements she'd patented in utero. We couldn't have been happier.

She grew up knowing she'd been named after me and the grandmother she would never meet, but she was still curious. "What does my name mean?" she asked one day, balancing on the back of the couch. "Not the 'her name is' story, but what the words mean."

I smiled, then laughed as she tumbled onto the carpet at the very moment the words left my mouth. "Graceful young woman," I said, then, between giggles, "Grace, for short."

Graced with a Visitation

By Elizabeth R. Kipp

I rise to this day with sadness and the bittersweet thought that today is my niece Sarah's birthday. Sarah was taken by the dreaded disease of addiction in April of 2014. She was such a beautiful soul with, among other things, the generous gifts of spirit and song. I feel her physical absence from this realm as a hollow recess echoing inside my heart, and I ache for the continued grief our family feels around her passing. I send prayers for Sarah and our family in hopes that we will all find a nurturing peace to fill that emptiness we feel reverberating with her absence. The prayer's grace eases into my soul.

I begin my early-morning routine and find my spirit buoyed further as I hear an early-rising wren burst into song just outside. I set myself to wash dishes by the kitchen window that opens to the west. A mourning dove sits in the walnut tree outside the window. Its head points in my direction. In this moment, I feel I am communing with this solitary bird perched in the tree in front of me. It seems that Sarah's spirit has stopped by and graced me with a brief visit. As our moments together end, the dove bows three times, its head still pointed towards me, and then lifts off, heading east.

It is fitting to have this particular bird share some space with me on Sarah's birthday. Beyond the symbolism of death in its name and its seemingly sorrowful song, this bird represents the message of life, hope, renewal, and peace. It is centered in optimism.

As I move into my day, having been greeted by the wren's joyful song and then visited by the mourning dove, I am heartened. Grace is present in all of this. We will find solace and peace to fill our hearts through all that we share – from the joyful to the tragic.

Jesus Walks with Me

By Pamela Forseth

I lay awake in bed in the wee hours of morning on June 6, 2008. I had been awake almost the entire night, tossing and turning, unable to shut off the "stinkin' thinkin'" that filled my head. I rolled over once again to look at the clock; it was 5:30 a.m.

I was so tired. I was so sick. And I felt more alone than I'd ever felt in my life. I didn't think I could go on another day. I prayed for help. The next time I looked at the clock, it was 7:30 a.m. In my mind, I replayed every moment of what I'd experienced over the last two hours:

I was in a temple with marble floors, marble walls, and stained-glass windows that ran from floor to ceiling. The light pouring through those windows was the purest light I had ever seen – glowing and glistening and filling the entire temple with luminescent radiance.

A balcony, also made of marble, stretched all across the upper portion of the room. I looked up and saw my entire family – even my mother, who had died nine years earlier. I also saw that the balcony was filled with angels. They were singing – a true angelic choir, creating music that sounded more heavenly than anything I could have imagined…even for angels!

Then a man walked in, dressed in a white cloak that tied with a rope belt. He had a small beard and mustache and medium-brown, shoulder-length hair with a slight wave. He held his hand out to me; I took it. Then I looked into his eyes and felt the purest, most gentle love I have ever experienced. There was no judgment, nothing but love in those eyes. At that moment, I realized it was Jesus.

I did not want to move; I did not want to leave that moment, for I felt safe and secure. But then I realized the message Jesus had come to give to me: In those times when I feel loneliness overwhelm me, when I think all is lost, remember that I am NOT alone! Jesus always walks with me, holding my hands, guiding me, and loving me unconditionally. He is with me no matter what. All I have to do is remember that moment, that feeling. It's there always.

Graced by a Goddess

By Michelle McDonald Vlastnik

"Every woman who heals herself helps heal all the women who
came before her and all those who will come after."
- Dr. Christiane Northrup

I was guided to start my Believe Circle project in 2012, and it really began blooming in a magical way in 2015 – once I let go, let God, and let life unfold.

On January 7, 2016, I met with the Council of Light and asked them, "Are there any beliefs or blocks in the area of receptivity or receiving that need to be addressed in my generational energy work?" I was told yes, the lineage on my mom and grandma's side was clogged with unworthiness. The women had given away their feminine power away by being who they were told to be or thought they should be.

Two days later, under the Leo New Moon, an energetic lineage clearing and celebration ceremony for all of these women was created by calling in Archangel Haniel, Jophiel, Goddess Artemis, and Isis, forming a sacred circle. My maternal female ancestors from present to centuries back were invited in. I could feel the energy build as each soul entered my invisible net of love – a safe haven to release old baggage of unworthiness, belittlement, disempowerment, or beliefs and experiences blocking their receptivity. I bestowed a blessing of unconditional love and Goddess light, filling their cup, honoring each one as she stepped into her power of Self.

We celebrated our ONEness and raised a glass of wine and toasted, "MY POWER'S TURNED ON!"

The next day, these words within a Sunday sharing called "Grace" by Cynthia Cebuhar sang synchronicity. She shared, "I believe the flow of grace is circular; receiving and giving, blessing and mercy, healing and wholeness, receiving and giving...and so it goes. Grace abounds. Grace surrounds." This quote was my validation from the Universe for my powerful healing work.

What Is a Miracle?

By Tiffany Andersen

Surviving a major accident...being thrown from the car onto the freeway at 65 miles an hour.

Walking again when the doctors told my mom I would never walk again.

Being days away from death...and surviving stage-4 cancer.

To my surprise, God had other plans.

These are obvious miracles...at least for me. But what about the moments when you know – without a shadow of doubt – you have received a message from the other side. To me, these are the most powerful of all.

With death knocking on my door – stage-4 cancer coming to take my life – I finally got it. I fell to my knees and prayed to the heavens above:

Dear God, I am not ready. I am not worthy. If you give me this one last chance, I promise to bring glory to your name. But Father, if you cannot use me for good, bring me home to be with you. I do not want to waste my life away again.

With tears in my eyes I reached for my Bible hoping I would receive a message from the other side; much to my surprise, I did.

Daughter, your faith has made you well. Go in peace. (Luke 8:48)

I knew, God as my witness, I would be healed. The physical part was yet to come. But I knew that, no matter how dark the valley of death I was to walk through, I would come out on the other side alive.

Many similar miracles have happened since God first woke me from a death slumber with cancer threatening my life. What a blessing it is to believe in such power given from above – the most precious of all gifts: faith, hope, and love.

My Spiritual Transformation

By Joanne Angel Barry Colon

My spiritual journey began on June 22, 2007, when my 12-year relationship came to an end, and it went into the fast lane when my mom crossed over to the spirit world on March 12, 2010. Her sudden death hit me hard, especially because she went into the hospital on my 41st birthday and died just eight days later.

After my mother's passing, I started seeing, hearing, and feeling her during Reiki sessions, and her presence became even stronger when I worked with crystals. Any time I needed guidance, I would call on my mother. Her answers came in many forms, such as seeing butterflies or numbers – especially 1024 (her birthday) or 312 (the day she crossed over).

Approximately two years after my mom's passing, my sisters and I cleaned out her closets and drawers and found a beautiful black tourmaline stone. We weren't sure whom it belonged to; however, I remembered my mother saying that my great-grandma was psychic, so I assumed it was hers. I sat quietly and meditated with the stone, asking to see the face of the person it belonged to. Later that day, my sister gave me a photo with my great-grandma's name on the back. When I saw it, I felt a tingling sensation throughout my body. That's when I knew my question had been answered. From that day on, I felt connected to my great-grandma and called on her for guidance as well.

Since these experiences jump-started my spiritual journey, I've been blessed with many other moments of grace. But I will always be especially grateful for the spiritual awakening I experienced through my connection with my mother and my great-grandma.

The Return of Martin

By Sally Pullinger

My beautiful daughter, Sophie, was two when her daddy committed suicide by fire. We weren't there. We weren't allowed to see. There was no closure. No one could help – everyone was lost for words or wisdom, devastated that such a deep and gentle man was gone.

The spirits were kind. The angels gathered around. We were gently guided here and there – to a magical homeopath, to a healer, to a circle of mediums. Someone was watching over me and my baby. But I was broken somewhere deep inside, sobbing inconsolably. I believed in God, but what could God do to help me? Martin was gone, forever gone. I couldn't see him, touch him, hold him.

I joined Ivy Northage's development circle. After six months, during the opening meditation, I heard voices: "Look! He's so tall and handsome…such blue eyes!" All up my right side, I was getting hotter and hotter, and inside, too – burning up, overflowing with tears. I wanted to cry, to scream.

Ivy came and held me close to her heart, telling me, "It is Martin saying hello. He loves you so much. He wants you to know it wasn't your fault. He says don't ever feel guilty. It was a momentary decision, a mistake. He so wishes he were still here with you and his beloved daughter."

As she held me, a deep peace came over me. Martin was alive, he loved us, and he was talking to me through this kind medium. She was confirming what I was hearing and feeling inside, and somehow it didn't hurt so much now, knowing he was still right here in his body of light.

Healing from this loss has brought me and my family such grace. We now live our lives working closely with all the spirits who encircle us, helping others also receive the love of angels and beings of light who show us that from the world called death comes a life and a light that never dies.

Spirit Awakened

By Judy McNutt

It was the summer of 1962, the first day of my school vacation. A pine-scented breeze through my bedroom window inspired me to take the half-mile walk down to the Strawberry Lodge to pester my friends for a ride on their horse.

Skipping along in the dusty gravel of Fossil Creek Road, all of a sudden I had the feeling that I was about to fly. I stretched out my arms and embraced the day. In an instant, the world brightened as if awakening from a long, cozy sleep. Sunflowers waved in the soft breeze, bees buzzed and zoomed around me, and sunlight warmed my shoulders and the top of my head.

Stepping off the road, I sat down on a smooth stone and looked up at the jubilant birds filling the robin's-egg-blue sky. Across the meadow, a woodpecker knocked and chipped at the bark of a tree. Two grey squirrels chased and fussed. Gnats clouded together, buzzing in the dappled shade.

In a matter of seconds, I took all of this in. Then I heard a voice say, "So it begins."

My stomach flip-flopped like a car at the top of a Ferris wheel. No one was there, yet the message was clearly meant for me. I experienced my first inner *Knowing*: "You will walk a different path."

I went home, crawled into bed, and confided in the secret section of my notebook.

One day, months later while brushing my grandmother's hair, I spoke of The Voice I had heard that day. She replied simply, "Well, now I know why I feel better when you are near me."

Although only 11 years old, I felt the grace within me awaken. The inner me instinctively knew that The Voice had spoken the truth. A door opened, and everything beyond the world spilled in.

Since my first Awakening, I have continued to connect with Spirit daily. When I listen deeply to the Grace awakened within me, I feel the presence of that blissful summer day.

Love Never Dies
By Sharon Hickinbotham

On January 9, 2014, I lost my brother, Darren, to suicide. As hard as it was to lose him, in many ways it was even harder to go on living without him – trying to find my joy and my purpose while feeling every hurt, every scar, and all the pain weighing me down. I missed seeing him and was constantly reminded of the broken link in our family chain.

Shortly after his death – while I was struggling to understand the *why* of his loss and the *how* of my own life – I had a vivid dream. He walked up to me, held me tightly, and telepathically said to me: "I'm not dead. I'm very much alive, just in another form, in spirit, and I am helping you always. You are never alone. But you need to move on, to live. I'll live within you. There are people who love you and want you be happy. That's what I want for you – love, laughter, and smiles." He continued to hug me until I woke up from the dream, my face drenched with tears.

Through that dream, I realized that Darren knows what I'm going through. He's helping me to get through my day-to-day struggles, to have confidence, to live, love, laugh, and be happy again. Since then, I've also found hope and solace through the endless signs from Darren in spirit, telling me that he is still with me.

My journey of grief has been incredibly painful and difficult, but it's also taught me so much. It's led me to offer intuitive readings and to help relay messages and guidance from loved ones in spirit. It's also led me to write and share my life stories with others. It's taught me that everything that happens in life shapes you into the person you are today.

Above all, it's taught me that love never dies.

A Cat, an Angel, and Grace

By Janet G. Nestor

I have a good friend and guide who is a dancing, prancing, tail straight up and wagging white cat. I first met him during a shaman-led soul journey. He and Archangel Michael created a fun-loving intervention that ended my fear of flying.

One day my white cat appeared during a flight, and he remained my travel companion until I learned to relax and laugh at 36,000 feet. The intervention began as I settled into my seat. I glanced out the window and noticed him sitting human style, legs crossed with one leg dangling over the edge of the wing. He was goofing around and doing funny things that he knew would keep my focus on him. I watched as the wind flattened his fur. At one point, I saw him sitting quietly reading a book. Traveling with him was like being the straight man in a comedy routine, which helped to put me at ease.

After many flights together, my cat stopped appearing. I felt empty without him, yet my thoughts were filled with mental pictures of his silly antics. The next time I traveled, I sat in the middle seat of three, enjoying the gift of extra space. Gradually, I became aware of a presence and turned toward the window to find Archangel Michael sitting in the seat beside me. We sat shoulder to shoulder for the whole flight and neither one of us spoke a word. Intuitively I knew why he was traveling with me. My eyes filled with tears that didn't fall as I experienced the transformational peace of his presence.

When I walked off the plane that day, I walked out of my fear, never again to be a white-knuckled passenger. Even in the midst of two mid-flight emergencies, I've remained free of the terror of flying.

Archangel Michael continues to be my friend and teacher, and I am extraordinarily grateful for his loving presence, which infuses me with strength. And just the thought of my white cat makes me chuckle. He left me with visions of absurd behavior that lovingly replace my fear with laughter. Together, they worked as a perfect team to help me to enjoy flying, which was definitely an act of grace.

A Dream that Spoke to Me

By Stella Tassone

My grandfather, my "Nonno," was a remarkable, hard-working man, and I loved and adored him dearly. One night, he came to me in a dream and told me he was on fire – burning!

I woke up in a state of fright, wondering how he could be burning. He wasn't cremated, so what was he trying to tell me?

Puzzled, I called my mum and described my dream. She told me my grandmother still lights a candle every night by a framed photo of him in her lounge. Perhaps it was that. She'd tell her to stop lighting it.

A few weeks later, I travelled six hours to visit my family home and go to Nonno's grave. As I walked towards his grave, I noticed the tomb beside him had a rose bush at the end. I also noticed it was black and had been burnt. I caught my breath, as the puzzle of the dream finally came together. I stood there at the end of his grave and began to cry – because what was once a beautiful rose bush had been burnt and because he had chosen to visit me in my dream. I truly felt him with me.

This was my first experience of connecting to someone who was no longer physically in this realm, which made me believe that there are many ways that loved ones who have passed over can still communicate with us. It is a moment of grace that will remain with me forever.

Why Do You Think God Is a He?

By Cat Williford

The noon hike into the Haleakala Crater on Maui Island wasn't as easy as it looked from the rim. Each time I thought of calling it quits, I felt pushed farther by an unseen hand I didn't believe in anymore. I was there alone to purge the grief around my father's death, which my kidney donation hadn't been able to prevent.

"Stop pushing me, dammit!" Perched on a rock for rest and water, I considered rant writing. Instead, rage bubbled out of me like lava. I paced around the rock.

"Fair and just? Merciful? B.S.! Lies. Stupid lies!" I yelled. "Daddy saved thousands of lives with his surgeon's scalpel, and You couldn't help us?" The image of the ICU nurse erasing Daddy's name from the board the morning he died played on a loop in my head. The scar that wraps around the right side of my waist was on fire, and my thoughts were running wild. "Six months of prayers for Daddy to live…come home…and You listen to the *one* prayer I barely whispered: 'I give up if he's ready to go'? You're nothing but an illusion for the masses, like the atheists say. Heavenly Father? Heavenly *joke* is more like it!"

Fist-shaking rage dissipated, I crumpled onto the hot ground, quiet enough to hear a lilting feminine voice behind me ask, "Why do you think God is a he?"

Certain the voice came from outside my head, I turned in a slow circle. Nobody. Nothing.

Oh, crap. I've cracked. I've really lost it now, I thought.

"Why do you think God is a he?" the feminine voice asked again with such gentleness that my tears seemed startled into submission.

For the first time in three years since the hell in hospitals began, I felt a calm sweep through me. Sitting statue still, years of Sunday school teachings melted like wax, seeming to drain out of me into the crater. I had actually tried to live the myth of savior, and it had led me here.

I went into the crater raging with grief and came out of it completely transformed, thanks to this loving voice, which I now refer to as the Divine Feminine, the Modern Goddess. Her Grace is forever rooted in my soul.

Blue Diamond's Graceful Call

By Laurie Cagno

As a natural-born singer with intuitive gifts, deep empathy, and a great passion for life, I've spent much of my life soaring high on my dreams and visions. But I've also had my share of pushing and pulling, fussing and fighting. At times, I've felt backed into a tight corner, trapped within my artist's ego – my head filled with noise and confusion. There was a time when I even doubted my own soul's wisdom, my inner song, my own voice.

Then I heard the message: "When the outside is silent, the teacher from inside our heart speaks volumes." So I sank into the silence, where I heard the whispers calling to me, bringing me face to face with my source – wise, blue-diamond eyes that saw right through my own warm, brown eyes, shaking me to the core, filling me with waves of love and clarity. "Sing, songbird, sing," I heard. "Heal those broken wings and fly. Watch, look, and listen as your soul soars and roars, moving mountains."

The whispers of Blue Diamond's graceful call return me to my true essence, revealing me to myself, filling me with love, transforming me with each breath I take. I am cut by the powerful silence, set free. Gentle, wonder-full tears bleed into me, seeping tenderly, covering and coloring me, filling me to overflowing through passionate kisses in my mind's eye.

I find my voice rising again in a tapestry of sighs and woes, highs and lows, as I sing in celebration. Yes, we bloom where we are, even when we fall. With a new dawn, light peeks through. And with eyes wide open, I see a glimpse of shifting tides as a new song arrives.

Your Inner Light Is a Beautiful Gift

By Wendyanne Pakulsky

Your inner light is a beautiful gift. It is like an elixir of grace, strength, and love that never lets you down. If you lean into this light, you will always have direction and strength to follow what is true to your authentic self.

I know this now, but there was a time when I was unsure – unsure of my direction in life and unsure of myself. I felt that my outer shell was crumbling, exposing an uncomfortable place deep in the centre of my being. Looking back, I see this as the beginning of a profound healing, but at the time it just felt scary. As much as I wanted to ignore what was happening, I couldn't. I had no choice but to honour the uncomfortable because it felt like part of my authentic self.

One night during this process, my grandmother came to me in a dream. She opened a door and entered my room. "Shine your light," she said. "It is beautiful, Wendyanne. Listen to what it is teaching you." She herself was shining brightly, glowing with an angelic radiance. "Believe in your inner self," she continued. "And know that the angels are always watching over you. You will get through this. Everything is going to be all right." Then she faded away and the door closed.

I knew that an angel had graced me that night with loving reassurance, giving me the confidence to follow my intuition and shine my light. After that dream, I knew that my recent experiences of feeling scared and uncomfortable were just part of a deep healing, pushing me into an energetic vibration of ever-increasing love and light. From that day forward, I knew that this inner light would unravel itself and guide me in any decision that awaited me. What a beautiful gift!

Angel Warrior
By Ana Gordon

On the last leg of a long journey, I arrived at the airport late at night, with only minutes to spare before my connecting flight home. I soon discovered that the airport was undergoing major renovations, making everything difficult to navigate.

Since it was the middle of the night, there was no one around to ask for help. I finally managed to locate a departure screen, which displayed my flight but not the vital information of a gate number. I felt a wave of exhaustion and frustration and was about to panic.

At just that moment, I looked up to see an unusual-looking man walking toward me. He was really big and tall and was wearing a plaid lumberjack shirt. He approached me and asked if he could help. I think he said, "What do you need," or he may have simply said, "The gate for flight such and such is 27, over there to the left."

You can imagine my utter relief! I went to make my way to the gate, glancing back in a split second to thank him properly, but he was nowhere to be seen. There were miles of clear walkway space in this cavernous airport hangar portal – it was as though he had just evaporated.

I have never forgotten this encounter. It delivered the exact information I needed at the exact moment I needed it, arriving out of nowhere.

To this day, I can clearly remember how totally at ease I felt in his presence, which invoked such a deep trust and complete reassurance that all was okay, which calmed me immediately.

Also, I know him. I have never "seen" him before or since, but I know he is my close guide who materialized into form when I needed him most.

This encounter showed me something essential about the blessed beings surrounding me. It has allowed me to feel protected, loved, and nourished in the embrace of the Divine.

Thank you, Angel Warrior – you have changed my life.

Chapter 2
Physical Shake-Ups & Near-Death Experiences

We both spent many years as skeptics, questioning whether there was anything beyond this physical reality. Over the years, however, through our own firsthand experiences and eye-opening (and heart-opening) miraculous accounts shared by others (especially stories of near-death experiences), we've come to believe that there is more to this life than meets the eye.

While every near-death experience is unique, many common themes emerge – showing that these are not merely subjective anomalies. Chances are, you've heard accounts of people who, while clinically dead, entered a realm of light and beauty, encountered angelic beings, felt an extraordinary sense of peace and love, and knew that dying was not to be feared. Jodi's grandfather and mother both had near-death experiences, which included these beautiful elements.

But you don't need a brush with death to experience a moment of grace. Oftentimes, a serious illness can inspire people to reflect upon their lives, re-evaluate their priorities, and make more soulful choices. An injury can also be seen as the universe's not-so-subtle way of encouraging (or forcing) you in a new direction. And physical shake-ups of all kinds can strengthen your faith in yourself, in your body's wisdom, and in the world beyond.

In the pages that follow, you'll find miraculous stories of near-death experiences and physical shake-ups that altered the authors' lives in dramatic ways. You'll read about illness and injury that initially seemed disastrous yet, over time, proved to be grace-filled turning points. You'll also read about people being given the chance to make new choices and change their lives forever. It's such an inspirational chapter, and we're so happy to share these remarkable stories with you!

The Day Grace Came Crashing Down
By Jodi Chapman

I always longed to be a writer. But I also longed for security. I didn't truly believe that I could support myself with my writing, so I went against my soul's calling after college and got a "real job" working as an editor for the government.

Shortly after I was hired a war broke out, and I ended up editing war documents, which hurt my heart every day. I was torn because I loved being able to support myself, but I couldn't squash the inner whisper saying that this wasn't my path. I tried hard to ignore it – telling myself that feeling secure was what mattered most. But it only grew louder – begging me to quit.

On August 31, 2002, the decision was made for me: I was in a horrible car accident that left me with injuries that made it impossible to edit.

Due to my injuries, I was laid off from my job and spent the next two years healing at home – visiting countless doctors who tried to put my body back together. During this time, I was very angry – at the woman who turned in front of me, at the insurance company, at my job, at my body, and at life.

I held on to this anger for years – until one day I realized that this was all an act of grace. Getting into this car crash was the best thing that could've happened to me. I wasn't going to leave my job on my own. I needed something this drastic to pull me away. My life was going in the wrong direction, and I needed a crash to (literally) stop it in its tracks.

It's now been almost 14 years since this happened, and I am happy to say that my life has improved greatly. I am a writer and have made a living at writing for the past decade. I'm on my path, and my soul is happy.

Grace came crashing down on me in an unexpected but completely loving way, and I am forever grateful.

One Day, Two Words, Three Moments of Grace

By Michelle Radomski

Rain streamed down the window and tears spilled from my eyes as the doctor shared two words that would turn our world upside down: *kidney disease.*

At the time, it was impossible to see how that one day and those two words could miraculously lead us to three moments of grace. And yet, that is exactly what happened.

The first moment came on a cold day in November 2009, as our very wise, very powerful, 13-year-old daughter listened carefully while her doctor gently and compassionately explained that she had a rare form of kidney disease. The disease could go one of two ways: Her kidney function could slowly begin to decline and she could potentially need dialysis and an eventual transplant, or the disease could just disappear through a process called spontaneous remission. There was no known treatment. We would just have to monitor the disease and watch its progress.

I felt the presence of grace as my child processed the information, took a deep breath, squared her shoulders, and simply stated, "I choose remission." She never wavered; she knew she would be healed.

My daughter might have been filled with certainty, but me?...not so much.

My mind raced with fear and my heart was heavy with pain. I frantically searched the internet for answers, relief, and hope. I cried. I worried. I screamed.

Day by day, I sank deeper and deeper into despair until, mercifully, I finally found my way to my knees. Grace met me there, and in a moment I will never forget, everything changed.

My heart opened wide to the Divine. Hope returned. I was able to connect with the place where I knew my child would indeed be healed. My business changed. I came out of hiding and began sharing my voice. And from this place of grace, I said yes to my passion and began creating my mandala art.

Three years later, on a sunny day in May, our third moment of grace arrived when we heard the two words we'd been waiting for: *total remission.*

Coming Back to Life with Grace
By Mimi Quick

The night had a chill, yet it felt warm at the same time, causing me to think, *Hmm, this is odd*. I was in the car with my brother, talking away, having fun as we always did. As my brother was speaking, I heard an inner voice say, "Look out!" But before I could even get the words out, we were hit by another car that had run a red light. I heard a loud crashing sound, and then I was immediately somewhere else.

I died.

My spirit left my body, and I was transported to a place that was foggy, cloudy, and very serene. I had no pain, and I felt nothing but goodness, love, and high-vibration energy. I wondered where I was, what I was doing there, and why. I understood that I was not in my body, but I also understood that it was not yet my time to be in this place.

I heard some chatter and saw two brightly lit silhouettes holding what looked like a piece of paper. They talked quietly, but I could not make out what they were saying. I wanted to know what they were talking about. I wanted to know what they were holding. I wanted all of my questions answered.

Finally, the beings came closer to me and said, "You have a choice: You can stay here, or you can go back."

Without hesitation I said, "My brother is there," and within a split second I was back in my body.

I felt pain in my chest from where the car airbags had hit me. Beside me in this smoking, mangled mess of a car, my brother sat slumped in his seat, unconscious. I called out for help, shaking my brother's leg. He started to wake up, and I told him everything would be okay.

And it was.

Glimpsing Grace in the Jungle

By Helen Rebello

I'll never forget the contrast between arriving as a lost soul at a yoga retreat in Sri Lanka and leaving 11 days later, deeply peaceful and irrevocably changed.

After a complicated hysterectomy 10 weeks earlier, I was sore, weak, and emotionally raw. Unused to feeling vulnerable, I had deliberately placed myself somewhere I couldn't run from because I knew I had a lot to process.

And so the healing began.

I fell down and got back up, cried my heart out, bared my soul, and said farewell to motherhood. Bit by bit, slowly and painfully, I started to rebuild with help from those around me.

On the day grace found me, we wrote down our deepest desire – I chose *presence*. One by one, we were then lovingly guided to use a focus to help us access our word.

I was guided to stand – to ground, breathe, and *be*. Using minimal words, my wonderful teacher instructed me to send energetic roots deep into the ground beneath the deck and to direct my gaze softly beyond the forest to the distant mountains. As I stood and expanded, the world before me slowly changed.

One moment, the world looked as it always does. The next, a silvery, liquid-like matrix formed between the trees, and everything shifted. Unwittingly, I entered a parallel world where life shimmered with depth, richness, and colour. I felt held, supported, and loved – and finally able to let go and move on.

It is hard to convey the deep peace, knowing, and profound grace I experienced in that moment. Everything I previously thought was important simply melted away. Just like that, standing on a deck in the heart of the Sri Lankan jungle, I glimpsed the magical inter-connectedness of everything. That was the moment I knew grace.

All it took was for me to allow myself time in nature to be present, grounded, and still – a rare moment in life that changed all subsequent moments.

A String of Grace
By Brenda Reiss

Saving my life took more than a moment; it took an entire *string* of grace. The string began at my grandson's Christmas concert, when I noticed that I couldn't see him. In fact, I couldn't see a whole section of his class. I had been so busy over the last few months – going through training and learning to build a business – that I had brushed off the constant headache and blurriness in my right eye, but now it went beyond that. I was going blind in my right eye.

This troubling realization led me straight to a doctor who wanted tests, and then to others who wanted even more tests. The string of grace continued, as doctors' schedules that had had waiting lists for several months all of a sudden had room for me. Spaces opened up and MRIs were taken on short notice. Specialists called in favors to one another. Doctors who were supposed to be leaving town stayed for me.

When I got back the results, grace was all that held me together as I heard the words: "brain tumor" and "surgery needed ASAP." This was Thursday, six days before Christmas. Surgery was scheduled for Monday.

Brain surgery wasn't in my realm of understanding. I knew that, as with any major surgery, there was an element of risk. But I also knew that not having surgery involved risks – including blindness and possibly death from a blood clot. I had the weekend to decide: Do I wait to see if I can heal myself holistically, or do I have a procedure to remove this tumor that's strangling my optic nerve and overtaking my pituitary gland?

I knew not to make this decision alone. In my shocked state, I prayed and said, "I need a sign about whether or not to have surgery, and I want it by tomorrow." Pretty bold, I thought, but I was desperate.

The final sign came through two holistic doctors who weren't supposed to be available but were. They both guided me to have the surgery, having faith that grace would work through the hands of the surgeon. And it did. I awoke from that surgery alive, able to see, and more grateful than ever for the power of grace.

Rescued by Hands of Grace

By Kim Steadman

I sat in my little child-sized lawn chair in the metal, flat-bottomed boat, playing with my paper dolls while my parents fished. In childlike, wide-eyed wonder, I surveyed the surrounding scene and absorbed the sights and smells of the warm Texas summer day.

Unexpectedly, a slight gust of wind swooped one of the paper dolls over the edge of the boat and into the water. I slipped my little arm over to retrieve it, but it was out of my reach. I stretched just a little bit farther...

Too far!

The splash of my body tumbling headfirst was met almost instantaneously by the sound of my dad diving in after me. The water was green, dark, and murky, as are many manmade lakes in Texas. I remember the rays of the sun being darkened by bubbles floating past my eyes as I sank deeper into the dark water.

My dad remembers that he lost sight of me almost immediately in the dark and murky lake. He dove in and swam down, trying to discern an outline of my body. I was doing my best to get back to the surface, but my dog paddling efforts were hindered by one thing: I was swimming in the wrong direction! Each little paddle took me farther away from the loving hands that reached for me.

Miraculously, my dad eventually felt my hand and was able to grab me. He quickly pulled me to the surface and tossed me upward to the boat and into my loving mother's arms.

I've known my entire life that I was spared that day. What could have been a tragic end to the short book of my life ended instead with a rescue by loving arms. I've often thought of that day as my personal daily reminder of God's Grace. It's been the guiding light that has taught me that there are days that you define, and then there are days that define you.

Grace also reminds me to make every day count.

How the Angels Saved My Life

By Catherine M. Laub

In 2005, I had one third of my large intestine removed due to a pre-cancerous polyp. After that, my irritable bowel syndrome got much worse. In 2007, I had a hernia repaired on the connecting spot of the original surgery. A mesh was implanted to hold it in place. Then, during a routine colonoscopy in the summer of 2012, my gastro doctor informed me that I had hundreds of pre-cancerous polyps in my colon and needed to have most of the remaining section removed.

Little did I know it then, but this "bad news" would actually turn out to be a life-saving development. A few months later, in October 2012, the angels saved my life by guiding me to a surgeon who went beyond the initial problem and found a much bigger one. I told my surgeon that I had been having pain in my abdomen but none of my doctors acknowledged it because they didn't feel anything there. So, during my surgery, he explored and found my implanted mesh strangling my small intestine and the tacks holding it in place beginning to puncture through the intestine. He told me that if he hadn't done the surgery then, it would have been only be a matter of time until the tacks punctured all the way into the intestine, causing a septic infection and, most likely, killing me.

My recovery took a lot longer than expected, due to the extensive surgery to remove the tacks and mesh. But, all along, I knew that my angels were by my side, guiding me. To this day, I continue to rely on them to get me through any situation.

Intuition as Grace in Action

By Vanessa Codorniu

Mystery and fear surrounded December 21, 2012. As an intuitive healer and teacher, I was overrun with questions about the Mayan calendar. Uneasy about our family trip that December morning, my mom and I decided to tag team. She said, "I'll pray."

"Okay," I said. "I'll add Reiki."

My older brother and his family led the caravan. My parents and I were in the middle car, with my brother and his fiancée behind us.

Dozing off in the back seat, I "heard" my soul offer a series of directions, starting with: "Ask your parents about their seatbelts." I did, and my mom put hers on. My soul continued: "Take off your metal bracelet. It will hurt your wrist." I slipped it off. Resting in the backseat, with my legs perpendicular, I had one between the front seats. "Move your legs so when something bad happens, you won't break your back." I moved immediately. "Sit up straight." Done.

Minutes later, I opened my eyes as the tires burst and we careened towards a gasoline truck! Stunned, I continued the dialogue with my soul:

Me: "Is this the way it ends this time around?"

Soul: "No, it doesn't end this way. There is still more to do!"

Me: "Is this what it feels like to die? Can we leave the body before I am fatally injured? Can I help my family through this afterwards?"

Soul: "No, you will be fine."

Because I had no seatbelt, I pressed myself tightly into the seat. Glass shattered. Veering away from the truck, we fell off the road and flipped twice. A metal divider finally stopped us. Landing upside down, I looked up at my parents hanging from the ceiling in their seat belts. We were alive!

Crawling out of the car, I heard, "Do not fear. Live your life fully. Do what you were born to do."

Living an intuition-led life literally saved my mom's life and my own. After the accident, I never returned to corporate work. Fears now seem smaller, life feels fuller, and my desire to share what I know to be true is stronger than ever! And I learned this lesson once and for all: Heed your intuitive guidance; it is pure, divine grace in action.

Showered by Grace

By Martina E. Faulkner

Years ago, as I started my journey through the refiner's fire, I was brought to my knees at a most inopportune time: I was in the middle of my morning shower.

While lathering up my hair, I found myself overwhelmed by grief, pain, and tears. My journey of shedding layers of imperceptible veneers had begun, and it was painful. Unexpectedly, with a mountain of bubbles on my head, I fell to my knees, sobbing.

Crumpled on the shower floor, with water pouring over my skin but not cleansing any part of me, I couldn't utter a word. I silently wailed as my tears mixed with the stream of soap and water from above. I could barely breathe. Immobilized, I watched in awe as my hands reached up.

Like a child drawing on a foggy winter window, my fingers knew what to do when I had lost any semblance of presence in myself. They wrote on the shower wall:

Help.

A single word inscribed in the mist was my call for assistance.

The effort it took humbled me further. As the water began to cool, with the bubbles all but gone and my shoulders hunched forward in a semi-fetal position, I felt a calm fall over me.

My mind began to settle as my heart returned to a steady rhythm. My tears, though still flowing, were a gentle trickle instead of a torrent. As I started breathing more deeply and steadily, I noticed my pain had eased.

My cry – my plea for help – had resulted in a warm embrace in the most unlikely of places. Mixed with the water from the shower, my tears had become diluted, free to flow out and away from me. I felt held.

I still use the shower wall to send messages to what I now refer to as my spiritual team. Whether they are messages of gratitude or renewed requests for assistance, there's a knowing that comes almost instantly the moment my fingers begin to glide across the steamy glass.

From Fatal to Fabulous

By Claire Peters

October 24, 1994, was a day like no other. It will stand out in my mind forever.

I had been getting sicker and sicker over a period of nine years, with various symptoms and health issues. Tons of doctors told me there was absolutely nothing wrong with me, that my bloodwork was perfect. I knew they were wrong. In truth, I was dying.

My daughter, Helene, begged me to go to just one more doctor, hers at the time. Just one more. I refused. I just couldn't be made to feel like a total dunce again when I knew the medical community was wrong. But Helene persisted, and she initiated what became my moment of grace.

Helene's doctor saw what was wrong and diagnosed me correctly. It now had a name: Cushing's Syndrome. With this syndrome, the body attacks the organs, causing them to fail. If left untreated (as so many doctors did because they didn't know any better), it can be fatal.

I asked for God's grace for the very complicated, nine-hour surgery to remove my left adrenal gland, which housed the culprit tumor causing major endocrine problems. The moment I remember best is when the Chief of Pathology came, clipboard in hand, to visit me at my hospital bed after the adrenalectomy. He introduced himself and told me that he generally doesn't visit patients – his job being in the lab. But he felt he just had to see the person whose pathology was so deadly.

Despite the dire nature of my condition, I did recover and I'm here to tell the tale! Twenty-one years later, I am 76 years old, happily married, a mother, grandmother, great-grandmother, and entrepreneur (life and business coach, speaker, bestselling author, and businesswoman). I am making the very best of this additional time in my life – given to me by the grace of God and my daughter, Helene.

Embodying Clear Vision

By Sharon Rosen

I've always engaged in practices to keep my inner vision clear, but my physical vision had become a mess.

Cataracts? At 56? I figured the slight lack of focus meant it was time for a prescription upgrade; it always had before. Ever since first grade, when Mrs. Wolf told my mom that I couldn't read the blackboard from the first row, I was used to ongoing micro losses of clarity. Most of my life, I've been so myopic that I reached for glasses before even getting out of bed.

The ophthalmologist was oddly excited about the diagnosis. "This will change your life," he said. "When we take out the cloudy lenses, we'll replace them with lenses to correct your vision. You'll see better than you ever have!"

I wept on the way home, imagining it. I've always been grateful that my vision could be corrected with eyewear, a modern miracle I tried never to take for granted. Wary of Lasik surgery and no longer comfortable in contacts, my glasses provided a safe, reliable solution.

As I contemplated my options, my vision grew increasingly cloudy and unclear. I was also losing depth perception, feeling like a little old lady going tentatively down my front steps. Where was the girl who used to move easily from boulder to boulder like a mountain goat when hiking? The ego I'd worked so long to heal and give its proper place was losing some footing, too. Still, it took me 18 months and increasing levels of blurriness before I scheduled my surgery.

Now I'm on the other side, surgeries behind me. I still need glasses for distance, but my near vision is perfect. I've gained full peripheral view and see things in true size, not about 25% smaller, as my stronger glasses made them appear.

I realize how much nuance and variation I'd been missing. When I gaze out at the rivers and mountains near my home, more colors and contours pop out. The acuity with which I see is astonishing.

On the other hand, the wrinkles, sags, and greys are also more obvious. With a relaxed and grateful heart, I bow and receive all that is now clearly revealed.

Body Wisdom
By Helen Ferrara

Waking during the night, my first sensation is one of pain – of stiffness and aching in the middle of my chest. I'm barely awake, but a fluttering of fear nudges me. (We've been trained "well," and certain symptoms evoke almost automatic responses.)

Giving more attention to my body, I become aware of pain along my whole left arm, the back of my neck, the middle of my back. My entire body feels stiff. Fearful words begin to coalesce within me (*What if...*), but they're interrupted when my right arm moves as if by its own accord, and my right hand begins massaging precise spots on my neck and back. Pretty soon, all the pain has disappeared; I curl and stretch, easing my stiffness.

From my side of the bed, I can see some of the sky. There's no moon, just a few stars in the velvety blackness of the warm night. As I lie there, fully awake now, I wonder at how my body knew just what to do.

My awareness feels expanded – it's as though I can "think" with every part of me and sense all that's around. A faint silver glow fills the room. All is peacefully silent throughout the house – the only sounds are the gentle breathing of my husband and daughters.

I shift my attention to the open window and sense the "breath" of the grass and plants in the garden. Though still lying in bed, I feel enveloped and supported by the night air. I'm in total comfort; nothing demands my attention, and I feel like all is right with the world – like everything has been taken care of and there's absolutely nothing to worry about.

From this vantage point of expansion and oneness, I feel timeless, and reviewing a cascade of brilliant insights seems the perfect thing to do. I don't worry that I might forget them; enjoying them, I trust I'll be able to access them again when the time's right.

By the morning, they're gone. I can't even remember falling asleep, but my appreciation for my body's wisdom and this grace-filled experience is everlasting.

Calm Amidst Chaos
By Alison M. Stokes

On the second anniversary of 9/11, I was attending a peace conference in Jerusalem, as the Irish delegate, when we got word that a bomb had exploded in Bethlehem, about six miles south of us. News of any damage or injuries was limited, as the people of Bethlehem, who were on high alert, had set up a blockade to limit access to their town.

We set off for Bethlehem but were stopped by the army before reaching the blockade. They were anxious about other explosive devices that might be in the town, while the medics were concerned for anyone who may have been injured. A message filtered through from the town that only a delegate from a neutral country would be allowed in. The message specifically requested anyone from Ireland or Switzerland to come through.

Amidst all the confusion and heated discussions at the blockade, I knew I was meant to be there in Israel at that exact time. It was as if I had been previously selected for this task. My thoughts were suddenly clear, and I felt a strange sense of calm and reassurance, knowing that everything would be okay without being able to explain why. I instantly volunteered to go in and assess the situation along with two other delegates.

After a briefing from the army and the bomb squad, we were allowed through the barricade. Luckily, we were able to confirm that the damage was limited and that no one had been injured. Amazingly, within a couple of hours, Bethlehem had returned to normal, almost as if nothing had happened. Yet I knew that something profound had occurred, which inspired me to proceed in a moment of angst and danger without any fear.

Looking back now, I can only refer to that moment as one of grace, for which I will always be grateful.

Why *Not* You?

By Giuliana Melo

"She wore her scars proudly, as if they were a dress made
with healing, golden fibres of heaven."
- Giuliana Melo

In 2011, I was diagnosed with stage-3 cancer, and I placed my life into God's hands.

I began to depend on God to fill me with confidence and to guide me in healing mind, body, and spirit. I became immersed in spiritual teachings. I developed a daily spiritual practice that began by offering thanks every day. I opened myself to receive blessings, and I prepared for their delivery.

Many times, I cried out to God, asking, "Why?! Why me?!"

Then one day, I heard the reply: "Why *not* you?"

That's when I felt the shift in me – an illuminated awakening so powerful that I intuitively knew that, no matter what the outcome, I was going to be okay. God and the angels had swept me up out of fear.

This was the power of grace. I didn't have to earn it. It was my divine right. It allowed me to pick up the pieces of my broken health. I recognized that the emotional component of my health needed healing, and because of my sensitivity, I needed to protect my energy. I had to learn to love myself enough to put me first.

As I reflect back on this experience, I ask myself: *What is grace?* To me, grace is the favour of God. It is divine influence in our life. It is the unconditional love of God. Grace heals us and is the strength to overcome whatever challenges we must walk through. When we acknowledge God and tap into grace, we heal.

I am happy to share that I am now cancer free, and I truly know the power of grace.

Learning to Love My Gus

By Lisa A. Stariha

"A CPAP machine? Are you kidding me? Seriously? Are you sure I have sleep apnea?"

I pelted my doctor with these (and many other) rapid-fire questions after receiving a diagnosis of sleep apnea. One of my health mysteries had been solved, but I didn't like the answer. I didn't want sleep apnea. I wanted something that was easily treated with medication. Yes, I wanted the easy way out.

For four years, I had experienced unexplained, life-disrupting, what-the-heck-is-going-on-with-my-body symptoms. After two years of seeing many specialists, I received no answers, only frustration and a mountain of medical bills. Discouraged, I gave up for a while.

Then I met a nurse practitioner who started me on a path back to health. Together, we created a treatment plan that included a referral to a sleep specialist. I resisted. For decades, I had searched for the answers to my daytime sleepiness and lack of energy with no luck. Why would things change now?

Ultimately, I relented and saw the sleep doctor. This doctor listened, *really listened* to me. When we finished, he smiled as he shook my hand and said, "Don't worry; we're going to help you." I nearly burst into tears. I had hope again.

After two overnight sleep tests, I became the proud owner of a CPAP (Continuous Positive Airway Pressure) machine. This device definitely takes some time to get used to. Is it fun? No. Is it sexy? No. Is it essential for my health? Yes. The machine blows air through a long hose that connects to a face mask. It keeps my airway open so I no longer wake up 27 times an hour gasping for air. I am finally receiving the restorative sleep my body desperately needs.

I knew it was going to be okay when I laughingly told a friend that I named my CPAP machine "The Snuffaluffagus," or "Gus" for short. While I don't love wearing the mask, I do love that I am taking care of my body. Gus keeps me safe and healthy, and I am forever grateful.

Life Starts at 21
By Yiye Zhang

Some say that life starts at 21. What started when I reached 21, however, is glandular fever. It began with severe fever for six months, then expanded to intense pains in my throat and stomach. My doctors said, "Sorry, but there is no cure."

Because I was new in London and living on my own, I didn't have friends to lean on. My passport was held in the Home Office, and my parents from China were not allowed to visit. Worse, I exhausted my sick leave and lived on my credit card, which was close to its limit.

I kept getting worse. Every day, I didn't want to wake up. I wasn't scared of illness, but I was afraid that there was no sign of recovery. Pushed into a corner without external resources, I had to go within. Initially, this thought terrified me, but the situation was so bad that I had no other choice. When I finally tuned in, however, to my surprise, I *loved* it!

One of the first things I experienced was a connection with my grandpa from the other side. Feeling his warm smile and hearing his tender whispers – "Everything will be fine; you will heal." – relieved my emotional pains immediately. Next, an ancient part of me intuitively guided me to meditate. Then I filled up my days by praying to Mother Mary, reading *Dao De Jing*, and enjoying bundles of laughter from watching comedies.

Slowly, I started to feel all the wonderful qualities that I had previously ignored: inner peace, love, and self-acceptance. And, for the very first time, I felt feminine!

I finally realised that real strength was not about winning a game, a medal, or a competition, but knowing at the cellular level that I am adequate, regardless of the circumstances.

Gradually, my health improved, and seven years later I got my immune system back. During that time, I immersed myself into alternative medicine and soul studies, which (conveniently) provided me with a solid foundation for the healing work I currently do.

Looking back, I see that my life indeed started at 21.

You Are Believed

By Autumne Stirling

In 2013, I participated in a highly specialized, nurturing, and diligent trauma program for individuals suffering from Post-Traumatic Stress Disorder (PTSD). It was a tremendous undertaking to engage in treatment of this caliber, and it was equally daunting to leave my country (Canada) to go to the centre in New Orleans. But I felt that I needed this type of intervention. My struggles to cope with my childhood trauma were overwhelming, and I had innumerable demons constantly stirring inside of me. I knew I needed help. I just had to open up my heart and go.

My mouth dry with apprehension, my hands shaking and drenched in sweat, I clutched my suitcase. Arriving at the treatment centre in early May, I left behind the snow and bitterness of our drawn-out northern winter and was greeted with a sunny warmth, verdant grass, palm trees, and tiny geckos that were cute as could be.

The change in scenery shocked my system, allowing to spring forth hope and optimism I had ceased to know existed within me. Within minutes, my attitude regarding how I was going to choose to spend my time shifted greatly. This was my chance to truly heal my heart and soul, to change my life. I could not let it slip away. I promptly decided to open up, let others bear witness to my pain, and to fully utilize every moment that was providently gifted to me.

With so many exceptional and compassionate therapists, trust came surprisingly easy, and my journey into my seemingly bottomless PTSD began. Weeks passed, and I settled into a routine. Some afternoons seemed to stretch into endlessness as I deconstructed my story, page by page. I was healing.

Towards the conclusion of my stay, during a particularly difficult session, my therapist said to me, "You know, you are so strong, you are believed, and you've got this." Tears sprung from within, an internal acknowledgement that she was right. I found grace in this moment, a grace that is intertwined within my spirit, never faltering, never doubting. New Orleans, you will always have my heart.

Alive by Grace, Living by Gratitude

By Colleen Georges

I heard a loud screech and saw a car coming full speed into my driver's door. Suddenly, everything was spinning. I didn't understand what was happening. I saw gravel beside my driver's window and stuck my hand out to stop the spinning. Then came a loud bang and impact, and I was sitting in my car...much farther up the road than I began.

Two men came and helped me out of my passenger's door and brought me into a nearby store. Almost immediately, a team of EMTs arrived. They examined me and found that I had airbag burns on my neck and small cuts from glass on my face. I'd also bitten the sides of my tongue off and I'd torn the skin off the side of my hand when I attempted to stop the spinning. But I had no broken bones, no internal damage, and no head trauma or other serious injury.

They said I was beyond lucky to be alive – much less relatively unharmed – after what had happened: Someone had made an illegal left turn, and hit a car, which crashed into my driver's door and sent me into a triple rollover. My car ultimately landed on its wheels in an intersection. Although this had happened on a busy street, my car didn't hit any other cars.

At the time (December 27, 1997), I was 22 years old and had spent several years questioning God's existence. This experience answered my questions once and for all: There is indeed a God, and he clearly had a plan for me. He could've taken me, but in his grace, he kept me here. I knew that I needed to be grateful for all I had and use the time he gave me to do good.

Following this experience, I got my doctorate in counseling, and gratitude became a center in my life. For over 15 years, I've practiced counting my blessings daily. For the last year, I've been counting them before bed together with my six-year-old son. One of his thankfuls each night is, "I'm thankful we have a good God." So am I.

The Grace to Heal Mind, Body, and Spirit

By Tanya Penny

It took three years, but I finally put the needle down for good. When I was diagnosed with Multiple Sclerosis (MS), my neurologist strongly recommended a medication that required me to give myself shots every other day. Not only do I dislike needles, but the medication caused flu-like symptoms for 24 hours. Needless to say, I was not thrilled, especially since it was only 30% effective in reducing the progression of MS.

During the next three years, I continued to have relapses and worsening symptoms despite the medication. Twice, I stopped because I felt it was not the right treatment for me. Eventually, I ended up back on it, due to fear of getting worse and pressure from my doctor and husband.

One day, after another horrible relapse, I went to give myself a shot and an inner voice said, "Stop. Put down the needle. There's another way." By the guidance, courage, and grace of my higher levels, this time I listened for good. I never gave myself a shot again and began my deeper journey into healing mind, body, and spirit.

Going against what western medicine tells you to do to heal (or, in my case, to "slow down the progression of") has not been an easy road to take. There were times when I wanted to go back to western medicine or, worse yet, end it all. But again, my higher levels graced me with healers, other earth angels, resources, and tons of guidance and courage to keep walking my path.

Today, I am happy to say that I had the grace and took that deeper journey. I am MS free and have also found my purpose: to support others to heal mind, body, and spirit, just like I have.

Another Breath

By Scott M. Dehn

I remember talking to God from what could have been my death bed. It was nearly six years ago, and I was struggling physically. I had dropped from my normal weight of 170 pounds all the way down to 117. My blood pressure was 70/40. I couldn't walk 15 feet without feeling exhausted. I looked dreadful and felt even worse.

As soon as my doctor saw my blood-pressure result, she sent me to the hospital. They stuck, prodded, tested, and IV'ed me for a week, finding nothing conclusive. I had post-shingles nerve pain, but that couldn't account for the severe weight loss. We were all stumped.

During that time, I talked to God, often, asking, "What do I need to do?"

I got the response: "Listen, my dear child."

I already listened daily, but this seemed to refer to another level of listening. "Alright, I will."

As soon as I opened up, the words and the *feel* poured into my consciousness like a fountain of understanding. "We are changing your life, Scott," God said in a soft but powerful manner. "We are sending you back to your roots, where you will lead more, become ordained, write a novel, and guide those who are seeking."

Those words were somewhat cryptic and confusing, but as I listened more each day, more was revealed. My mysterious illness improved, and I was able to follow the guidance. I returned to the area where I grew up, got ordained, and am currently offering spiritual guidance and writing two novels about learning. I now see fewer people from my prior spiritual community but touch more lives, helping new seekers. I feel I have realized my calling, my purpose.

This divine gift came from a state of grace – something beautiful that is effortless, divine. Something that bestowed upon me a divine favor, supported me in becoming healthier, and gave me direction. This gift showed me that I had more work to do and gave me the strength to do it. I feel blessed to have been given another breath.

Grace Saved My Life

By Linda Dieffenbach

Once there was a young girl who believed that she was worthless. She carried tremendous pain from events that were beyond her control, yet she could not see that it wasn't her fault or responsibility. Not knowing this, she took in all of the blame and shame and made it her own. In the depths of her pain, she believed that the only solution was to end her own life and free the world of the burden that she believed herself to be.

I was that young girl. So blinded by the pain from personal trauma and not having the resources to cope with any of it, at the age of 15, I had resolved to end my life. I put together a plan, got everything in order, and set off to school one day with the intention of leaving mid-morning to commit suicide.

I do not believe that there has been any day in my life more surrounded by grace.

It was not just one moment of grace or one person that saved me, but so many people and events showed up to change my plans. People and circumstances got in my way at every turn. Despite the numerous changes, I was still determined, and I began taking pills. Miraculously, friends showed up at my door, having realized my plans, and took me to the emergency room.

And then, as I was lying in my hospital bed being treated, I was visited by a constant stream of friends and loved ones. I learned that I was loved and that I had value. I felt a powerful stirring in my soul as I took in this truth.

This experience changed the trajectory of my life. As I healed my own wounds, I committed myself to helping others who are lost, in pain, and alone – helping them heal from the pain of their past so they, too, can find their own value and learn to love themselves. Grace saved my life.

There's Always a Why

By Felicia D'Haiti

When wrestling with the "why me?" of being diagnosed with cancer, I originally concluded that there was no good answer. I thought I lived a healthy life. Not knowing how to deal with this question, I decided to put it aside and not even think about it until answers began revealing themselves to me.

One such answer was given to me recently. Months into my treatment, my dad called to pass along a message from a family friend. She was sitting with another sick friend who had been in a coma-like state for a few months. The sick friend suddenly woke up, said, "I'm praying for Felicia," and then went back into her sleeping state. It was at that moment of hearing her message that I awakened to part of my answer. I realized that this is part of my life journey, and to move through the journey without learning from it would be tragic for me and for everyone I come into contact with in the future. It reminded me that I was not alone on my journey, not forgotten, and that there were many more people praying for me and thinking of me than I even realized.

One of the most difficult parts of this journey has been in learning to receive, as I am used to giving freely but have not been comfortable with receiving. At each point on this journey, whenever I've become discouraged, a loving word, a touching card, or a generous act has lifted me up. All of these moments have reminded me that there can be as much joy in receiving as there is in giving. The acts of kindness that I have acknowledged and received over the last six months will leave a lasting impact on my life and encourage me to openly welcome the ebb and flow of giving and receiving in my daily life.

The Comeback
By Kimberly McGeorge

"You never know what lies ahead." I used to say to my clients. I meant it as an encouragement, in a positive way. But I never anticipated that I would be the proof that it can also work negatively.

At the height of my career, having been divorced for 12 years and making an independent living for myself and my four daughters, I realized I was deeply miserable. I felt exhausted, hopeless, and empty. Life had no meaning. Money had no meaning. Work had no meaning. After continuously giving for the last five years, I had nothing left to offer.

I succumbed to that feeling. I could barely stand upright. For the next three months, I spent most of my time in bed, which was the only comfortable place to be. Thankfully, my caring parents came to stay with us and did most of the parenting.

It felt like I hit rock bottom and there was no way up.

Slowly, with rest, good nutrition, love, and support, the dark clouds started to part. I decided not to go back to my old profession with all the people who caused me pain. I took a job as an office manager and felt good about moving forward without looking back.

Then one clear morning a year and a half later, I woke up with the feeling that God had spoken to me. "Come back to work," he said. "People need you." Only later did I learn that my clients and others I had served over the years were thinking about me and praying for me to come back.

As soon as I went back, it felt right. This is my life's main work and purpose, aside from being a mother to my gifted girls. I am here to serve, to hold the light, to teach, and to expose truth.

During the past year since this happened, my business has been very successful: I earned more and donated more than ever before, and have been offered television shows, movie parts, and media exposure. And above all else, I'm no longer afraid and I practice grace with complete self-love every day.

Motherhood, Cancer, and Grace

By Lynne Newman

At one point in my life, I thought I knew what it meant to live a graceful existence. I had expectations for how I would shape my life and visions of how I would live it. I thought that I had control of my life, and it looked pretty amazing. After all, I am a passionate, hard-working, and caring person.

And then life took several unexpected turns.

Following fertility struggles and two miscarriages, in 2009 my husband was diagnosed with metastatic melanoma. We had only been married two years and had just announced that we were expecting our first child. Our lives were turned inside out and flipped upside down shortly after Mark's 30th birthday.

It was supposed to be a special time in my life, a time to be nurtured and to be taken care of. Unfortunately, this was not the case, as my husband's diagnosis took priority. I had to be there for him while being pregnant, delivering a child, and becoming a first-time mother. Life got pretty complicated.

Mark and I both mourned the life that we once dreamed of. We experienced feelings of guilt, shame, anger, and sadness. It was hard. It rocked us to our core and challenged everything, including our marriage.

As the years have rolled on, we've continued to focus on healing and have found our way as a family. Yes, despite the messiness of dealing with advanced cancer while parenting, we feel more aligned and awake to what matters in life. For this, I am grateful. I have simplified and deepened my well of compassion. I know that I am more than my story. I give myself permission to cry and not have it all together, and also to enjoy life and trust in what will be.

Simplicity. Surrender. Trust. To me this defines true grace.

Love's Grace: Air Hugs and Kisses

By Bonnie L. Boucek

I took a strangled breath, closed my eyes, and asked, "Are you sure?" Everything stopped. I didn't want it confirmed. Dread filled me. I already knew.

"Yes," the doctor said. "You have fibromyalgia. There's no cure. You'll never retain a job. You'll spend the rest of your life on pain medication."

Being diagnosed with fibromyalgia – a medical condition with chronic widespread pain and a heightened, painful response to pressure – is terrible in and of itself. For a mother with small children, it becomes a nightmare. Imagine waking up to discover you can't hug your child. Visualize your little one running to you with an "owie" and wanting comfort, but you cry out in pain. Contemplate your kids being afraid to hug you because they might hurt Mommy.

It was bad enough that I was always in pain, always tired, and always on edge. Now, I was a mommy who couldn't help her children, let alone give them hugs and kisses. I wondered: *What kind of mother am I? Useless? A burden?* Feeling like a failure, I stayed away from everyone.

During my self-imposed exile, I continued to beat myself up emotionally. Nothing I did helped ease the pain from fibromyalgia or from letting down my children. My faith was shaky at best.

Then one morning I woke up feeling different. Peace surrounded me – warm and soft, relaxing and calm. It felt like home, like being held and comforted by a parent. I sat there, healing in the glow of God's love. That's when it dawned on me: I didn't need to hug my children physically for them to know I loved them. The thought fluttered into my soul: my heart could convey its love with air hugs and kisses.

This newfound knowledge lifted a heavy weight from my heart. I've found that I am a good mother after all, and my children give me the strength to face each day with love.

The Universe Always Responds

By Michelle Marie McGrath

When the doctor told me I was pregnant, I knew with absolute certainty that a baby was not going to materialise from this experience. How did I know? I could not "see" a child; it did not feel real. So how would it manifest into my physical reality? I also knew because, for months, I had been asking the universe for all that was not in alignment with my highest truth to be dissolved, and I knew that having a child was not aligned with my truth.

As much as I knew this to be true, it still made me wonder about myself. What did it say about me that I didn't want to have children? Was something "wrong" with me? After all, society tells us that being a mother is the highest calling of womanhood, yet I never experienced a ticking clock, hormonal craving, or the feeling that I was missing out. As much as I enjoyed children, I was never convinced that motherhood was right for me. Since childhood, I sensed that life contained many meaningful paths, motherhood being just one of them. It's not that I felt strongly *against* motherhood; I just never felt the need to make it happen for me.

The doctor told me I was pregnant, which then led into an intense few months of fatigue and nausea. My body felt alien, as though it belonged to someone else. My dreams were vivid; I repeatedly saw myself inside Noah's Ark, tossed around on a violent, grey sea. What was this really about?

On the way to my dating scan appointment, I said to my husband, "A baby is not going to be born." He gaped at me like a fish with glassy eyes. At the appointment, I was told that I had a molar pregnancy (a growth in the uterus which, although not an embryo, triggers symptoms of pregnancy).

The doctors were baffled. I did not fit any of the specific categories of women who experienced this condition. They had no explanation. But I knew: it was the course correction my soul had been asking for. I had gotten off track, but as always, the universe responded appropriately, getting me back on track and reminding me to listen to my soul. No, there would not be a physical birth, but this was exactly the rebirth experience I needed.

Sharing the Journey of Healing

By Catherine M. Laub

I quit high school when I was 16 due to health issues. Because of problems with my colon and bladder, my disposal system was working overtime. I was embarrassed leaving the classroom so many times to use the bathroom. I sought medical care, but the doctors couldn't do much for me. Eventually, I returned to school and made an arrangement with my teachers: to keep my embarrassment down, I was permitted to just walk out of class without raising my hand to draw attention to myself.

In this way, I managed to graduate, but I remained self-conscious long after high school. I had incredibly low self-esteem and almost no confidence in social situations. I was always worried that everyone was talking negatively about me, and I eventually learned that many of them were – including my own siblings! During conversations, people would often just walk away from me, leaving me feeling empty.

My low point came in 2014 when I attempted suicide. Through grace, I survived. And, thanks to this extreme wake-up call, I reached out for help. I joined supportive organizations, received holistic treatment, and began to leave the house more often, making new, supportive friends. Also, out of emotional self-preservation, I distanced myself from my unsupportive siblings.

This last year has been one of great growth. Grace has brought me a long way regarding my physical and emotional health. I'm now opening up about my journey – the struggles as well as the successes. By doing so, I hope that I can help others with their own struggles and encourage them to seek help.

So far, the response has been overwhelmingly positive. I recently shared a personal triumph on Facebook: "I had a full week and actually left the house 5 times for events. I have come a long way...I am so proud of myself!" In just two days, this post received 46 likes and many uplifting comments, which has been a tremendous boost for my self-confidence. I wrote in response: "Thanks, everyone! Your support means a lot to me! I am overwhelmed with such love from all of you. When I just saw how many of you liked my post, I finally acknowledged to myself how much I am really loved."

Living in the Light

By Robin Chellis

I felt the end was near. I could feel my body shutting down. I had been in and out of the hospital. My body was weak and depleted. I was exhausted, and I longed for peace – to no longer suffer endless symptoms and pain.

As I lay in bed, my mind became euphoric. I had crossed the veil. It was beautiful. I felt the oneness of all things. I felt God's infinite love. I was pure space, pure light, pure love, pure expansion. It was beyond words. I was home.

I soared for a while, having a conversation with God. I came to new understandings. I was given a choice to stay or go back.

I knew in that moment that there was no judgment in anything, and I had pure choice. I knew without a shadow of a doubt that I could stay in that light and expansion, or I could go back to my body. I knew that either choice was perfect.

I no longer feared death – for in death, you are in God's pure presence. It is the space of you. You see your true light, and the light that is in everyone, reflected from the eyes of God.

I wanted so much to stay in that pure spaciousness of complete peace and love, but I knew I had more to do on Earth. I knew I had a bigger purpose. I was here to share light with the world. I knew that it wasn't time for me to leave my earthly body. It was time to radiate my light – time to help others see and share their brilliant light. I still had things to do, to learn, to teach, to experience. I knew that I could bring a piece of Heaven back to Earth, and that we could live Heaven on Earth.

I returned with a newfound strength and resiliency – a new grace, a gift from God, allowing me to continue living in the light.

Chapter 3
Everyday Grace

S ometimes grace arrives in miraculous forms: visions, visitations, messages from beyond, near-death experiences, and extraordinary healings. These are the "goosebump" moments – the stories that make the metaphysical headlines, so to speak. And yes, these experiences are miraculous and inspiring, and they deserve to be celebrated, savored, and shared.

But these aren't the only forms that grace shows up in. Sometimes grace appears in quiet, subtle ways – often in the midst of seemingly "ordinary" moments. In fact, it is grace that allows us to see the extraordinary within the ordinary – to see that, in one sense, there are no "ordinary" moments. Every moment is infused with divine grace.

While not everyone experiences what is generally considered a "miracle," we can all experience the miracle of everyday life. We can all appreciate the beauty of the world around us, the love we share with one another, and the magic that life brings us in every form!

We've both experienced supernatural miracles. But this doesn't mean that our lives are dull or lacking in grace 99% of the time, when these miracles aren't occurring. Quite the contrary – the majority of our everyday, "mundane" lives is infused with grace. And because this is where most of life occurs, these are the moments that make it beautiful, worthwhile, and thoroughly amazing.

The pieces in this chapter show how grace appears in seemingly ordinary situations: eating a cookie or sharing a sandwich, painting or dancing, watching your children, or simply breathing. You can even experience grace by doing exactly what you're doing right now: reading a book! We hope that the experiences shared here move you and inspire you to see the many moments of grace in your own life…every day!

In the Garden

By Dan Teck

I opened my eyes and found myself sitting in a wondrous garden. Above me shone a brilliant, golden orb – too bright to look at directly but somehow gentle even in its immense power. It warmed my face and illuminated the breathtaking scene before me: a stunning explosion of colors, arranged in a way that surpassed the work of any human artist. Fairy-like creatures flew around me, their brightly colored wings shining in the light as they communicated with one another in their flute-like language of whimsical melodies. The entire garden danced with life. The air itself felt alive – caressing my skin in a way that simultaneously warmed and cooled me.

Feeling completely at peace with where I was and also eager to explore this paradisiacal setting, I stood up and took a few steps. The mossy surface cushioned my feet, yielding to me while supporting my entire being. As I looked around, I encountered hidden treasures that I hadn't noticed at first: tiny buds on the verge of bursting into bloom, subtle decorative touches, and near-invisible winged creatures dancing above and around me.

The most magnificent part of this garden, however, went far beyond sensory beauty: Although I was completely alone (aside from the winged creatures), I was able to communicate with others who weren't there in physical form. I became aware of their thoughts, emotions, and most meaningful experiences – "hearing" them almost as if they were communicating telepathically or describing it all in person, or as if I were living it along with them. They shared profound truths – stories occasionally touched by pain and heartbreak but ultimately leading to higher levels of grace and glory.

Their words and experiences were still swirling inside me when I encountered someone who seemed to be part human, part angel. She spoke just a few words to me, but I felt unconditionally accepted and cherished, filled with a love that I knew would last forever. With a heart filled with gratitude, I kissed my wife on the forehead, refilled my coffee, and went back out to the patio, where I continued to edit the latest batch of pieces for *365 Moments of Grace*.

When the Student Becomes the Teacher

By Denise L. Roseland

"You gonna eat the rest of that, Miss?" He often showed up in my classroom during lunch to catch up on missing work. He seemed to be sick a lot and missed school often.

"Eat what?" I responded.

"The rest of that, Miss."

I looked down at the last two messy bites of my mostly eaten sandwich. Another day of ham, mayo, and cheddar on flavorless bread. "Umm...no."

"May I have it?"

"Are you hungry? Surely you don't want my mostly eaten sandwich."

"I don't mind. It looks good."

"Okay. Help yourself. How about you take this apple off my hands, too." I fumbled in my desk drawer to retrieve an apple some community group had handed out to teachers the previous week.

"Sure. Thanks, Miss!" He started eating as if it were the finest gourmet meal, and I excused myself to go pick up some copies. As I walked down the hall, my eyes welled up with tears.

Work had been stressful the last few months. The school district was struggling through incredible budget challenges. The impasse over the terms of the teaching contract had created a divide among colleagues. The community and families were tired of how it was impacting opportunities for students. I was constantly irritable after months of living under the dark cloud of all that resentment and anger.

As I packed my lunch that morning, I was complaining to my partner: "I just want time for a bowl of homemade soup and a delicious salad. Not overly processed crap smashed between pieces of bread."

The very sandwich I had complained about was an amazing treat to my student. The shame over my lack of gratitude welled up and rushed out with those tears. I stood sobbing over the copier for several minutes before I could pull myself together to go back to my classroom.

"You okay, Miss?" he asked as I walked back into my room.

"Yep," I said. "Wanna meet me in here for lunch tomorrow? I think I'm making a pot of homemade soup tonight. Can I bring you some?"

"I'd like that," he said.

Touched by Grace Through the Written Word

By Holly Worton

Ten years ago, I did not believe in Grace. I did not believe in God. I did not believe in anything other than practical, tangible things. In 2006, I moved, along with my ex-husband, from Mexico to Argentina. The day we arrived, the owner of a bookstore spontaneously gifted us a book: *The Way: On The Way with a Contemporary Master* by Juan Sgolastra.

My ex went home and read it immediately, enjoying it immensely. I avoided the book; it looked spiritual, which meant that it held no interest for me. If books can repel a person, this book definitely repelled me.

We had moved to South America to expand our business, and as we got to know people in town, I noticed that several of them wore a small sword necklace. In their homes I would see a strange symbol hanging above the front door; once I saw the same symbol above the entrance to a restaurant. After a conversation with one of our new, sword-wearing employees, she brought up her "meditation group," which was apparently linked back to that book that I had been avoiding.

One day, while driving through town, my ex announced that we were going to the Wednesday meeting of this meditation group. I instantly flared up, insisting that I had no interest in going. Yet I accompanied him anyway.

I was extremely uncomfortable with the exercise that evening, yet afterward, I felt a sudden euphoria and returned home bursting with creative energy. I played music, danced, and painted until late into the night. I returned once more to the group, but still had no intentions of joining.

It wasn't until months later that I finally picked up that book and read it. Halfway through, I knew that I would be joining the group. I just felt it deep in my gut. I was sitting on the deck of our cabin, which was nestled on the edge of the woods overlooking a pristine lake, and it hit me. I stopped reading and knew in my heart that I had made one of the most important decisions of my life. Grace had touched me.

An Object Lesson from a Contact Lens

By Lori Thiessen

It was Monday morning after a four-day swim meet, and swimmers, parents, and the coach exhaustedly filed into the bus heading home. I was looking forward to the 10-hour trip. My marriage was falling apart, and I needed time to think.

I fought off sleep but finally succumbed to an awkward, fitful, head-propped-on-pillow-propped-on-window dozing.

I woke, neck stiff and vision blurred in one eye. Uh-oh…that could only mean one thing: one contact lens had slipped out of place during my nap – probably due to my unconventional head position. Gently, I poked and rubbed my eye to shift the contact back into position. Not good. I couldn't find the contact. It wasn't in my eye. Panic welled up. My vision is bad, and my lenses are special order and expensive. The thought of being half-blind for a few weeks plus the cost of a replacement lens was frightening. Horrifying. I'd already spent money on this trip, and there was none left for a new contact.

I couldn't accept the loss and started the search over again. First, my eye, then the pillow, clothing, upholstery, floor, window sill, everywhere. No lens. Despairingly, tears blurring my fuzzy eyesight, I gazed out the window at what I assumed was mountain scenery.

About an hour later, the bus stopped. There were bathrooms available in the lower level of the visitor center across the road. We all trooped out across the parking lot, across the street, through the gift shop, and down the stairs. I waited my turn and was last in the washroom. As I removed my coat, I heard a faint sound and looked down. There at my feet was my contact lens. Completely intact. Perfect.

That clear in-my-head-but-I-swear-audible voice spoke to me: "If I can take care of your contact lens and return it to you in perfect condition, do you not think I can also take care of *you*?"

My reply was gratitude and relief beyond what words could express. The grace of God's love surrounding me was everything I needed to carry on.

And They Slept
By Marla David

My daughters have grown up; but when they were younger, especially as babies, I waited until they were fast asleep, then I would tip-toe into each of their rooms. I stood next to each one, with that inner smile only a mother could have. I would watch and listen to the rhythm of their breathing. I would take a breath in and then sigh quietly, in total contentment. This, to me, was the definition of peace.

Sometimes, I sat in the chair. It was humbling. I felt blessed and privileged to be a mother. There was such pureness in that moment. I felt only love and grace.

I think it was the late Dr. Wayne Dyer who wrote that children at a young age are between Heaven and Earth. This concept has long fascinated me and made me think of my own children. Where were they when they slept? What did they dream of? Is this why people are spellbound in the presence of babies?

Wanting them to be in complete comfort, I would ensure that their cover was on correctly, sometimes pulling it up further to better support or protect their little frame. Running my hands ever so close to them as I tucked their favorite stuffed animal under their arm, I whispered my love to them – total, unconditional love, when you love completely with heart and soul, with no expectation of anything.

My little angels were unaware that their mother was present. If they knew I was there, it would have jarred them awake. When they did stir slightly, I stayed ever so still, not wanting to interrupt their blissful sleep.

I still went into their rooms as they got older. It kept the fire burning, that feeling of grace, that awe, especially on difficult days. Always, when I felt comfortable, I left their rooms, and they slept.

Pen to Paper

By Susan Elizabeth Schoemmell

Sitting in my second writing class at a local library with the same instructor from last year, I was overjoyed to learn and practice new techniques of writing and sharing stories with others. Our first assignment was to write without stopping – do not edit; just let the words flow. Patty then gave us several themes to conjure up thoughts that would bring life to the words we wrote. This exercise went well for me, and the words flowed freely onto the yellow legal pad set before me.

When our lesson in free-flow writing ended, Patty shifted our focus, introducing a few examples of poetry. I was decidedly disappointed, as I really did not feel that this would inspire me to practice my writing skills. I felt deeply out of my comfort zone. My thoughts began to wander, and I was relieved when our lunch break was upon us. Patty then announced our assignment during lunch: we were to create our own poem. Panic set in as I feared failure and a blank page. I considered how easy it would be to not return to class after lunch.

I walked to my car and pondered how my joy and glee had turned into confusion and anger. I was befuddled about how to get inspired and write a poem in less than one hour. I sat in my car, munched my sandwich, and sipped from my bottle of water. Then something urged me to try. A soft whisper came: "Put the pen to the paper, and let the words flow."

After a few attempts at using different words to convey my thoughts, I started with: *A soft breeze beckons my spirit to walk in tandem into His loving arms.* Something was missing. I stared out at the rain falling gently on the car window and recalled how Patty had indicated that a simple, subtle description could be powerful. I finished the poem, which I called "Invitation":

A soft, gentle breeze,
Beckons my strong spirit,
To walk in tandem with Jesus,
Into the loving arms of a forgiving Creator.

I learned a lot that day. I put pen to paper, and a world of possibility opened up to me.

The Gift That Helped Me Find My Voice

By Lesley Pyne

For many years, blending my voice with others – with friends and family, in church, at school, or *anywhere* – filled me up and brought me more joy than anything else. Then 14 years ago, after undergoing six unsuccessful rounds of in vitro fertilization, I lost my voice and felt like grace had left me, too. I was silent and alone, grieving my childlessness. I allowed it to control me, always looking at what was missing in my life rather than at what was still there.

Then one day I met other women like me who knew what this silence felt like. I started to speak, tentatively and quietly at first, and I slowly started to rediscover my voice. For 10 years, I struggled to find my true voice. I also started a personal-development journey, learning Neuro-Linguistic Programing and joining a choir. I could feel my voice slowly getting stronger. In time, I felt strong enough to set up a business supporting childless women.

The more I've written and told my story, the stronger my voice has become and the more I've helped others. Last year, I was interviewed for BBC National Radio and was asked how I feel now about being childless. Before I could stop myself, I said these words: "Childlessness is the biggest gift in my life because without it I wouldn't be who I am and have the wonderful life I have now." The words shocked me, and I was flooded with joy and grace, just like when I used to sing.

My life isn't the one I hoped for, but now that I accept it and the gifts it brings, I experience joy and grace everywhere. And when the music starts, I feel my voice rising strongly and joining with the choir to make beautiful harmonies, and I know: *This is me. I've found my voice.*

Grace by Cookies

By Katie Kieffer

During a seminar, I began feeling that I was made to come to Earth as punishment. They made me come here and were watching me. Who "they" are, I have no idea; but they left me here with an implant of shame.

Sitting in the client seat, I felt increasingly exposed as we moved through an exercise in finding root beliefs. The practitioner and teacher worked intently, gently, without judgment, guiding me through the web of my subconscious mind. My desire to melt into the floor was intense. I felt naked, all my secrets laid bare. As blocks of shame were cleared away, the nakedness ceased to matter. I felt a major shift and wondered what it would look like in action.

On our break, I began to understand what it really meant to be the observer. I felt my body stand up from my seat at the narrow table and walk to the snack counter. It felt as if my mind hovered inside my body, detached and watching. Delicious Moravian cookies were beckoning me – we all devoured these for days. I watched myself open a sleeve of cookies, taking two. Never before that moment would I have taken what I perceived as bold action. I would have waited longingly for someone else to open the cookies, and later maybe taken two. I may have deprived myself of them altogether, as I often did in such situations.

As I enjoyed those cookies, I contemplated what I had just done. The fear of doing wrong was absent, quite an odd sensation. All my life I had a clutching, hollow pit in my stomach. Fear of punishment ruled as if every thought, feeling, and action would bring grim consequences.

That was gone! In its place was confidence, a sense of wholeness and Divine acceptance.

Now, head up, shoulders squared, I claim who I am and my Divine right to be here. No longer do I anxiously stare at the floor, avoiding soul-piercing eyes as I once did. I now know I am worthy of all the beauty and kindness this life and Earth offer.

Tears of Grace Add to the Morning Dew

By Preston Klik

At 1 a.m., I stepped out into our garden area, barefoot, to read. Lights shimmered on the gnarled wood fence, pavers, and fire-pit. My toes tingled, feeling the moisture of the long grass. The flowers and weeds were sprinkled with dew, as was our old chaise, which I settled into. Its wetness added coolness to the already crisp fall air. I began reading a "mindfulness" book but quickly set it down. Inspired, I chose to engage the Now, not abstract text.

What a beautiful night! What a wonderful moment to be alive! Eyes closed, my awareness shifted to senses and emotions: The cool air entered my nose and throat. As my body pressed against the dew-dropped chaise, moisture seeped into the cotton of my clothes. I listened to the night: The muffled sound of airplanes and cars. The gathering whine of two motorcycles in the distance. A coyote howl? Magical.

Eyes open: Christmas lights glistened on the dew. Our Buddha statue held sacred space. The corrugated metal façade of our home provided a geometric background to the many beautiful plants, weeds, grasses, and colorful flowers that overran our little parcel of nature. Random dark holes in the earth marked where squirrels buried their treasures. A gorgeous night on planet Earth.

Thoughts arose: *I'm alive! What did I do to deserve this beauty? Am I worthy of all these gifts?* Surely *this* is what they mean when they say we're born into "original blessing," not original sin. Surely *this* is evidence of "this precious human birth" and the "Sacred Cycle" – as gratitude ascends, grace descends.

Our new home astounds me. My wife, sleeping in our bed, gathers her energy for the coming day of helping others heal. This amazing woman loves me. *Me!?*

There's an abundance of food, shelter, clothes, music, books, the internet, health – everything I need. Plus four loving cats. I've honored the vow I made years ago: I lead a life worth living. My life is full. But not finished. I've more to do, more to become, more to experience. I am blessed.

Filled with gratitude, I wept. My tears added to the morning dew.

The Moment I Surrendered

By Allen Vaysberg

Lisa held out an eye mask and asked, "All right, who's next?" At that moment, I knew it would be me. I didn't *want* it to be me. I even *prayed* that it wouldn't be me. I sat there in agony until our eyes met and she said the words I so dreaded: "Allen, you're up!"

I sheepishly took the mask, put it over my already-watering eyes, and desperately tried to get my bearings. Lisa Williams had just performed a beautiful live reading in front of our Advanced Mediumship Class, and I was supposed to follow *that*? Are you *kidding* me?

Even though my eyes were closed, my senses were in overdrive and I could feel 24 pairs of eyes looking at me. What's worse is that I also sensed a camera that was recording the class 10 inches from my face. This was the closest I had ever come to a do-or-die moment. I only had two options: One was to get up and run away and feel completely justified, because I was surrounded by Lisa Williams and a group of experienced professional mediums. I came here to explore my abilities, not for *this*!

The other option was to surrender.

I took a deep breath, told my angels and my guides, "You got me into this; you'd better bring me something," and then I let go.

I started seeing something, grabbed onto it, and shared it – only to realize that it didn't relate to anyone in the group. This was it. I was ready to give up, but Lisa didn't let me. "Go on, continue."

I let go again and saw a house, a bed, and a child. Then I heard a name. Someone in the group said it was meant for her, and I broke down. I felt the emotions of the child and the emotions of the message, and it overtook me. I was doing the reading while crying, and I could hear the rest of the group crying along with me.

Sometime later, I was done and it was the best reading of my life. I had learned to surrender.

Gazing Grace
By Sophie Maya

In my 40s, I began noticing how uncomfortable I felt under any kind of commercial lighting. My head felt like it was plugged into a light socket, my heart raced, my energy drained, and I became spacey. I didn't understand what was happening, but being in those environments was no longer an option. So I began spending more time in nature, which helped alleviate the symptoms I'd been feeling. Before long, I also noticed an unexpected side effect: I started to feel the thoughts of others when directed my way.

I know this may sound nuts. I questioned the validity of these experiences, too! I asked healers and therapists for advice, but no one was able to offer me any helpful insight. Instead, I often felt judged or even considered crazy. But a little voice within said, "Move away from the thought-energy of judgment. There's a gift in this experience. You just have to unwrap and receive it."

So I decided to try an experiment: Whenever I felt pain in my head and sensed that it was coming from someone else, I checked in with that person to see if I had upset them in some way. I found that I was often correct! Sometimes they weren't willing to admit their feelings at first, but because I showed up genuinely concerned about them, they eventually confirmed that they had been upset with me. I also discovered that when others were thinking kind thoughts about me, my energy felt light and joyful.

The biggest gift I received from these experiences was to see the power that our gaze has upon another's life. We often hear that our thoughts create our reality. Now I see that our thoughts can affect others' realities, too – for their betterment or not – blessing and uplifting another or casting a spell of darkness.

Now, when others show up unkind or disrespectful toward me, I look into a mirror, hug myself, and tell myself what I need to hear. After I've shored up the love within myself, I send it out to them, too, gazing grace upon both of us.

If I Can Experience Grace, Honestly, Anyone Can

By Sue Kearney

I'm here to tell you that if I can experience, see, recognize, and share grace, so can you.

I did not seek grace. In fact, I was sure that the closest I would ever get to grace would be to learn and practice restraint of tongue and pen. To zip my lip long enough to replace my default responses (born of bitterness, anger, and a chip on my shoulder the size of Utah) with something softer, wiser, and more loving, because my thoughts were dark, and I felt so wounded and stuck. My words rang of deprivation and entitlement, not love, generosity, or gratitude.

I got clean and sober in 1991 and spent the first 10 years with a black cloud over my head. Miserable sober is not fun.

I really didn't believe that my thinking would ever change. I was actually happy that I had come far enough to think before speaking or writing, even if that was all I was ever going to get.

And then two things happened:

The first was on my way to my sister's for Thanksgiving (a 90-mile journey), when I got stuck in stopped traffic less than 10 miles from home. Instead of thinking my usual, *I hate this freeway, I hate living where I live, I hate my life,* my first thought was actually, *I hope no one is hurt.* When I realized that my thinking had in fact changed, I was surprised and jubilant. (Me, jubilant? Why yes!) I danced around in my car and enjoyed the rest of my ride. No black cloud present. Or necessary.

The second moment of grace occurred one day when I found myself talking to someone in a milling-about crowd. I noticed that I was engaged with the person, not looking over her shoulder to find a cooler, more socially advantageous, hipper person to talk to! But wait, there's more. I also found myself (after a too-long pause, but still) saying, "How are you?" back to her. At that moment, conversations ceased to be only about me. I have learned to be less self-centered and to actually listen.

Grace.

Dance with the Divine

By Yiye Zhang

I still remember that afternoon six years ago when I heard the news that my job was at risk. Headquarters had decided to restructure the entire company, and our team had to go.

To say it was unsettling would be an understatement. I was only six months away from getting permanent residence in the UK. If I were forced to stop working, it would eliminate all my previous 4½ years' record, and I would have to start from scratch to collect "points."

I found myself furious and filled with angry thoughts: *This is so unfair! I've worked so damn hard. We are a high-performing team – why us? Why me? I put all my effort in for what – nothing?!*

Gradually, this anger triggered immense self-compassion. My inner voice whispered: "Stop stressing yourself even more. This is a perfect time to quit being a workaholic. Do something different in the evenings, like dance, and let go of the rest."

Within one week, I got a text message from an old friend: "Let's check out the salsa class at Pineapple Studio." I went, shaking off all the anxiety. One casual class turned into weekly classes for six months. I watched myself moving from the absolute-beginner group to the intermediate ones and then the advanced one. Then one dance style led to two – I picked up Brazilian Zouk.

When I was dancing with my partners, it felt like I was also dancing with the Divine. As I danced with the Divine, my fear around permanent residence subsided until it didn't feel like my personal problem anymore.

Then the restructuring date approached. Surprisingly, I was rewarded with extra bonuses, and I got my permanent-residence stamp from the Home Office just two weeks before my old job disappeared!

I became good friends with my Zouk teacher, who then left London. At his leaving party, out of the blue, he gifted me a book by Sonia Choquette, who has since become my spiritual teacher and the alchemist of my new lightworker career. Even now, I continue to dance with the Divine, and I can feel grace beneath any challenge I face.

Healing with Gratitude

By Shelley Lundquist

Sitting with a client who'd survived many years of domestic abuse, I listened and watched as her tears slipped silently down her face. Despite having found the courage to leave her husband and start over, her fear was palpable, her wounds were raw, and she was exhausted.

"I don't know how I'll manage on my own," she whispered.

"It doesn't matter if you don't know how right now, only that you decide you will. We'll get you there. And you're not alone," I reminded her.

I knew all too well how she felt. Thankfully, I also knew a powerful force of love and healing: gratitude. Creating a gratitude journal had helped open my eyes to life's awe-inspiring abundance and open my heart to my own healing long ago. I now keep a stack of them at hand for clients and anyone else who I think could use one.

At the end of her session, I opened my desk drawer and handed her one. She accepted both the gift and the task I gave her to find at least five things in each day for which she felt grateful. "I suppose I can try," she uttered, skeptically.

"I suppose you can," I smiled back. I knew that finding five things in a day when you're focused on suffering can seem a daunting task, so I simply offered, "They are there. If you pay attention, you will find them. Look for a smile. Listen for laughter. Feel the warmth of a hug. Notice the sun shining. Hear the birds singing. You get the gist."

When next I saw her she was much more at peace. I was grateful she'd taken the task to heart.

"I did it with my daughter," she laughed. "It was so much fun! We made her a journal and filled them in together every night after dinner. She made it easy when I was having trouble! 'Silly Mommy,' she giggled. 'You have *me*!' And with her name at the top of my list, there was no turning back."

So began her journey of healing.

Catching the Big One

By Karen L. Wythe

It was an ordinary day like any other when my ex-husband and I, both nature lovers, decided to go out to the Wiscoy Creek and do some trout fly fishing. As I waded into the creek, Bob walked downstream to a spot just out of my sight. I stood casting out and reeling in. It was a perfect spring day – mildly warm and partly cloudy with the sun peeking in and out. Every breath of air seemed revitalizing. The water was clear, and I was sure I would catch a fish.

I began the poetic motion of fly fishing – casting out and reeling in, using finesse to make the fly landing on the water mimic the motion of an insect skimming for a drink. Breathing in and feeling good, I raised my arm to cast. As I did that, a ladybug landed on my bare arm. I could see it as I followed the cast. At the same time, I saw a groundhog come out in the sun on the bank before me. Glancing at the sky, I noticed the beauty in the movement of the clouds. Catching a fish had become irrelevant; I was enjoying just being in the creek. Suddenly, I became aware of the brown trout at my feet. Time stood still. In that moment, there was a shift in my reality. I became one with all that is.

That was a day of grace for me. It is an experience that has stayed with me. It was not a day I caught a fish. No, it was a day I glimpsed into the Oneness of all Creation.

A Backpack Filled with Grace

By Michelle Wangler Joy

Several years ago, I felt painfully bored with my life. I wasn't confused; it's just that what I wanted felt too scary: I wanted to travel the world by myself, with just a backpack, for many months.

This vision thrilled me, yet it also terrified me. I was filled with thoughts of doubt and fear: *People will judge me. I'm being irresponsible. I'm wasting money. I'm wasting time. What if I get really sick? What if I get kidnapped? What if I get lost? What if, what if, what if???* I tried ignoring my inspiring vision, but the vision was relentless.

Finally, after years of fighting my internal battle, I decided that following my vision was more important than letting fear dictate my life. I set a date. I displayed inspiring travel photos around my house. I hung up a world map, placing tacks in all the places I wanted to go. Picking up extra jobs, creating an extremely strict budget, and holding tightly to my vision, I saved thousands of dollars within a timeframe that amazed me.

I was away for almost six months. I rode camels through the deserts of Egypt, uncovered pottery fragments dating back to 750 B.C. at an excavation site in Greece, hiked the Swiss Alps, received blessings from monks in Thailand, jumped out of a pink airplane in New Zealand, and made lifelong friendships in many countries all around the world.

These experiences have enriched my life in so many ways. Through them, I came to believe in myself. It's been five years since I've returned, and I feel like I'm still traveling with my backpack that's filled with grace because I continue to grow, evolve, and move past fears. And I know that I always will.

Two Hearts, One Magic
By Meilin Ehlke

Slowly, the door opened and I heard my son, Tilo, tiptoe into the living room. *Beautiful how he remembers to move quietly as a mouse when I am on a conference call*, I thought, taking my attention away from the fascinating discussion. *But why is he still up? It's almost midnight.*

Our eyes met, and I felt him express, *Please don't send me away. I can't sleep, and I don't want to be alone.* Somehow, I resisted the urge to send him back to bed as he slid into the armchair across me.

It was clear in the way he sat down that he contemplated staying until the call ended. *Oh, no. It is far too late*, I thought. I didn't want to miss a moment of this magnificent teaching. We needed a magical solution for both our needs to be met. I was pulled back into the conversation happening overseas as Tilo anticipated what would come next. A few minutes later, my awareness moved to the stack of paper I was writing my notes and impressions on.

Automatically, my hand pushed a piece of paper across the table, inviting Tilo to draw with my favorite pencil. Happily, he began sketching an intricate form.

I sensed his rising anger after a while. Frustrated that his drawing didn't turn out as he wished, he rigorously tried to cover it up. "Don't worry; you can create something new out of what you started," I whispered. "Let me play with it."

Disbelief on his face, he passed it to me. My hand scribbled over his lines, shading in areas to give his scratched-out area balancing pieces. Voila! A new picture emerged. He noticed the new direction the image took and demanded it back.

Happy, my attention returned to the call. Suddenly, with a contented smile on his face, Tilo rose, presented our co-creation to me, and left to go to sleep. I sat there contemplating that graceful connection – a moment that fed both of our hearts, inviting us to see each other in a gentle, tender way while supporting what we both desired.

Breathe, Listen, Breathe

By Twyla Reece

The morning sun gently lit the room. Breathing deeply from my heart, I asked, "How can I serve today?" Continuing to practice heart-focused breathing, I felt the peace of the moment and gratitude for the day. Then the phone rang, I read my emails and reviewed my to-do list, and I was suddenly multi-tasking. The ease began to deflate. Breathe...*Oh, there I am.* Stretch...a few yoga postures...move my body...walk by the to-do list...momentary anxiety...breathe. So went the morning, weaving in and out of awareness. The morning ritual of being human.

On this particular day, a day that I had planned to be quietly productive, I found myself scattered to the wind. A simple, quick errand turned into a day of grace-filled detours. I was in the right place at the right time to help a woman struggling with crutches. She had been in front of me in a store. I was aware of her but not connected to the extent of difficulty she was having.

It was not until I saw her in the parking lot that I saw that she needed help. On crutches, and in obvious pain, I thought she was walking to her car, but no, she passed the cars and began to walk down the street. I gently got her attention, offered her a ride and, after helping her get groceries, drove her safely home.

From there my day continued to twist and weave, creating a tapestry of order that went beyond my to-do list. It was not until later, in quiet reflection, that I realized how grace-filled my day had been.

How easy it can be to get caught up in the day, in the busyness of activity, and go into spiritual amnesia: the condition of forgetting that we are connected to each other and the Source of all that is.

On this day, however, I was reminded to pause and ask myself: *How can I be of service today?* I remembered to breathe, listen, breathe, and follow the breath of guidance. This is the beginning of grace.

Kayak Empowerment
By Carol Ann Arnim

A couple days after a Faster Emotional Freedom Technique (FEFT) tapping session, I begin to hear the word *kayaking* in my mind. I ignore it because I would never kayak, since I fear deep water. Yet the word keeps repeating, so I think to myself, *Okay, Carol Ann. You are being told something, so pay attention.* To my delight, three days later I find myself booking a kayak outing.

When the big day arrives, I'm feeling confident. I know I can do this. But then I see that two single kayaks are being taken down to the beach. An inner rumble of fear rises up when I realize that I am about to head out to sea in a kayak all by myself. Holy cow! This is not what I envisioned! I thought the tour man was going to be steering, leading our way in a double-seated kayak.

After a few moments, he asks me, "Are you ready for this?" I mentally tap, and confidence returns. I am soon seated in a kayak by myself, paddling into the water. Holding my fear of water in check, I do my best to get this contraption going the right direction and to stop heading me back to shore. Slowly, I get the hang of it. A smile spreads across my face as I silently express gratitude to my FEFT tapping for boosting my confidence and guiding me to this new experience.

Then I let out a gasp of disbelief and awe as I see what I am paddling toward: Confederation Bridge – the very one that I'd once been afraid to cross! That bridge, which once held me in a vice of terror, was now my friend. The day I finally crossed it with a smile was a huge milestone for me. How divinely perfect that I am now transcending another fear, sitting solo in a kayak, blessed with a joyous heart.

Tapping out my fear has gifted me this experience of liberating empowerment. Thank you, tapping, and thank you, kayaking!

Thanksgiving Space and the Flow of Grace

By Saira Priest

For the Thanksgiving family meal at my mom's home, I assigned myself to bring four dishes, although she asked for only one. If that was not a big enough challenge, I chose to make some new and untested recipes. The pressure was on.

My usual worries when preparing food for others are whether or not the food will turn out well or if people will like it. Those things did not worry me that day. Somewhere in the back of my mind, however, a different concern was forming. The refrigerator was overstocked for the holidays. I had bought at least two of everything I would need, as well as extra items, just in case. Where would I put everything after it was prepared? Most of it needed to stay cool. I knew Mom's fridge would be full, too. Supplies were coming out and going back into the refrigerator as needed for the different dishes. I let my concern go and focused on cooking. With anticipation and excitement for the upcoming gathering that evening, the day of preparation seemed to flow effortlessly.

The food came together lovingly. First, a bowl of colorful confetti salad large enough to require two hands – imagine my delight at a completely open bottom shelf. Next, a platter filled with wild rice and roasted chestnut dressing – the middle shelf was available. A traditional family dessert on a round flat plate slid right onto the top shelf. In popped the round dish of orange-cranberry relish.

Finally, a leftover jar of fruit needed a home, and I was sure there was no more room. But when I opened the door, there was just enough of an open space on the top shelf. With my mind cleared of the details of food preparation, it shifted toward the awareness of how my concern was easily answered, time and again. Grace opened up each space. I was filled with joy and gratitude at the realization that during the entire day, I had been in the flow of grace.

Truly Being in the Presence of Art

By Felicia D'Haiti

My discovery of the importance of seeing art in its original location came on a rainy day in October. My friend and I had taken a train to Venice for the weekend. Knowing we only had a couple of days there, we planned to visit only major sites and museums that we had pre-identified. Yet there was one rather large and imposing church that we passed several times near our hotel that never seemed open. Our curiosity was piqued.

On our last day in Venice, we rose early in an attempt to enter the church before morning services. Yes, the doors were open! We quietly crept inside. There we saw several marble-sculpture tombs and monuments, a carved-wood choir loft, and numerous paintings – all beautiful but nothing out of the ordinary. We stepped farther into the church. As I rounded the corner of the massive choir loft, I was awestruck. There it was – a painting that I had only seen in poor reproductions.

The *Assumption of the Virgin* painting by Titian seemed to fill the entire front of the church. It was massive and beautiful. As I moved closer to the painting, I suddenly felt overwhelmed and inexplicably drawn into the image. I felt as if I wanted to cry because I was so awed by its unexpected beauty. As I became more absorbed in the work, I could almost feel the velvety texture of Mary's robes and the light fluffiness of the clouds. I felt the airiness and weightlessness of Mary's statuesque figure as she rose into the heavens effortlessly. And I could experience the wonderment of the onlookers in the painting as they witnessed her assumption.

It was at this moment that I understood how a painting truly could be alive. As I was drawn into the painting, I felt as if a spark of creativity, joy, and beauty had been ignited in my life that I wanted to share with everyone I met.

When Grace Requires Forgiveness

By Joan B. Zietlow

Some years after my divorce, I made a career change to a new position with extensive travel. Prior to this, I had rarely traveled via plane, so I assumed that my recent anxiety was due to being an inexperienced traveler. Unfinished conversations never crossed my mind. Before long, however, I noticed that each time I prepared for a trip, my mind continuously played a broken record: *What will I do or say if I run into my world-traveling ex-husband?* The girl-in-every-port scenario had come to a head, and I just bailed.

Before this, I had been unaware that how I dealt with conflict was avoidance and denial. Given that I was raised in a family with parents who never expressed any conflict or affection and what my dad said was law, I was hardly equipped to handle conflict in any other way. Identifying and voicing feelings was totally foreign to me. Forgiveness? Who, *me?* Discussing conflict and working out a compromise wasn't a tool in my toolbox.

Through counseling, classes, and lots of self-help books, it became apparent that my unforgiving heart was holding me captive and keeping my power and sanity in the hands of my ex. As I learned how much power I continued to give him, I looked for ways to take it back. Facing my fear of confronting and just talking to my ex, I tracked him down. I thanked him for all the things he had introduced me to: steamed artichokes; pomegranates; orange coffee; making a soufflé; running a crane; riding my motocross bike; and, most importantly, self-worth, confidence, trust, and self-respect. I let him know how much richer my life was because of him. Even though there were many things that hurt me, they no longer carried their charge. I could now, with a sincere heart, wish him health and happiness.

After talking to my ex, thanking him for enriching my life, and letting go of all unforgiveness for him and for myself, I never worried about seeing him again. We remain friends, and I can finally travel in peace.

Every Moment Is a Moment of Grace

By Sharon Rothstein

There are times when I am so caught up in the fast-paced happenings in my life that I find it difficult to recall even one single moment of Grace. I must then become quiet and notice that everything always works out for me. This is when I say to myself: "Is not *every* moment a moment of Grace – another platform to rise up to my own desired outcome, request, or need? My beloved Grace is always available to me. Exactly what I beckon appears with the greatest of ease."

Sometimes I wish that Grace would speak to me and say, "My beloved child, know that the best outcome will always manifest for you, although it may appear in a way other than what you have imagined or intended. Say often to yourself, 'I expect the best to happen,' and allow me, Divine Grace, to wave my magic wand around you. Let go and have faith in my assistance. I have your back. I am Grace Almighty, your powerful protector and guide. There is no issue or concern that you may be facing that I do not have the perfect solution for. I will assist you in varied ways. I will manifest as emotional, physical, or financial relief and comfort, my love. Think of me, your Grace, in each moment, and I will meld with you in everlasting peace of mind."

When I am able to slow down enough to hear Grace's message, I realize that what comes my way *every* moment is my moment of Grace. I am not to judge so harshly. If something appears as my good, I will be joyful and content. When a situation appears as an obstacle, I will step back, take a deep breath, recalibrate, and ask Grace to provide my appropriate solution.

I know that, in every moment, Grace caresses my soul and provides the necessary tools for the blueprint of my journey. I simply must slow down this merry-go-round in my mind and enjoy these precious moments of Grace.

Hologram of Grace

By Karen Bomm

My splash pierced the silence when I dove off the boat into the refreshing mountain water. This was my time to take a quick swim after several long slalom ski runs of pure glass.

My husband relaxed in the early warmth of the sun as it was too early for the families of recreational boaters to get their crews fed and moving. It was only us and a few quiet fishermen on this divine lake.

Every summer, we celebrate Heaven on Earth as the sun rises and sets on this magnificent high desert. Instagrammers worldwide come to photograph the shadows dancing on Lake Abiquiu, its surrounding red rock, and expansive blue sky that becomes an ocean in its own right.

This is where Georgia O'Keeffe painted her beyond-belief landscapes. Each view represents another painting, with the southern vista offering a mesa called Pedernal Mountain, rising 9,862 feet to become the north flank of the Jemez Mountains and the Coyote Ranger District of the Santa Fe National Forest. This was our paradise – just 30 short minutes north of Santa Fe – where we could absorb this section of New Mexico, The Land of Enchantment.

But today was something more. My plunge into the water became draped in a three-dimensional Hologram of Grace. It was surreal. I felt a primal energy infuse all of my senses. *Was I experiencing Kundalini rising or a blissful awakening?* I was the lake, the sky, the wind, the sun, the water, my husband, the boat. I was all things, and my senses were magnified, aroused. My instinctive energy force was hyper-aware. It was like a deep meditation as I breathed in and out. My body became one with our living planet. The only words I know to explain these extended moments, as my senses overwhelmed me, are *bliss* and *grace*.

My moment of enlightenment was undisturbed when I heard my husband gently ask, "Are you ready to head over to Ojo Caliente to soak your bones?"

"I am! Thank you for this day."

Finding Light

By Dana Ben-Yehuda

I found my soul while dancing in the empty aerobics room at Gold's Gym. There was nothing unusual about that day; I was doing what I'd done hundreds of times before, an hour or two every day for a year – practicing for my lesson, moving backwards and forwards across the floor. Dancing a box step: rising on my toes, lowering, forward, side, back. I felt content, just repeating these simple movements and finding balance in my body, noticing the way my feet traced the floor.

Then I caught a glimpse of myself in the mirror as I was dancing. My face had a smile on it that reminded me of the smile in my baby pictures: pure, happy, completely open, and shining light. I smiled out at myself, radiating love, and saw my soul shining out from my eyes.

Right then, I knew that dancing is what makes my soul shine.

I couldn't have seen myself without that mirror, although everyone at the gym knows I dance. They often mentioned it when they'd see me. Even though the room was often empty at the time, the walls were full of windows. And when they'd mention my dancing, I could see their faces lighting up. The sensation was like one candle taking light from another…finding light.

This experience drove home one of the most important, grace-filled lessons I've ever learned: Whatever it is you're doing when your face is shining, do *that*! If you're a dancer, dance! If you're a singer, sing your heart out. Hold a baby and smile. Look at a flower and let the beauty wash over you. Be a candle to light someone's joy. The light they reflect is your own soul.

Enjoy the Journey

By H. Michelle Spaulding

Growing up as a military brat turned me into a restless, modern-day gypsy. I'm an adventurer and explorer by nature. I never felt grounded or at home anywhere. Yes, I had immediate connections to places, but not a sense of "Ahhh!"

So I set off on a quest for a town that my heart and soul resonated with – a quest that lasted over 20 years! I experimented with Arizona, New Mexico, and Colorado. I looked for areas that were creative, artistic, spiritual, Native American influenced, culturally diverse, free thinking, college towns, environmental, wellness centers, hippie dippy, elegant and sophisticated, in the mountains, and a day's drive to the ocean.

After over two decades of searching, my inner gypsy finally found contentment in North Carolina. For the past two years, I have been recuperating peacefully from a chronic illness in my colorful island cocoon in coastal North Carolina. In my desire to create the lifestyle of my dreams, I had also been looking for a retreat in the mountains. A few weeks ago, after searching high and low, I found my "Shangri La" in Asheville, NC.

In Asheville, I finally felt the lightbulb go on. I'm now ready to explore the possibilities that crafting a life here could provide. I'm not going to hop right in and try to make something happen. I'm going to let God and my wise inner voice guide me – my heart, not my head.

I'm in my second half of life, and time is moving rapidly. The moments are to be savored and enjoyed. No more plowing and trailblazing through life. I no longer have to plant the flowers; I can take time to smell the roses already blooming and finally enjoy the journey.

Opening Up
By Kaylyn Gelata

I am an avid writer. I've been putting my life onto paper since I got my first journal at the age of 10. For most of my life since that time, the journal and pen have been my way to sort out my life's challenges and emotions, which can feel like a chaotic mess when not let out.

There was a period in my early 20s, however, when I stopped journaling – a time when I was struggling in my life more than ever. My journal sat on my bedside table, and every night for about eight months, I would look at it and look away, afraid of opening it…and myself. On some level, I knew that opening up would be good for me, but I also sensed that it would hurt.

This principle is true with the heart and the hips. Through my yoga practice, I learned an asana designed to open up the hips: the pigeon pose. Everyone knows it's good for you, but it can feel so painful – especially when your hips are tight. But this is when it can also be the most helpful. And the more open you are with this pose, the less it will hurt the next time you go deeply into it.

The same goes with the heart. Have you ever done a metaphorical pigeon pose in your soul – really tried to stretch yourself and open up – with a really closed heart? It's very hard to do. That's how I felt about opening up that journal after my unintentional hiatus.

Finally, however, I asked myself why I was so afraid of the very thing that had always been there for me when I was lost. I faced my fear, cracked open the journal layered with dust, and began writing. And writing. And writing. The more my hand cramped, the more I felt myself opening up. The more it hurt, the more I cried. And the more I cried, the more I remembered why I used to write regularly.

In that moment, I remembered that while regular exercise will keep my hips open, regular exposure of my heart will keep *me* open – open to realness, pain, hurt, and love. Expressing what is hard hurts, but the alternative is staying tight and closed and never really feeling my way into that deep stretch. There is freedom there, at the bottom of that stretch… in both hips and heart. When I stretch, I am whole.

Divine Whisper of Self-Acceptance
By Milada Sakic

Grace is my favorite energy, and I call it into my life every day. It helps me to experience flow, creativity, and self-acceptance. I adore co-creating with this energy, hearing its divine whisper, and trusting that it is my friend and my partner.

It has not always been this way, though. As a recovering perfectionist, rather than calling in grace and self-acceptance, I used to call in perfection and faultlessness, saying: "Dear Guides, help me make this excellent and perfect...before I let it go into the world." This approach led to the opposite of grace: tightness, heaviness, stress, and stagnation.

Nowadays, I invite grace into every part of my life. If I am working on an article, planning my teaching schedule, or getting ready for a client, I consciously make room for grace. I take a walk, stretch for a moment, and move energy in my body. As energy flows, grace comes through, softly bringing enlightened gifts: a breeze of inspiration, insight, clarity, ease, spaciousness, stillness, and loving presence.

Inviting grace into my daily routine has transformed my life. My to-do list now has three items (it used to have 10). I know that as soon as I create a sacred container (e.g., set an intention, create a title, or schedule an event), grace is nearby. Most importantly, I have learned to trust that gentle twinkle of insight that comes through as a divine whisper, so breezily, so gently, so beautifully offering a suggestion: "You can take action on it, or you don't have to. It's up to you. You can make yourself wrong or not. You don't have to be that which feels heavy. I am here to help you breathe in more ease, flow, self-acceptance, and presence. Choose me if you'd like."

I no longer feel a need to make myself wrong for making different choices. When grace comes through as a divine suggestion, I simply say, "Thank you. Thank you. Thank you." And I smile and then take action.

I know that grace is here to guide me into alignment. How do I know it is grace? Because it feels like lightness, ease, flow, expansiveness, acceptance, breathing space, inner peace, alignment with love and truth, feminine strength, me.

Countless Moments of Grace

By Janet Dhaenens

This book has changed my life! I've been writing a long time, and I am so excited at the idea of having my writing published. It's been a gradual journey to greater clarity, marked by countless moments of grace.

I used to ask my son for help with my writing. Sometimes, he would ask, "What are you really trying to say here?" He knew me well enough that, at other times, he would simply say, "What you are trying to say here is…" and then proceed to say it concisely and clearly. I wanted to organize my thoughts like he could!

I have many pages of handwritten notebook paper. I'm surprised sometimes when I read something I wrote years ago, because often I am saying the same things now. The difference is that now those ideas live IN me. I embody them, rather than just believe them to be true. As I have practiced walking my talk, slowing down enough to explore what it means to take responsibility for what's happening in my life, I have gained a deeper understanding about myself.

Bit by bit, I found words that felt like a match to what is inside. At times, I experience the words flowing out effortlessly! I feel confident and realize that what I have learned can be helpful to others. I'm eager to share.

Writing these pieces has brought aspects of my life into focus in a different way. In addition to the clarifying practice of putting my thoughts on paper (and sharing them with others), simply contemplating what to write about has helped me realize that there are *so many* moments of grace in my life – they occur *every day*! Here is another one now: my recognition that countless moments of grace fill my days. Through slowing down to notice them, I find more and re-experience ones that already happened. And I feel deeply blessed!

Embracing Dreamtime Messages for Healing

By Tia Johnson

While I have been an avid daydreamer since I was a girl, it was my nighttime dreams that captured my imagination and wonder. For example, a dream from my childhood was a message about boundaries. The dream involved my uncle's first wife, her family, my family, and me. We were happily holding hands, walking through my neighborhood, and admiring the scenery. I turned around and noticed a shadowy figure approaching us. Sensing danger, I tried to lift everyone up to fly away, but it didn't work. I was only able to lift my family in the air; however, since we were holding hands, we never flew away from the shadowy figure. Thus, we were at its mercy.

Reflecting on that childhood dream of trying to uplift the entire family helped me to heal from my belief that I can fix every family issue. I learned that not all problems are *my* problems. The other message that came from this dream was knowing that I can set boundaries and break away (let go of the hands) from a negative situation. While I deeply cared for the well-being of everyone, it wasn't my problem to solve. Also, since I had this dream, my uncle has divorced his wife and moved on with his life. So, in a sense, the dream prepared me for the future rift between the families.

As I reached adulthood, I became more accustomed to having dreams that served as dress rehearsals for waking-life issues. Now, I create time to gracefully journal and occasionally reflect upon dreams as a method of self-evaluation. I'm constantly learning ways to improve my life, and I'm thankful that my dreams provide a platform for me to address issues in my life that I may otherwise unknowingly suppress. By embracing the messages of my dreams, I have been able to heal from negative mindsets and establish healthy boundaries.

Graceful Presence

By Amanda Dale

As I sit at this rest stop with pen to paper, many thoughts, feelings, emotions, and streams of energy flow to me and through me. It's been a while since I was last inspired to write, and I've missed this piece of myself. Now, however, I feel an overwhelming sense of comfort, joy, and delight as I place pen to paper and center my awareness in this present moment.

My attention is drawn to the sounds of trucks rolling fast along the highway. I hear crisp crackles as the 54-degree wind tosses my hair and gently brushes against my skin. I hear birds chirping and people stopping for rest before re-entry to the highway. I notice very dry, light-brown leaves hanging sparse in the abundant, precisely lined trees.

As I become increasingly aware of all that is present around me, I am also reminded of the still and quiet inner presence. I breathe in, deepening my breath, each one deeper than the last. I visualize my muscular, skeletal, and other integral body systems; DNA, molecular, and cellular structures; my lungs; my entire physical and non-physical essence. I see my love light shine and expand beyond me – to the air above me; to the space that surrounds me; to the depth of the earth beneath me; to all land and water; to the sun, moon, and stars; to everything known and unknown. I am one with this essence, and this essence is one with me.

I take another deep, cleansing breath as I choose to release the past. The past is done and gone, along with any remaining expectations of myself or others. I feel as though I've relinquished control of the uncontrollable. I experience a moment of re-alignment with my mind, spirit, and body. I know that my essence flows in perfect time, always.

In another precious moment of grace, a ladybug lands on the table and walks across the paper I am writing this experience on. I smile with joy and gratitude, feeling the magnificent presence of peace.

Finding Grace in Challenges

By Heather Nardi

Like most people, I have experienced numerous challenges throughout my life. I dropped out of college, became pregnant out of wedlock, watched my teenaged daughter suffer with anxiety and depression for eight years, and I've also suffered from my own anxiety and was clinically obese for 17 years.

We all have stories of challenges and difficulties. Some are very different from my own, and others might be similar. These stories – my own and others' – have often led me to wonder: How come some people use their deepest, darkest, and even tragic experiences in a way that helps themselves or others, while other people become stuck in their stories, unable to move out of the darkness?

Then, one day while I was journaling, the answer came to me: *Grace!*

Grace is so powerful that not only can it redirect your own life, it can also improve the lives of others. Grace is that feeling of unconditional love, when you are at peace with yourself and feel complete gratitude for anything and everything. Grace is the kind of happiness that accepts everything, while feeling that situations can be better.

I know that even just one of my experiences could have kept me stuck. I chose to be a positive thinker, looking for the good in any situation. But it was more than this that allowed me to move forward. I've also experienced grace.

Grace has helped me see my family's difficult journey as an opportunity to speak out and share with others – something I wasn't able to do until recently. Grace has helped me to grow and also empower others. Grace has helped me find ways to give back to others while supporting myself in a safe environment.

Grace is not something we can hold; it's a process that helps us grow, align our inner and outer purposes, and bring more abundance into the world. And while grace often awakens gradually, we can experience it at any moment of our life – even in the midst of the most difficult challenges.

A Grace-Filled Memory
By Karen Hill

Getting out of balance in my life happens so easily, which is why I pray and meditate on a regular basis – to quiet my mind, take a break from my daily stressors, continue on my spiritual path, and get centered with the universe.

During one meditative experience, I find myself sitting outside, silently becoming more relaxed, the warm sun beaming down on my face. I sit peacefully, pondering a moment of the past:

I see myself as a child, entering the woods on a hot summer day. The trees cool my body as I skip along on the trail with my friends. I see the creek and would love to get in and play, but my mom has told me not to get into it because she does not want me to get wet. Therefore, my friends and I decide to swing from the vines that are hanging from the enormous trees. We swing and swing again until, suddenly, we crash into the creek and (of course) get wet! We cannot stop laughing; we are having so much fun. We play in the woods all day until it is time to go home.

I am filled with gratitude remembering this sweet memory from my past. It was such a time of grace when I first experienced it; and now, through this meditation, I am given the opportunity to laugh and smile once again. The worries of today melt as I focus on the magical moments of my life.

Everything As It Must Be

By Karen L. Wythe

It was a small miracle that a co-worker and I were gifted tickets to see the Dalai Lama at Cornell University in Ithaca, New York. For two days, we managed to free ourselves of all responsibilities and embark on an adventure. It was one I would remember for a lifetime.

We set out, trusting we would find our way and find lodging for the night of our arrival. Finally reaching Cornell, we easily found visitor parking near a building that thankfully had a ladies' room right inside the door. As we left, we saw a sign that pointed to event seating in another building. Everything seemed to be going perfectly.

Upon arrival, however, we found that our seats were already filled. We were redirected to the gym in yet another building that had bleacher seating and a 12-foot screen. Disappointedly, we entered the near-empty room and found our pick of seats across the room.

The room filled with excitement. As I looked out, passing right in front of me was a man I knew, Roger, looking forlorn. I called out to him, and a look of relief swept over his face. He explained that he had been locked out of the main seating because he left his group to see the other exhibits on campus. Happily, he sat in the last open seat next to me. He explained all we needed to see after the lecture. Through Roger's guidance, we went on to the campus museum exhibit. There we met people who told us of a unpublicized lecture by the Dalai Lama the next day. We were also guided to lodging still available.

In the morning, we got up extra early to be at the beginning of the line. It was a cold, rainy day. Standing outside the library doors, I gazed at a sea of colored umbrellas lining the library stairs behind me. In that split second, we all became one. It was a beautiful, blissful moment. An overwhelming sense of unity and peace filled me, and I felt filled with joy and the grace of knowing that there is a peace that passes all understanding when we go with the flow of life.

Grace and Our Creative Process

By Ambika Talwar

How we long for grace to enrich our lives, especially when difficulties seem insurmountable and we sink into the black hole of our own shadow. But dark intensities also reveal the presence of grace. She arrives in unexpected ways to remind us of what is true.

Years ago, feeling trapped in a job that had lost its luster, I desired to write but felt constrained and tired. I went to a park and sat by the pond. As I looked across the ripples, She appeared as Mother Saraswati, assuring me that I would write.

Poems flowed and I developed my painting, but I was not satisfied. I hungered for creative consummation in other areas. Somehow, the creative life would always win out.

I had written poetry since my college days and felt called to expand my creative horizons. Walking the stairs to a friend's place, I was stopped by a single thought: *In two years, you will make a film.* That morning I'd mused over a story's cinematic potential. The film was completed in 2000. It won an award in Belgium!

In the years that followed, my understanding of the connections between grace and our creative process continued to deepen. Following a vision in 2003 that illumined our intimate cosmic unities, I recognized poetry as a process of awakening. I also understood that the subtlest thought or touch creates vast ripples, which heighten our awareness of our sacred capacities.

In 2006, after being weakened by a series of injuries and studying energy medicine, I realized that wellness and art are inspired by the same creative process, for language ignites, inspires, and re-forms. All my visions and the creations that followed were touched by the presence and force of grace – and brought to life by action, allowing my passions to emerge into wholeness.

Now, grace reveals with utter simplicity that truth empowers. What holds me back are my fears and judgments. What moves me forward is my inner voice of grace. I simply ask that grace keep me in humility as I journey forth, recognizing our unities and our sacred purpose to express our creative vision and awaken to the human heart's greater intelligence.

Fly at Night

By Monica Laws

There is a kind of magic in the air. The boats are in the bay. Children are off in the distance – at the carnival, riding the roller coaster, screaming with delight. The smells of barbeque, corn dogs, and funnel cakes permeate the air. Hundreds of people in front of the stage share the positive energy, the vibes of awesomeness.

Kempenfest is an arts and music festival at the park by Kempenfelt Bay in Barrie, Ontario. My children and one of my best friends have been attending with me for a number of years. During one particularly memorable year, we were able to experience an outdoor live concert by Chilliwack, a band that has been around since the 1970s. I grew up listening to them. Years later, they are still sharing their music at local festivals like this one.

It is special when a band leader can touch hearts and souls with his endearing stories. During the concert, frontman Bill Henderson spoke like a friend. It was like he was talking to each of us alone, almost like sharing life stories and experiences around a campfire.

The song "Fly at Night" became an opportunity to express that his closeness to the audience while playing music has been one of the most important things in his life. These four men in a rock 'n' roll band get high on music every night. They provide a release from our mundane lives to be present in the moment, to feel the pure joy of being alive. The band and audience connect together. "And when we look out and see you there, you seem much closer and you feel so near."

I was so grateful to share this with my teenaged children and best friend. They understood. They got it. They danced and sang and stood with me in moments of peace, beauty, and connectedness. I looked at them and felt such overwhelming gratitude, love, and joy.

The Importance of Home
By Emily Herrick

With one innocent question, my husband, Michael, changed the course of our lives. We had been living in East Hampton, New York, happily married for almost six years in March 2014. Life was very good, yet we both sensed it was time for a change. Our community and home were beautiful, but the area was beginning to feel less and less like home; many small beach homes were being torn down and replaced with huge, impersonal mansions that were rarely used. We craved a sense of community.

Michael and I, big food and wine lovers, have a tradition: I read a food-related book out loud to him many evenings after dinner. We had just begun reading *Growing a Feast* by Kurt Timmermeister, the story of a dairy farmer on Vashon Island, Washington. Intrigued by Timmermeister's pastoral descriptions of life on the island, Michael asked one morning, "What about where that guy lives?" I answered, "What guy?" and he replied, "The guy in the book."

We started researching Vashon online and within minutes were exclaiming over how perfect it seemed for us. I discovered a house that had gone on the market that day that looked like a great fit. I called a realtor who said, "If you're serious, you're going to have to fly out here this weekend. I can almost guarantee that house will be gone by Sunday."

We were on a plane to Seattle several days later. We made an offer but didn't get the house. Six weeks later, we returned and bought a piece of property. Six months after that, we arrived on the island and began the process of building our dream home. We have never looked back, never been happier, and never had a regret. That moment of grace, when my husband asked the question that led us to the life we truly want to live, was a pivotal moment. We found what *home* means to us.

Chapter 4
Signs of Grace

S ometimes grace has a playful, yet powerful, way of showing up in our lives – a way to grab our attention through objects or events that are meaningful to us. We both tend to be on the skeptical side and oftentimes need a lot of proof in order to believe that we're receiving a sign and that it isn't simply a coincidence. Because of this skepticism and our need for additional proof, we've received an extraordinary number of signs throughout our lives from our angels and loved ones on the other side, which we're so grateful for because each one helps us remember that we are never alone and that we are always connected to something so much bigger than ourselves.

We were absolutely devastated when our Norwegian Elkhound dog-ter, Xena, passed away from cancer a couple of years ago. She was our entire world, and we felt lost without her. She immediately began appearing in our dreams, in song lyrics, and on dice! Shortly after her death, we had a numerology reading that said her number was a five. After the reading, we began rolling fives all of the time when we played backgammon each night, which had been part of our routine for years and was when we missed her the most. We loved that she was letting us know she was still with us. Even to this day, we roll an exceptionally high number of fives, which always reminds us that she's right here.

Receiving signs such as these brings us so much comfort. And in this chapter, you'll read about many other signs that others have received as well – signs that helped them to see and feel that their loved ones on the other side and their angels and spirit guides were right next to them. We hope these pieces help you see the signs in your own life as well. They are always there, and when we're open to noticing and receiving them, magic happens!

Angelic Intervention

By Mathew Hart

We had long fantasized about moving from Toronto to Los Angeles; but my career kept us in Canada, and my wife, Nola, had never actually been to L.A. In March 2006, however, when my work suddenly dried up, we took a spontaneous trip. Everything fell into place quickly: flights, childcare for our youngest daughter, dinner dates, business meetings. The only thing that proved difficult was our accommodations until, without us asking, a professional acquaintance offered us a furnished rental property she owned in Santa Monica that was going to be vacant during our visit. And so it came to pass that we ended up staying for free in a beautiful apartment with a spectacular, unspoiled view of the Pacific Ocean. Amazing? Yes. Angelic intervention? Perhaps. But there's more.

On day three of our trip, we decided to take a drive along the coast in search of a neighborhood that we thought we might fancy living in. Interestingly, we had only been on the road for five minutes when a street sign suddenly caught my attention. "Look, Honey," I said, "Hollister Avenue."

"I saw that," Nola replied, adding, "Why don't you pull over and I'll take a picture."

You see, our two teenaged daughters had recently started their first job working for a retail chain called Hollister – a new chain in Toronto, selling, of all things, youth-oriented Southern Californian casual wear!

There was a line of traffic behind us and nowhere to pull over, so we couldn't stop. Nevertheless, we were just discussing the idea of phoning home to tell the girls about the sign when the very next street sign caught our attention: *Hart* (our surname)! We began to chuckle at the "coincidence" when the next street sign came into view: *Fraser* (Nola's maiden name)! With that, we literally gasped out loud while tears welled in our eyes as we immediately recognized an incredible moment of grace and validation.

One year later, we took a leap of faith and made the 2700-mile move to "The City of Angels."

Just Believe

By Sylvie A. Savoie

In September 2004, I was brushing my teeth when I noticed the lump on the side of my throat. Though it would be another month before the official cancer diagnosis, my instincts had already brought me there. Meanwhile, as I waited for the final results, it was becoming increasingly difficult to stay calm.

One morning while making breakfast, I was suddenly overcome by a growing sense of urgency. It felt like I was running out of time. Unable to stand still any longer, I grabbed my portable CD player and went out for a walk.

"Maybe this is the beginning of the end," I caught myself thinking.

I began sinking deeper into despair, when the song playing in my headphones caught my attention. It was "Bring Me to Life" by Evanescence. I had always loved the rhythm, but this time the words seemed to speak to my core. As the singer pleaded with her lover to stay, it felt as if my body was begging my very soul to not give up. Every word fueled my will to live.

When the song ended, I looked down to hit replay and noticed a blue sparkle at my feet. Initially I simply walked over the decorative glass pebble. All I wanted was to return to the comfort of the lyrics. With every step, however, I felt a growing pull to go back.

"It could serve as a reminder of my newly found strength," I thought to myself.

With that in mind, I turned around and began to scan the ground. Once in sight, I quickly grabbed my little symbol of hope. I flipped it over to get a better look, and tears filled my eyes. Printed in gold letters was one simple word: BELIEVE.

From that moment on, everything else fell into place. To this day, I have yet to meet anyone who recovered as well from the same procedure. As for my little stone, it greets me morning and night on my bathroom counter. It is my reminder to have faith that whatever I really need will always, somehow, come to me.

The Ultrasound Miracle: Hello, Bella!

By Angie Carter

My daughter, Bella, was only 19 months old when she passed away unexpectedly. It wasn't long after her transition to the spirit world that she began sending me signs that she was still with me. I began finding rocks in strange places, such as under furniture and inside of toys. Rainbows began appearing frequently, often in places with no explanation. Electronic devices would start up and Bella's toys would turn on, sometimes when the batteries were dead. Her favourite doll was motion activated and would talk when no one was in the room. This was her way of letting me know she was still with me, and I continue to be comforted by her presence.

Last July, I discovered I was pregnant. I was very anxious about the pregnancy and fearful of how I would react to a new baby. I felt a strong need to know the baby's gender to help me prepare emotionally. I felt Bella's presence during our ultrasound and knew she was with us. When the ultrasound technician told us we were having a girl, tears of joy began to flow uncontrollably. Shortly after we left the hospital, a rainbow appeared in the sky – confirmation that Bella was with us.

I had posted a few ultrasound photos on Facebook, and a few weeks later, a friend told me to turn one of the photos sideways and look behind the baby's head. I couldn't believe my eyes when I looked and saw there was a face behind the baby. But what I saw was not just any face; it was Bella's face! I layered a photo of Bella taken a month before she passed and placed it over the ultrasound. It was a match! Bella's eyes, nose, and lips matched up perfectly. Even wisps of her hair are visible in the ultrasound photo!

I have experienced many miracles since my daughter's transition, but I have never seen anything so incredible. I know Bella is with her baby sister, and that helps fill my broken heart with love.

Please visit www.angiecarter.ca to view the incredible photo.

Butterflies from Dad

By Bryce Goebel

The phone rang at 1:37 a.m. I didn't need to see the number. I knew. Mom was calling because Dad had passed. I was numb as my husband and I dressed, packed a bag, and prepared to drive home. *Home.* The word took on a very different meaning now. Logically, I knew Dad was no longer in pain. His spirit was in a better place, but my heart was grieving. I had lost my teddy bear. He was more of a dad to me than my biological father ever was.

The morning was a blur. I retrieved Dad's belongings from the hospital and made arrangements at the funeral home. In the midst of all the activity, I needed some quiet time, so I snuggled into Dad's favorite spot in the garage. In my grief, I was also angry with him for not saying goodbye. My grandfather had said goodbye when he transitioned; I expected the same from Dad.

I thought about his last words to me, spoken just 36 hours earlier: "I love you. Take care of your mom." I realized that he *was* telling me goodbye. He was tired of fighting.

As I continued to think, Dad appeared (a special but not completely unprecedented experience, since spirits have been part of my world since I was a child). "Why didn't you tell me?" I demanded.

"A man has to have some secrets," he replied.

"Are you okay?" I asked.

He gave me a big smile and said, "I can finally take a deep breath." I had to laugh.

Dad promised he would send messages to show he was near. A few days later, I noticed a white butterfly on his swing. The love I felt was overwhelming. I knew it was him. He was keeping his promise. The tears began to flow.

Butterflies continue to appear in the most unexpected places. They give me hope. Each one reminds me to BE love. To be thankful. To smile often. To give whole-heart hugs as often as possible. And to be fully present in each moment, because you don't know how many more you have.

A Glimpse of Christmas with Mom

By Tae Lynne

Christmas was my mother's favorite holiday. She decorated the house inside and out – including the bathrooms! Holiday music blasting from the stereo, Mom would bake 10-15 varieties of cookies every year. We didn't have a lot of money, but she always made Christmas special with stockings that overflowed with goodies.

Sadly, on December 19, 2004, after a four-year battle with cancer, the doctors told us Mom would pass within one to two days.

We kept vigil at her bedside. Slowly, the clock ticked to day five...*Christmas Eve*. Mom took her last breath that morning. I believe she was hanging on for one last Christmas with us!

Eleven years later, Mom's spirit continues to grace us with her presence. She likes to turn on/off lights at my father's house and appear in family pictures as a glowing orb. Once, while taking Dad's picture after his skin-cancer procedure, her essence covered his face in *four* shots. Out loud, my sister explained to her that we needed a clear picture of his scar. She was gone in the next image!

Another time, I huddled in bed, sick and in pain. "Mom, I need you," I whimpered like a small child. Feeling a depression on the bed behind me, I turned over, expecting to see the cat. Nothing was there, but I could feel her familiar embrace comforting me.

Perhaps the most meaningful sign was when she left my father several quarters on their bedroom dresser. She had often done that so he could roll them up in wrappers. I thought about the significance of the quarter – 25 cents. Christmas is on the 25th! I believe Mom left Dad this token so he'd know it was her and that she is always with him.

My oldest sister now carries on the cookie-baking tradition. I decorate my house from top to bottom, and my middle sister finds joy in filling the stocking for the kids. We all sing Christmas carols at her graveside every December 24th.

Mom hasn't really left us; she lives on in the holiday traditions she lovingly bestowed upon us.

The Feather Delivered by Angels

By Nukhet Govdeli Hendricks

I will never forget that day. It was a beautiful, sunny day in May with bright blue skies. Before I took off to meet with a dear girlfriend for lunch, I was reading the posts on my Facebook page when I saw yet another person talking about finding a feather, a loving sign from the angels. I would be lying if I said I wasn't a bit envious. Although I have been talking to angels all my life, receiving and channeling messages easily, I had yet to find a feather.

As I drove to the restaurant, I was still thinking about the feather. I knew I just had to ask the angels about this, so I did: "Why is it that I have never found a feather, which everyone else seems to do so easily?"

My question was met with giggles and a question in return. I heard the angels say, "Although you have always been able to communicate with us easily and we have been sending you so many divine signs that we are always with you, you *still* need a feather to be assured?"

"Yes," I answered. "I *really* want a feather of my own!"

By then I had reached the restaurant. I parked my car and went inside to meet with my friend, while, in the back of my mind, I was still preoccupied with the idea of a feather of my own.

We had a delightful lunch and caught up on each other's lives. When it was time to go back to work, I said goodbye and walked to my car. As I reached to open the driver's side door, I saw it. Directly below the driver's-side door, a beautiful, bright, almost-seven-inch-long white feather was lying on the ground. Tears welled up in my eyes while a big smile took over my face. Then I heard the lovely angelic voice that had a hint of smile: "Satisfied?" she asked. I was *beyond* satisfied. I felt truly touched by angelic grace!

Ever since that day, I have been finding white feathers in unexpected places. They are my signs of angelic grace, letting me know I am never alone. But that first feather remains my absolute favorite.

Kleenex from Jesus
By Meredith Fjelsted

On the seventh day of my mission trip to Ecuador, we arrived at the remote place where we were meeting with a group of Quechua people. I was tired. I was cold. But those feelings faded away as I looked in awe at the magnificent mountain in front of me. It had rained the night before, and the clouds were drifting upwards, circling the mountain. It was absolutely breathtaking. The clouds looked as if they were made out of angels, surrounding the mountain's peak. I started to cry. Two of the local indigenous women put their arms around me and spoke to me in their native tongue. I couldn't understand them, but it didn't matter. I was in awe of the indigenous people's beauty as much as I had been of the mountain's. The women wore beautifully embroidered, handmade clothing with matching ribbons in their hair. We smiled at each other, through our tears, as we all cried together while we looked upon beautiful Mount Cotopax.

I realized that I didn't have any Kleenex to wipe away my tears, so I quietly asked those around me, "Do you have a Kleenex? A tissue? Anything?" Nothing. I knew on these mission trips one had to bring one's own tissue, as it was rare to find any. But, in my tiredness, I had forgotten that morning to bring along any for the day. When I went to sit in my seat, to my astonishment, three perfectly folded Kleenex were sitting neatly on my chair. Their fragrance of roses was so abundant that I smelled it before I had even seen the Kleenex! I looked for someone to thank, but my gift-giver couldn't be found.

It was impossible to obtain Kleenex in the remote mountain village, but I knew that day that I had been blessed by Jesus. He had left me three perfect Kleenex and supplied the means to dry my tears. Tears of love.

Bird Messengers

By Marla David

I recently asked for signs or messages from my late dad and – *wow!* – it's like someone opened the floodgates. At first, I wondered if I was making more of things, then I thought that perhaps these synchronicities had been happening all the time and I just hadn't noticed. But once I noticed, they didn't stop!

One of the recurring signs comes in the form of birds. Dad and I used to watch birds together from the back porch. He was the one who pointed out the first red-winged blackbird I'd ever seen. So it was fitting that, while visiting his grave, I saw a red-winged blackbird sitting right on top of his stone!

After multiple red-winged blackbird sightings/signs, I began to look for them. One such time was at a gallery this past fall, when I had the privilege of having Robert Bateman, an artist and naturalist, personally autograph a print for me. I wanted to get a print of a red-winged blackbird, but they didn't have any; so I got a winter scene of a cardinal instead. Then, while waiting in the line, I overheard people saying that cardinals were messengers of someone from the other side coming to visit. I hadn't known that, but since then, I see the cardinals come to our bird feeder all the time, especially that beautiful male, strutting his red plummage.

Not long after the gallery event, I received a telephone call saying that Robert Bateman had agreed to do a private commission of a red-winged blackbird for me!

My dad's bird messages continue to be received loud and clear.

Surprise!

By Katie Power

No, I can't be pregnant! I'm too young for this. I have goals. I have plans. I can't be a mother! My face fell in disbelief as I stared down at the stark pink line that had sealed my fate. My body froze, yet my mind went haywire. I tried to convince myself that it wasn't real, but a deep and unshakable inner knowing told me otherwise: I was 18 and going to have a baby.

Unlike the father, I took the news very badly. I was devastated. The question of whether or not I should keep the baby continuously plagued my mind. I was terrified and didn't know what to do. Eventually, I went to an abortion clinic and learned that I was already midway through my first trimester.

The appointment for the procedure was to be scheduled on the would-be father's birthday. How cruel would that be? I went home and cried in turmoil. Feeling depleted and overwhelmed, I pleaded to God to just give me a sign – to do something (*anything*) right then to let me know if I was supposed to have my baby.

Astonishingly, the CD-ROM drive on my desktop computer immediately popped open! I was stunned. That had never happened by itself before (nor has it since)! At that moment, a divine wave of inner peace and calm overcame me. Something surreal was happening, and all of my hesitations and doubts were being lifted. *Oh, thank you, God. Thank you!*

From there, everything started to fall into place. Hurdles soon vanished and miracles abounded. In fact, the best one of all appeared in my loving arms seven months later. On April 12, 2002, at 4:07 p.m., my now-husband and I welcomed our first beautiful and beloved baby boy into the world. Two years later, our family was complete upon his brother's cherished arrival on May 20, 2004.

Through all of this, I've learned that blessings often do show up in disguise and that each of our lives are being discreetly guided and looked after. In the end, everything is just as it should be.

A Concrete Sign of the Divine Hand of Grace
By Christine King

Travelling back from town late one evening, the train carriage was completely deserted. I'd just spent time with a good friend, telling her all about a fascinating program I had been co-facilitating with a colleague. It was a combination of metaphysical and spiritual awareness and non-predictive hand analysis. Detailed research has led to the understanding that the lines and markings on our hands are connected to the neural pathways in the brain. A powerful diagnostic tool by itself, when it's combined with spiritual understanding it can be invaluable in helping people find their purpose in life.

As I settled down in my seat, I started to think about whether or not we should repeat the program. The first one had been an amazing success, but we weren't sure we would have enough attendees the second time around to give people the same interactive experience that the first group had so enjoyed.

Knowing that the next stop wouldn't be for at least 10 minutes, I decided to meditate on the subject. Closing my eyes, I began to communicate with the Divine Presence within. I said something to the effect of, "Infinite Spirit, Higher Self, guide me in this decision. If we are meant to run the program again, please make that so clear to me that I cannot possibly mistake it."

Well, I was in no way prepared for what came next. I was jolted out of my meditation by the noise and shaking caused by the train arriving at the next station. As the train came to a stop, I stared out of the window at another train pulled alongside us. I could not believe my eyes: there on the window, perfectly aligned with where I was sitting, were two large perfect hand prints formed from cement mix!

Needless to say, I took this as the go-ahead, and we ended up with another fully attended program. We joke that Divine Grace gave us a really "concrete" sign and definitely had a "hand" in the entire process!

The Green Coat
By Lucy V. Nefstead

Oh, how I treasured my new winter coat. I loved everything about it – the shiny material, the length, the warmth, fit, fabric, buttons, and especially the color: green. I had saved and sacrificed for this coat, and now it was mine! I was the luckiest, happiest lady in the world.

One winter evening, shortly after buying the coat, I invited friends over for dinner – a married couple down on their luck. Both had lost their jobs and had no new prospects in sight. The wife, wearing a thin, threadbare coat, lamented that her "coat money" had been used to buy food. She was cold and had no income.

My heart sank, not only for my friend but because I knew what I had to do. I had another warm coat besides my "green beauty." It wasn't pretty or new, but it was warm. This friend had very little. She deserved more. I had her try on my green coat. The fit was perfect, as was the price: free! She cried with joy as she hugged the coat – now *her* coat – to her.

My heart sank again as I watched her leave, wearing my treasured coat – now hers. Yet I knew I had done the right thing. I thanked the Universe for the opportunity to give with love. I prayed to God and the angels to open my heart. I sent her love, repeatedly, and released the coat to her.

Then the bizarre happened: People began giving me coats – friends, neighbors, co-workers, and people I didn't even know. Some said they thought of me when they saw a particular coat; others felt I needed a coat. Merchants gave me remaining coats. The list of coat circumstances goes on and on. The coats came in all colors, lengths, sizes, and fabrics. To this day, I give coats away; and, just as fast, more coats come to me. I am truly "the coat lady."

Of the innumerable lessons here, the one that resonates most deeply with me is this: Whatever treasure you release with love and no expectation, it will return to you a hundred fold. So it is written, and so it is.

Wings of Grace

By Kristy Carr McAdams

It was a cold February morning when I received the phone call. Lois, a 48-year-old relative, had left her earthly life. As I hung up the phone, I cried and prayed. I told God I was overwhelmed. Drying my tears, I went to my computer in the kitchen. An incoming mass email message popped up with the heading, "Pretty sure you need this NOW." The email message was about a meditation called, "From Overwhelm to Calm."

Feeling like I got an email from Heaven, I went to my Facebook page. As I started looking at images, a white peacock photo popped into my news feed. It looked like a picture I had taken some months earlier in Florida, at the Fountain of Youth. The rare white peacock symbolizes immortality and can also represent Christ – a beautiful sign, as Lois was a very devoted Christian.

Getting up from the computer desk, I grabbed a yogurt to lunch on and headed for the kitchen table. As I settled into my chair, a movement outside the window caught my eye. I had to smile as I saw a blue bird sit at eye level, in a bush, 10 feet in front of my seat.

Three days passed, and the day of the funeral arrived. Needing information about where Lois's service would be celebrated, I read the address and name of the church for the first time. I giggled out loud. The New Life Church was on Blue Bird Lane!

Returning home after the funeral, I took off my winter coat. The infinity scarf I was wearing had an inch-long, white feather around the area of my heart. As I chuckled out loud, I said, "Okay, I know Lois is well. Thank you for the signs." With a tear in my eye and a smile in my heart, I felt like I was hugged by an angel.

A Vision on a Mountain

By Alicia Isaacs Howes

In April 1999, I started my walk in the Sangre de Cristo Mountains with an unusual destination. I was practicing an exercise that my healing teacher had assigned. The turnaround point I'd chosen was to feel differently from how I started.

With each step, I was to say out loud a worry or fear. I began the walk weighed down with grief and guilt after a miscarriage just two weeks earlier. So I found it easy to keep a fairly normal walking pace with a torrent of thoughts like, "I got pregnant too soon after surgery," "I didn't take my vitamins," "I'm not meant to be a mother," and "Maybe I'll never have another chance."

It was a relief to let all this out. After about 10 minutes on the path, I started to slow down as I had to dig around more to find a different worry. And then, a few feet in front of me, I "saw" a beautiful baby boy, wearing just a nappy. I could feel the warmth of his body and breathed in the special sweetness infants have. He was long, with fine blond hair and seemed to be about three months old. I was mesmerised as I watched his tummy going up and down with each breath as he lay there calmly in mid-air.

As the vision faded, I realised I'd reached my destination. I felt deeply peaceful.

In April 2000, our nine-pound, two-ounce, blond baby boy was born! With all the joy of his arrival, I didn't think about that vision on a distant mountain until six weeks later. Elliott, who was growing very fast, lay on the changing table, patiently waiting for his new nappy. As I turned back to him, my breath caught as I finally recognised him as the one who'd come to visit me on that path. A moment of grace on a Colorado mountain stretched all the way to a dirty nappy in Chicago.

The Monarch

By Nicole Black

I was only 28 when my mom died. Too sad to comprehend, I cried and begged for a sign of her existence. A short time later, a beautiful white butterfly appeared. And each time I would feel sad or hopeless, I would look around and there would be a beautiful white butterfly.

Things were good until my dad got sick. And then the white butterflies started to appear even more frequently. It was as if they were saying, "Fear not, it is not his time yet."

Then came the morning when I left him at the hospital, and I *knew*. I didn't want to go. I dragged my feet. I moved as slowly as I had ever moved. In fact, I was driving slowly down the freeway when the butterfly appeared. It was almost as if she hovered right in front of me before flying over the hood of my car. Impossible – or at least highly improbable that a butterfly could fly into the wind at almost 60 mph. When she fluttered out of view, I craned my neck to see, but I knew that she was gone. I knew that she was going for my dad and that he, too, was gone. My chest cavity filled with energy, and I knew that he was at peace now. The phone call moments later confirmed what I had already intuited.

Some time passed, and I cried every day. I wanted to see him so badly. I wanted to believe that he was here. He was my best friend, my confidant, my father. When I saw the most magnificent monarch butterfly in my backyard that afternoon, I cried even harder. There he was, and for one moment in time, I felt as if he looked into my soul and told me that everything was going to be okay. And it is.

The Summer I Learned to Trust Completely

By Nukhet Govdeli Hendricks

As a non-profit executive, I don't just *believe* in miracles...I *count* on them. So, when we hit a very difficult time during the summer of 2014, my faith was truly tested.

We had just gone through a very successful rebranding. Financial support from our donors had been strong, but when summer rolled around, our finances hit a wall. Regardless of what we were doing, we were unable to generate the revenue we needed for our programs and would soon run out of our savings.

By August, I was beginning to feel the exhaustion setting in from worrying about cash flow and from the sleepless nights I spent wondering what to do. During one of those restless nights, after tossing and turning for hours, I finally started to drift off to sleep when I heard a voice say, "Trust. Simply trust."

Sleep was impossible after hearing that. I left my bed and started to journal. I was guided to write down my intentions for the organization, including a dollar amount to be manifested by the end of the year: $380,000. Not knowing what else to do, I surrendered and wrote down that number.

From that night on, my mantra was "I am trusting; even if I am really scared right now and find it very hard to trust, I still trust." This went on for another two months. Just when I thought I would need to take drastic financial measures to continue our operations, a trust officer (yes, that's his actual job title!) called to let me know that a gift was left to our organization in a loving donor's will. And the amount was more than $380,000. I was speechless, in awe of the miracle. I knew we were touched by divine grace.

Ever since then, on every December 31st, I write down all my personal and professional intentions, including the revenue I want to generate for my organization. Then I surrender it to the Divine to create the miracles while we do our part: work with love and then TRUST...fully and completely!

Hello, Grace

By Sharon Rothstein

The train comes on time. Hello, Grace. My interview goes well, and I am divinely hired. Hello, Grace. I ponder a question, and it is answered through the lyrics of a song on the radio. Hello again, my Grace. A book that I contributed to becomes an international bestseller overnight. Hello, Grace. Hello!

Thank you, Grace, for showing up in my experience as often as you do. I need you each moment. Thank you for your bank account of Grace that is always full and overflowing. A deficit of you, dear Grace, is not even a possibility. Hello, dear friend that saves this soul over and over again, each moment, day, week, month, year. I am always seeking that next "hello" from you, a sign that we are connected, confirmation that I can do this human life. I allow you, Grace, to appear and wash my fears away, right in this moment. When you present that next signal or a-ha moment, I say, "Hello there once again. Hello to my positive synchronicities at the most opportune times."

When you prompt me to offer Grace, I become your channel. I elicit right words or actions in assisting others. I always bestow your gift of Grace through attention to mankind and contributions to this blessed world. How many times in a day will I notice your presence?

When my day ends, I lay my head on my pillow and chant, "Hello, Grace, my majesty, my revered partner. I bow down to you in awe. I remain in a state of gratitude, Grace, for your provisions, large and small. I offer appreciation for the beating of my heart and for you allowing me to awaken each day with another chance to receive and offer a moment of Grace – another day to say hello."

Nana

By Shannon Leigh Brokaw

Ellie, as some people called her, will always be the picture of grace to me. She loved me, her strong-willed granddaughter; and I loved her, my feisty Nana.

Nana didn't exactly grow up the richest of children, but what she did have was a loving home. How blessed they were, she surely knew.

Nana later married her Army love and had two kids. She was a devoted mother and military wife – living overseas at one point when her children were still young.

Many years later, she faced a painful separation; and while this hit her hard, she still acted out of love for others. She was the first to help someone in need; if they didn't have something to eat, she would share what she had or make sure there was a meal available. If someone needed socks or clean clothes, she would find a way to help, even though she was on her own and lived off of a small pension.

When I was young, she lived in a tiny, one-bedroom condo on the ocean, which my siblings and I called home for numerous summers during school breaks. I never knew how much appreciation I held for those moments until it was too late. Her small abode was also a second home for the many friends she had made who became an extended family. She always spread happiness to everyone.

In her 80s, we witnessed external and internal worlds collide during her battle with Alzheimer's. It was so hard to say goodbye to the Nana I knew. I wondered who I was going to get a reassuring hug from when life pulled the yoga mat from beneath my feet.

On an afternoon walk with my dogs – in the midst of a breakup that spiraled me to a new, all-time low – I longed for a hug from Nana, the kind of hug that said, "Everything IS fine." Out of nowhere, a hummingbird (Nana's favorite bird) flew onto my path. I felt a true love permeating. At that precise moment, I knew that I would always be okay, no matter what, because that was how she lived her life. She had passed the torch of grace.

Awakenings

By Tiffany Andersen

I once heard a message so powerful it had to have come from the realms only angels can cross. As I sat in my living room with a broken heart and tears coming down from years of pain, I surrendered myself to receiving the Light.

I turned on a radio and heard a message that was so clear that it pierced my heart: "Wake up, oh sleeper. You have been on the other side of the fence for too long. Arise from the place you are, and come back to your first love!"

This message, spoken by Pastor Greg Laurie, tore open my soul and awoke in me the love of something so powerful that it cannot be described with mere words. Never before had I experienced it. Would I ever again? I had to know.

The next day, for the first time, I offered one simple prayer: *God, speak to me.*

With the Bible on my lap, I did what I had never before done in my life: I opened it to read...with a pure heart. And just like that, I connected to the other side, as God spoke to me for the first time with these words:

Awake, O Sleeper, rise up from the dead, and Christ will give you light. (Ephesians 5:14)

How could it be? It was the same message I'd heard Greg Laurie speak on the radio just the day before!

The power of feeling a presence that comes from beyond this dimension was something new to me. This connection came from pure light, pure love, and a hope that there is truly something beyond what human eyes can see.

Editors' note: We arrange the pieces without dates based on what we think will create a nice flow. Imagine our pleasant surprise when we reviewed the final proof and saw that this piece based around Ephesians 5:14 "randomly" appeared on 5/14!

Do You See 11:11?

By Mathew Hart

Back in early 2005, not a day went by when I didn't inexplicably turn to see a digital clock at exactly 11:11 or 1:11. I found it mildly amusing at first; but on August 22, 2005, when it had happened too many times to count, I immediately went to my computer and Googled "1111." I got many hits sharing a similar theme: the angels use the 11:11 time prompts to let us know that we are loved, that we are on the right track, and that we are not alone. I felt comforted by this and continued to receive these time prompts on a regular basis.

About a year later, however, another overwhelming day of time prompts occurred. By this time I was seeing 1111 and 111 on clocks, watches, receipts, addresses...everywhere! Seeking more clarity, I meditated and then sat for a channeling. Here's what the angels said:

"It is with great pleasure that we share with you the reason for the 1111 sightings that have been baffling you. The sightings are not so much to urge you to take action of any sort as much as they are for your enjoyment. They are reminders that we are all on the same spiritual path together and we all share a common objective to bring peace and understanding to the planet at this time. Many souls are working towards this common goal, and many of them are participating as you have been in the sightings of the 1111. This is all you need to know at this time regarding this phenomenon."

Two weeks later, it dawned on me that having an inherent sensitivity to 11:11 was not just about acknowledging and enjoying the presence of the angels (and our common goals) but was also a recurring act of grace that teaches us, by example, to trust the signs and synchronicities that guide us along our path.

11:11. How simple! How amazing!

You're on the Right Path

By Yiye Zhang

My heart was pumping, hands sweating, knees shaking. I locked myself in the office toilet, crying out my anxiety. I had just wrapped up the goodbye email to my ex-colleagues, coming out of my "psychic closet" in front of a group of analytical brains. To put it mildly, I felt vulnerable.

My head was going crazy: *What am I thinking, leaving this lucrative career to start my spiritual business?! Who do I think I am?*

Peeling off my outer layers and labels – physics and math graduate, accountant and financial analyst – I claimed my truth that I was an intuitive and spirit guide to the core. I'd ignored my intuitive gift for so long that I felt torn apart inside. It hurt so much to watch my passion and purpose sliding by.

I finally followed the pull from my most authentic self by leaving the corporate world behind. But there I was, hiding in the toilet, so frightened that I repeatedly doubted my decision.

Life never feels dazzling when the ego is running the show. I knew that I had to switch the "channel" and let Spirit lead. I took a few deep breaths and prayed over and over again: "Dear Spirit, please show me a sign."

I felt a bit calmer, then followed my vibes and wandered to the Foyles bookstore in central London. A "testing" oracle deck card by Doreen Virtue on the shelf caught my eye. I pulled out a card, which read: "You're on the Right Path – keep doing what you're doing, because it's working." What assurance! I could certainly feel the wink from the angels.

A few days later, my brand-new website attracted initial attention, and I even received a voluntary payment from one of my pro-bono customers. Also, I learned that the company wanted to extend my work for a few more months with a pay raise, which was just enough to invest in a few business courses that I'd wanted to join. Of course I said "YES!"

When we leap into our most authentic selves, the Universe always over-delivers. I asked for one sign and instead received many.

My Magical Money Envelope

By Michelle Anne Gould

I could tell you stories of terrible lack that would make you cry. I have been there. I recall a time in my life when I was sitting on the floor, breastfeeding my newborn baby, eating only rice, and having to choose between buying nappies or paying my bills.

These days, I choose to experience the magic of money, like when I've received unexpected gifts, complimentary extras, or even money appearing out of thin air! While I feel so lucky and grateful for all of these blessings, there is one deeply treasured incident in particular that fills my heart, as I know it was a gift from the Universe. I was handed a magical money envelope.

I had only a few minutes to get to my appointment with a client, and I could not find the office. I had driven past four times and walked the street twice. "This is not funny!" I muttered out loud, becoming more frustrated. People looked at me as if I were crazy.

With a sigh, I dropped into my heart and called upon angels to guide me. I heard a message: "You need to have a clear destination; it won't matter how you get there."

I stated out loud, "I'm going to office B, and I will be on time." A moment later, the office appeared.

My efforts to get there had left me frazzled, so I took a few deep breaths to compose myself. I was able to give 150% of myself to my client that day – feeling totally present and in a wonderful energy of love. As I left, I was handed an envelope, which glowed a wonderful shade of pink. I gratefully accepted it.

Later, I got out the envelope to fully receive and bless my money. As I kissed the envelope, I realised with a jolt that it was a plain white envelope. My mind flashed back to when it was handed to me; it truly had been pink! I smiled knowingly. Inside was double my expectation.

Moments like this have helped me develop an abundance mindset, and I continue to fall deeper into faith each day. I love finding the wonder and abundance that is all around us.

Grace in the Sky
By Farah Joy Rupani

Valentine's Day 2014 started off feeling like the most dreadful day of my life. On this day known for great love, I felt unloved and more hopeless than ever.

A distressful accident had resulted in four months of recovery away from my husband and my home. I wasn't sure that I would be able to get my life back to normal again anytime soon. Feeling extremely discontented with myself and disconnected from every person who I called family, I contemplated how I could ever love and appreciate my life again.

My dejected heart was hungry for a miracle.

During silent meditation that afternoon, I felt nudged to step out of my home. I thought about surprising my daughter, Reyah, by picking her up from school, which I had not been able to do in months. I braved down the steps of my apartment on my own with my left foot in a fracture boot and the right in an ankle brace. I drove to Reyah's school with great anticipation of the joy she would feel when she saw me.

After picking Reyah up, I noticed three unsupervised little girls standing outside, which seemed unusual. I wondered what they were up to. As I approached, the girls yelled in excitement, encouraging me to look up at the sky. My eyes were curiously glued to the cloudless blue sky when I realized that someone was skywriting. I stood there in tearful amazement when I noticed the phrase being written: *I love you.*

Joyfully reveling in this meaningful synchronicity, my soul instantly knew that this message was divinely meant for ME. Unloved as I had felt that day, God had gently nudged me to step out at that particular time because He wanted to remind me of His love for me. This miracle of love was His testimony and a revelation for me. Suddenly, it became very clear to me. In any moment, I can *choose* to begin anew with loving my life again. It was a moment of pure grace that I was meant to receive.

Graced by Feathers

By Cynthia Helbig

I began awakening to the world of spirituality in the early 1990s and was soon voraciously reading any book I could find on the subject. My logical, critical mind struggled with this new information, yet something urged me to read more.

One Sunday morning, propped up in bed with a copy of *Past Lives, Present Dreams*, I read how feathers began frequently appearing around the author, Denise Lynn, after her Native American teacher, Dancing Feather, passed away. Denise told how feathers also began appearing for people who had read her books and attended her seminars. Feathers, she explained, carried the wisdom of Spirit. She even suggested that they would soon appear to me, the reader of her book. It was up to me to interpret their message.

This concept was brand new to me, and I grappled with its validity. I stared out my bedroom window to the garden outside as I pondered Denise's words. As if on cue, tiny, white feathers began to float down from the sky. I counted nine before they stopped. Was Grace confirming to me that what I had just read was the truth?

I wanted to believe, but surely it had to be pure coincidence that feathers had shown up right then. A flock of birds must have just flown by!

A few days later, I pulled my chequebook out of my bag. There, stuck between the pages, was a beautiful brown-, fawn-, green-, and blue-coloured feather. I froze in surprise. How did it get there? Where did it come from? Even to this day, I have no explanation.

I realised that this feather was both pure magic and a message, saying loud and clear: "Trust in the mystery of Grace."

Since then, I have been graced with many feathers and many signs. My faith and trust in the divine design of Grace is now unshakeable. What a journey this has taken me on – one of healing, self-discovery, and empowerment. Eventually, it led me to my passion: meditation. And it all began with a feather.

Calling My Grandma in Heaven

By Courtney Long

Granny and I loved chatting. Even though we lived 2,000 miles apart, the distance between Ohio and Arizona seemed small during our long, meaningful phone conversations. We talked about everything under the sun – family, my romantic ups and downs, her favorite sport (baseball), you name it.

When she turned age 92, Gran declined quickly. I scheduled a flight to see her one last time, but my heart sank when my dad called and said she was dying that day, just hours before I would arrive.

Thankfully, my dad held the phone to Gran's ear so I could say goodbye. Through my tears, I told her how much I loved her and that I would still be calling her in Heaven.

Gran did not know that I can communicate with angels and souls who have passed, but in that moment, I imagine her soul knew exactly what I meant.

After she passed, I saw the numbers 333 and 222 numerous times on the clock and license plates. In those moments, I thought of my grandma, but I wasn't sure why. I figured the angels were trying to comfort me while I grieved.

The night before Gran's funeral, a thought popped in my head: *I'll always be able to reach Gran at 419-474-3339.* Suddenly, something clicked: Gran's phone number contained a 333, and my phone number contains a 222!

Holy Toledo! Through these 333s and 222s, the Universe was validating that I could indeed "call" my grandma – just in Heaven instead of on Earth! I realized my grandma was trying to tell me that she was okay and still with me. As tears streamed down my face, a deep wave of comfort washed over my soul.

My grandma helped me know that Heaven is not far away. It is a higher dimension of light (like a higher-frequency radio station) that is all around us. Our departed loved ones are very close, and they want us to know they are okay. In fact, anytime we want to talk to them, they are just a "phone call" or a thought away.

Our Monarch

By Jenny McKaig

As I lay beside my love in our tent, I gazed softly at the glow of light pouring through the mesh, landing delicately upon us. We had enjoyed a fun and wonderfully relaxing camping trip. No cell phones, no computers – just us and nature. Conversations by bonfire. Toes in the sand. Tiptoeing over dunes that opened onto the lake beyond where we set up camp. Our boat, at sunset, breezing with the radiance of red-orange decorating the sky, and our sweet black lab, so excited to jump into the expanse of clear, cool water.

As I lay there reflecting on the trip, an orange monarch, his wings beautifully embossed with black design, found his way between the tent and the rain cover. As we packed our things and started taking down the tent, our butterfly fluttered near. He didn't fly away when we took off the rain cover. He rested as we packed, staying with the tent, then danced around me as I picked up the last pieces to pack them into their case. As we drove back to civilization, our monarch followed the truck for quite a while before he flew away.

When we reached cell-phone range, I turned on my phone and saw multiple messages from my family. "Call Mom," read a text, then voicemails from my mother, brother, and sister all saying the same thing: "please call."

I got the news as we drove down that rural country road: "Your grandfather passed. We've been trying to get you since yesterday."

I felt a well of emotions. Then, just like that, our monarch appeared at the side of our truck, flying as we drove along that long rugged road. It was as though my grandfather came to tell me first: "I'm gone, but I'm still here. Hello and goodbye. I love you."

It was my grandfather, monarch of our family, father to 14 and grandfather to 30. Even though I was worlds away from him, his spirit found me anyway.

Our Hearts Are Connected to Everything

By Afzal Khan

Life is beautiful. Life is a mystery. Life is amazing. Life is more than you think you know.

Over the past few years, these truths have been driven home in amazing ways for me. It all started on a cold morning in January 2012. I was on my way to work, waiting alone at a tram stop. As I stood beneath the shelter, something caught my eye: a damp patch in the perfect shape of a heart.

The rest of the pavement was completely dry, except for this heart shape. I looked up and noticed that rain had gathered on top of the shelter from a few days ago. A crack in its roof allowed small droplets of water to fall to the pavement below, miraculously forming a heart shape.

It was beautiful. I was amazed. I got out my phone and took a picture. Normally I wouldn't do this, but the experience was....well, a miracle!

About three months after this, I had another experience of seeing heart shapes. I had an indoor house plant that I would water before leaving for work. One morning, I went to water the plant and saw that it had grown two leaves that were connecting to form a perfect heart shape. I was amazed and ran to get my phone to take a picture.

After this experience, I began seeing hearts almost everywhere: in food, tea bags, plants, water, you name it...and I took hundreds of photos. Seeing these hearts has changed my life. I love how they mysteriously appear, like love notes, as a surprise.

I've shared this story with others who now also see hearts everywhere. Is it grace? Absolutely! And perhaps it will happen for you, too.

Chapter 5
Animals & Nature

D an has always loved camping, hiking, and being in nature. Jodi, on
the other hand, rarely enjoyed nature and has spent most of her
life indoors. A couple of years ago, however, her soul said that she
needed to move to the beach in order to heal physically and emotionally.
We have learned to listen when her soul speaks, so we moved to the
Oregon coast as soon as we could.

The miracles that we've encountered here already have been
extraordinary. In just a few short months, she's healed more than she
had in years and wants to spend as much time near the water as possible
because she loves the ocean's transformative, healing energy. We can
feel sad, angry, or overwhelmed and immediately feel these emotions
being replaced with love, joy, and vitality within minutes of being near
the water. It's that powerful.

In addition to the grace of the ocean itself, we love the animals that
we see there. We were recently at the beach when a bald eagle flew right
over us and circled for a bit before flying away. On that same visit, Jodi
saw a sea lion bobbing its head in the ocean. We always love watching
the seagulls play in the water, and we've even spotted a few whales
swimming just off the coast! We experience each of these as moments of
grace – moments that help us feel connected to nature and to our world.

In this chapter, we share many such moments – some in nature,
some with animals, and some with both. Some moments are peaceful
while they are happening; others feel tragic while they are happening,
and the grace comes later. At their core, though, they all show how close
each of us always is to grace. It's in our dog's smile and our cat's purr.
It's in the ocean's beauty and the mountain's vastness. It's everywhere,
and we're so blessed that we get to experience it so often.

The Healing Magic of Alchemy Farm

By Ingrid Koivukangas

I drove up to the overgrown driveway and tried to peer through the blackberry brambles and wild roses to see the house. Instead, I "saw" a burst of golden lights, like tiny fairies, greeting me. After years of working with deep intuition and Nature, I knew I had arrived somewhere very special, a place of wonder. We called the realtor – even though the sign wasn't even up yet!

Later that day, as we rambled through the forest and fields, I was overcome with a sense of peace. It felt like the land was welcoming us. I said a prayer, asking Spirit to help us make this place our home. Opening my eyes, I looked down and saw an owl feather at my feet.

Within three months, we sold our house and moved – just in time to pick the first apples from the orchard. We were visited by families of deer, a troop of plum-loving raccoons, giant owls, feral cats, and the most memorable: a tiny green frog that hopped up to us while we sat on the deck. We decided to call our 10-acre property "Alchemy Farm" – a place of transformation.

Over the first five months, we lovingly brought the house back from years of neglect. Somehow, I also managed to finish writing the first book of the *Hunters of the Dream* trilogy. With our first spring on the horizon, we began planning our farm gardens. I was going through the list – 70 blueberry plants; a small vineyard; 150 willows; a greenhouse for tomatoes, peppers, and melons; a medicinal garden; a field of flowers… – when I stopped in amazement. Tears filled my eyes as I thought about the many difficult challenges I'd faced in my life and the countless times I'd said, "In my next lifetime, I'm just going to be happy. I'm going to marry a good man, live on a beautiful farm, grow fields of flowers, and write books."

I am here. I have arrived. I am still in *this* lifetime. This beautiful land with its alchemical magic has quietly led me through a transformation to a place of deep gratitude and grace. I am home.

Healed by a Dolphin

By Josie Wood

My husband had died in a car crash just over a year ago, and today would have been our wedding anniversary.

I needed to do something fresh and different to demonstrate I was ready to heal, let go of grief, and embrace life. I felt pulled to go on a spontaneous adventure – to visit a beautiful part of the Northumberland coast where there were reports of a wild dolphin that liked to swim with people.

After a three-hour journey, I reached the small harbour where the only boat visiting Freddie the dolphin was about to launch with one seat left. Previously, I thought I might catch a glimpse of the friendly dolphin from the harbour wall, but here I was setting out to sea.

The boat was hired by a group of people who had swum with Freddie often. They were all kitted out in wet suits and dry suits, ready to plunge into the cold North Sea.

It seemed Freddie was expecting us, as after only 15 minutes of the sea spray blowing through our hair, we saw him giving a welcoming leap. The boat stopped, and people took turns swimming with him. My heart and soul exploded with delight and joy to watch the fun and harmony between humans and the wild dolphin who obviously adored sharing his love of life. My day was complete. Seeing Freddie like this was more than I had hoped for.

Then one of the swimmers asked if I would like to borrow her dry suit, put it on over my clothes, and swim with Freddie. My heart raced with excitement and nervousness as I lowered myself into the water, finding myself in a moment of exquisite grace that still fills my heart.

With the other swimmers, Freddie was playfully lively; however, he seemed to sense exactly what I needed, and he swam to me very gently. He rested just below the surface of the water gazing at me.

For an eternal moment, I was blessed by the peaceful presence in his eyes, as if he understood *everything*.

When the Ocean Calls

By Nathalie Dignard

One sunny November morning, before my daughter's soccer game, I went for a walk during warm-up. Holding my steamy travel mug with both hands, I listened to the birds filling the early morning with their lively tune. As I closed my eyes, I smiled and let my senses take it all in.

I was near the ocean but couldn't see it from where I was standing, yet I felt its powerful pull. The ocean was calling my name, loud and clear. Like long-lost lovers, we needed to see each other… *now*. As I smelled the salty air, something started bubbling up inside and my heart expanded.

I paused on the train tracks to get closer to my muse. Standing there, I became very aware that on the one side was where I had been, and on the other side, where I was going. My heart was beating in my ears as I picked up the pace. I couldn't get there fast enough! "Go touch the ocean," said a voice within me. So I ran right into the arms of creation.

By the time I reached the ocean, happy tears flowed down my cheeks, and I was bursting with joy. She held me in that moment, rocking my soul into the light. I let the water kiss my shoes, and I laughed out loud as the rhythm of the tide transported me deep into the experience.

BLISS! Magical, transformational bliss!

Elevated to my most vibrant self, I had just found love, THE love. A communion with life like never experienced before. The heart-flutters, the butterflies, the expansion, all my magnificence reflected back at me. In that moment, I realized, *I am totally in love, and I am not even in a relationship right now!* Bliss cracked me open!

The ocean gifted me with a powerful moment that I can now reconnect with at will. It left me feeling madly in love with life and truly, madly in love with me.

St. Henry

By Roxanne Beck

"You're the best dog in the world," I told him, the tears streaming down my face.

Henry was special. Like most border collies, he was beautiful and brilliant. But he wasn't just smart – he was *saintly*. He loved everyone, and everyone loved him.

In my 20s, I adopted him from the Nashville ASPCA, and for four years we lived in a little duplex with a huge yard. Then I moved to Manhattan to pursue my acting and singing career. I felt guilty about taking Henry with me, but knew he'd rather live in a tiny studio on the Upper West Side than be left behind.

For the next 10 years, I temped in law firms to support myself. Henry waited patiently for me to get home every day. We'd go to Central Park on weekends, where he would happily bask in the sun or chase rats (there were a lot of them). Eventually, I met a jazz musician and married him. When we moved to Westchester County, Henry was 14. I felt grateful that in his senior years, Henry finally had a yard again. By this time, he was arthritic and almost completely deaf, but his loving, sweet personality was as constant as the Northern Star.

Not long before his 17th birthday, Henry had a stroke. He started spinning around in circles, unable to walk in a straight line. The vet put him on steroids, and he got a little better...but it wasn't enough. One cold, February night it became clear that it was time. We put Henry in the car and met the vet at his office. While we waited for the drugs to take effect, I leaned over and held him. After a couple of minutes, I felt something powerful *whoosh* through me and fly straight up toward the ceiling. *What was that??* When I stood up, he was gone.

There's no doubt in my mind that it was Henry's spirit leaving his body. It was a moment of grace I'll always be thankful for, because I feel sure I'll see him again.

Winter Morning Awakening
By Jack V. Johnson

I trudged down the snowy driveway with my younger sister and brother to wait for the yellow bus that would take us to our new school. The sky was socked in with low, heavy clouds, and my breath made its own clouds with every exhalation. It was the middle of my fifth-grade year, and my family had just moved from a house outside a small northwoods Wisconsin town to a house outside a not-quite-as-small farming community nearly 300 miles south. As a bookish introvert, I struggled to make new friends. Almost as much as I missed my old friends, I missed the forests and lakes of my old home, the bear snuffling outside our windows at night, and the deer bedding down in the field behind our house. Those memories contrasted sharply with the farms and farmers of my new home.

Such was my state of mind on that dreary winter morning. Then, from the corner of my eye, I caught a glint of light and looked up to find every icicle, every snowflake, shining and sparkling gloriously where the morning sun had burst through the clouds. I stood transfixed, and it felt as though a translucent shell had cracked and fallen away from me, revealing the world with a brightness and clarity I had never seen. In that moment, there was no Jack, no farm, no woods, no sun – there was only the All, only the One.

I came back to myself in a rush, and all too soon I boarded the bus and headed off to another day of fifth grade. But those few crystalline moments of Oneness had profoundly transformed my understanding of the world and my place within it. Even as I write this, decades later, I can feel the shining lines of light that connect us one to the other, and all of us together to the rest of the universe, and I feel the loving touch of grace upon my heart.

Serendipity Kitty

By Alexa Rehrl

"Be careful! You know she will fall in love with the first cat she sees!" said my father-in-law to my husband when we mentioned our intention to adopt a cat. Of course I disagreed, but he was right!

Our first trip to the shelter (just down the street from our house) was only meant to be educational, but I was immediately drawn to the very first cage. Inside was a fluffy, black cat, fast asleep. His name card read: *Olivier, 9 years old.*

While I skimmed his information papers, he opened his eyes, stuck his paw up to the glass, made eye contact, then promptly fell back to sleep. His little bean toes were still squished up to the window. *It's a sign,* I thought.

This was not an adoption day, but the head volunteer forgot some paperwork, so we were able to meet Olivier. She told us that people hadn't been interested in him because he was older and had black fur. He wasn't open to being petted, which worried my husband. But Olivier seemed to be an extra sensitive cat, and shelters are stressful.

The next day, I returned on my own and stayed with Olivier for two hours. He sat next to me but would not climb onto my lap. However, when another cat did, he seemed jealous! That was enough for me to ask for the adoption paperwork. I believed in the little guy.

We didn't know what would happen when we brought Olivier home. But the moment I opened the cat carrier, he walked out, explored our condo, then climbed upon our bed and started purring! We joined Olivier, and he finally let us pet him.

Next, we brought out his favorite toy, the laser pointer. He chased that red dot at full speed the length of our condo several times. What freedom!

By grace we found Oliver; and one year later, we are truly a family. He teaches me to honor my own sensitivity and reminds us that all souls desire love – even those housed on four legs!

Loving Signs Through Nature

By Fiona Louise

Using Doreen Virtue's *Talking to Heaven* deck, I asked my deceased friend Jack for a message. The card I pulled depicted a monarch butterfly and the words, "I send you loving signs through nature."

The next day, I sat in the garden thinking about him and felt grief welling up inside. I asked the universe for a sign that he was with me. Within minutes, a monarch butterfly flew over to me and landed on my thumb. It stayed there for a few seconds and then moved to the cup I held in my hands. It sat on the rim of the cup, looked up at me for several minutes, and then flew away. I felt such peace and love flow through me. For several days afterwards, I felt that way, and I was so grateful for the connection.

The following year, Wayne Dyer passed; and during his tribute they showed a video in which Wayne tells the story of a monarch butterfly landing and staying on his hand for 2½ hours. Wayne believed it was a message from his deceased friend Jack. Wayne talked about the lesson he'd learned from his Jack about being in a state of gratitude. The butterfly reminded him that he wasn't alone, and for several days afterwards he felt such peace and contentment that someone described him as "walking grace."

Hearing this story, with its similarities of experiences and feelings both Wayne and I felt, gave me an even stronger sense of peace. It also helped me process the grief of Wayne's passing.

The day after hearing Wayne's story, I walked into the garden and two monarch butterflies flew toward me and over my head. I said a silent hello to Jack and Wayne, and smiled, thinking about this connection.

My moment of grace, just as it was for Wayne, was a message that we are not alone; that we are all loved, guided, and connected; and that the deceased live on, not just in our hearts but as universal energy we can experience whenever we have the need.

A Wolfhound Saves the Day

By Faye Rogers

For many years, I've been passionate about the wisdom of animals and all they have to share. In 2007, I turned this passion into a profession, as I stepped into a new career as an Animal Communicator/Pet Psychic. My enthusiasm was running sky high, and I felt that I had finally found my true purpose.

Around that time, I received an important message from a special member of my animal family: Torino Wolfhound, a light red brindle with hairy whiskers and beard, big strong legs, and deep dark brown eyes. Today, Torino is an elderly fellow, but back in 2007 he was approaching his second year (in wolfhound years, the sparkly youth of "teenager-dom").

One day that year, completely out of the blue, Torino urgently advised me to get in touch with my dear friend in the USA. He wanted me to tell her that it was very important she did not use the steps at her back door. While this felt like a crazy and weird message to receive, I passed it on. I felt the energy of *complete trust* in this unexpected message.

So, from my house in Christchurch, New Zealand, I emailed my friend in America: *Hey, Torino wants me to tell you to check your back steps before you use them; it's really important that you don't use them.*

My dear friend replied back with big hearty thanks for Torino Wolfhound and his message. She shared: *Faye, it's really dark when I get home, and one of my nightly rituals is emptying the kitty litter tray. I carry the tray perched in front of me and walk down the steep back steps. If I hadn't gingerly checked the steps, I would have had a really nasty accident. It turns out the electrical cabling from my night light had fallen and was strung across the stairs. A death trap was waiting for me! By the Grace of God, I am still here.*

I'm so pleased to have been the human messenger for this warning from dear Torino. He reminded me that regardless of what form we walk in, we are all connected in Oneness, and Oneness is Grace.

Sacred Feminine Blessing

By Joni Advent Maher

Last Mother's Day weekend, I was in my kitchen when I heard a loud, unusual whirring sound outside. As I stepped out my front door, I caught sight of a two-by-four–foot swarm rounding the corner. My husband, just returning from errands, was more than a little disturbed.

We returned inside to watch the tiny yellow-and-black bodies in a moving cloud outside the window. After a while, the activity died down and I returned to the kitchen without giving the matter much more thought. Within 24 hours, however, we discovered that the swarm had built a hive in our foundation.

Assuming they were wasps, my husband was hell-bent on eradicating them. He tried fumigation, sprays, and shoving my daughter's bright green Play-Doh in the cracks of our mortar. Rather than eradicating them, however, his efforts drove them inside. They began emerging through the air vents into our guest room! That's when we first noticed (thanks to our close-up looks) that they weren't wasps after all, but honeybees, which seemed extremely fitting.

Honeybees are a symbol of the Divine Feminine. Long devoted to the Sacred Feminine, my passion had recently blossomed into a deep desire to share Her mysteries and gifts with other women. I *knew* that these honeybees nesting and crawling into our home had come as an affirmation of my devotion and mission of sharing Her with the world.

Upon learning that they were honeybees, we found a beekeeper who could safely relocate the hive. Over the next six weeks, the honeybees were drawn from our foundation into a temporary hive so they could be moved to their new home in the country. When finished, their extraction was so complete it was as if they had never been here.

Imagine my surprise 18 months later when a lone honeybee buzzed in to join me and my daughter in the kitchen in the dead of winter. The bee arrived the month I was moving my group space, the Sacred Sisterhood Sanctuary, home to the very guest room the honeybees had consecrated. I couldn't help but feel the visitation was a wink and a blessing from the Divine Feminine.

Divine Dialogue with Sasha Kitty

By Lore Raymond

Mom and I left the vet's office that night drowning in a tsunami of grief. The decision was made to end Sasha Kitty's suffering. While struggling to drive home through torrential tears, I heard: "I left something for you." It was Sasha Kitty. She repeated herself two more times.

The next morning, still grieving and still wondering what the "something" was that she had left for me, my soul craved comforting. I started my spiritual practice of Divine Dialogue Writing™. As I had done for years, I invoked the angels, asking: *What do I need to know for my best and highest good now regarding Sasha Kitty?*

After shuffling the Doreen Virtue Angel Cards, I pulled the *All Is Well* card with this message from Archangel Jeremiel: "Everything is happening exactly as it is supposed to be with hidden blessings you will soon understand." At that moment, Mom walked into my bedroom. She wondered what angel message I'd received. So I showed her, and she reported that she'd received the *exact* same message that night.

Repeating the question before drawing another card, I received: *Hello from Heaven!* with Archangel Azrael sharing a message that my loved ones in Heaven were visiting and to let go of any worries and embrace their blessings. A quiet whisper followed: "Sasha wants to work with your guardian angels to help you be peaceful, so watch for other signs from Heaven."

Two weeks later, I pulled the *All Is Well* card again. "You're too funny, Sasha Kitty," I mused. "The *All Is Well* card was just returned to the deck; I've had it on my desk since you left. Now it shows up again! Did you know it's the two-week anniversary of your new cat adventure?"

"I know," I heard her whisper.

"I miss you."

"I know," she said.

"Hope all is well."

"It is. Chirp." (Her sweet acknowledgement sound.)

So, what was the "something" Sasha Kitty left for me? It was the unwrapped gift of knowing that life continues after death. She's just in another room – for where there's love, communication continues...even with the furry, four-footed ones!

Sunrise

By Sheila Callaham

I sit on the front step of my house, facing east, coffee in hand, waiting for the sun to peek through the fog that hangs thick to the first light of dawn. My favorite time of day.

Closing my eyes, I breathe in the morning air, clean and crisp, and listen to a chorus of birds. I make out the distinctive notes of a Carolina Wren calling, "Jeremy, Jeremy," against the backdrop of the loud metallic chirps of cardinals. A moment later, I hear the musical song of a robin, blending with the clear whistles of a tufted titmouse. Echoing in the distance is the soft cooing of a mourning dove beckoning for a mate.

I put down my cup and stand on the walkway just as the sun breaks through the mist to greet me. With a deep inhalation, I stretch my arms over my head and slowly exhale as I bend from the waist for a sun salutation. At this moment, I connect with all of Mother Earth – the birds, the trees, the ground beneath my feet.

Lifting myself upright, I move slowly, intentionally through several salutations, allowing my connection to this moment to deepen. Birdsong continues, a dog barks in the distance, and I stand after the final bow, just in time to see the passing of a blue heron across the top of the trees.

I smile in thanks and gratitude for the gifts of nature, the beauty of the horizon, the assurance of each sunrise, and for the moon cycles that push and pull at the ocean tides. I give thanks to Mother Earth, ever constant in her perpetual show of grace.

Kelly, a Spiritual Vehicle of Love

By Jody Rentner Doty

Monday morning was like so many: hurry up, get ready for work, pack lunches, get the kids up and dressed and into the car. That's when I heard it, the unidentifiable noise that brought me to my lowest point. I had backed the car into Kelly, my 15-year old golden retriever. I didn't see her, and with her aging hips, she just couldn't move quickly. The rest is a blur, a vague recollection of two construction workers hearing me scream and gently lifting my injured dog into the car, and then the words from the vet, "I'm sorry, Ma'am, with her age and condition, she's just too old and broken to fix. It happens more than you know."

Kelly was my unconditional love. She was always there for me; she was also a nana dog to the kids and a friend to each member of the family, even our new kitten who she let nurse on her elbow. Kelly was much more than a dog; she was pure love.

I took the kids to a friend's house, came home, and collapsed on the couch, uncontrollable tears streamed down my face. I cried for hours until I felt something wonderful. I saw Kelly's beautiful face appear before me. She told me it was her time and not to be sad. "Yes, but did I have to be the vehicle of your demise…literally?"

My question was answered with the most indescribable feeling I've ever experienced. I can only liken it to being held in the palm of God. A warm wave of love filled my body, washed over my face, and instantly dried my tears. It was peacefully calm, unconditionally forgiving, a love so powerful it transcended all human emotion. I smiled. I couldn't help it. I suddenly felt joy on this, the worst day of my life.

Even now, I feel Kelly watching over me. Her spirit is a beacon of light that reminds me daily of the power of love and the gift of forgiveness.

Today Is Different

By Donna S. Priesmeyer

I woke up much earlier than usual this morning. On most days, I would have gone back to sleep, but today I sensed a need for quiet time in the hours just before dawn. I got out of bed, walked down the stairs, and noticed an unusual brightness. It was the glow of the first snow of winter, falling softly and gently, glistening in the moonlight.

As the darkness gave way to the dawn, the view from my front door took my breath away. It was a moment of pure grace. I gazed outside – my attention captivated by the falling snow creating a thick, white blanket over the lawn. As the sun rose, ice on the trees began to twinkle like tiny Christmas lights, magically ignited by nature. Had I gone back to sleep, I would have missed this moment – an interesting metaphor for spiritual awakening!

Earlier in my life, this wintery scene would have triggered early-morning angst. Missing work on a snow day at the TV station where I worked was incomprehensible. It was our responsibility to report school closings and cancelled events. We were expected to come in early. The challenges of getting to work – frozen car doors, dead batteries, road closings, traffic accidents, etc. – added to the stress. Such were the days of my live-TV career. It was an exciting time in my life, but one in which I had to forfeit the simple pleasure of staying home on a snow day.

Today is different. Today I can stay home, sit by the fire, appreciate the beauty of the snowfall, ponder, and write. And as I do, I am blessed with a revelation:

Grace is like a cup that is filled to the brim with so much love and joy that it spills into every area of life, providing inspiration for new and fresh forms of creativity and expression.

Gentleness of Grace

By Gabriele Engstrom

Last year, my 17-year-old cat's health was slowly on the decline. Since I am a healer, I used different varieties of healing on him. He would perk up and be happy for a period, and then his health started to decline again. I knew my time with him was getting shorter, and I was waiting for a sign to act. I did not want him to just disappear, as cats often do. Suffering was not an option.

One Sunday morning, I had just come back from a walk and was relaxing on the sofa when an inner voice told me to go into the garden, which I did. I saw a little tree snake, with the head pointing in the direction where my cat was lying. It was impossible for the snake to see my cat since he was hidden behind a huge potted plant, and the distance between the two was quite large. I had never seen a snake in my garden since I moved in.

Then a very strong voice said, "Do something about your cat." I was stunned. Was this a sign? Again, I heard, "Do something about your cat." Next, the little green snake slithered away. It was late, so I decided to wait until the next day, hoping that his health would improve.

Unfortunately, it did not.

The next day, he was worse. My kind neighbour drove me to the vet, who took one look and said, "OH!!!" Usually when I took him to the vet, he would investigate everything. Not this time. He knew.

His passing was, may I say, beautiful. He was purring peacefully, as if he was thankful and joyful that I let go, allowing him to move on.

Of course, I grieved for my little furry friend. At the same time, I was grateful for the clear guidance I received. It showed me how help comes from so many different areas. I just had to be open and accepting and to allow grace.

Look Up to the Sky

By Marcia Sandels

I arrived at this moment of grace near the culmination of an unforgettable tour of southern Europe. After three weeks of traveling by land, sea, and air, I looked at the night sky over our lakeside lodging in Greece and realized that I was viewing the same awe-inspiring sky that covers our entire planet! From this location, to where I live in the Midwest USA, this same sky – stars, moon, sun, planets – interconnects our physical world across oceans, continents, mountains, deserts, and city, state, and country boundaries. Wondrous magnificence!

Humanity has established a necessary interrelationship between different regions by way of natural resources, commerce, production, and communications. Our countries are interdependent upon one another worldwide as we progress into the expansiveness of creative ideas, inventions, and technology, which is tremendous.

We are one tribe, the human race – a truly diverse combination of a multitude of colors, cultures, ethnicities, languages, and beliefs – all existing on planet Earth. We coordinate and share our accomplishments for the benefit of humankind. God loves variety – as evidenced by the richness of our ethnic and cultural diversity. God is Love.

Each of us is an individualized, multi-faceted, multi-talented soul creation of our Divine Source. And yet, we are one with each other, made in the image and likeness of God, through Spirit, the Breath of Life. *We live and move and have our being in God.* (Acts 17:28)

Remembrance of our oneness is the key for harmonious living. God is Life. The sky is limitless – vast, infinite, expansive. The grace of God can be found in all of Creation, everywhere.

In that moment in Greece, I opened my eyes and heart to the sky and felt the preciousness of all of life – in humankind, plants, animals, minerals, *everything.* It was miraculous and such a blessing to witness and celebrate.

The Love of a Dog

By Kathy Proctor

Four years ago, I decided I would search for a dog. I have always loved dogs from afar but felt that they would be too much work for me. I recognized that I would be the primary caretaker even though my young son, Matt, and my husband, Steve, were willing participants. I spent six months poring over the internet. I was obsessed with the search but unclear why. My life was full with a job, husband, child, home, and extended family. In many ways, I had all I needed.

I finally found him. His name was Diego, a young German Shepherd mix who was enthusiastic, sweet, and handsome. Never in my wildest dreams could I have anticipated what a gift Diego would be to all of us.

Less than a year after we got him, my husband was diagnosed with a virulent cancer. From the beginning, we were told there would be no cure. Steve bought some time with surgery and treatments, and we focused on the positive whenever possible; but eight months after being diagnosed, my husband died.

The world we had known fell apart. I became a single parent with a broken heart. Throughout all the turmoil and pain, Diego was a constant loving presence. He was my steadfast companion, often absorbing the grief, offering a snuggle when I felt alone, and creating laughter with his playful antics. He was the glue that bound us together as the family we had known and the people we were becoming.

Diego was by my side as I cleared out the memories of 20 years from our family home and again when we moved to a much smaller home down the road. Both houses had fenced-in yards and enough wildlife to occupy him. We all made the adjustment well and are finding our way together.

Recently, when I was reminding Matt that we are now a family of two, he looked at me and said, "No, Mom. There are three in our family: you, me, and Diego." How true it is.

Even in the Deep of Winter

By Elizabeth R. Kipp

The calendar has now moved just beyond the winter solstice, so each day grows a little longer and the light radiates a little stronger. I sit with the day, knowing we are deep in the grasp of winter and ever so slowly moving towards spring. Though this process of lengthening days just doesn't seem to happen fast enough for me, I find some measure of solace in its steady progress, no matter how slow it might appear. Like life itself, I learn to measure progress by how the Divine reveals it, not by how I want it. I find that when I sink fully into the present moment, time suspends itself. I am here, right now, regardless of the season. When I presence myself in the stillness of the moment, I am graced with peace and comfort, so all concerns slip away and vanish.

I rise from a short respite this afternoon to the joyous song of one of our neighborhood wrens – my spirit guide, who I have named "Joy Bringer." This bird carries only a few grams in weight, yet it produces a resounding voice that ricochets throughout these woods as if it were being broadcast through Nature's loudspeaker. That such a sweet and bold sound can come from a creature so tiny is a testament to how great the spirit can truly be. Grace reveals itself in so many ways to me. A moment with this beloved spirit guide in the deep of winter warms my heart, no matter what the temperatures outside might be.

A Gift from the Ocean

By Gabrielle Taylor

At first, all I noticed was its small, white edge, sticking out of the sand near my toes. The pure white contrasted with the red patches of worn-off nail polish and the dark wet sand. After digging it out and picking it up, I felt that the shell's sharpness had long since smoothed by years of being washed over by the sea. I also noticed a splash of colours on its soft inside – little gifts of pastel pink, purple, baby blue, and a streak of yellow. My mood immediately lifted.

My husband and I were spending a week at the ocean. It was our way to recuperate and heal. Life lately had all felt like too much: working so hard to keep up with the house, the bills, the kids, and ourselves, all while coping with the terminal illness and recent passing of his father.

But when you're exhausted and your heart is grieving, the ocean doesn't necessarily make it any easier to relax. Dark grey clouds loomed overhead, heavy with water. *The sky is crying with us,* I thought.

I held and caressed this precious shell for quite a while. It was soft and luminescent on the inside, showing off a slight and gentle inward curve. But the outside was dark grey with a rough surface. This was where life was, I thought – in the underbelly of things, beneath the harder, dark, and prickly shell.

The shell spoke a thousand words to me. It told a tale of tenderness, of years of a secret and beautiful life under the ocean, of a long-preserved vulnerability. Its appearance served as a reminder to once again pay attention to the tender and sensitive zones of life – those vulnerable parts that can get wounded but which have the resilience to heal again. "I am you," it whispered.

On that day when life felt so full of sadness and loss, this tiny shell helped me remember the preciousness and joy that comes when I welcome my sensitivity.

I looked up to see my husband walking toward me, a smile on his face. And for an instant, the clouds seemed to part.

The Gift of Grace from an Angel Cat

By Marianne Soucy

In the summer of 2012, my beloved cat, Kia, died. She died all alone in an animal hospital the same night we admitted her. I will never forget the call my husband and I received from the vet at 5 a.m., telling us she was dead. The guilt we felt for the way she died was devastating.

My moment of grace happened when I reached out to Kia in my pain and she responded with messages of unconditional love, forgiveness, and wisdom. Kia's special messages have truly changed me and my life. It was as if a door opened, giving me direct access to grace for much more than just a moment; this grace has stayed with me to this day.

As I wrote this piece, Kia also sent me her insights on grace:

My moment of grace was when you brought me home – when you took me into your life and your home.

Grace to me is peace – the deep peace you feel when your soul is touched. When you're met with unconditional love at a time when you have forgotten or lost hope that there really is such a thing as grace.

Grace flows to you each time you allow a message from us to come to you, each time you open your heart to my love and teachings. Without what happened, this wouldn't have happened either. Consider that. It is only because of your pain, you began those writings. They are your connection to grace. Through them, grace flows to you and to those who read the messages.

My biggest wish is that I can truly embody Kia's love, forgiveness, wisdom, and grace and become a vehicle for the great light and the angel that she is. She is greatly missed, but she will always be in my heart. Our souls are connected, and I will honor that connection always.

Strange Bedfellows
By Annalene Hart

One evening while I was watching TV, my mother went to empty the garbage and left the front door open longer than usual. I didn't think much of it until I sensed something moving in the living room. *Something definitely is not right*, I thought to myself. But it wasn't until I got up and headed to the kitchen that I was jolted by a jarring realization: there was a perturbed bat flying around in our house! By this time, my mother was also witnessing this distressed intruder flying from our 16-foot ceiling and dive-bombing down inches away from our legs – making us both scream in terror.

What happened next is a bit fuzzy, but I do remember saying to the bat: "It's okay, Sweetheart, we won't hurt you." The next thing we knew, the bat had collapsed on the short throw rug by the foot of the kitchen sink. My mother asked if it was dead, and I said that I didn't think so, as I studied his suddenly small figure. What had so recently looked like an impressively large-winged creature had now apparently shrunken to less than half its size. It looked so vulnerable lying on the rug that I suddenly felt an enormous, overwhelming sense of compassion for this bat and its plight. My mother and I each took an end of the rug and carefully angled it outside the porch door, allowing him to fly free into the night.

Sometime after this incident, we noticed that a bat had claimed one of the wooden slats on the outside of our kitchen window. We couldn't help but wonder if this was the same bat we had rescued. Soon, he acquired a buddy who would sleep a few inches from him: a hard-shelled bug! They became steadfast companions.

Every time I see these two friends, I remember the moment of grace when I first felt connected to this "wild" creature. It was so touching that the bat trusted us enough to stop fighting and just let go in a heap on the floor. Yes, he was exhausted, but his peacefulness let us know that he felt safe with us – and it changed my perspective in a way that lasts to this day. Even as an animal lover, I never expected to share heightened moments of communion and grace with a bat!

Communicating with Buddy

By Carolyn McGee

I have always been blessed with the innate ability to empathetically connect with animals. As a child and then again when I started my pet-care business, I would have detailed, two-way conversations with the animals, not completely accepting that I was actually understanding what they were saying and vocalizing it for them.

When I began my angelic-communication journey, I realized that I was not making up the conversations; they were real. However, I was blocked around communicating with my own animals. My heart dog, Buddy, was so patient and loving with me, supporting me in my awakening journey. I knew his health was failing, and I was afraid on some level to hear what he had to say.

Two days before it was his time to transition, I heard him clearly and distinctly state that he loved me and that it was time for him to move on. It was time for me to let someone new and human into my heart. Buddy had been my constant companion since shortly after my divorce. He was the one that comforted me when my kids went to their dad's home for the weekend. He was the soothing presence when I had a challenging day and needed unconditional love. I knew that he was right about me not risking my heart with a man because he completely filled it for me.

As sad as I was knowing that I was going to lose him in the physical form, I was thrilled that I was now open to communicating with him. I knew his unique tone and was comforted that we had an open communication. He is now on the other side, continuing to support my spiritual development and ability to connect with life of all types. He is my angel dog guide helping me to connect deeper with other people's beloved animals in spirit. His graceful spirit continues to support and love me.

Embrace Love

By Sheila Sutherland

It was a blizzardy night in December. I stopped in the lobby of my building to check my mail. When I looked back outside, I saw a big fluffy cat, pleading with me to take him in from the cold.

I couldn't just let this cat into the building; I didn't know who he belonged to, so I left and went upstairs to my apartment. I felt tortured. How could I leave that poor thing outside to freeze on a night like this? I called people in the building to see if they knew where he belonged. No one knew. Maybe he was the stray that I always heard fighting in the back alley.

I went back, and he was still at the door. I scooped him up, not knowing how my other three cats were going to take to this new intruder. As soon as I put him down in my apartment, his whole countenance changed. Fear took over, and he turned into a wild cat!

The following days were filled with growls, hisses, and being struck out at. The cats and I were all stressed and felt in danger. After two weeks of never being sure if the cats and I were going to be attacked, the decision had to be made. Although the thought broke my heart, I decided that he would have to go to the SPCA.

When I came home from work that day, I saw that he had taken over the top of my fridge. I walked over and put my face right up to the edge of the fridge, knowing that I could be in danger of being seriously clawed. We looked at each other, and I said, "What are we going to do?" I saw his big, furry paw lift up, and I braced for impact...but instead, he placed it gently on my cheek. In that moment of grace, of us staring deeply into each other's eyes, fear was replaced by acceptance and love.

From that moment, Sebastian has become the most loving, adoring cat anyone could ask for. He's shown me that in every experience, we can choose fear or love, and I've seen the beauty that comes into our lives when we embrace love!

The Inspiration of Nature

By Tamiko S. Knight

As day-to-day life unfolds, people often look for inspiration to keep them going. Many turn to traditional sources, such as family, friends, and community associations. But when I ask myself what most inspires me, I always come up with the same answer: nature.

Observing the way water flows over and around rocks and logs helps me overcome obstacles in my own life. The different hues of the sky inspire me to connect with my emotions. The seasons inspire me to adapt and change. I look at winter as a time for rebirth and renewal of life. I use it as a time to reflect within the cocoon of my thoughts, thinking about how I can metamorphose and improve as an individual.

Sometimes inspiration comes from the biggest animals and natural forces – such as whales deep in the ocean. At other times, I'm inspired by the smallest insect. One of my most inspiring moments occurred while visiting a park on a windy afternoon. I was feeling particularly discouraged at that time, and I found myself looking down at the ground a lot. At one point, my eyes focused on an ant that was getting slapped around by the wind. The interesting part was that no matter how hard the ant got blown around, it still held a firm grip on its food, which was twice its size! I found it truly amazing how it took shelter in the cracks on the ground in order to continue toward its destination. That moment changed my life forever. It made me realize that if a tiny little ant could carry such a heavy burden yet maintain the will to keep going, even in the face of such adversity, surely I could, too.

In that moment, nature became my most inspirational teacher. Since then, I have come to believe that if a person really wants to learn, they only need to take a seat in the class of nature.

Beloved Guide Dog's Spirit Flight

By Carol Ann Arnim

Shortly after my hubby, Robert, transitioned, I was blessed to become a puppy raiser for Guide Dogs for the Blind. I began training a sweet dog named Laverne, and after 10 months of advanced training, the school chose to release her to me. While I am not physically blind, I have always felt that she was my own guide dog – helping me to see clearly through my grief. Because of our close connection, I chose to change her name to Spirit.

A few weeks prior to her 13th birthday, I intuitively sensed that she wasn't going to be with me much longer. I was sickened and unable to imagine life without her.

To help me through her upcoming transition, I purchased the most beautiful angel with flowing ribbons, since Spirit had always felt like an angel to me. I have been gifted with messaging from Archangel Michael, who has been talking to me all my life. Shortly after buying this angel, Spirit also began communicating with me daily.

I realized that, due to what Spirit had done for me all her life, I must now allow her to fly away in grace with a smile on my face. With help from Robert, who occasionally buoys me with conversation from the other side, I knew that I would be fully supported when the time came. Somehow, I knew I would be able to watch her die with calm, total acceptance.

In one of her many visions, Spirit told me to see a daffodil and go inside of it, *becoming* the daffodil. "Feel yourself as the daffodil; embrace all this beauty, allowing it into your heart." Her comforting messages gradually eased the pain of her coming death, and I felt stronger and believed that I could do this.

When the day arrived, we were both ready. Tibetan prayer flags draped her body as I released her. She flew free on the wings of butterflies, and I had a peaceful heart. While our journey here on Earth had ended, our journey together in spirit will continue forever.

Grace in the Saddle

By Shirlzy Everingham

Over three years ago, I fell off a horse and smashed my ankle. After months of treatment and rehabilitation, I was finally fixed...physically. But what followed was three years of fear. I was scared to get back on a horse. I was scared of falling over on uneven ground. I was scared each time I stepped into the horse boxes to clean them out, which was quite a problem since I had to clean out 20 boxes each day! For a time, I stopped riding altogether, but I began to feel invisible and ordinary. Without horses, I just wasn't *me*.

So, to help myself feel better, I started on a journey of prayer, self-discovery, writing, and mindset programs. I also reflected on my journey with horses and realised that the grace and validation of my own horsemanship was still inside of me. I could still feel it making me sparkle. Feeling this, I realised that I wanted to help people step out of the ordinary and into their own "sparkle"!

While doing my daily devotions one day, it hit me why a certain horse was in our herd: Grace brought me this horse! Tangles, my horse, just seems to know stuff. I have watched many people ride Tangles. If an experienced rider is on him, he does all the right things. And when a non-rider gets on, he just plods along, knowing that the rider cannot handle anything more. He knows exactly what each rider needs. He knew what I needed, too. He wanted me to trust him – and myself – so that I could once again experience the grace of being back in my riding boots.

Through my journey, I've learned that grace is everywhere, just waiting to emerge, and that God sends us what we need every day of our lives. Clearly, what I needed at that important time in my life was Tangles, my grace horse. His grace holds me while I saddle up for the ride.

A Soulful Awakening from Echoes in the Night

By Nancy Merrill Justice

I turned to look, but to my horror, she was gone. I began a frantic search and called out her name: "Lacey! Lacey!" My voice faded as fear lodged in my throat.

Suddenly, a loud screeching sound pierced the night air, becoming echoes that would soon fade into an eerie calm. In a daze, I overheard my neighbors say, "Definitely a coyote who caught its prey."

In that cruel moment after my cat Lacey had escaped out of the open garage and lost her life, my soul awakened – and with it came a blessing. As I processed my guilt and grief, I realized I had been living my busy life unconsciously – on autopilot with checklists of never-ending "to-dos" that allowed me to ignore unwanted feelings and make thoughtless mistakes in judgment. I was drifting through life when this painful, life-changing moment of truth catapulted me into a new level of soulful awareness.

I began my transformation with one simple commitment: to be more consciously aware of my thoughts, feelings, and actions throughout each day. I would need to slow down, so I did. With each passing day, I became calmer, more focused and deliberate. I began feeling more deeply as I listened to music. I became more influenced by art. My soul filled with creativity, and I began writing. I was more present – in touch with myself and with others.

I realized how easily I could slip back into my old habits, so I incorporated a new habit. I noticed that when taking daily nature walks with my two dogs, my mind easily let go of life's chatter and I would feel a wonderful sense of peace and calm. I also noticed that an abundance of creative ideas would seamlessly flow through my mind. So I began recording those ideas on my iPhone while I walked, creating "walking journals" that I use in my soul-connected writings.

Some souls are awakened gradually over time. My soul awakened in a moment – from echoes in the night. I will forever be grateful to Lacey for helping me reach a new level of awareness.

A Rose Filled with Love

By Patsy Hillman

A prize-winning rose that had been planted in a cottage garden is now rooted deeply and has grown very tall. It has climbed virtuously towards the sun's warm rays while stretching its prickly stemmed, viny arms out wide. It clings to a white, wooden-picket fence and covers an arched trellis gateway to the garden. Its beauty is breathtaking. An abundance of delicate flowers – deep orange and candy-apple red – fill the vines, looking like an exploding ball of fire.

Warm, powerful southern winds blow under the trellis arbour, opening the blueish-green wooden gateway to the garden. The wind carries the strong scents of lavender and rose, which now fill the paths of the cottage garden. The rustling leaves and the whistling wind play together like an orchestra, while the carefree roses sway and dance to their song. A few rose petals let loose and hitch a ride on the winds. Some petals swoop and swirl as if riding a roller coaster, while others float gracefully downward onto the flowerbed below, coming to rest on a blanket of purple lavender and lush green trailing ivy.

The warm winds have quickly dried many of the fallen rose petals, curling them up. Within time, they will turn into rose dust, returning to Mother Earth.

During my meditation, I sit in deep serenity, visualizing the cottage's healing garden. I take a deep breath, smelling the scents of lavender and rose oil warming in the room next to me. In my mind's eye, I see the abundant rose vines, and I reflect on how similar we are to this delicate flower. Roses symbolize love; they come in a variety of sizes, shapes, and colours; and each one is beautiful and unique. It doesn't matter where our roots have been planted. God loves all. Each of us is a rose filled with love – and love is what makes us bloom fully and gracefully.

Beloved Cat: The Grace of a Peaceful Passing

By Aprile Alexander

A year ago, I assisted my feline soulmate, Benares, to pass on with dignity.

Benares, my "miracle worker" cat, had saved my life on three occasions. He and his sister, Ganges, filled our lives with delight and unconditional love. After Benares's diagnosis, I talked to him and cried. A single tear formed in his right eye. He was given just six weeks to live, but thanks to love, prayer, warm-hearted veterinarian care, energy clearing, and his own sheer determination, he amazed us by living five years more.

Finally, Karen, his veterinarian, recommended euthanasia, saying, "I've done my best to give him a good life, and I want to give him a good death." This was a painful decision for me and his dad, Murray, but when Benares was ready to pass, he let us know very clearly.

On the day of the home euthanasia visit, we waited for Karen and her assistant, Jenny. Benares rested on my lap, under the colorful blanket I'd crocheted for him over the previous few days. I felt such love and great sadness, but I also knew that all of us, including Benares, were in agreement: this was the right way.

The injection was so gently administered that I did not even realize the instant of Benares's passing. Afterwards, I sat with him for a long time, feeling very deep peace, knowing that all was well with our beautiful boy. Murray took a photo of Benares and me; a friend seeing the photo later said, "Benares looks as though he's sleeping. You look like a madonna and child." Yes, yes! In the sacredness of that moment, I understood beyond a doubt that Benares was whole and free.

I wrapped his body in the crocheted shroud, allowed his sister, Ganges, to see him, then I looked out the window and said, "Thank you." A massive release of energy went whooshing out of my chest, as if Benares were leaping to new beginnings. I was flooded with a shockingly fresh energy of love, joy, and profound gratitude for the true grace: absolute knowing that we all live on.

Furry Angels

By Sarah Berkett

As an animal intuitive, I have experienced many moments of grace with animals. I have a deep respect and love for them, and I am constantly amazed at all the wisdom they share with us. I have learned to love and accept animals for the magnificent spirits they are – not as dependents, siblings, or children, but as partners in the joys and sorrows of life.

Growing up, my father and uncle provided me with so many special souls: dogs, cats, bunnies, turtles, baby chicks, horses, and even a piglet. And while I have loved all of them, I have always had a spiritual connection with dogs.

When I look into the eyes of a dog, they speak to my soul. They never seem to tire of watching me, of being with me while I live my life, or sitting by my side and entering into the spirit of the moment. My dogs always seem to know where I am, even when they cannot see me. We trust each other – a trust that does not come from emotionalizing or because they were rescued, but from pure acceptance and understanding.

Throughout my life, I have had my share of pains and troubles. I keep my soul and emotions close to the surface, and the dogs in my life have been able to see them, sense them, and smell them. I always smile when I think of them and feel gratitude for the time I've shared with these furry angels.

For me, getting a dog is a spiritual experience. In June of 2012, after losing my beloved Beamer, I set off to meet a rescue dog named Sasha. As I pulled into her foster mom's long driveway out in the country, I could clearly see in the distance a beautiful spirit running towards me. I knelt down slowly as she stopped in front of me, smiled, put her paw into my hand, and kissed my cheek. We looked into each other's eyes and shared a tender moment of grace, as I realized that Sasha was sent to comfort me and move me forward in my spiritual growth.

Field of Grace

By Joni Advent Maher

During a recent rough passage in my life, a veil was lifted as I sat on my yoga mat with the bright winter light pouring through my sunroom windows. I had spent the morning in prayer and movement as an attempt to regain my center after having lost it 10 minutes into my day.

My cramped, furtive mind and despondent mood persisted despite my efforts. I couldn't shake the hollow funk or the sense of disconnection that left me feeling like my whole being was covered in a papier-mâché shell that made it difficult to breathe. I sat back, losing hope.

Then, as naturally as a change in the wind, I found myself beyond the veil in what I can only describe as a field of grace. I experienced myself in a soft field of light with grace raining down on me in a form resembling mimosa blossoms. These soft, white blooms floated down on me, slowly opening my numb and desperate heart like a summer rose.

The field began to gently flutter and shimmer, which reflected my inner experience. I felt light and spacious. I was finally able to breathe deeply. I looked out at the barren trees and saw the oak mirroring me. Her few remaining brown leaves fluttered in the breeze. My recently troubled mind became as still as a pond on a summer's day. I was free, open, and receptive.

After some time, I moved into the rest of my day. As I often do, I chose a Medicine Card to support me. While not completely surprised, I was somewhat taken aback when I chose the Swan, who represents grace. Soft tears began to flow from my eyes as I quietly acknowledged to the Universe, yes, I will fully recognize that I am completely held in grace.

The next morning, I awoke feeling a little off. I walked over to the window and raised the blinds. Big wet, white snowflakes were gently falling from the sky, covering the earth and trees. Gazing out, I was instantly returned to the field of grace.

When Grace Purrs Sweetly

By Denise L. Roseland

It is 4:45 a.m. and I am awake. Working.

It's worth noting the time because I am serious about sleep.

Still, I had this regrettable moment of weakness last night. Tomas curled sweetly next to my belly, purring ever so sweetly. I didn't have the heart to put him out. That would have required waking him. Okay…I would have had to get out from under the toasty covers.

But now, I can confidently say that I should have plucked that beastly cat from the cozy quilt and tossed him out when I had the chance.

Before you judge me harshly, let me explain Tomas. He prefers to live in his own magical kingdom (our backyard). Still, as dusk falls and the lights come on in the house, he wants to be part of the family routine – cooking, eating dinner together, helping the kids with homework. He waits patiently at the patio door until one of us lets him in. He hangs out. He escorts each of the girls into their bedroom for bedtime snuggles. When we finally turn in for the night, he lounges on our bed with us, purring contently. For a while. But he simply refuses to stay in for the night. Rain, heat, or cold – sometime around 4 a.m. he wakes and begins wild, bounding laps around and over the bed (including over the sleeping humans) to encourage us to let him outside.

And so, that sweet purr set the stage for a 3:45 a.m. wake-up otherwise known as triple-pounce-to-the-liver that ended with knocking a full glass of water onto the hardwood floor.

And so here I am reviewing a client's revenue plan after letting the cat out and cleaning up the wet floor. And thinking of the thousand things I didn't finish yesterday, and the thousand more that will emerge this week.

I look out the window and see Tomas sleeping like a baby on the patio. On his back, feet up in the air. Aww, is that a smile on his face? In this moment – despite my premature awakening and overloaded schedule – the love I feel for him puts everything else into perspective…even his early-morning antics.

Becoming Dr. Doolittle

By Isabella Rose

As a child in elementary school, I was fascinated by the movie *Dr. Doolittle*. I remember thinking, *When I grow up, I want to be just like him. I want to talk to the animals, too!* Reflecting back over the years, I see how much I have shared in common with Dr. Doolittle's love of animals – starting with our pets.

Each pet that enters our lives becomes an intricate part of the family. Each one is just as special as the other. Like any family member, each pet brings his or her unique personality, yet some qualities always remain the same. Pets are the perfect confidants, nurturers, defenders, and protectors. They love without condition, lend a listening ear without judgment or discrimination, collect tears in their fur, make fun playmates, and sense when danger is near. These qualities develop a mutual bond that can never be broken.

Now that I am older, I see the beauty in *all* creatures big and small, furry and smooth, feathered and scaly. I have reconnected not only to the beauty of all creatures but also the openness to receive the messages they send when I am present in the moment.

Every day, I hear and see their messages all around me. The crow that caws outside my window every day reminds me to listen to the ancient wisdom within myself. The swans in the nearby lake share their messages of grace, beauty, and transformation. The deer in the field or on the side of the road remind me of my childlike innocence and gentleness. The cardinals I see in the trees, or flying by as I drive, remind me of my connection to the spiritual realm and my ancestors. The hawk who is my spirit guide and represents my late aunt, whom I see frequently throughout my travels, brings me messages that guide me further and further towards my dreams.

Although I didn't become a veterinarian like my childhood movie-hero, I have cherished my interactions with many types of animals over the years; and I've always appreciated the love, companionship, and grace they have brought into my life.

The Magic Stick

By Maria T. Rothenburger

It was just a stick. I sat among the lavender in my backyard, whirling from fathomless sorrow, when my eyes rested on its smooth, straight form.

Actually, it wasn't just a stick. It was *his* stick.

Bailey, our gregarious Yellow Lab, was obsessed with that thing. He was a true Labrador, and we often joked that he would retrieve it endlessly...or until he collapsed from ultimate exhaustion. We thought the latter to be impossible. But Bailey had died unexpectedly three months earlier, just short of his eighth birthday, and I sat in one of his favorite spots that spring, reeling from the loss of this pure soul.

After six years of failed attempts at making a baby, I questioned whether my frail psyche could handle another devastating defeat. Our marriage was broken, we had lost friends, and I walked around in a sort of gray haze most days. But, despite my behavior – how loudly I yelled, how irritated I got, or how I allowed infertility to fade the light in me – Bailey's love never diminished. He calmly and simply waited for a game of "stick."

When I looked at his beloved plaything, I felt instant and profound anguish for all of the missed moments with Bailey. His unrelenting exuberance, lolling tongue, and bottomless appetite failed to delight me in his last years, and my heart shattered then because of it.

What was I doing? This wasn't living! How had I given infertility so much power?

I dragged myself through the proverbial dirt, but I knew Bailey was there encouraging forgiveness. "Be gentle with yourself, Mama. And be willing to play stick any time! I love you. Now go, and Be Here Now."

I had a profound shift. Infertility would no longer steal my moments! I would not lament the past or worry about the future. I promised Bailey I would change, and I did! My new way of being helped facilitate the healing of our marriage and the adoption of our gorgeous son – not to mention our new Lab (who's presently addicted to tennis balls).

Dear Bailey, thank you for your magic stick.

In Praise of Stillness

By Nicole Levac

Walking in nature helps me invite a gentle, soothing energy into my life. It helps me connect with a part of myself that is calm and peaceful. It also reminds me that stillness is not a place of inaction; it is a state of being that is essential for a soulful life. My time in nature always graces me with amazing lessons, such as the moment a few years ago when I learned the value of stillness.

After a night of restless sleep, I felt my body full of tensions, my mind overly exerted, and my spirit agitated. I knew I needed to find some peace, ground myself, and regroup if I was going to be able to go on with my day. I knew I needed to envelop myself in the healing energy of nature, so I buckled up my snowshoes and set out into the powdered snow.

Freedom, exercise, and peace allowed me to release the stress, the tensions and fears, along with the weight of what had occupied my life and my night. The more I released, the closer I felt to nature. The closer I felt to nature, the more I was able to receive its wisdom and goodness. And the more I allowed myself to become enveloped by the beautiful external environment, the more I connected with an inner stillness – a place of serenity, quiet, calm, and tranquility that allowed me to slow down my body, mind, and spirit so that I could be one with myself and with nature.

Sharing in this wisdom of stillness allowed me to feel that special moment of grace because I knew I had been heard, supported, recognized, and recharged. I was ready to go back to my life knowing that stillness was available whenever I needed it, thanks to Mother Nature.

From that place of stillness, I could face what was happening in my life and trust that I would get through it – whole, grounded, and solid in who I am.

Chapter 6
Loving Grace

For both of us, many of the most profound, life-altering, soul-awakening moments of grace in our lives have involved love – especially loving each other! (Sappy, but true!) We cannot imagine our lives without the moment we met, the first moments we truly connected, the moment we fell in love, the moment we shared our feelings for each other, the moment we got married, and so many other moments of love since then. Sharing this love has been the greatest blessing in our lives.

Love takes many forms – each beautiful and worthy of celebration! In addition to romantic love, there is the love you feel for family, friends, spirit, and self. Love can be shared in a supportive community, with people you barely know, or even with complete strangers.

There are also infinite ways to show your love: It can be demonstrated by being there for a friend in need, by allowing your child to find their own path, or by saying "I do." Love can be experienced by remembering the past, embracing the present, or opening yourself up to new possibilities in the future.

In this chapter, you'll read about moments of grace involving all types of love, experienced and expressed in all types of ways. There are loving tributes to parents who have passed away. There are stories of children filling their parents' hearts with love and awe at their innate wisdom. There are stories of reconnecting and rekindling old love and stories of letting go with love and grace.

We hope that these pieces touch your heart as much as they've touched ours – charming your inner romantic, filling you with delight for the myriad forms of love all around us in the world, and inspiring you to cherish all types of love throughout your own life.

Love Conquers All

By Lisa Anna Palmer

My father, Corrado Cattelan, was larger than life. He was our rock.

In 1953, he left Italy to come to North America, where he started a cement-finishing company with my Uncle Aldo and worked hard to provide a good life for his family.

When he was diagnosed with lung cancer on March 5, 2007, we felt like the foundation beneath our feet had crumbled. I began every morning with a three-hour cry before heading out to see him. When he entered the hospital for the last time, we congregated by his side every day to pray until the illness swallowed up his earthly existence.

Dad passed away on April 25, 2007, at the age of 74, but not before he taught me one final life lesson that is now stored in the deepest recesses of my soul.

In his final days, my father kept pointing to the little red light on the oxygen monitor that was placed on his index finger. He repeated in laboured whispers: "Love will conquer cancer...love conquers all."

I couldn't fully grasp the meaning as I watched him fade. I simply responded through my tears, "I love you, Papa."

One day, years after his passing, while I was feeling particularly low and searching for answers, my father's words came back to me: "Love conquers all." In that moment, I realized that every piece of advice my father had ever given me was still in my heart, and nothing – not even the most aggressive lung cancer – could take those gifts away. This moment of grace brought me solace, as I finally understood that although Dad had passed years before, our love for him continued to grow, and his words were still there to help guide us. Though losing him so soon was not the outcome we had prayed for, in the end, love did conquer cancer.

I hope that my dad is resting in peace, knowing that the foundation he built for us remains solid. Our love for him and his million-dollar smile will remain in our hearts forever.

Filling the Void
By Jen Flick

I was placing the finishing touches on my three-year-old daughter's stylish bun. This was the night of her first ballet recital, and I couldn't have been more excited. As she covered her delicate face with a soft bathroom towel, I gleefully applied sparkle spray to complete her special hairdo. Seconds later, my daughter lowered her petite hands and gazed into the mirror. Drawing a deep breath, she turned to me and exclaimed in wonder, "Oh, *Mama!*"

My heart leapt in my chest. The emphasis she placed on the word *Mama* woke up something inside of me. An immediate realization followed: I am actually *living* this moment. Having lost my mother when I was four years old, I'd never experienced ballet class or sparkling hairspray as a child. At a deeper level, I'd never learned the extensive beauty and intense emotionality this word carries with it. Most of my life had been devoid of all things "Mama."

Looking into the wells of my daughter's infinitely adoring eyes, an awareness took root. I was a *mother*. Surely, I realized this the day she was born, and certainly I had been mindfully, wholeheartedly engaged in each day of her life since. But this moment was different. It stopped me in my tracks.

Suddenly, an otherworldly voice came through. It was a whisper – kind, gentle, and as fluid as a soothing summer breeze. It softly announced, "She came to heal you."

Now I was the one to draw in a breath. Goosebumps covered my body. What an incredible, sacred, holy gift. This precious three-year-old, in her fluffy tutu and sparkling hair, *came to heal me.*

It's been 11 years since I heard that wise whisper, and not an hour has passed that I've doubted its message. Piece by piece and day by glorious day, my daughter has been filling the void with joy. I give thanks and praise for her life, and I will forever honor that profound moment of grace.

Missed by an Inch
By Star Staubach

Two weeks after my 30ᵗʰ birthday, single, and recently out of a four-year relationship, I was in flux. I appreciated where I was and who I was, yet I wanted my fairy godmother to appear and grant me the man, marriage, and family of my dreams. As a child, I imagined myself married well before the age of 30. Despite that, I was the most content I had ever been. Yes, I looked forward to reaching the next level, yet I appreciated where I was. I had the awareness of the desire for love, but I didn't feel desperate to find it.

After a night out with friends who encouraged me to try online dating, at 1 a.m, I sat myself in front of a computer and created an online profile. It made me pause. What *do* I want? What do I have to offer a relationship? I sat with it. I pushed myself to answer all of the questions, sharing in authenticity.

Two weeks later, he contacted me. Looking at his profile, I could have sworn that he cut and pasted from mine to his. On paper, we were extremely compatible.

In the few online exchanges we shared, I found myself excited and curious to know more. I cut to the chase, asking him to call me. We talked for two hours straight. We even discussed the taboo topics of religion and politics. Who was this guy?!

Days later, we met in person. The intensity of our connection made it challenging for me to keep eye contact.

I wondered why he hadn't shown up in my search results when I posted my profile online. I combed over every detail. I searched through *every* man who had been suggested to me. He wasn't there.

I finally figured out why: When asked what height I wanted in a partner, not really knowing what to put, I replied with 5'10" as the shortest. My husband is 5'9". Thank goodness *his* filter let me in and he found me – I nearly missed him by an inch!

The Pecan Lady

By Elaine Lockard

I have a tradition of baking Sugar and Spice Pecans every year for Christmas. Not only do friends and family receive them but also people who I want to thank for being in my life that year.

In 1985, I met a very special lady who became not only an important spiritual mentor and teacher in my life but also a very dear and close friend. Her name was Reverend Beverly – or "Rev Bev," as she used to call herself. We shared many, many happy times and happy memories.

Around 2001, I noticed some changes in her that she would not talk about. They were subtle at first, but over a couple of years it became very apparent that something was wrong. It was then I learned that she had been diagnosed with Alzheimer's.

It was devastating! This vibrant, active, intelligent lady was having her mind slip away, and it quickly became necessary for her well-being that her son and his family move in with her. Each time I called to talk with her over the next year, she knew less and less who I was – until one day, she did not know me at all.

Then a remarkable thing happened! Her son, as he was trying to help her understand who was on the phone, said that I was the lady who sent the pecans. He said it was as if a light bulb went off – she got a twinkle in her eyes and remembered me!

From that day forward until she passed, as long as she was told "The Pecan Lady" was on the phone, she knew me and could talk coherently to me, even if only for a minute.

That one act of love broke through the walls of her disease and brought her, her family, and me a ray of happiness in an otherwise dark time.

Nothing can stop the power of love! It will always break through any barrier!

Through the Cracks

By Scott Fjelsted

Dropout. Breakup. Depressed. Broken. My life as a 23-year-old, defined in four words. Living with my parents after dropping out of college, I would often be gone partying for days, and when I was at home I mainly slept. I can only imagine how hard it was for them to see me live like this, especially since my siblings were living successful lives.

I have heard grace defined as "unmerited favor" as well as "a gift given although undeserved." I certainly was in a place in my life that had no merit and wasn't deserving of anything, yet grace was there even though I couldn't see it. However, I can see clearly now.

The most unlikely person gave me the most profound gift of grace at possibly my lowest point. My dad never uttered the words, "I love you." Hugs could be forced upon him if the person was persistent enough. Tears were only seen a couple of times at funerals.

During one of my multi-day stints in bed, depressed and alone, my dad entered my room. After saying he hoped I would get out of bed and get a job came the words, "You can stay here as long as you want." Only these weren't mere words. They were spoken with a tenderness that I had never heard from my father before. Even though it was only a glimmer, this light of grace pierced through the cracks into my soul.

I didn't hop right out of bed that day, but the healing did begin. As I turned my life around, those simple words from my father opened me to grace from our Heavenly Father as well.

In a world of deadlines and timelines, a world that tells us we need to be at a certain place, have a certain amount of money, retire by a certain age, or that we shouldn't have this or that habit anymore, I now know that our Heavenly Father waits patiently for us and, through eyes of grace, echoes the sentiments of my own father: "Stay here as long as you want. And when you're ready for a change, I will help you, regardless of where you are or what you have done."

Grace of Self-Love

By Christine Arylo

Love yourself. Sounds like a good idea, but how do you do it, or tell if you are doing it well? Unfortunately, most of us don't grow up learning about self-love. It's not until something happens as adults that we realize we are lacking one of the most essential ingredients of our happiness.

I was 30 when I realized I didn't love myself. It happened two weeks after my fiancé ended our engagement and I found myself alone one night having a terrible case of heartache. You know the feeling? Like your heart has been ripped out of your chest, leaving a big hole of emptiness?

After breakups in the past, I had always thought the feeling of emptiness was because the other person had left my life. This time, however, the voice of grace came through and changed my life forever. Like a beam of love, grace broadcast into my ear, "Christine, that is not *him* missing inside your heart; that is *you* missing! Yes, you have self-confidence and self-esteem, but you don't *love* yourself!"

Grace spoke truth. I had never considered loving myself. I mistakenly believed that if I was confident, had lots of friends, and was successful at work, then I was all good. Wrong.

That night, I made two promises to myself that I have continued to keep, foundational vows of self-love:

1. I promise to love myself more and more every day of my life.

2. I promise to never settle for less than my heart and soul desire.

That night, I know that grace saved my life, for its words gave me the wisdom I knew deep inside but had never been shown: every relationship and situation in our lives is affected by our abundance or lack of self-love. I have since dedicated my life to practicing and teaching self-love to adults and children around the world. We cannot control others, but we can control our relationship with ourselves. Your relationship with yourself is the most important relationship you have; value it with all of your heart.

Birth of a New Relationship
By Janet Dhaenens

I asked my son, Aza, "Have you talked to your sister about being at the birth?"

"What do you mean?" he responded.

"I asked her about it, and she told me she wasn't sure she wanted me there."

"She asked me if I would be with her for the birth," Aza said. "I just assumed you would be there, too."

I felt crushed. Amaryllis wanted her brother there but not her mom. I felt like crying, but I didn't. I sat with the way I felt. A couple hours later, after dinner together, my son's girlfriend asked me how I was doing. I told her how I felt and why.

She sat beside me on the couch, and I cried. I didn't try to understand or figure anything out with my mind; I just let myself feel the pain that came flooding up. I felt I've never been a good enough mother. I felt sad for the closeness I've always wanted with Amaryllis and haven't had.

Then new thoughts came in: a birth is special, but it's only the beginning of a new life. The greatest gift is the relationship I will get to have with this new granddaughter. The greatest gift is now that I no longer have Amaryllis deeply connected to me feeling I'm wrong, our relationship is changing. I feel the potential for more connection and a sharing of great joy between us.

These thoughts felt good. I was thrilled. I even had the thought that I really want to support Amaryllis in this expression of letting me know her needs. A desire to be a mother who accepts and supports her child, loving and honoring the part of her daughter that doesn't feel safe with her mother, arose strongly inside me. I suddenly knew that the greatest gift I could give her would be to love her all the more for her choice to honor herself and what feels good to her. I am in the process of giving her this gift, and it feels wonderful!

It Was Time

By Brenda Reiss

It was time for a divorce. This marked the end of my third marriage – definitely my last, I told myself. I'd noticed a painful pattern in these relationships, and the common denominator was *me*. Now, it was time to bring awareness and healing to the issues that kept repeating themselves. So I decided to do just that by not dating – just focusing on me. And I did that for two years.

It was a time of intense self-exploration. I read self-help books, attended workshops, went into therapy, and experienced many beautiful personal-growth modalities. I learned about codependence, loving myself, and growing closer to the gorgeous Spirit that I tried to run away from most of my life. And I experienced the full range of emotions – from being on my knees with gut-wrenching pain and grief to laughing with girlfriends and eating dessert for dinner.

After two years, I felt that it was time to practice what I had learned, and that meant dating. I knew I didn't want to be alone the rest of my life, yet I was scared to dive into a new relationship. Maybe the healing didn't work. Maybe I would still choose the same type of person, leading me right back into my old, unhealthy patterns. But, through my worries, Spirit kept whispering ever so softly that I was okay. I would find love again, especially now that I was learning to love myself.

After quite a few unsuccessful forays into the dating scene, I told Spirit I was done and that I must have misunderstood about finding love. I was disappointed, yet I was also enjoying my own company for the first time in my life. Spirit works in funny ways, though. No sooner had I given up looking for a man when I found one. The moment we were introduced, my heart knew that this was *him*. We both knew. I felt a calmness and a safety that I had never felt before. As tears of joy filled my heart, Spirit whispered, "See, I told you."

Physician, Heal Thyself

By Tanya Destang-Beaubrun

As I admired the breathtaking October foliage, my heart filled with gratitude. Attending this retreat was the fulfillment of a long-held dream.

I knew that at some point we would all have to tell our life story, and I was ready to tell mine. The story was that, after 20 years of practicing family medicine, I'd realized that I was not happy with how healthcare was being delivered. I felt the burning desire to offer my patients something more – to optimize their wellness by integrating health of body, mind, and spirit.

As a family physician, I already took care of their bodies.

As a newly certified health coach, I would take care of their minds.

At this retreat, I would be taught how to care for their spirit.

Over the years, I'd listened to many life stories, held many hands, and wiped away so many tears. That night, as I sat in the midst of our group healing circle, my tears flowed freely.

I cried for all the patients I'd been unable to save. *Had I failed as a doctor?* I cried for all the times I had missed being present for my family. *Had I failed as a wife and mother?* I cried for all the times I'd felt not good enough.

As the tears rolled down my face, I was comforted by the gentlest of angel hands caressing my back. That's when it hit me: I'd been so busy taking care of everyone that I'd forgotten that I, too, needed to be held, to tell my story, to have *my* tears wiped. I needed to let go and be open to receive. I realized that in order to become my best self, I had to learn how to receive as much as I had given all these years – to remember that the comforter needed comforting, too.

That was my moment of grace, my miracle, for that was when *my* life story became clear. That was the moment when this physician learned to heal herself.

When Our Child Said No to Our Faith

By Serena Low

The Sunday after my daughter turned 13, I went into her room as usual to remind her to get ready for church. She was in bed – sobbing. She said that she could no longer call herself a Christian and would not be coming to church anymore.

In that moment, I felt like a parenting failure. We had read our children Bible stories, talked about God at home, enrolled them in a Christian school, and taught Sunday School so we could be involved in nurturing their faith and involvement in church.

Part of me felt hurt and betrayed. Yet another voice inside was reminding me that even in this crisis, I had a choice: I could play the drama queen, or I could make this the turning point of our relationship.

Through tears, I told my daughter that I was sad and disappointed, but I respected her decision. I assured her that we would always love her just because she is ours, even if she made choices we did not agree with. This was a very hard thing for me to say and mean – I grew up in a family where affection and approval depended on obeying the rules.

The look on my daughter's face was priceless. She confessed that she had held back from telling us earlier because she was afraid we would kick her out. I knew then that I had done the right thing, and I can only attribute my response to God's divine grace.

We have now modified our Sunday routine so that one of us can stay home with our daughter. We have also informed close friends and family so that they are mindful in their conversations with her. It took a crisis to remind me that my love for my daughter does not depend on her following the path I desire for her. She needs to do the right things from her heart. It is time for her to go on her own quest for meaning and answers, and I have faith that in God's own time, she will find them.

By the Grace of Bev

By Annie Price

Bev was in her early 50s, an extremely bright and successful psychologist with a full practice. Abruptly, she was forced to give up her practice, along with her independence (including driving) and much of her identity. In the prime of her life, with her mind still sharp, Bev had been diagnosed with the most aggressive form of Alzheimer's.

I can only imagine how difficult those early days must have been for Bev, her family, and her friends. I came into the picture a few years later, as one of three caregivers supporting Bev in her home.

Bev has taught me a thing or two about being present in my life. This wise, gentle soul reminds me to pause and enjoy the grace-filled moments in every day. That's what Bev has now: moments.

One of the first things I assisted Bev with was putting together a batch of her homemade granola. She uses a big, wooden bowl to mix up all the ingredients. When I was going to chop up some pecans, Bev put her hand out to stop me – saying we needed to break them up (and other ingredients) with our hands. She did all of this with much consideration.

When everything was ready to mix together, Bev put both of her hands into the mixture and paused to look at me, trying to explain that we "put love in it." When I finally got it, I blinked away my tears. All the careful handiwork was her very consciously putting her love and her very *being* into this special batch of granola. Bev used to say, when preparing meals for family and friends, "The love flows up from the heart, down through the arms, to your hands and fingers – putting the looove in it!"

Life can get way too busy, and we forget to just *be*. When walking Bev's dog, we feel the shining sun. We marvel at the vibrantly colored bush. I appreciate Bev's delight in spotting her favorite heron by the pond.

With Bev, I've found so many simple moments of grace to enjoy.

Editors' note: You can find Bev's granola recipe here: http://goo.gl/ksvqes.

The Winds of God's Grace

By Lore Raymond

"The winds of God's grace are always blowing;
it is for us to raise our sails."
- Rabindranath Tagore

"It's freeeeezing here in Virginia!" I complained to my sister, Cathy, second-guessing my decision to leave the relative warmth of my Florida home. "What a crazy way to start New Year's Day."

"I love coming to this Buddhist temple," Cathy said. "I thought you'd love it, too."

Perhaps because my soul had been yearning for peace ever since my husband and I separated, I decided to brave the cold and follow Cathy inside the temple. We tip-toed into the empty, majestic sanctuary in shoeless silence, meandering around the room's perimeter, which was lined with huge crystal boulders. We found ourselves standing before an altar for Tara, the Mother of Liberation. While my eyes feasted on the glittering offerings of brass bowls filled with fruits and flowers, Cathy turned to me and asked, "If you died tomorrow, what one thing would you regret never having done?"

I immediately replied, "Not having a daughter." Where did this answer come from?! Was this the voice of a workaholic, career-focused, 44-year-old?

"You need to leave an offering before we go," Cathy suggested. I prayerfully took off my amethyst necklace and placed it on Tara's altar.

With my "sails raised" through this prayerful intention, I later headed to the island of Roatan, Honduras, for soul-searching. I decided to leave the USA and begin teaching again. Sitting in my third-grade classroom was a bright, brown-eyed little girl. In time, we came to know and love one another as mother and daughter. Born of my heart, she's a February baby with amethyst as her birthstone.

Today, Nazlie is married to Brian, and they're parents of Blake, my first grandson – also born in February! How could I have ever known how beautifully the winds of God's Grace would bless me?

Are You Willing to Bear This?

By Susan Mechley Lucci

"Are you willing to bear this for her?" Those eight powerful words shifted everything. Devastated by the latest teenage explosion directing 100% of the blame at me, I sought sage advice. Grace flowed, transforming my immense sadness, opening me to another perspective.

Managing three teens during their high-school and college years has been *the* toughest challenge of my 50 years. Gone are the days when they leapt into my arms, eager to share delight and distress. Caught up in the busyness of modern life, they are rarely home, rarely separated from their phones. I still hold on to family dinner; I light candles, cook healthy meals, and play music. Dinnertime conversations – once the juicy highlight of my day – typically devolve into teen angst, judgment, or complaining.

I feel their intense pushing away, individuating as required for healthy ego development. Moms raise babies to fly from their nest. Sure, there are still wonderful memory-making moments, but there are also painful arguments. I find myself missing their toddler days, passing day after day together at the zoo or in the park.

I work hard to maintain peaceful relationships among and with these three wonderful creatures I've mindfully mothered for two decades. There are times when I feel like the end of a swimming pool they are forcefully pushing off against to swim faster out into the world. Their launching into the next stage necessarily mandates big changes, some of which are quite painful to those left behind.

And yet…every so often, when I can see no way through, grace magically slips in between our stuck places, shifting perspectives, transforming us, reminding me that loving them is letting them go out into the world on their own.

For me, a single question – *Are you willing to bear this?* – awakened an appreciation for the whole process and graced me with a holistic perspective. Yes, in fact, I can bear *even this*, trusting that, as everything continues to change, all will be well.

When Love Knocks

By Natasha Botkin

This would be my first Christmas alone. I had hoped to enjoy a meal at my favorite restaurant, but I discover they have closed early. The owner apologizes for my inconvenience. "No apologies are necessary," I tell him. "Go enjoy your family. Merry Christmas to you."

I am back on the road, zipping along, tears streaming down my face at the realization that I am going to be alone. Me, the one who always had a place for others to go.

I do not even recall turning into the parking lot or climbing the stairs; yet here I am, knocking on his door. His vehicle is there, but he does not answer.

Ruefully, I head home. Just as I open the door, I receive a text: *Was that you knocking at my door?*

I reply, *Yes,* and he says that I can come over.

My heart dances over to his place, and as I am waiting for him to answer the door, I hear him speaking to someone: "Just wait until you meet her; you'll love her." He opens the door and our eyes meet, our hearts speak – no questions, no worries – for in that moment, it is the two of us, a love that cannot be defined.

A small speck of black meows hello, and he closes the door. It is obvious that he had other ideas for his night, and yet he opens up talking and chatting – just where we left off months ago.

As we settle in for the night, the moment of unconditional love shines as our hearts speak. There is no need for words. I needed him, and he allowed me to come. We snuggle, and as he sleeps, I lie there, so thankful for our graceful moment of love.

A Graceful Moment of Pure Love

By Jodi Cross

My hand rested on the wooden cradle as I watched my baby – smiling, drinking in this peaceful moment – when I suddenly became aware of a gentle, loving presence standing beside me.

I was alone in the house. I knew there was no one within a two-field radius.

My sense of calm changed to feelings of awareness and clarity. I had felt and seen energies before, so I was aware that if I changed my energy, I might not be able to stay connected to this energy, which felt so special.

I sensed a male presence. Without moving my head, I used my peripheral vision to see his profile. Wow! He was so beautiful, dressed in radiant white robes from head to foot. His beautiful, love-filled eyes looked straight at my baby.

My first thought was, "NO! Please don't take her!" I could feel panic spread through me. I just wanted to gather her up into my arms and say, "No! She's mine. Please let her stay." As I went to move to pick her up, I was unable to. It was as if I was frozen, yet I could still move my eyes and think my thoughts. I looked back at my baby, love filling my heart so much that I thought it would burst. I looked back at our visitor, and I felt the love within him flow through me.

I knew we were safe.

His gaze never left my baby. His love for her was total. I felt so honoured to be gifted this vision. As that thought went through my mind, a voice filled the room: "Blessed are the pure in heart, for they shall see God."

I completely understood the message.

At that moment, my love for my baby had been so pure that I had been given this most precious gift, a vision of His pure love.

Love Without a Catch

By Judith Clements

"Beauty without grace is the hook without the bait."
- Ralph Waldo Emerson

In the beginning, my understanding of grace had three different sources: the blessing spoken before meals; the famous Princess of Monaco; and the one most revered by me, those elegant rituals of ballet. As I grew up, however, other life lessons took precedence over grace.

During my in-between years, I became preoccupied with the beauty and appeal of "approval." Beneath beauty's deceptive allure were J-shaped rusty devices, many with multiple sharp barbs. Even the single-barbed hooks could be masterfully disguised with appetizing bait. For decades, I impaled myself swallowing the fisherman's bait – hook, line, and sinker.

The preferred bait, guaranteed to lure me into dangerous waters, was that rare combination of warm, gentle, male attention. I felt neither beauty nor grace in my feeding patterns. Yet, actually, grace was evident, for I managed to avoid predators while growing into a sizeable and wise adult of my species. Migrating into the greater lakes, I joined others. We shared joy, comfort, and beauty in synchronous movement. Still, I was a lonely one among the many, seeking deeper, intimate connection.

My supreme moment of grace came with a hook of an entirely different nature. The highly skilled sportsman, sans camouflage gear or hidden agendas, dropped his hook into the water. "Trust me," he whispered as the smooth and shiny stainless-steel hook drifted slowly down in front of me. Cautiously examining its naked simplicity, I noted its distinct lack of barbs. Yielding to my curious inner minnow, I swam into the curve of its hook, which perfectly cradled my body. Through grace, my rapid ascent and the strange, loud noises did not trigger my desire to struggle and escape. The whirring reel and the ever-brightening light felt oddly reassuring.

Under blue skies and a tropical sun, I released all fears of survival. Both the sportsman and the sportfish were hooked, attached to a gift of grace. Beauty had manifested by grace without a baited hook! Our profound gratitude nearly exceeded the boat's weight limit!

Three Words of Grace

By Beth Frede

At 43, I was living a relatively peaceful, happy life with my little family. I had a great marriage, healthy children, and creative work I enjoyed. But even though outwardly I seemed to lack nothing, inside I felt a deep longing that had been there since childhood. *Something was missing.*

I was the second of three children, and both my older brother and I were adopted. As a child, I didn't understand why, despite a loving, stable upbringing, I still felt fundamentally different.

I loved all things creative – art, piano, sewing, crafting – but none of my family shared my passion for these activities or my serious, introspective personality. I felt loved but also acutely disconnected, separate, and often invisible.

While I'd never hidden my adoption or felt embarrassed by it, I'd always believed that my life had begun the moment I'd been adopted and that nothing before then had mattered. Looking back, I was trying to wish away my past out of love for my parents. I didn't realize that by denying my start in life, I was also denying my true self. But the older I grew, the more I wondered about my original family. *Who was my birth mother? What about my father? And why was I given up?*

Eventually, I just *had* to know. I contacted the adoption agency to learn what I could, filled out the required paperwork, and waited (impatiently!) to hear back.

Six weeks later, a caseworker called. While she couldn't reveal the names of my biological family members, I did learn some things about them. I discovered I have a half-sister, and I finally learned why I was given up for adoption. But surprisingly, the smallest note had the biggest impact. The caseworker wrote: "Your birthmother's hobbies are: *painting, sewing, decorating.*"

Instantly, a sense of connection seeped into my bones. I wasn't random; I came from somewhere! Those three simple words gave me the grounding roots I'd been missing, and those roots gave me wings to fly.

Love Heals

By Sharon Hickinbotham

Everyone says, "love hurts," but that isn't true. Loneliness hurts. Rejection hurts. Losing someone hurts. Love heals. Love lifts you up. Love casts out fear. Love washes away your pain, allowing you to shine and feel wonderful again.

I have felt the hurt of loss and loneliness when I lost my brother to suicide in 2014. I have also felt the healing power of love, through his daughter, my niece, Emilie.

Despite the tragedy that she has endured, Emilie has a loving personality. Her energy is uplifting and inspiring. We both experience strong intuitive voices and the power to connect to nature, our loved ones, spirits, and divine love. I am blessed to be a part of her life, to be her Auntie and her friend.

When Emilie was just 10 years old, she wrote a song for me called, "Which Way Does the Wind Blow." Here are just a few lines from this heartfelt, original song:

Don't hold back, just let yourself flow with the wind.
Let the wind choose the right path that you know and trust.
Let it cleanse your body, feel the new flow…

It meant the world to me to hear these words from my niece, who wrote freely, straight from her heart, guided by spirit. This is a special gift that I will cherish and hold dear to my heart always. Her love and wisdom – shown through this song and throughout her life – has also taught me that spirituality and love come in all ages.

Our loving connection sometimes feels like that shared between mother and daughter, best friends, or even twin sisters. Oftentimes, one of us will sense that the other needs a friend and "randomly" give a ring just when one of us needs it most – lifting our spirits with a chat or laughing and sharing stories.

Although this love cannot bring back Emilie's dad, it can help to heal some of the hurt from this loss. No matter how painful it can be at times, we know that we share this healing love forever. And we know that we have our own guardian angel watching over us.

Graceful Step-Parenting
By Chrysta Horwedel

The holidays are a sacred time of joy, love, and family traditions; yet the hustle and bustle of planning that accompany the season can be challenging for a step-parent. Feelings of love inspired by the season are easily replaced by frustration and annoyance, which is exactly what I was experiencing this time around.

I found myself sitting in my most comfortable chair, surrounded by the beautiful holiday decorations, yet I was stressed to the max. I realized that I couldn't handle this on my own. I needed something to help clear the emotions that burdened my sensitive and hopeful heart. So I asked for guidance.

Suddenly, in that very moment, every thought and emotion halted. All attempts at planning ceased. Then something beautiful happened: As I became still, I began connecting with my breath. Within the stillness, I sipped cool air through my lips and then, as if a switch were being flipped, the answer became clear: It was up to me to take the high road and to have the courage to step out onto a new path.

Being a step-parent is complicated, and the holidays seem to bring even greater opportunities for ambiguity and complications. Not this year, though. My resolve was clear. This year, my frustration would be replaced with grace. I would operate from a place of love and compassion, and I would do so first and foremost for myself. I had to take the journey back to this place of grace. It didn't matter if others would acknowledge or accept me for extending an olive branch. What mattered was that I was taking a stand for my family; for my place in that family; and, most importantly, for myself.

You Are Loved

By Bianca Lynn

I was brought up Christian. I went to church as a girl. My father was a minister, as was his father. Yet I always felt disconnected from my religion. It just didn't provide what I wanted – whatever that was.

I left the church behind when I went to college. I began exploring different paths: satsangs, meditation, studying with modern-day Essenes, energy work, breathwork, participating in sweat lodges and vision quests. I even visited different churches from time to time. Through these, I had some experience of spiritual satisfaction, some peace, and perhaps even a sense of the Divine. I had moments of feeling free, refreshed, and renewed. But most of the time, there was an underlying lack of confidence. I carried anger, a feeling of doubt, and a sense that something was wrong (probably with me).

In 2012, I was invited to an energy-training class. A long breath meditation was part of the course. As I lay on the floor after the breathing, my body started to shake slightly, and I began to weep. I was overcome by a sense of peace that literally shook me to my core. It was as if I was enveloped in a beauty and love that I did not know existed.

"Are you okay?" my friend asked.

"Yes," I choked. I was more than okay. I was loved. I knew it in every cell of my being.

How can I share my experience in a way that others can understand or, more importantly, *feel?* I do not know. What I do know is that this brief moment left me with a sense of comfort and peace. I know all is right in the world.

Sometimes I still feel pain, sadness, and heartbreak. Sometimes I am clumsy, judgmental, or angry. But underneath it all, I know that each and every one of us (including me and including you) is special, perfect, and completely loved.

Walking Our Path

By Lacey Dawn Jackson

He lived in Ireland. I lived in the northwestern United States. Our lives were full of adventure. We traveled Europe and lived in a van while exploring New Zealand. We lived here. We lived there.

I was missing home terribly. Being so far away, I found myself getting depressed and insecure about our relationship. At the same time, he had stepped back as well. We still went to bed each night saying, "I love you." We still laughed and had great conversation. We both felt it, though.

The summer came and went. It was time for me to go back to the States. I was sad but filled with relief. As I watched him walk away from the train station, I wondered if I would ever see him again.

Once I arrived back home, I knew it couldn't continue. I felt angry because my feelings had changed and his had shifted as well. I didn't think it was fair to spend so much time and energy in cultivating a relationship when our feelings had changed.

One day after we finished talking via Skype, I knew I had to do something. I sent him an email telling him that I couldn't be in a relationship any longer. I felt like my heart was breaking. I walked outside to get some fresh air. I had this overwhelming feeling of love and grace come over me as I stepped off my porch. Within my soul, I knew I had done the right thing for both of us. Every time I would find myself wondering if I had made a mistake, I remembered back to the moment I stepped off the porch and God enveloped me. It was a feeling I will never forget.

A few weeks later, as we talked and got some closure on our relationship, he expressed feeling relief as he had read my email. I realized that in that moment God sent his Love to cover both of us because we were hurting. God let us know that there was indeed another path for each of us to follow. It just wouldn't be together.

Grace: Much More Than a Name in the Sand

By Jane Hamilton

My daughter, Grace, is by far the greatest creation of my life. Long before she was born, I was drawn to writing her name in the sand on holidays (which I now understand to be part of the manifestation process). She really is our little miracle, a joy, and a gift from the Universe.

Her father and I met by accident when my college tutor's car broke down on a dark country lane and we waited together for the recovery services. A short time later, our "knight of the road" arrived and, after diagnosing the fault, guided us to a nearby pub to await recovery. That knight and I were married within the year!

We started trying for a family immediately but, after three unsuccessful years, resorted to IVF. I also practiced Reiki daily, placed healing crystals around our home, and prayed to the Universe. I promised that if we had a child, we would bring them up to be good, kind, and a shining light in the world.

Sadly, treatment failed. I returned to the fertility specialist who, because I was now 42 years old, gave me a 1% chance of conceiving. When I left the clinic that day, in front of me was a small girl in a brightly coloured raincoat splashing in a large, round puddle. I didn't know if this was a sign from the Universe or a cruel twist of irony; either way, my heart was heavy.

Some weeks later, during an evening phone call with my sister, she somehow sensed I was late. I put it down to the after-effects of treatment, but she suggested I test anyway. I told her not to wait up.

But she did wait up, and I did call her back…because, amazingly, the result was positive – I was pregnant!

Our lives changed from that moment on, and in 2008 our perfect miracle girl was born – six pounds and four ounces of pure joy. The name Grace suited her perfectly, as it embodies miracles, soul connection, purity, love, and light, which is what our beautiful daughter brings us every day. My Mum, Elizabeth, passed away in my 30s, so we named our daughter Grace Elizabeth, meaning "gift from God."

We love our beautiful Grace, and we thank you, beautiful Universe.

My Genesis
By Colin Hegarty

When I was 16, I was given the opportunity to travel to Baja, Mexico, for a youth mission's trip through my church. For a week, we would serve as helpers at the "Genesis" campground. This ran sort of like a summer camp; they brought in different orphanages each week and different youth church groups to help out.

We arrived a day early to settle in and get accustomed to the area. The next day, a bus full of bright-eyed orphans arrived. As they got off the bus, their faces beamed with the biggest and brightest smiles. That's when it hit me: this was a luxury to these kids. It was like a vacation for them. I had grown up going to summer camp, hating it really, but I never knew how fortunate I was to get that opportunity.

After a little meet and greet, each member of our church was paired up with an orphan (*niño* or *niña*) so we could serve them throughout the week. Sure, there was a bit of a language barrier, but our group learned a bit of Spanish beforehand to hold small conversations.

I was paired with a shy little *niña* named Tania. Throughout the week, she would sit by herself when we had group games. I would sit with her for a while, but she told me to join the game and have fun. She never wanted to join, but she always cheered us on from the side, giving me a smile when I looked at her.

During the last night, we had a big campfire, singing songs and reflecting on our life-changing week. After the fire, we all went to bed with tears in our eyes, not wanting to leave the family we had created in only six days. Tania gave me a big hug and handed me a note that said:

To: Colin

Colin, I love you, thank you and I will never forget you and that you and God loves me. Goodbye.

From: Tania

My True Love and the Gift of Acceptance

By Gail Butt

At 16, in a college classroom, I met eyes with a boy who would change my life; I just didn't know it then.

By 33, my plan for life didn't seem to be working out. I wanted to be married with kids and live in a gorgeous home with a successful career; but instead I was single, living at my parents' house, and so unhappy in my job.

One day, I found myself with an energy healer for the first time. During the session, she asked me to pick a card. It read, "I move through the cycles of my life with joy and acceptance." This left with me with more questions than answers: What cycle of my life? What joy? Acceptance of *what*? Hopefully not that *this* was how life was going to be!

A few weeks later, I returned and drew another card. The healer looked at me in amazement. It was the same card, something she said had never happened two sessions in a row before. "Someone is definitely trying to tell you something," she said.

She was right. Two months later, my life was changed. I was in love…with the boy from that college classroom! Although he had been a very special part of my life for all those years, I had given up hope that he would ever be anything more than a great friend.

With that love came a new start and a transformation of every area of my life. It brought me more joy and happiness than I ever thought possible, and it brought me acceptance that life has a plan greater than mine and will bring me exactly what I need, exactly when I need it.

My true love brought me that gift of acceptance, brought me a soulmate to share my life with, and made all my dreams and more come true. As I write this, we are expecting the birth of our first baby, and I will soon be moving through a new cycle of life with joy and acceptance.

In My Brother's Room

By Monica Laws

The hospital stood in the city amongst acres of trees and trails. I visited with my brother following a routine surgery. He was groggy and a little out of it but very happy to have my company.

When he was given the go-ahead to finally sit up, the nurse gave him basic instructions: "If you feel faint or nauseated, lie back down." She didn't stay. I postponed heading home. I just could not leave him all alone. It didn't feel right at all.

At first, sitting up for five minutes was plenty. The next time, I gave him a pillow to hold on to and rubbed his back. I put him in the chair so he could lean back. His fingers tingled, and he began to yawn. The nurse said it meant he needed to lie back down for at least another hour. It was my time to leave. I leaned over to kiss him goodbye and say I love you as he lay there snuggled up with the blanket.

He called me the next afternoon. He was thankful and happy that I had been there that first bit of time after the surgery. He was up walking that day and felt better. His wife and stepson had just left from their visit. He was thrilled with the Valentine's card from his wife. "Wanna hear what it says?" he asked.

"Yes, please. Of course!" I said.

He read the card with enthusiasm and explained the pictures that went with the silly captions. He was so happy with that card, and he shared it with me. He was vulnerable and open. I felt closer to him than I had in years. His love for her shone through so much when he read to me. And I felt that love. It was beautiful.

Was my moment of grace being there to support him as he recovered? Was it being able to share in his happiness and the love he felt for his wife? Or was it realizing that it really was okay that it was me there that first day and no one else? Or maybe they were all moments of grace – his, hers, and mine.

Choosing Love
By Shelley Lundquist

"Will you please stop doing that?" I snapped at my daughter, exasperated. So, instead of sitting down at the table, she finished dishing out her plate of food and promptly went to eat in her room.

Minutes before, I'd been so looking forward to sitting down at the dinner table together and hanging out.

I sat down disappointed, more in myself for losing my patience. In many ways, my daughter is very much like me. At times, she drives me batty with her procrastination, her teenaged habits, and the disparaging darts she dispatches in my direction on what seems like a daily basis.

Thankfully, I know that whatever irritates me is about me and that the only behaviour I can control is mine. I also know that how I project myself into the world around me communicates my intention.

When I'm coming from a place of love, compassion, gratitude, peace, creativity, and clarity, everyone around me can feel that energy and doors open in welcome. Likewise, when I feel irritable, anxious, or emotional, I communicate that too; and, as I just saw with my daughter, doors close because *I* am closed.

I had communicated intolerance and received the same in return. It didn't matter if I felt I had a valid reason to be annoyed. Indulging that did not get me what I wanted. Energy always ripples outward, and if I want a specific outcome, I know I must be vigilant in how I show up and make sure it is in alignment with the message I want to deliver.

When dinner was done, I knocked on her door.

"I'm sorry I was impatient, sweetie. I missed you at dinner."

"I'm sorry too, Mama," she granted.

"Want to go for a walk?" I asked, hopeful.

"Nah, but I'll play a cards with you," she smiled.

"Deal! Sealed with a hug."

Every moment I pause, step back from emotion, and gently reframe my thoughts to choose love, truly is a moment of grace.

My Father Saved My Mother's Life

By Catherine M. Laub

In January 2012, my father told me in a dream that he would not make it to the end of the year. Even though he was 83 and had a heart condition, I was horrified. I then learned that he was having more heart issues and was going to have a heart catheterization in April. There was a risk for him, so my husband, Tony, and I went to be with him for this test, along with other family members. The test went well, and he was told that he needed a defibrillator and that they would schedule an appointment once his insurance approved it.

In May, Daddy fainted in his home and hit his head. My mother was in another room and rushed to him. She couldn't revive him and thought he was dead. Her heart was palpitating, and the paramedics in the ambulance asked if she needed to be checked. She said no, it was just the stress. When I found out this was happening, I immediately went to the emergency room.

I was even more upset when I recalled my dream. The day was long, and Mommy was still having chest pain and kept telling the doctors to only worry about taking care of Daddy. I saw her take a baby aspirin midday. I was alone with both my parents when the doctor explained that Daddy would get the defibrillator implanted on Monday. With that, he asked if we had any questions. Mine was, "Yes, can you ask my mother about her chest pains?" Within 10 minutes, Mommy was admitted and brought to the catheterization room. It was discovered that she had been experiencing a heart attack all day, and she received two heart stents. I am amazed how strong she was to last all day in such pain!

I told my mother that my father, in essence, had saved her life. She could have been driving or sleeping while the heart attack occurred, but my father had such a wonderful connection with her that his soul provided a way to keep her safe – by getting her to exactly where she needed to be on that day: a hospital!

Dedicated to my parents, Michael Luciano, Sr.
(deceased December 2012) and Carol Luciano

What Feels Comforting?

By Janet Dhaenens

"Now I'm feeling insecure. I have the thought you are only doing this because I asked you to, not because you would choose to do this on your own."

I was taking space in circle, meaning everyone's attention was on me. We were doing an exercise of exploring what we wanted, asking for it, and receiving it. I wanted nurturing. I asked each person in the group to do one thing for me: "I'd like to lie down and put my head on your lap. Are you willing to hold my head and run your fingers through my hair? Would you lie down against my back and cuddle up close to me? Would you rub my feet and legs?"

Each person agreed to my request and I felt good receiving, but then thoughts that I was taking too much time and attention arose. "I feel like I'm wrong to want attention."

My peer coach suggested I ask each person how the experience felt for them. Their responses were expressions of joy and appreciation.

I was so pleasantly surprised that I had to ask them if I was understanding correctly: "You mean it's okay for me to want and receive loving care and attention, just because I want it and I ask you for it?"

I heard a resounding "YES!" from everyone. This was my first time in circle of deeply receiving nurturing attention from others. From this experience, I understood that I don't have to keep repeating my past experience of feeling wrong for my desires. I saw I could no longer honestly repeat old stories about being alone and feeling uncared for. I had a new experience of feeling deeply cared for by people I'd just met.

I knew that this was a practice; it would take time for new experiences to enter my "experience pool" and dilute old painful memories. But I was clear that this was what I wanted and that participating in circles would give me ongoing opportunities to have more of these positive experiences. I also knew that each person's desires could be different, yet their requests being met would help heal their pain – and that, together, we could create new experiences that bring joy to each of us.

Pistachio or Vanilla?

By Karen Packwood

My teenage daughter and I had just spent a joyful New Year's Eve together. We explored the beautiful seaside town we were visiting, went to an indoor circus, and ended the evening with party poppers and everyone singing "Auld Lang Syne."

Thirty minutes later, however, we were in our respective hotel beds when a torrent of tears began pouring from my eyes. I didn't want to spoil my daughter's evening, but it was no use – the dam had broken.

"Why are you crying, Mum?" she asked. "Is it because of...?"

The mere mention of my ex-partner, who had recently ended our relationship, was enough to intensify my sobs. I scrunched up under the duvet, under the delusion that if I hid myself, my daughter wouldn't notice how wrecked I was on what was meant to be a celebratory night.

"Do you want to talk about it?" she asked.

Her simple question took me aback. I'm the adult and am meant to soothe my child in times of distress, not the other way around. I paused and questioned what to do: stay "grown up" or give in to my need for comfort? But before I made my decision, she hopped into bed with me, cradled my head in her arms, asked about my feelings, and truly listened to the answers. I was deeply touched by her tenderness...until she asked a question that utterly confused me: "Which do you prefer, vanilla or pistachio ice cream?"

I wondered: Why this sudden non sequitur? And then I realized that she was using a tactic to take my mind off of my problem, not to diminish it but to help me feel better. And it worked! I found myself chuckling through my sorrow! "Pistachio," I replied. "How about you?"

"Vanilla," came her reply. " Are you feeling better now?"

"Yes," I replied.

"Good. Let's go to sleep then," she said matter-of-factly, leaping back into her own bed and snuggling down.

It might not sound like much, but when your heart is breaking and your child leaps in to show you love and support in such a kind and compassionate manner, you can't help thinking how blessed you are.

You Are Safe

By Autumne Stirling

As a survivor of childhood trauma and a difficult divorce, trust did not come naturally to me. I didn't even take any particular notice of my defense system. It was just the way things were, the way I had always been. The walls I constructed to protect myself were so impenetrable, I thought I had been cursed with an inability to have faith in anyone or let them get too close to me. My defining characteristic was much like Willie Wonka's Chocolate Factory: no one ever went in, and no one ever came out.

Following a divorce and the cessation of my relationship with my family, I began the journey of single parenting and what I believed was the end of romantic relationships. I simply was no longer interested. I focused my energy on my son and myself, utilizing coping mechanisms learned in trauma treatment. I slowly discovered how to fulfill my needs and take responsibility for my own happiness. This was a process and a monumental milestone. For the first time in my life, I felt truly untroubled.

Then I met him.

He was different from anyone I had ever known – a beautiful soul whose eyes shone with kindness. His touch was soft and loving. He listened and understood me. He showed me more love in small moments than I had ever been shown in my entire life. Still, I was guarded and mistrusting. My feelings had nothing to do with him and everything to do with my past. My history was defining my present, but I no longer wished to be impermeable.

One day, he said to me with so much loving fierceness, "You are safe. It's okay. I'm right here. You will always be loved." Grace had landed right in front of me; his words and heart changed my world. I now truly believe I am worth it, I am loved, and I am right where I belong.

Healing Grace of Caring for My Dad
By Carolyn McGee

One time when my parents were visiting me, my dad fell and hit his back on a big planter. At first, we thought he was just bruised, but we quickly realized that he had broken some ribs. Because of his chronic obstructive pulmonary disease, anything related to his breathing was an especially big concern.

After some surgeries, he needed to go to a nursing facility for rehabilitation before he could go home. Since my parents live about seven hours from me, it became necessary for my mom to go home while I became his caretaker.

My dad was physically and emotionally unavailable when I was a child. He often traveled and has a speech disorder called aphasia where what he thinks he's saying and what he actually says are not always the same. It made having in-depth conversations challenging between us. Now, I was responsible for ensuring that he got the care that he deserved and needed.

I went every other day to visit him for the months that he was there. Having that time together shifted our uneasy relationship to one of gratitude and connection. I was able to be there for him in a way that I never felt he had been for me.

He started telling me stories about his childhood and his travels. I learned more about his dreams, how he felt, and what was important to him. I started to understand his language better. We suddenly knew what the other was going to say. We laughed. It became clear to me that even though he wasn't physically with me and my sister very often when we were growing up, he was constantly thinking about us and truly did love us very deeply.

This time of caretaking for my dad graced me with the gift of connection without childhood filters. My heart opened wide to accepting him and our relationship without reservations or expectations.

My Heart Grew Three Sizes That Day

By Laura Freix

Exhausted from a long night following a month of chaos, I rolled over and tried to ignore the phone. Still, I wondered who would be calling so early. I knew it must be important, so I dragged myself out of bed to check. It was a dear friend; her son was in trouble. I could feel my own emotions well up in empathy, as my son had had similar struggles of his own as a teenager. She was seeking advice on what to do. *Without consciously choosing the words,* "Do you want me to come with you?" came out of my mouth. I do not know where the words came from, only that I was meant to go. Within the hour, I was on the road for the over-200-mile journey.

What unfolded in the days that followed was a series of tiny miracles that reminded us we were not alone in this. Without going into all of the details of the weekend, I could simply see connections that my friend could not. It began when she gave hundreds of dollars to a stranger so that the woman could see her son. She did not do it for any personal gain, but my friend's random act of kindness was witnessed and positively impacted her son's situation. My son, who understood firsthand what it meant to be given a second chance, was able to use his connections to help my friend's son get a job interview and pay it forward. Things had come full circle, and I had a knowing every step of the way that things would work out, that we were supported by the Divine in each moment.

In life, there are friends you can count on for love and support in any situation, friends you can trust with your most vulnerable truths. Until that moment, I did not know that I could *be* that friend for her. By stepping up to the plate when she needed me most, my life and our friendship has been forever transformed. I was able to connect to my higher self in a way I never dreamed possible. And while I don't feel that I've ever been a "Grinch," I feel that, like the famous Dr. Seuss character, my "heart grew three sizes that day."

Trusting God, Trusting Love
By Teresa Salhi

On March 10, 2009, I stepped off the international flight from the United States to Tunisia, Africa. All day, I'd been filled with joyful anticipation, even during the 14-hour flight. However, as I looked around and saw signage only in Arabic, I began to get nervous. "Dear God, you guided me here. Now what?"

The answer came back: "You belong here."

I'd come to meet someone I'd been communicating with online about goals and dreams, including helping African children. Although our countries, religions, and beliefs were miles apart, I felt a deeper connection that transcended our differences. Still, meeting in person required ignoring doubters and putting aside fears. It required trust.

As a young girl, life taught me to be strong, trusting, and open to new experiences. I was the new student each school year because we moved often. Mom was married to her second husband then, but he was Daddy to me. He came and went a lot, which was hard on Mom, so I had to be strong for her.

Now I, too, had been married and divorced twice. Was I following the same path? Through pain and loss, I felt my trust begin to subside. During my lowest point, when my ex asked me to choose between him and my child, I questioned myself: Was I being naïve and trusting too easily?

But as I stood alone in this Mediterranean-city airport, thousands of miles from my home, I trusted that this was indeed my destiny. I felt God's guidance unfolding.

My phone rang, and it was my friend. He was only a few steps away! Never before have I seen a more beautiful man holding a more beautiful bouquet of pink roses – my online friend with mutual interest in African children, now turned escort…*soon to be much more.* The next seven days were magically infused with new beginnings and deeper levels of trust.

As I write this now, it's February 14, 2016. I sit across the table looking at my beloved husband. Exactly six years ago, he arrived in the U.S. with only a backpack. Yes, I am married to the man from the Tunisian airport. The lesson? Trust God…*and true love.*

It's Safe to Be Me

By Janet Dhaenens

My partner said, "I feel uncomfortable about the way you interact with other people sometimes. Some things you say are beyond their understanding, and I think they get scared."

A part of me relaxed. We were on the phone, she in her home in Prince George, Canada, me in my home near Sandpoint, Idaho, United States. I sat down to take in what she said; suddenly, I was in tears!

In every other intimate relationship I've been in, the person I was with didn't meet me with this level of honesty. Instead of opening up, they moved away from me. Some part of me knew this meant it is truly safe to bring *every* part of myself into this relationship. If we can talk about the uncomfortable emotions that we trigger for each other, we can work with them. If we can't acknowledge and talk about them, they could be what cause us to go in separate directions.

Celeste and I met through a mutual friend. We were both totally surprised to fall in love! I've been in many relationships with men and have two grown children. At the time we met, she was 18 months into learning a new way of life after her husband of 48 years passed. Her two children are just a few years younger than I am.

The first two years of our relationship were mostly by phone. I was not allowed into Canada because certain officers at the border did not believe I could live on so little money and thought I was trying to get into Canada to work or to live permanently, illegally, with Celeste. Because Celeste has MS and her ability to travel is limited, we spent only a few weeks together during those two years, when she came to visit me.

Hard as it was, we now see that time apart as a gift; it slowed us down, gave us time to learn more about ourselves, and helped us create a solid foundation from which to find a way through our differences. Both of us feel valued and honored, giving and receiving love with openness and honesty. And I've learned that it's safe to be me...*all* of me.

Raising Successful Children

By Millen Livis

When my daughter was born, I was clueless about how to raise a successful child. I was overly protective, trying to keep her from making mistakes. But this approach neither shielded her from adversity nor helped her become self-confident. She was shy and suffered from peer pressure and bullying. The scariest moment was her admission of suicidal thoughts.

This was quite a wake-up call for me that forced me to rethink my approach to parenting. I want my child to succeed in life, but do I always know what is best for her? I often try to protect and advise her so that she won't make mistakes, but will an overly protected child become a resilient, confident, and self-reliant adult? Most of us have learned lessons in life through trial and error, by falling and getting back up, learning from our mistakes. I decided to give my daughter an opportunity to explore, to fall, and to get back up on her own.

This approach was put to the test when she decided to quit her Ivy League college after one year because she felt that she didn't want to become a speech pathologist. In the past, I might have tried to talk her out of this decision, to "protect" her and encourage her to continue on what seemed like a safe path (and not forego the significant financial investment she'd already made!). Instead, I supported her courageous decision to be in integrity with her inner wisdom.

She eventually found her path and is now a successful child and family psychotherapist. She especially connects with children in an amazing way because she can relate to their emotions. Her most painful childhood experiences became her best credentials for helping her clients!

Through my own trials and errors at parenting, I've learned that, despite my motherly inclination to protect and the cultural pressure on pushing our children to become "stars," the most important values I can instill are self-love and the courage to be authentic and unapologetically unique. Successful young adults are not necessarily those who were protected or "saved" as children; they are those who are at peace with who they are and are able to confidently walk along their own unique path. And successful parents are those who love them unconditionally.

Soul Kiss

By Jeanette St. Germain

The morning sky was filled with pastel hues of pink, yellow, and baby blue. There was a glowing softness in the air, a cozy warmth that blanketed the rolling hills just outside my neighborhood. As my feet stepped from the hard concrete sidewalk to the parched, winter grass, my heartbeat quickened, my breath drew short. Even with the sleepy dawn stretched out like some lounging tomcat, I could feel the buzzing current underneath, an electric pulse ready to pounce at any moment.

I peered out across curving pathways and mini lakes, searching for the spirit that matched my own. My awareness expanded, and I became acutely aware of every color and sound around me. There was an insistent pull at the center of my chest, some unseen, magnetic force guiding us together.

His physical form suddenly appeared directly across from me, with only a small section of lake between us. At the same moment, our eyes met and we hurried to close the gap. It was surreal, as if time froze and all rational thought escaped us. There were no adolescent fears or human hesitations, no boundaries between our souls. All of creation felt poised, leaning in to witness something of great cosmic origin.

Before I could even think to feel shy, his arms were around me. We spun in a circle and embraced heart to heart. With a sigh he pulled back slightly, laughter sparkling in his honeyed eyes. Our gaze locked, bridging some etheric chasm, and then his lips were on mine in a deep first kiss.

It was pure joy, completely natural, a perfect fit. Waves of infinite love exploded all through us, and behind closed lids we shared visuals of spinning galaxies and engulfing flames of liquid light. We watched in awe as spiraling energies flowed from our hearts and merged into one radiant beam, encircling us in the heart of the divine.

We were only 16, suddenly thrust into a kind of soul-awakening first relationship. In the end, the intensity of it burned too deep, too bright for the understandings of this world. Even though this memory is from long ago, those moments of love shall stay with me forever.

A Mighty Grace Is Delivered
By Annie Price

I was 42 when I got pregnant with my third child. My husband and I knew that my age posed higher risk of having a Down Syndrome baby, but we accepted this possibility. Still, we were relieved when our girl, Ceara, was born without this condition. What we didn't know at the time, however, was how many moments of challenging grace had just been delivered into our lives.

For the first couple of years, she seemed fine for the most part, yet we felt a creeping doubt that something wasn't right. By the age of three, it became painfully obvious that Ceara had some delays. I didn't yet understand what this meant. I was afraid, and I couldn't find any answers.

Finally, a professional provided the diagnosis of Moderate Autism. While overwhelmed with the confirmation, it was also a strange comfort to know. There was much for us to learn in assisting Ceara.

At one of her first therapy sessions, I watched through a glass as the therapist showed her a card with picture of an eye and a pair of motioning hands. She pointed to each, saying slowly, "I want…" When she prompted Ceara to repeat these words, I got it – how pictures were going to help Ceara communicate. I went home and laminated piles of pictures.

Ceara would receive speech therapy and other therapies for several years. She wasn't going to follow the normal developmental milestones; she would hit them in her own time, in her own way. Through our experiences with Ceara, we've gained a deeper compassion and sensitivity of individual differences – many moments of grace that we wouldn't have known without her in our lives.

Now a teenager, Ceara continues to both challenge and surprise us with her ongoing development. Her biggest hurdles are understanding social cues and appropriate behavior. Even with her unique struggles, she's just one dramatic, willful, *normal* teenaged girl!

A Mother's Love

By Sharon Hickinbotham

I'm blessed with a best friend who I call Mum. From the time I was a baby, throughout my childhood, and now as an adult, I've always been able to count on her loving support and her arms around me to make me feel safe. The support she's given me has helped me to be strong and hold my faith. She's pushed me to believe in myself, follow my heart, and not to give up when times seem hard. The bond I share with my mother grows stronger with each passing year – right up to the present. The days when she rings or texts just to say "I love you" and senses that I needed a friend always bring a smile back to my face. She is my angel, and I love her to the moon and the stars.

I've always cherished this connection with my mum, and for years I've longed to share this bond with a child of my own – to be able to pass on the deep love that my mum has given to me. This part of my journey, however, has not been easy. My body has had to go through many renovations – including three laparoscopies, endosalpingiosis, and having adhesions and a tube removed due to endometriosis. I have not yet been able to conceive, but my faith remains strong.

No matter what cards are dealt to me in the future, however, I have already become a stronger person from my experiences. I have also learned an important lesson: even though being a mother would be a wonderful gift, my intuition tells me that I am to use my motherly gifts in other areas of my life – being there for my nieces and nephews and my animals (who are like my children), experiencing love in all areas of my life, enjoying the here and now, and living happily with those I love deeply. Even without being a mother myself, I can give and receive a mother's love.

Finding Joy in Minutes of Awareness

By Janet Dhaenens

Celeste and I were on the phone, as we are every morning when we aren't physically together. "I'm thinking about my next trip to see you," I told her.

"I'll run right down and open the door!"

"That's what you'll do," I said. "But what are you feeling underneath your words?"

"Excitement. Anticipation. Love. Gratitude," she responded. "What are you feeling?"

I share with her: "I love it when others want to know about my emotions, because when emotions are being shared is when I feel most alive! I feel love. I feel cared about by you. I feel nourished and grateful for the depth of our connection.

"Because your physical condition causes you to live your life at a slower pace, you invite me to slow down. I appreciate the permission this gives me to engage in self-care. Here at my home is the feeling of endless work to do! A part of me loves this familiar physical work, yet along with it is the pattern of overriding the messages my body gives me about what it needs.

"I appreciate the deep reflection and heightened awareness my time with you invites. We often trigger each other's fears, and we always find our way through the emotions that come up for both of us. As we find places of connection in our differences, I feel more deeply nourished. I feel freedom. I feel free to be me, confident that you will not judge me and leave.

"You help me see clearly how rich and full of joys and challenges my life is. I'm able to appreciate and value the challenges as much as the joys now, thanks to the safety of you being there (and not taking what I say personally) while I explore my thoughts and emotions. Your presence in my life is a priceless gift!"

Through my tears of gratitude, I hear Celeste's response: "You give me that same gift. When you share, I feel you are speaking what is in my heart if only I knew how to put it into words."

Assume the Best, and It Will Be So

By Mary Meston

Catching a peek at my phone between flights of a business trip, I was delighted to see a message from my eldest nephew. You see, I am not very close with my brother's children. The fallout from his divorce has created an ongoing challenge in his relationship with his children. He has made persistent efforts to participate in their lives, but without similar intentions on his ex-wife's part, he's been fighting an uphill battle.

My delight diminished quickly as I read the content of my nephew's message. He shared a story he wrote about his grandfather, who died when my nephew was only eight. While the story's intention was to convey the unrelenting strength of my father – a survivor of the Great Depression, a WWII and Korean War Veteran, a hardscrabble laborer, and a gentleman farmer – he cited severely incorrect facts about his character and his choices.

How could he write such things? Where did he get these ideas? I was certain his mother was influencing him yet another time to stir up the pot. With outrage, I hastily penned a terse response correcting the most disparaging and incorrect facts. Luckily, however, I was unable to send that angry text as the cabin doors closed.

I ruminated during that long flight – thinking of all the wrongs and hurt I felt for my brother, for myself, and for my family. And when I couldn't be angry anymore, a calm came over me. In that moment, I heard something say, "Open your heart to him. Your nephew is trying as best as he knows how. Assume the best, and it will be so."

I took that moment to forgive all the years of tension, strife, and misunderstandings. I reworded my response with compliments and gratitude. Without anger or judgment, I shared corrected facts and even more stories about his grandfather. That change of mind initiated an ongoing dialogue where we continue to share wonderful stories, building a family relationship I thought was never to be.

Committing to Love and Finding My Soulmate

By Viknesvari Piche Muthu

I was 29 years old and had not yet been in a relationship. I kept falling for men who were not ready to commit. Often, I found myself providing emotional support or fixing their problems.

Along my path, I connected with a Love Coach. At first, I was afraid of the financial commitment for her coaching program; however, I realised that if I desired a committed relationship, I needed to commit to myself first. I trusted my intuition and faced this obstacle by saying yes, committing to a self-love ritual, and working through limiting beliefs.

After working with these practices for a while, I felt strongly guided to connect with a man on a dating site. I found his energy very attractive, and I told myself that I had nothing to lose. From the start, I loved our connection and enjoyed spending time with him. He embodied many values that I desired in a partner.

After a while, however, we began to communicate less often. I felt really sad that I did not receive the connection that I desired, even though I knew in my heart that he was still interested in me.

My Love Coach encouraged me to continue dating. This was a big stretch for me. I slowly released the hurt and allowed my healing process to begin. I chose to let go and focus on my growth. I had fun dating other men, and my confidence as a woman grew!

Frequently, however, my thoughts and feelings returned to the man I'd connected with on the dating site. I trusted my intuition and attempted to reconnect with him. By Divine Grace, we had an amazing date on his birthday, the 25th of December! We both expressed our feelings for each other, naturally and easily. Soon, we were together and deeply in love.

I am so happy that I chose to follow my heart's voice! This man whom I love treats me like a queen. He is more than everything I have ever wanted! In his words, "Our love is eternal, undefined by terms, limitless." We are blissfully committed to each other. I am so excited to be living my life with him.

By committing to love, I found my soulmate, as well as a message of hope for others: *you, too, are meant for magnificent love!*

Sown on Rocky Ground

By Chris Anderson

Like a seed sown on rocky ground, I have struggled to navigate the terrain of my own heart. Although many aspects of my life have been thorny, I have learned to live according to my own values and cultivate a life of love and meaning. I have grown to feel safe, explore my gifts, and make peace with my shadowed past.

Post-traumatic stress disorder, depression, anxiety, self-loathing, and anger wreaked havoc on my psyche for many years before I was courageous enough to view myself through eyes of love. When I made my healing a priority, I found the courage to look deep within. What I found inside was a small child who had been brutalized, betrayed, held hostage, and forgotten.

She was locked away because I had abandoned her! She was dirty, shoeless, and in rags, and would not even look up at me. With great humility, I knelt down and reached for her. We clung to each other for hours as she sobbed, releasing her burden of pain and fear, sharing her intense loneliness. When she finally lifted her wide eyes up to mine, her lifetime of sorrow poured out of them, and my heart shattered over and over again. We held each other until all of our tears had fallen, then we opened our hearts to forgiveness…and we found peace.

Life hasn't been perfect since I've forgiven myself, my abusers, and my past; however, I now feel whole and am no longer so afraid. Self-limiting beliefs now trigger immediate self-awareness and receive compassionate correction. I have a tenderness towards myself that I didn't know I deserved, and I have found a way to love myself, shadows and all.

Grace Has No Color

By Lore Raymond

"He taught us that grace has no color."
- Marlene Owens Rankin (about her father, Olympian Jesse Owens)

Attending Judson College in Marion, Alabama, felt like running a race! There was the sprinting over two years and 10 months to secure a BA degree in Elementary Education, running a marathon through student teaching and an 18-hour course load to graduate, and dashing to complete wedding plans. The race's prize? Graduation, a wedding, and my first job as a fourth-grade teacher in Selma, Alabama.

The school of 400 African-American students remained segregated in 1974 despite the Civil Rights Movement. No academic training could have totally prepared me for teaching these 34 children. The *real classroom* wasn't only about teaching how to solve math problems – instead, students sought me to teach with a compassionate heart and soul. I felt responsible for resolving rotting, aching teeth and hungry, growling tummies.

Like a committed runner, I persevered. Sometimes cheering and even jeering could be heard from the stadium's crowd. Yet, after three years, the finish line of my first teaching job was in sight! Military orders were transferring my husband and me to upstate New York.

Arriving on the last day of school, a navy bandana covered my stringy hair and framed a makeup-free face. *Almost there…just a few more boxes*, I thought.

Then a student found me, pleading, "Miss Lore, you need to come to the teachers' lounge." Reluctantly, I put aside my packing and followed him to the lounge. There, lined up side by side like the ribbon at a finish line, were seven mothers of my students dressed in their Sunday best. The principal's wife stepped forward, explaining, "We'd like to say goodbye and thank you for loving our children as much as we do." With gratitude, each gifted me with a hug and a travel gift.

"Thank you," I blubbered before returning to packing. I realized that, on this day, these mothers had taught *me* a precious lesson: Grace has no color, nor does gratitude or love.

The Alaska Daughter

By Sophia Ellen Falke

"You must be the Alaska daughter," the elder ladies of my mother's church said as, one by one, they gently reached out and touched my arm. It was my mother's funeral service. I was "the Alaska daughter" because two years earlier I had taken my mother on a 10,000-mile camping adventure from my home in Tucson, Arizona, to the Arctic Circle north of Fairbanks, Alaska.

It was 1989, and at 75, it was Mom's first camping trip. I almost didn't invite her, wondering if she would be comfortable on a 2½-month trek with few of the amenities of home. I was driving my ¾-ton pickup with a self-contained camper in the truck bed – complete with a three-burner stove, a small refrigerator, heat, comfortable beds, and, most importantly, a toilet and large water tank. But would that be enough?

At first, Mom was nervous. Early in our trip, she asked that we leave a campground before settling in because she didn't feel "right" there. It meant driving two more hours to another camping area, but I happily did so because I had promised Mom we would leave any place where she didn't feel safe, no questions asked. As we continued to explore the amazing wonders of the western United States and Canada, however, she started looking for more rustic campsites – remote places where the sky was clear and the stars would come down to greet us each night.

We followed in the steps of ancient people; walked on glaciers thousands of years old; looked in the eyes of aging totems; fished for salmon on the Kenai Peninsula; met caribou, moose, badgers, and bears; and beheld beauty that took our breath away. During one particularly grace-filled moment, we stood on a bridge 100 miles north of Fairbanks and watched a brilliant, shimmering sun sink over the western horizon, setting the Yukon River on fire with reflected yellows and reds.

For all the beautiful moments of the trip, however, the most important part was sharing our love and joy of being together and creating beautiful memories to last a lifetime. For Mom, that lifetime was two more years. For me, the memories still live in my heart.

Chapter 7
Earth Angels

M any of us have had the pleasure of meeting someone who embodied grace, who emanated joy and love, and who had goodness just oozing out of them. Sometimes this person showed up as an answer to our prayers, and other times they seemed to appear out of nowhere. They always know just what to say and do to help us, and our life is positively transformed from their being part of it.

We call these people Earth Angels. They are the people who seem to leave a trail of happiness wherever they go, and they definitely make our world much brighter and more loving. It's almost like they have one foot here on Earth and the other in Heaven. We believe that these special souls are helping to change the world – one grace-filled moment at a time. Earth Angels are the types of people who pay for the upcoming person's order at the drive thru, who donate anonymously to a special cause, and who leave a note in the bathroom stall that inspires rather than deflates. (Jodi just read a note such as this the other day that said, "You are absolutely wonderful, and you deserve everything in life.") Earth Angels are the human embodiment of grace.

You'll know when you've met an Earth Angel because you'll instantly feel lighter, happier, and more open to life. You may find yourself in awe and grinning from ear to ear after being around one. It doesn't matter if they help you in a small way or a huge way – the impact is always the same: you feel loved, seen, and appreciated.

In this chapter, we are thrilled to introduce you to many of these angels. As you'll see, they come from all walks of life and offer grace in all types of experiences, but one thing that they all have in common is their ability to lift others and to help them expand in some way. We hope you'll feel uplifted after reading these pieces. We sure have been!

The Angel in My Living Room

By Maria T. Rothenburger

The vacuum cleaner glided quickly over the kitchen floor as I pondered the next task I would have to do. Dishes, laundry, mopping, toilets; I had a thousand things on my list and only a bit of time in which to get it all done.

That's when the pesky thoughts started: *You can't finish it all. And you know what? You can't ever finish things, never mind finish them on time. You can't do enough, be enough, or accomplish enough, and you're fooling yourself if you think you can.*

I continued to beat myself up: *You only think you're a good mom. Look at your son over there — you've got him distracted on a tablet so you can "get stuff done." How sad. Your clients are only marginally helped, and you're an average wife at best. You can barely put together a decent meal most of the time. Shall I go on?*

I nearly brought myself to tears with my self-professed mediocrity.

I was already plenty annoyed when I heard the familiar, "Mom?" coming from the living room. What could he possibly need now? He isn't hungry again already, is he? Sheesh!

"What, babe," I said in my best I'm-trying-to-keep-it-cool voice.

He barely looked up and said, "You know I love you, right? Like, forever?"

The vacuum stopped moving. I couldn't help but be shocked by the exquisite contrast to my self-deprecating thoughts.

I was loved no matter what.

I was concerned about laundry, but there was an angel sitting in my living room reminding me that getting things done didn't matter.

"I love you too, babe. Like, forever."

Gray-Haired Grace

By Lisa Miles Brady

"Oh my goodness, I *love* your hair!" I exclaimed as I wheeled my cart into the ethnic-food aisle. I blurted it out so quickly that I actually startled the woman parked in front of the taco shells.

"Why, thank you!" she smiled back, putting her hands on her gloriously gray bob cut, as if to make sure it was all there. Then she came close and whispered, "It's a wig. I'm going through chemo."

Without missing a beat, I gave her a hug and said, "Well, angel, you make cancer look good." We both laughed at the absurdity that the fight for her very life could be so easily camouflaged with bronzer and a good hairpiece.

"I've been through four rounds. None of them worked. I'm starting a clinical trial soon."

"I'm sorry. How have you tolerated the treatments?"

She spoke about losing her hair and the irony of getting excited to see once-dreaded chin and lip hair again. She lifted her hair slightly to show me her eyelashes and eyebrows with all the pride of a new mother showing off pictures of her first-born child.

"I have pancreatic cancer." We stood there in silence, looking into each other's eyes. In that silence, we honored the gravity of the diagnosis. Without another word, she knew I understood that this clinical trial was her last hope.

I didn't flinch. I didn't say it would be okay, because I really didn't know. Instead, I held her gaze and asked her name.

She seemed relieved. "Lois," she replied.

"I'll be thinking of you, Lois."

She touched my arm and smiled as we parted. She'd been Seen. Held. Heard. Loved. Her touch conveyed just how much that meant to us both. As I continued down the aisle, I held back tears, reveling in the gift I'd just been given. Lois taught me that we can choose to *be* the grace we wish to see in the world, even while doing mundane things, like grocery shopping. We grant grace in the moments we recognize someone else's humanity. Or their beautiful gray hair.

Pizza Night

By Monica Laws

I have an angel in my life – a guardian angel. She is my sister, and she has been an angel and an amazing support, help, and friend throughout the years.

In November of 2003, she invited me to Pizza Night.

The ladies drink some wine; eat appetizers; and talk about life, love, family, work, health, sex, children, and everything under the sun without holding back.

We aren't pizza connoisseurs. We do take pictures with the pizza-delivery dude. We take pictures of ourselves and keep memories by writing in a journal. Beyond that, I believe the real point is that "It's not about the pizza!" It's about sharing together. We always call our Christmas get-together a "love fest." It's about our connection and our unconditional love and support for each other.

The girls welcomed me that first night with open arms. Reeling with pain from a recent separation, they provided love and support and included me for the next time! There are now seven "Pizza Girls." No more members, although we do occasionally have special guest stars. It is so very special to be a Pizza Girl. We have had people ask to join, but membership is closed. It is a close-knit group that is 100% committed to seeing each other at least every few months, no matter what. We make sure to schedule it ahead of time and prioritize this time together.

Many years after my first Pizza Night, I look back on everything we have gone through together. I am so grateful. I am so happy. I am so blessed. I know that it is rare to have this kind of a group with this kind of a bond. Thanks to my Angel Sister, Silver, for inviting me that November night. And thanks to all of the Pizza Girls for welcoming me with open arms that night and always having my back.

In 2003, everything changed. Who I am today is so much more than who I was then. I am happier. I am more confident. I feel beautiful. I am a goddess. I am a Pizza Girl.

The Miracle of Olivia

By TaraLynn Majeska

I stood there, seven months pregnant, in the dark quiet of the hospital corridor, staring at the suddenly illuminated plaque that captured my attention as I was strolling by. Could it really be true?

Quickly, I scanned back to the year of our baby Olivia's life and death. She had spent a lot of time up here. Oxygen tanks sustained her breathing, and a multitudinous medical staff compassionately attended to her needs. Through it all, I held the vision of a book with her picture on the cover titled, *The Miracle of Olivia*, as well as the hope that it would proclaim her miraculous healing. Instead, I had to face the heartbreaking reality of her death and let her go into the arms of God.

Thoughtfully, her nurses commissioned Brother Bartholomew, a cancer patient, to create a wood-inlay plaque in her honor. When it was presented to me, I didn't understand why there were three children in the picture when it was meant for one, but I was grateful for the beautiful remembrance. Sadly, the artist died two months after Olivia.

Now here I was, examining it with a whole new awareness. One of the girls with a scarf around her head had to be Olivia. She gazed up at the sky, holding a heart in one hand and the handle of a wagon in the other. The second girl, with long brown hair, resembled Hannah, my two-year-old daughter. She helped Olivia hold the wagon handle, and grasped a wooden staff in her other hand as she glanced back at the small boy riding happily in the wagon. I had just found out that the baby I was carrying was a boy, Benjamin.

So there it was, the presence of my three children – two known long before their arrival, their physical features and personalities emanating through this prophetic image. God's message was pure grace: that I would have more children who would be healthy. This was a source of profound comfort, love, acceptance, and inspiration that helped me move forward, knowing that everything was going to be okay.

In the Wink of an Eye

By Marian Cerdeira

Feeling rushed and frazzled during the busy holiday season, I walked into a convenience store with clear intentions: get in, make a purchase, and get out...quickly!

As I hurriedly searched the aisles, I passed a woman and, for an instant, our eyes met. There was something in her eyes, but I missed her "message" until we met at the checkout counter.

As I paid for my purchase, my wallet opened upside down, and its entire contents of change flew out everywhere! I looked down in shock. Then I noticed the woman behind me picking it up and smiling. As I apologized, she calmingly assured me that it was no problem to help me. Another gentleman reached down, picked up more of my change, and gently handed it to me. As I thanked him, again all I could feel was an undeniable kindness.

I finished my purchase and turned around to the lovely woman with the beautiful smile and thanked her. I said, "I hope you receive a blessing today."

She looked at me and said, without hesitation, "I already did: I woke up!" I looked directly into her eyes this time and explained to her that I realized I was meant to meet her that day, to hear her words, and to receive the "gift" she shared with me. She looked at me, smiled once again, and winked.

I could feel her angelic presence, her love and compassion, fill the physical space we stood in and touch my soul. In that short, beautiful interval of time, I was reminded that love and deep compassion are everywhere.

Snow Angels

By Karen L. Wythe

Shortly after moving into student housing at Houghton College in West Seneca, New York, a lake-effect snow blanketed the area. *A good day to stay in*, I thought. However, I had just found out that the only way to get my phone turned on was to venture to the phone company's office in Hamburg. (This was before cell phones and the internet.)

Bundling myself up, I got into my white Volkswagen camper van and started out – frequently having to scrape my windows on the inside from the frost that built up. (Volkswagens just weren't made for Western New York's cold weather). I was traveling along what looked like country roads, surrounded by fields of white, when I noticed a big snow plow barreling along behind me. Already stressed over having to scrape the windows, I thought, *Please let me get far enough ahead so I don't get plowed into.*

Quickly scraping and hurrying down the road, I turned onto an unplowed road, thinking that I had driven out of harm's way. As the snow began to come down harder, however, I felt my tires spin out of my control. I was being sucked off the road! While I prayed, "Please help me," I landed in a very deep ditch.

I continued to pray, shifting my plea to: "Please get me out of here!" I hadn't even finished praying when a guy came up to the side window. "Don't worry, little lady, we'll get you out." Then I heard more men talking, and before I knew what happened, these three "snow angels" in their tow truck pulled me out. I hadn't been in that ditch for more than three minutes before I was rescued! Thanking them and God, I was happily and safely on my way.

A Miraculous Phone Call

By Linda Graziano

I have bipolar disorder and have experienced great depths of depression. On one such day in 1998, I felt myself heading into a downward spiral – crying and thinking very negative thoughts about myself – when the telephone rang. It was MaryAnn, my best friend from high school, who I hadn't talked to in about a year. After saying hello, I immediately began to feel paranoia. "Who told you to call me?" I asked.

"No one," she replied. It took some convincing until I truly believed that she called me on her own. After that, I started crying and told her I was very depressed again. She recommended a really good book: *Conversations with God* by Neale Donald Walsch. "It will change how you think about things," she said.

I thought, *Hmmm…the title doesn't sound very appealing.* But then I realized that no one told her to call me at that moment, and it occurred to me that this could be a "God" moment. I also remembered that I kept passing a sign at a church that read, "There is no such thing as coincidence. It is God working anonymously."

That call changed my life! I was in a serious depression when the phone rang, and by the time I hung up, I was rejoicing in life's miracles!

I bought the book, and it changed the way I looked at life. It began my personal-growth reading journey that keeps my bookshelves full!

My bipolar disorder is not cured, but I have discovered what keeps me well. In addition to medication, I connect to my inner self/soul. I also find joy through my work as a life coach, helping others connect with their heart and soul. It continues to be an amazing journey, and it all started with one phone call.

Waking Up to Humanity

By Bianca Lynn

September 11, 2001.

I arrived at my office at 8 a.m. The morning was beautiful, the sky was blue, the air was comfortably warm, and there was a slight breeze. Shortly after I arrived, I noticed a strange odor. My windows faced south, looking over two buildings in lower Manhattan. Above them floated streams of computer paper and bits of debris. I couldn't make sense of it. *A popped incinerator on a building,* I thought. *What else could it be?*

Over the next hours, the world and I learned what it was.

It was a hard day to live through, as was the aftermath in a world turned upside down with uncertainty, fear, and pain. But you already know that story. What I want to share is the other side of it – the beauty that emerged from the ashes of a horrific act.

That day and in the following weeks, people who usually ignored or competed with each other helped each other. People reached out to everyone they loved or had once loved to ensure they were okay. People spoke to strangers on the subway genuinely, admitting to being wounded and raw. People stood at an intersection holding up signs of support for workers heading downtown to repair utility lines. For months, news stories of kindness emerged.

In October, we were allowed back to our office. Lower Manhattan was a war zone, and the fires continued to burn in the Trade Center site, making it hard to breathe. Yet what I remember most was that people were a little kinder. The streets and buildings were brighter. They had more sunlight hitting them because the towers were gone.

I wouldn't want to live through that day again. It is a day that continues to define many lives of those who are still suffering. Yet, with all of that, it was also a day that allowed us to experience our full humanity and that woke us up to our own magnificence, compassion, and grace.

Gratitude at Glendalough

By Karrol Rikka S. Altarejos

My excitement was laced with anticipation. I was a mere three days away from my first trip abroad without friends or family. Becoming slightly obsessed with the idea of "being prepared," I created list upon list. With all the plans I was making, you'd think I was *moving* to Ireland instead of spending just a week there. Throughout all of my running around, I ignored the pain that had begun to manifest in my ankle, attributing it to minor physical fatigue.

The day arrived and, determined to have an adventure, I waved goodbye to my parents who had come to send me off. I boarded the plane with a slight limp in my step. By the end of the flight, my left shoe felt tighter. My ankle continued to swell, and my discomfort magnified with each passing hour.

That evening in my hotel room, armed with aspirin, ice, and pillows to elevate my leg, I prayed and performed Reiki, hoping for a miracle. The next morning, the improvement that I wished for had not come. I couldn't put any weight on my ankle without feeling excruciating pain. Worries and fears flooded in as the possibility that my journey would be cut short became more and more of a reality.

With careful, purposeful steps, I hobbled along the wooden walkway, occasionally leaning on the shillelagh gifted to me for support. I looked out beyond the precipice and took in the view of the valley. The sights; sounds; and crisp, fresh air at Glendalough were more beautiful than I had ever imagined. Tears rolled down my cheeks as I felt overcome by waves of gratitude.

In the days following my injury, I was assisted by guardian angels in the form of tour companions – the doctor who taught me how to wrap my ankle, the constant care of newly made friends, and the tour guide who assured my safety – who became my trip's saving grace.

The Gift of Kindness
By Shelley Lundquist

Out on our evening stroll, my partner, Sean, and I took a detour to the store just as they were closing up. We quickly collected what we needed and headed to the checkout.

As we approached, the cashier informed the woman in front of us that her card had been declined. Visibly embarrassed, the woman asked if she could run to the bank a few doors over to see how much money she had left in the account. With a shake of her head, the impatient cashier told the woman the doors were already locked as the store was closing.

Rattled, the woman started sorting through her items to see what she could put back. "You're holding up the line, ma'am," she was reminded, as if that somehow helped.

"That's alright, Mama. I don't need any juice or cookies," came unexpectedly from the little girl beside her who was clearly up past her bedtime. "Let's put those back." The woman's eyes teared up, as did mine.

I checked the register. Her bill totaled $74.36. I looked to Sean, who nodded without reservation. How blessed I am to have a partner who is such a kindred spirit!

"That's okay, sweetheart. You don't have to put anything back," I told her. "We're happy to help."

I'm not sure who was more shocked – the woman or the cashier. (We had to tell the cashier three times before she seemed to understand that we were serious.)

At first the woman objected, then she allowed herself to accept the gift. "I'll pay you back, I promise," she stammered. "Thank you so much!"

"No need for that," I told her. "Just pay it forward and help someone else when you can."

The little girl was smiling from ear to ear as she waved goodbye. And so was I on the walk home.

Giving is always as much a gift to the giver as it is to the recipient.

On the Night Train

By Christine Schwarzer

He was a stranger on the night train. I was traveling from Hamburg to Freiburg on a beautiful Friday night. I had taken an empty seat in an empty cabin. The curtains were already shut by the previous passengers, and I made myself comfortable, expecting a calm and quiet night of snoozing and perhaps dreaming. But then he appeared.

"But *she's* there!" he screamed to the conductor. My face must have shown my lack of enthusiasm for having my oh-so-quiet little sanctuary invaded by anyone, especially a drunken stranger. "Oh, God," I thought. "This is exactly what I need right now!"

The conductor had apparently directed him to the seat next to me. So again, the man entered the cabin, this time with his wife and four children.

In time, the four children were all sleeping on the floor, next to our feet. I noticed that they were more serious and quiet than usual children, yet they seemed to be content. The family that I had judged so harshly were refugees from Afghanistan. The man and I communicated with gestures, broken English, and a lot of appreciation for each other. With simple words, we tried to connect our very different worlds.

This family was so loving and peaceful – to each other, to their children, to me, and to the young woman from Australia who later entered the cabin. It was so bizarre how peaceful they all were, given all the war, trauma, and pain they must have endured. Their graceful presence manifested in every little thing they did and the way they lovingly touched their children.

That night, this family from Afghanistan gifted us simply with their presence – two rich, young women from the "modern" world, who seemingly had everything. It was then I realized we had nothing in comparison. Despite all our wealth, we were poverty-stricken. Clinging to our mobile phones because our society is so afraid of genuine human connection, of community, of love. Acting out of fear because we are so afraid to love. That night, I learned to accept my friend's offer: his presence, his care, his love for a stranger, and his grace.

Grace in Drops of Water

By Marihet Hammann

It is just after sunrise in Pretoria, South Africa – another hot, sunny, mid-summer day. The streets are abuzz with commuters – myself among them – finding our way to work. I tune in to my favorite radio station, looking forward to hearing the usually quirky host who keeps me company during my daily journeys.

This morning, however, the host's mood is different. I feel urgency and sense distress as I hear the announcement: "Today, we launched an initiative to transport and donate water to Lichtenburg – an area that has been severely affected by the recent drought. At the moment, the situation is so dire that people are fighting about water in parts of South Africa. We are doing a call-out to all of you, our listeners."

I am touched by the announcement and say a silent prayer for those affected by something as basic as a drop of water. *There, I've done my good deed for the day. I've responded to the call. All is well.* With these thoughts, I reach my destination and turn off the radio.

That is, until I get into my car at sunset for my commute back home and what I hear changes my life forever. The radio station is experiencing a crisis: people are continuing to drop off water, and there is not enough space to store it all. This is quickly sorted, but then a bigger crisis arises. The three trucks being loaded will not be able to deliver all the water. The host announces: "Listeners, we need more trucks and no more water."

The situation appears surreal. In the process of me trying to make sense and gather my thoughts, it hits me: Isn't this a profound witnessing of a nation paying it forward? People from all walks of life in South Africa are in harmony, paying it forward by collaboratively dropping off 2.5 *million* liters of water.

This is a moment of grace…in each drop of water.

Meeting Adaline

By Ana Gordon

Just when you least expect it, the world has an astounding capacity to transcend the ordinary. For me, meeting Adaline, "Star Child," was one of those moments.

On a cool, blustery day, I put on my blue parka and went for a stroll with my husband. Glad for the fresh air and to be connecting with David, we walked to our local park.

Then I met Adaline.

We were passing the playground area, when all of sudden this little yippy pup comes bounding under the fence around the swing sets, making a beeline for me. Within seconds, I found myself patting his tummy, wondering who this being could be – full of such unreserved exuberance, unbounded joy, and recognition.

As I stood up, I saw a toddler, about 18 months old, climbing over the lower rung on the fence determined to reach me. She kept gazing at me intently, as she made her way with arms outstretched for me to pick her up. I glanced at her mom for the okay to pick up her child, recognizing how keen Adaline was to get into my arms and connect.

As I held her, I experienced what was probably the most telepathic exchange I have ever had. I felt a connection that filled my heart with awe, wonder, and delightful appreciation for the Divine in action in my life. Upon hearing her name, "Adaline," spoken, I felt a deep recollection well up in my being, simply hearing the resonance of it.

Such a gifted one, the name that came to me was "Star Child." Perhaps she was the first in a wave of advanced souls, messengers for those who care to see.

So I held Adaline and listened to all she had to "say" for quite some time – probably 20 minutes in actual time, yet one of those transcendent encounters where time seems to fall away.

It heartens me to have met Adaline, a most-needed sign of grace for me – deepening my intuitive capacity and allowing me to relax with all that occurs in wonder.

The Eyes of Grace

By Faye Rogers

In 2011, I was a guest speaker at the Holistic Happy Horse Day in Christchurch, New Zealand. I was there to talk about Animal Communication and Animal Healing. Many of the people attending the event were feeling vulnerable and fearful due to the earthquakes that had hit the city a month earlier. Many attendees had lost jobs, homes, and amenities, and were facing the unknown. Some of them had also lost family, friends, and animal companions when the city fell.

One couple bought their eight-year-old daughter, Grace, especially to meet me. Grace is wheelchair bound, severely handicapped, and unable to speak. But as I gazed into her beautiful eyes, our souls connected and all I could sense was completeness and love.

As we connected, I could feel her communicating with me in a way that transcended speech or words. She shared that she is the Universe whilst walking the physical plane of reality. She shared profound insights about fear and love. She shared that she personally did not experience fear, and she hoped that one day the whole planet would ascend and live beyond fear. Her dream was that the world would only live with beauty, love, and respect.

Grace shared that her purpose is to be a teacher of love. She wants others to learn how to embrace a deeper love for themselves and for others. Her message was of exploring our own beauty, as she explores her own beauty. She wants all of us to be greatly touched by others, just as she is greatly touched by others – to be in touch with the Greater Universe, just as she is in touch with the Greater Universe.

Love was woven through all that she shared – the truth that love is the key to everything, that *we are love*. As a child of the world and the Greater Universe, she only knows how to live with completeness and love.

Grace may be a child who is physically challenged, but she is a child who feels all and sees all. She IS Love...and GRACE.

My Awakening Miracle

By Maya Demri

The journey to my higher self began with a desire to heal from my painful past, but it really blossomed thanks to the Oneness teachings. These teachings have brought powerful transformation and healing into all levels of my life. As I discovered my soul's inner strength and my ability to stay connected to it and to the divine, it became possible for me to heal from anorexia, abuse, and suicidal thoughts.

The Oneness movement originated in India by Sri Bhagavan and Sri Amma, who are considered to be living avatars. Together, they founded the Oneness University in India, where thousands of people from all over the world come to study the Oneness teachings, which inspire people to become aware and to find bliss. Many of the teachings involve meditations that use the image of a golden ball that radiates within oneself until it expands all over the universe. That golden ball is ONENESS, an image Amma and Bhagavan envisioned when they were kids, which they later understood as the powerful light that connects all beings.

My own discovery of Oneness started as a part of my human will to survive deep emotional, mental, and spiritual suffering. Born into a dysfunctional family, I survived nine years of incest, as well as verbal and emotional abuse throughout my childhood and into young adulthood. My pain led me to anorexia, cutting, and suicidal tendencies – but it also led me on a spiritual pilgrimage, as I looked for something or someone to save me from my pain.

I went to workshops and speaking events until I connected with the woman who holds the Oneness meditations in New York. She invited me to her Oneness meditation circle, and I was hooked! The Oneness circle and the blessing (called *deeksha*, which blessing-givers send through connection with divine to others) is incredibly healing for the body and mind. It's a process of awakening and rewiring the brain from unhealthy coping mechanisms to healthy ones.

For me, finding these teachings was a moment of grace that led to many more. I can say without a doubt that Oneness saved my life.

Grace Walked In

By Jody Wootton

I grew up feeling like I was "10 feet tall and bullet proof," as the old cliché goes. There was no challenge I couldn't face, no obstacle I couldn't overcome, and no place I wouldn't go in order fill my life with adventure. It wasn't until I really experienced grace in my life that I changed my thinking of how this world really works.

I've experienced several spiritual shifts in my life, but the one that really stands out is when my son was born. This was truly a moment of grace. It was a long labor, which kept me in the hospital for several days. I was so grateful that he was finally born, but I soon realized that he would not eat. We thought that we asked all the right questions to all the right people, but we had no luck. He was losing weight each day – precious ounces for a baby so young and fragile.

On the third day, grace walked into the room in the form of a maternity nurse. She said, "Let's do what we've got to do." Without a moment of hesitation, she put together a syringe and catheter tube, filled the syringe with life-giving milk, and placed the tube into my son's mouth. Ever so gently, measuring each drop, she filled my son's belly. It worked! Finally, his hunger pains were satisfied.

I never felt so much peace and loving care from a complete stranger. She was truly a saving grace to me, to my son, and to my family.

In this moment of healing, I once again felt like I was 10 feet tall! And although I now realize that I'm not actually bullet proof, I do know that I am always surrounded by grace.

Rocky Road with a Topping of Grace

By Saira Priest

"A new smoothie shop opened down the street!" I told Bill, my mentor. He had never heard of a smoothie before, and I was excited to show him. Along the way, a tall homeless man with foggy eyes asked me for money – "for ice cream," he said. Bill, a successful corporate executive, carried on his usual expedient gait towards our intended goal.

"You want ice cream?" I asked, driven by a deep desire to be of service, but too busy at work to do much else. With money, I hesitated; but ice cream I could do!

Torn between wanting to introduce a new treat and helping the tall man, I shouted at Bill, asking if he would mind having ice cream instead. His constant thoughts of negotiating future deals interrupted, he simply shrugged. The tall man, too, was surprised that someone was actually taking him to the shop.

Though an understandable fear of danger arose, I chose to stay with safe thoughts of love and compassion. "Come on!" I waved enthusiastically, as if to two old buddies.

While we waited in the long line and considered our choices, the man known as "Spirit," who was unaccustomed to attention, carried on a scrambled narrative of his journey on the rocky road of life. I was able to make out some grief over the loss of his mother and sister.

"Are they not with you still, watching over you, *Spirit?*" I asked, reminding him of his namesake.

While we sat to savor our summer sweets, we dove deep into that silent place where only souls can meet. Satisfied with the tasty treat, Spirit's once-glazed mocha eyes shone brightly as he looked into mine. "We really talked here today, didn't we?" he asked with his speech now crystal clear. I nodded a smile. We both stood up and hugged.

Leaving the shop, Bill finally spoke. "There are a lot of panhandlers on the streets."

Grace quietly spoke through me, "There's a lot of pain to be handled on the streets." And, thanks to ever-present grace, there is a little less pain to be handled on the street today.

A Mother Named Grace

By Gretchen Oehler Hogg

It is so much easier to embrace our most cherished blessings if we have at least one role model who sets the tone for our life. My mother, Grace, gifted me with this divine blessing. She had a heart-warming spirit and wisdom that radiated unconditional love, which rippled out to so many others.

After her death, I realized not only her profound impact on my life but also the powerful life lessons discovered in the deep chasm of loss. I had to cross a great divide to arrive at a place where I could see that her death has been my greatest spiritual gift in life.

I think of my mother as the very essence embodied in the expression of being in the "State of Grace." As Pope Francis has said, "Grace is not part of consciousness; it is the amount of light in our souls, not knowledge nor reason." My mother personified the essence of this definition. She was the compassionate, listening ear and collective mother figure for everyone. She shared pearls of wisdom, endearing smiles, and warm-hearted hugs.

Each of us experiences life lessons about love and spirituality. Oftentimes, however, it's often not until we reach a certain age, achieve significant milestones, or experience dramatic loss, that we're able to recognize these lessons. Sometimes it's at those major turning points, such as becoming parents or losing a parent, where we garner a deeper understanding and truth about love.

The State of Grace I learned from my mother is the essence I strive to emulate in all my roles – personally, as a mother, grandmother, wife, sister, and friend, and professionally, as a Soul Coach®, energy healer, and light-worker. Like my mother, I guide and support people who are on journeys of self-discovery and transformation, guiding them to embrace their deeper truths and life lessons for their soul growth. As Wayne Dyer says, "If there is truth in that we choose our soul families and tribes, I chose so perfectly for my lifetime lessons." I am blessed to have had a perfect role model. Thank you, Grace.

What Being in Circle Means

By Janet Dhaenens

The first day of our in-person training, I totally screwed up in my effort to facilitate the circle. Later, I realized I had gone into that interaction feeling like I was wrong, so it's no wonder I didn't do well. At the time, though, I just felt bad. Other members of the circle shared how they felt, and I sat with how uncomfortable I was. No one else was judging me. I was the one judging me!

By the end of our circle time, I felt better. It was the end of the day; as others were gathering their things and leaving the room, I found myself in tears again. My roommate saw me; when she realized I needed support, she called several others to join her. They stood in a circle around me, accepting my emotion.

I realized what happened. While I was in circle, I was able to receive the acceptance others had for the part of me that makes mistakes and can't figure everything out. But I was usually so rejecting of that part that once the circle time ended, I couldn't hold the acceptance and went back into self-criticism. I shared this realization with my new friends, and after a few minutes, I stopped crying. They invited me to join them for dinner, and I welcomed the company. I felt myself readjusting to this new feeling of acceptance.

This was the beginning of huge changes inside me through leading and participating in circles. Sitting with others, when each person shares how they feel, creates a deep connection I always believed was possible and now experience often. When I feel others accepting and valuing me, it's easier to feel that way about myself.

I've found the most valuable part of circle work for me is hearing how others feel when they witness me "falling apart." That feedback helps because I realize I'm not alone in my fears, my harsh self-judgment, or my struggle and desire to be different. Sharing my experience with honest, truthful people, who also want more self-acceptance, is continuing to change my life.

Anything Is Possible, According to Susan

By Tanya Levy

I could hear myself arguing with the emergency-room doctor as he told me it was not a viable pregnancy. I kept saying, "But I don't have any pain like last time." It was 2 a.m. My obstetrician happened to be on call, and she came down to see me. She told me later that from the time she talked to me until she walked to the chart she decided not to give me the medication that would have ended the pregnancy. Something stopped her. I convinced the doctors to give me one more ultrasound.

I went to my hospital room to wait. Through the curtain, my roommate, Susan, started talking to me. She asked me if I thought for sure I had lost the baby. She told me that she'd had several losses and then had a special procedure and went on to have four children. Then she said the words that really stuck with me: "Tanya, anything is possible." The nurses kept coming in to check on me, but it was Susan who talked to me all night long. I couldn't see her through the hospital curtain, but her voice was that of an angel.

The next morning, ladies from my prayer group showed up. They prayed with me and one of them said, "I have a feeling that your baby is okay." Just then, the technician showed up to wheel me down to the ultrasound room. They wired me up, and I heard it, as loud as a cymbal – my baby's heartbeat: "Ba-boom, ba-boom, ba-boom." When I got back to my room, the church ladies and Susan cheered.

For the rest of my pregnancy, on my mirror were the words, "Anything is possible, according to Susan." And it is. Grace came to me that night in the form of Susan, whose faith got me through my darkest hour.

My miracle baby is now a six-foot-tall teenager who reminds me every day that anything is possible.

The Knowing
By Lisa "The Link" Rizzo

There have been so many moments in my life when I felt the presence of grace. I remember one time when I was very young, I was sitting on an upstairs porch, singing my heart out to the sky. It was a rainy day, but I was enjoying being in the company of my spirit guides. When I looked down at the street, there were about seven or eight people standing in the rain listening to me sing. I immediately stopped singing, but they asked me to continue…so I did!

My guides shared with me the deep significance of that experience: it only takes one moment to change someone's day…or even their entire life! From that day forward, I've known that a single act of kindness goes a long way. In that moment on the porch, not only did I experience the joy of singing – for myself, my guides, and also my audience on the street – but I also enjoyed the kindness of the people who asked me to continue. Thanks to their praise and encouragement, I felt a great warmth run through me, which I still feel today when I recall the scene.

These days, I often get asked why I feel the need to help others – especially those who couldn't care less about what I'm trying to do for them. "Why do you waste your time and energy with people who have hurt you so much and continue to use you for their own purposes?" people ask.

When I hear such questions, I often remember that moment of singing on the porch, recalling the warmth I felt, and knowing how much difference a single moment of kindness can make. Now, as a medium, I'm able to offer help on a deeper level, giving others a look at something beyond this earthly plane. I'm also equipped with a "Knowing" – my guides tell me who I should work on the most, and they also tell me when it's time to let go and move on. With this Knowing, my soul is at peace, resting in faith that I am helping when I can, sharing what I am called to share, and doing what God intended.

Reclaiming My Inner-Child Warrior
By Lisa McDonald

I was 40 years old when I found myself plunged into the abyss. My marriage reached its breaking point, and I was catapulted into a cross-Canada relocation with my two young children, then aged three years and 18 months, respectively.

In spite of the challenges I faced with this new reality, I never lost sight of the blessings and the privilege it truly was to remain a fully-focused, stay-at-home mum. I will be eternally grateful for the precious gift of time I was afforded, which allowed me to raise my sweet children, albeit on my own.

As my youngest child approached school age, however, I knew I would soon be expected to return to work. I had maintained contact with colleagues from my previous vocation and knew that a position would have been graciously extended to me. Despite the allure of security, I fundamentally believed – with every fibre of my being – that returning to my old job was not a viable option for me.

As crunch-time crept up closer and closer, I searched my soul for a new game plan that could financially sustain my children and me, allow me to remain fully accessible to them, and honour myself. I knew that I had a choice: I could allow fear to guide me backwards, or I could move forward into the unknown. I asked myself what kind of legacy I wanted to leave for my children, and the answer became clear. Tapping into my inner warrior and a child-like spirit, I decided to pursue my dream of writing children's books.

As I moved forward with this passion, I was blessed with help from every side – including a wonderful publicist, mentors, illustrators, and numerous speaking invitations – helping me enjoy tremendous success and the ability to share my work on a larger scale than I had once thought possible. Now, as I move forward to my next adventure – writing transformational/personal-development books for adults – I feel immense gratitude for everyone who has supported me throughout my journey, including my children (who have remained my "true north") as well as my own inner child and inner warrior, who remind me of what's possible when we choose to move beyond fear and live passionately.

Pregnancy and Rebirth

By Jovon Renee

When I was a little girl, there were nights when I would lie in bed sobbing, crying out to God: "Why is this happening to us? What did we do to deserve this? Please make it stop!" I would hide under my blanket, trying not to listen to the screams, the threats, and the sound of our things breaking. I lived in fear, scared to death that one day my mom and I would lose our lives by the hands of this monster.

It wasn't safe to be me, so I hid behind a false façade and became somebody I was not. I quieted my voice and my truth because I believed I was worthless. My light dimmed, my hope diminished, and the free-spirited little girl inside me died a little bit every day. I felt powerless.

As an adult, I dreamed of breaking this cycle by becoming a mother and providing my child with what I didn't have: a safe, loving home. This dream was so strong that I never gave up on it, even when I was unable to conceive a child. I sought out fertility treatments, but the option presented by my doctor didn't feel right to me. "How is my body supposed to produce its own hormones if I'm taking them?" I asked my doctor.

"It's not," he replied. "You'll *always* have to take them."

I again felt powerless. This wasn't what I wanted, but what was the alternative? Do I accept what I'm being told, or do I listen to what feels right to me and take matters into my own hands?

I chose to take back my power. Through a series of synchronicities, I was divinely guided to use Traditional Chinese Medicine and visualization. One morning months later, I woke my husband out of a deep slumber to share the news with him: "I'm pregnant!"

Even when my son was a just a desire in my heart, I felt him guiding me back to myself. Intuitively, I heard him say, "Momma, I have come to remind you of who you are: a powerful creator!"

Through the process of conceiving and giving birth, I also rediscovered my voice, my truth, and my worth. I broke the shackles that had been holding me back. No longer was I powerless, nor was I ever. I had been reborn, and a whole new world opened up for me!

The Question That Changed Everything

By Suzie Welstead

I've had two big turning points in my life. The first one was when I ran away from home at the age of 17. The next one was triggered by a suggestion from a counsellor at my son's school.

For years, I never addressed my emotions. I just shoved them down and got on with my life. There were a few times when I did try to open up to others, but it was never well received, so I bottled up even more. What I didn't realise was that keeping my feelings inside and not addressing them wasn't healthy. It was also keeping me stuck.

One day, I went to help out at an event at my son's school. While clearing up afterward, I had a conversation with the school counsellor, who asked me something that left me no choice but to deal with what was going on inside me: "You don't like yourself very much, do you?"

This question released years' worth of pent-up feelings. I immediately started crying. I knew that I had to change something in my life, but I wasn't sure what. The counsellor suggested that I become a life coach, but I didn't feel ready or even capable. I thought I needed a lot of qualifications after my name, as I figured that people would expect that. But the counsellor helped me see that my life experiences would enable me to help others and be a great coach.

I took the suggestion, and I now love who I am and the coaching work I do: encouraging women to love themselves and to build a life they love.

Grateful for Soul Connections

By Christina Araujo

As a young girl, I was very timid and never liked to talk to others. I was the only child for the first seven years of my life, so I had a lot of time to stay in my own world. When I became a teenager, I always had a couple of close friends who I spent time with on a daily basis; but I never enjoyed associating with too many people because I was so scared to speak with them or, oftentimes, even *look* at them.

This all changed when I was 24 and I made a deep connection with an 85-year-old Indian woman. I had never felt a connection like this before in my life. We met at an event at a community center. At this time, I was still very quiet, sat away from the crowd, and focused on being in my own world. She walked over, sat next to me, and started telling me her life story. Caught off guard, I gave her my undivided attention and maintained eye contact with her. As she told me her stories, I felt all of the emotions she was feeling, and I could see her story through her soul. She had a beautiful spirit that had been searching for people to genuinely listen and love her for all of her life.

Without thinking, I began to tear up because of what a strong woman she was and how she hadn't let anything break her apart. I thought that this was astonishing, and I wanted to know every detail about her life. After listening for three hours, I felt myself float out of my body and into her story, watching everything. I never once stopped listening or tuned out.

After that moment, I became a social butterfly. I was excited to connect with every soul that I came in contact with. I realized that I love listening to others and learning about how they grew into the people they have become. I now do this by showing up everywhere I go – fully present with my mind, heart, and soul. To me, this is the true meaning of life. All of it is amazing, and I am in love with it all!

Chapter 8
Divine Interventions & Timing

Most of us have experienced moments when we felt like we were in exactly the right place at the right time. We've also experienced moments when something didn't feel right, so we avoided a certain path and later found out that our intuitive hunch was correct. And sometimes, we've felt the hand of grace step in and intervene in some way – either moving us toward or away from something. In all of these moments, we can look back with awe at how divine the timing truly was.

We've experienced all of these scenarios, where it felt like the hand of grace was helping us along. We frequently think about how every single thing had to line up in just the right way for us to meet on a remote dirt road in New Mexico in 2001. (Dan had just moved from New York one month prior.) If just one piece of the puzzle hadn't been in place, we wouldn't have crossed paths, and our lives would have been much different.

We've also been blessed to have avoided potentially horrific situations, thanks to divine intervention. Jodi was once at a stop light that had just turned green. Just before pulling through, a book fell off her seat. In the split second that she took to lean down to grab it, a car sped through the intersection, running a red light. Had she gone right away, she would have been collided into. Years later, a car did run into hers, which left her extremely injured for years. Thankfully, it was a rare moment when Dan wasn't with her since the windshield sliced the passenger-side air bag and he most likely wouldn't have made it. We are so grateful for each moment together and also for the roles grace and divine intervention have played in keeping us together.

In this chapter, you'll read many awe-inspiring moments such as these, which show that everything is always happening in perfect timing.

Intercepted by Grace

By Susan Mullen

We were teenagers enjoying a road trip with our parents when things suddenly became very scary: While sitting in New Jersey traffic, I was horrified to see my older sister's face swell to an unrecognizable size. Cathy collapsed, struggling to breathe.

This was back in the days before cell phones or GPS systems, so we had to find our way to the nearest hospital the only way we could: by asking directions. I remember the speeding, then the toll booth attendant pointing "that way." And I remember that the recent traffic suddenly thinned out, the sky got brighter, and within just a few minutes we were there.

We had two nurses, one physician, and one receptionist all to ourselves in a quiet, empty emergency room. They saved her life. As soon as we exited the hospital property, the weather was once again dreary and we were back in traffic.

As we drove home, we all recalled the same details of the seemingly ethereal experience: the weather changed, and the hospital was surrounded by incredibly colorful, lush greenery. It took just minutes to get there, the parking lot was empty, and two nurses were already outside waiting for us. (One was even holding a syringe of epinephrine – how could she have known?) The emergency room was pristine, white, and *vacant*. There were no clocks or ringing telephones. In fact, there wasn't even a waiting room.

Then Cathy asked, "Mom, what were you holding in your hand?" During her extreme distress, Cathy's consciousness had left her body, and she saw Mom clutching something in her hand. None of us knew that my mother, a registered nurse, was prepared to do an emergency tracheotomy.

While between dimensions, she described feeling weightless and extremely peaceful, and she saw an unknown woman in light. Cathy was in control and could float toward her or back to us. She chose to return to her body when she saw me crying.

Incredibly, the insurance was never billed. Even more incredibly, Mom later searched for but never found the hospital – because it simply didn't exist! But divine interceptions do.

Grace On-Air

By Tara L. Robinson

"I've been planning my suicide for the past 10 days, but I just decided I don't want to die," said the shaky voice on the other end of the phone. With my mouth (and heart) wide open, I marveled at the divine synchronicity of events that had led to this moment. It was clearly a profound act of grace.

I hadn't expected to be on the radio that day, and I certainly hadn't been expecting to have this conversation with a caller in crisis. I had expected to be on a plane traveling back from Dallas this particular Tuesday afternoon during the weekly radio show I co-host. However, at the last minute, my travel plans had been canceled, which had changed my availability for hosting the show and had made it possible for me to interview Dr. Wayne Dyer during a teleconference earlier in the day. I was now sharing with my listeners about my conversation with "The Father of Motivation."

This particular caller explained that he was driving from Detroit to Nashville and had been flipping through the radio channels as he passed through Cincinnati when he heard me talking about asking Dr. Dyer about The Serenity Prayer. This subject had spoken deeply to him and was exactly the sign he had needed to reconsider taking his life, since a copy of this prayer had been hanging on his refrigerator for a long time.

A line in this popular inspirational prayer says, "God, grant me the serenity to accept the things I cannot change." Upon hearing this powerful reminder, my caller had decided to see his challenging circumstances through the lens of grace instead of trying to change them by ending his life.

For this life-saving moment to occur, everything had had to align perfectly: my travel plans, my interview with Dr. Dyer, the hosting of the radio show, and the fact that the caller "happened" to land on 88.3 FM at that exact moment. Although *Waves of a New Age* can be heard globally online, the range of the local airwaves does not cover a large area. Traveling north to south like he was at the time, there was a very tight window when he could have picked up a signal for our show. But anything is possible when it is time for a moment of grace.

Shukraan (Thank You)
By Linda Lynch-Johnson

It was a life-or-death situation on so many levels that November night in 1979. I was concerned for my son, Stephen, who had gotten the flu, which made his asthma critical. The local medical office could no longer control his condition, so they urged us to take Stephen to the hospital in Dammam. My husband needed to drive us because in Saudi Arabia women are forbidden to drive. But he had a bad stomach virus that made him unable to move. Now what? We had to get our son to the hospital.

We had an instant moment of grace when our neighbor stopped by. We explained the situation. He wanted to help but didn't have a vehicle. My husband told him he could drive our car. In America, this would have been a simple solution. However, Saudi law forbade a man from driving a car he didn't own and also forbade a woman to be traveling at night with a man who was not a relative. But my son's health demanded we go anyway. So we set out, praying we wouldn't be stopped.

However, insurgents from Iran had taken over the holy city of Mecca, stopping in the villages of Safwa and Qatif. Retaliations had begun against the villages and traffic was diverted, stretching our 30-minute drive to an hour. As we finally neared Dammam, we saw red tail lights ahead. The military was stopping traffic and searching every vehicle.

My son's life-and-death situation was now mine and our neighbor's. As a non-relative, he could be beheaded. I could be stoned as an adulteress. My son's breathing had become desperate, and he was starting to turn blue.

I was frightened, and then I remembered a prayer I had learned years before: *Let go, and let God.* So I did. As we approached the checkpoint, I spoke what Arabic I knew and pointed to my ill child. The guard waved us through without asking for our identification. We arrived at the hospital in time, and my son's life was saved.

Rise and Shine

By Charise A. S. Harkin

Since early adolescence, I have struggled with depression and anxiety. My condition grew significantly worse in my 40th year, when I found myself chronically plagued by negative thoughts and frantic emotions. Nothing or no one could guide me through this internal tempest back to safe shores.

Unable to work, I became reclusive, reckless, and self-destructive. Numb to the joys in my life and distant from my family, depression and anxiety trapped me behind my front door and under my bed covers. I felt immersed in a raging ocean without any glimmer of hope or happiness.

At that time, I didn't know that I was experiencing the flooding storm of bipolar depression. I just knew that I was drowning in tribulation. I was consumed with dark days and nights, many times confusing the two (often unable to change out of my sleepwear).

For two long years, I committed myself to practicing mindfulness therapies as well as a regimen of prayer and meditation. And then, on an ordinary day, I was granted an extraordinary moment – a sense of calm. I felt the warmth of a gentle presence, something I had not experienced before – the love of an infinite spirit gracing me with unexplainable strength, allowing me to start my expedition to healing and wellness.

With this divine energy came the gift of gratitude. Within days, I could smell the intense, fresh fragrances in the cool air. Within weeks, my thoughts became colourful, as did my dreams. My prayers shifted from requests of aid to thankfulness for my good fortunes. I could now recognize the power of positivity and feel this transformation in my heart.

By no coincidence, I have been blessed with forgiveness and countless earth angels placed in my path to support my journey. I've been guided to reconnect with my faith and my family, and I've been inspired to share hope with the flawed, broken, and beautifully human. And I've been reminded that stars shine brightest in the darkness and, with God's graces, so can we.

Good Friday = Bad Weather

By Courtney Long

Rainy days may have a bad reputation, but I experienced a rainy day in 2002 that shed light on a life-changing spiritual discovery.

As a child growing up in Michigan's fickle weather, I never knew whether to expect clouds, sunshine, or rain. However, my mom and I noticed one consistent weather pattern we could count on: Good Friday, the day Christians grieve Jesus dying on the cross, often brought gloomy, gray, rainy weather. Two days later, Easter Sunday, often brought delightful, sunny, springtime warmth, reflecting the joy of Jesus rising from the dead. I marveled at the magic of this year after year.

When I reached college, I met classmates of various religions – Judaism, Buddhism, Taoism, and Islam. This led me to question Christianity. *If there are so many different religions*, I wondered, *how can one be "the" answer?* I saw beauty and truth in them all.

After feeling close to God my whole life, I suddenly felt afraid and confused. During this dark, cloudy time in my life, I was on a quest for my own spiritual truth.

My search led me to Madrid, Spain, to work as an au pair. My host family took me skiing in the Pyrenees Mountains for Easter. Despite perfect, sunny skiing weather the entire week, I woke up on Good Friday to a rainstorm. Clear across the ocean, on the other side of the world, the weather was sad and dreary, just like in Michigan.

Waves of tears washed over me – not because I couldn't ski that day, but because I realized this was a message from God. Despite my questioning, God was still there to comfort and love me. I realized in that moment that I didn't have to choose a manmade religion. My religion was LOVE.

Joy and excitement bubbled up within me as I awakened to a new understanding of who God is – a powerful force of love that flows through everything in this entire universe, including me and including the weather. I breathed a sigh of relief, knowing that with God (a.k.a. "Love") by my side, there would now be infinite sunshine in my life.

Canvas Is the Portal to My Spirit

By Aeriana Blue

To help build my photography business, I often volunteer to shoot various events for the opportunity to fill my portfolio. Last year, I photographed a "Wild and Free" painting retreat for women in Texas. I was invited to paint as well. I accepted the invitation and gave myself the opportunity to truly be Wild and Free!

I painted on a canvas as big as I was, mostly with my hands – layers and layers of new experiences, textures, and feelings. I was painting from my soul with wild abandon and no fear! No one judged me – even I didn't judge me! If it didn't feel right or look right, I could just paint it again to allow something different to come up.

The entire chain of events, from seeing a friend's post to my arrival in Texas, was classic divine intervention! Spirit put me in the right place at the right time so that I could experience grace. What started out as a business venture turned into a spiritual marker in my life.

Before this experience, I had been working for years on developing my connection to Spirit. I'd taken the classes and done the "work" but still felt no reliable connection. In the end, all Spirit was waiting for was for me to let go and allow it to move through me naturally.

I am pleased to say that it is now doing exactly that. I am painting, still with my hands, and people are actually *buying* my art! By letting go, I invited Spirit to work through me. I am forever grateful for the opportunity to connect easily and with grace. I don't judge the images and messages. I know in my heart they are always right. Each time I come to the canvas now, it is an amazing and soul-enriching visit with Spirit.

The Day He Felt My Pain

By Pooja Shende

On the morning of November 28, 2000, I was waiting to join the road on my scooter right outside my apartment when a rickshaw coming from the wrong direction crashed into me. To my good karma, many people rushed to help me, and my family came to my rescue. I was rushed to the hospital, where I was told that my left knee was damaged and needed to be operated on. The operation was done by Dr. Nicolas Antao, who has been a blessing in my life.

After the operation, when I thought that the worst was over, came the tough part: I realized that I could not bend my leg even one degree and would have to undergo three months of physiotherapy. The sessions were difficult and painful, but I continued to work on improving my leg with a "never give up" attitude and my belief in Shirdi Sai Baba.

After nearly two and half months, my leg showed great signs of improvement, having gone from 0° to 100° bend. On one particular day, however, I just could not tolerate the pain and screamed my heart out. Then I suddenly saw Shirdi Sai Baba sitting on his throne, which started shaking as if there were an earthquake. That moment made me realize that even he (God) could feel my pain. That is when the miracle happened. After I got down from my physiotherapy table and was asked to practice walking, I realized that I could now walk without support. I was back on my feet! Hurray! Everyone in the room, including the physiotherapist, started clapping and was in tears. I did not realize that so many people were watching me closely and praying for me. That was one of the best days of my life.

I thanked each and every person who was there with me during this difficult time: my husband, parents, relatives, friends, doctors, nurses, and all the unknown people who silently prayed for me. And I thanked Shirdi Sai Baba for this experience, which allowed my belief and bonding with myself and with him (God) to become stronger and stronger.

Beyond the Veil

By Roberta L. Marhefka

It had been at least 25 years since I'd last seen or spoken to Mary. We were close friends in high school but parted ways upon graduation. She went off to college, and I moved across the country with my family.

So when I received her call out of the blue after so long, I was pleasantly surprised. Mary had seen my name in the small Colorado town paper and wondered if it was me. Strangely, we both had eventually moved to Colorado and had lived only a few miles apart for years.

I looked forward to a happy reunion, but to my dismay discovered Mary's son had recently committed suicide. He had jumped off a tall building. The fact that he had been a vivacious, popular young man in his 20s made this tragedy all the more shocking to her.

Having been a spiritual life coach for years, I immediately knew why Spirit had brought us back together at this time. After a little coaxing, she was willing to allow me to use Reiki energy and hypnotherapy/ breathwork to help her find some relief from her grief. I know that everything happens for a reason, but I never imagined what would transpire during her session.

Her son came to her and explained that he was so sorry, that he had not taken his meds and was not in his right mind. It was not intentional. He was with God and was doing God's work from the other side. He had not left her or the family. Their love was so strong that they were able to continue going through the veil and kept communicating on their own afterwards.

He continued to send her signs that he was around her. It was whenever she was meditative or on her walks that she was able to notice the clouds shaped like a heart or the stones on the roadway also shaped in hearts. Their ongoing connection helped her to move forward and accept her loss because she still felt him in her life.

The grace of God is a blessing to behold and what I call a real-life miracle. It was so gratifying to assist them in their healing. Knowing I was used as an instrument for love is, for me, a miracle of my own.

The Light of Paris

By Star Staubach

Sitting in a business event, surrounded by a group of women, I pulled out my crystal ball (something I'd *never* brought with me before that night) and I spoke my BIG wish, the wish that made my heart leap, the wish that made me feel dreamy: "I want to go to Paris, kid-free, with my husband for my 40th birthday."

I said it, and then it happened: a woman near me was blowing her nose with an unusual designer tissue. Others saw it first. "Star! Look! Janet's tissues have *stars* and the *Eiffel Tower* on them!"

The table erupted in laughter and squeals of excitement, "It's a *sign*! You're meant to go to Paris!"

A few days later, crystal ball still in my purse, I went to dinner with friends. I was laughing, "I have this crystal ball in my purse, and it is *heavy*!"

"Star, why do you have a crystal ball in your purse?"

I explained the story. I showed them the tissue adorned with stars and the Eiffel Tower.

"Star, you know that we have a timeshare in Paris, right?"

"WHAT!!?? Tell me more!"

My friend proceeded to check availability on his smartphone, "It's available January 9-16th. Would that work?"

My birthday is January 10th.

"Because of off-season, the condo is only $127 for the entire week."

In that moment, Paris went from a distant dream to a very possible reality. It was that conversation that gave my husband and me permission to search for flights, discovering that we had 50,000 unused Skymile points ($500 toward a flight). When we inquired about childcare, my father said, "Book it; we'll figure something out. Either the kids can come here or we'll go to your house." I began the process of weaning the baby (who was still nursing and waking at night).

I was in Paris for my 40th birthday and received the lesson of a lifetime: by stating my wish out loud, I allowed grace to appear and assist me in creating a magical moment.

Wrapped in an Energetic Bubble

By Rozlyn Warren

There have been several close calls in my long, interesting life; and all but one have been wrapped in fear and followed with harsh memories and what-might-have-been shakes.

The lone exception occurred while I was traveling on the interstate. At this time in my life, I had been learning about and practicing creating my own reality and determining my vibration for several months. I was consciously aware of how amazing life is, had an intention for a beautiful outcome for the appointment I was traveling to, and was vibrating at such an amazing level that my body was buzzing. I was, as they say, "tuned in, tapped in, and turned on"!

Suddenly, I found myself being moved from the outer lane of the three-lane highway onto the emergency strip. I remember thinking, *Isn't this interesting?* – my new energy-neutral phrase when something surprises me. Then I noticed a super-sized recreational vehicle towing a car occupying the space where I had just been.

I thought, *Hmm...* and sped up until I could pass him, knowing intuitively that I couldn't slow down and let him pass me because then I would be going too slowly to safely re-enter the flow of traffic.

What amazed me after all of this was over was that there was no fear, no drama or trauma! My high vibration of love just moved me over and told me what to do, and I just got on with my beautiful day!

Even knowing that, at the speeds we were traveling, if we had touched each other in any way there would have been a horrendous crash, there was and even now is no fear...it just seemed so natural.

For the other driver, who apparently had never seen me, what a shocked look he wore as I swooped in front of him from a lane that isn't supposed to have any traffic! It was, for me, a beautiful example of living in the grace of love.

An Unscheduled Left Turn

By Brenda M. Wiener

My husband and I both grew up attending church on a regular basis because that is what you did. This Sunday was no different. We were preparing to attend church services with our two children.

Having moved almost two years earlier, we were still attempting to fit in with our new church. It was not going well. My children and husband didn't like the church we were attending, and if I was honest with myself, neither did I! As usual, by the time we got on the road to church, we were running late. I was upset and so was everyone else in the car.

I longed for something different. I knew deep inside that something more was possible. I started asking everyone I met where they attended church. Interestingly enough, I kept getting the same answer. Everyone told me they loved this particular church with its Bible-based teaching, sermons, music, and wonderful people. I was ready for a change. I just did not know if I was ready for a whole different denomination. In fact, it had never occurred to me to even consider changing. I had attended the same type of church my whole life. I was even teaching Sunday school at our current church. Now, all of a sudden, it was a possibility. What would my husband and children say? What would my family say? What would my friends say?

As we stopped at the stop sign, I looked at the clock and saw that we were almost 15 minutes late. Somewhere I got the courage to ask my husband to turn left instead of going straight ahead. Everyone was in an uproar. I offered that we could go home or we could check out this new church. Reluctantly, everyone agreed we would check it out.

The decision that day has changed my life. I know in my moment of frustration, the courage to make the request to turn left, instead of going straight ahead, held a quiet whisper of grace for me. I am now on a journey of faith I never knew was possible.

The Darkest Hour Is Just Before Dawn

By Christine King

Many years ago, in utter despair, I watched helplessly as my whole life disintegrated around me. Left widowed and broke, I languished in my one-room rented apartment. The misery was indescribable.

One day while I was sitting alone, the shrill sound of the telephone pierced through my sorrow. I picked it up and heard the voice of a friend. In contrast to my deep unhappiness, she oozed excitement. "I had a dream last night," she blurted out. "You and I were taking a training course in hypnotherapy. It's a sign! We must do it!"

Indignation suddenly replaced my self-pity. She knew I had lost everything and had no money, so why was she even suggesting this? Undeterred by my negative response, she proceeded to say that no money was required yet because the deposit wasn't due for a few weeks.

Despite my sarcastic response that I had no way of getting funds, albeit in a few weeks' time, she came back at me with the most insane advice I'd ever heard: "Just sign up, Chris, and the money will come."

I had always prided myself on being a very down-to-earth person, but for some reason, my rational mind went on vacation that day and I ended up enrolling in the course.

Three days later, there was a knock at my door. A neighbour stood there with a piece of paper. She handed it to me. "This company is offering a week's work mailing out flyers; would you be interested?" I took the job.

That one week turned into several more, which paid for my course deposit. Then the manager, hearing that I had some experience in advertising, offered me the junior marketing role.

This regular work and increase in salary ended up funding my entire training. Over the past 35 years, I have added psychotherapy, soul psychology, healing, metaphysics, EFT, and scientific hand analysis to my skills. I was also guided to set up a Metaphysical Society, which has trained hundreds of people, consequently touching the lives of thousands.

All credit is due to Amazing Grace working beautifully in Divine right timing through that life-changing telephone call.

Divine Timing: An Unexpected Gift of Grace
By Cynthia Starborn

The news on the other end of the line from the French Embassy in New York hit me like a thunderbolt: Due to budget cuts, my teaching job in France, scheduled to start that fall, had just been eliminated.

I hung up the phone feeling numb. I was on a family vacation in Wells Beach, Maine, the summer after my first year in graduate school. Since the spring, I'd been excitedly preparing for a dream opportunity to teach English in France the following year. How could things suddenly go so wrong when everything had felt so right?

After breaking the news to my parents, I ran to the beach and spent several grief-stricken hours sitting on a rock at the edge of the Atlantic, staring at a point just beyond the horizon that I couldn't see, a point called France where I still felt in my heart I was meant to be.

At some point, with my heart still aching, I mustered up the strength to walk back to the cottage my parents were renting that week and back to a chapter in life I hadn't planned for. Unable to register for graduate classes that fall since I'd taken a leave of absence, I arranged with my summer employer to continue working there that fall and did my best to enjoy full-time office work.

In October, my older brother, Steve, unexpectedly had to have back surgery and spent many weeks in the hospital. I realized, humbly, how grateful I felt to still live close enough to visit him.

One day, my younger brother, Mark, picked up a message on my parents' answering machine from a French woman inviting me to come teach English at her school in Normandy. Apparently, all the other English assistants had just quit. I called her back excitedly and said I could start in two weeks.

Two days before I was scheduled to fly to France, Steve came home from the hospital.

I was amazed at the grace of divine timing, this mysterious grace that had somehow orchestrated my dream trip to France at the perfect time.

Square Peg, Round Hole
By Karen Hicks

Much of my youth was spent searching for that which would make me special. I had an emptiness inside that I longed to have filled. How lucky for me then to have met "Robert" (a pseudonym) when I was 19 and attending university.

One of the more life-changing experiences we shared as a couple was a pathway to faith. We belonged to a strong faith community, and the Church became a big part of our lives. Through our understanding of what we assumed was God's plan for us, we became engaged.

As the days passed and wedding plans got underway, I began to doubt if the marriage was the right thing to do. In my mind, though, of course we *had* to get married; we had found God together. Doubt grew each day, and I continued to resist what that little voice was telling me: that this marriage was not to be.

I remember that magical night. It was only a few weeks before the wedding, and I was so afraid. I felt I had no one to talk to or turn to. I was sitting cross-legged on my bed, deep in worry and praying for help. My thoughts were jumbled. Warm air began to circle my body, and a feeling of peace filled me from top to bottom. It was a transformative moment.

Though I was nervous to take the action I knew I needed to take, because I understood that I wasn't alone, I found courage. I called Robert and told him we couldn't get married. It was as simple as that. This courage would carry me quite a while as I navigated through an exile from our church community.

Upon reflection, I see that the "square peg" in this situation was my mistaken belief of what my path was "supposed" to be. Now that I've learned to listen to the little voice that guides me, I have fewer square pegs, more ease, and a lot more grace!

Archangel Michael and the Hand of Grace

By Ana Gordon

It was a blustery winter day, and I was in a hurry, dashing off in my sturdy, trusty Toyota Highlander. As I headed toward the neighboring town, huge drifts, high winds, and ice were everywhere. Still, I had four-wheel drive, I am a good driver, and I trusted that all would be well.

What I did not anticipate was hitting black ice and having my car spin 360 degrees in a few seconds, but that's exactly what happened.

I was taking the entrance ramp onto the highway. These are usually icier in these conditions, so I was careful – but still likely driving too fast. As I reached the ramp's downward curve, I felt the car literally move out from under me.

Everything seemed to slow down.

I can still recall the Technicolor brilliance of everything around me as I allowed the car to spin itself miraculously to the right direction with me intact.

As my car spun out of my control, I felt the divine presence of Archangel Michael. It felt like he just reached down and, like an adult handling a Tonka toy, righted my car – putting it back facing the right direction and miraculously intact.

In that moment of divine intervention, I felt such grace, and the feeling is still with me right now as I recall it.

I am, of course, grateful to have avoided a potentially serious car crash. More importantly, however, I am indelibly imprinted with this hand of Grace, which has impacted my entire life – so much so that I now work wholly as an intuitive and call upon the archangels every single day.

May whoever calls upon Archangel Michael receive blessings. He with the valiant sword, he of the fearless heart.

The Universe Really Does Listen

By Marie Spencer-Rowland

I had moved to the United Kingdom only a few months before and, through an unfortunate chain of events, suddenly found myself without a home. Trying to find somewhere to live in London was beyond stressful. I was all of 21 and had never done anything like this solo. I viewed place after place, but all of them were being snatched up, sometimes even just as I was getting to the door to view them. I tried to stay positive by telling myself, "The right place will come up," but living in limbo was hard and money was extremely tight.

After living like a squatter for several weeks, I made up my mind: If I didn't find somewhere to live *that day*, I would take it as a sign that I was not meant to be here. While travelling on the train into London, I looked up at the sky and made that point very clear to anyone who was up there listening. I had enough cash in my purse to buy a one-way ticket back to Australia, and if I couldn't find somewhere to live that day, that's exactly what I intended to do.

Less than an hour after making this declaration, I found somewhere to live. It was cheaper than I had budgeted for, closer to work, and a beautiful property. Everything fell into place that day, leaving me no doubt that everything happens for a reason.

Living in the UK turned my life around. I *was* meant to be here. Shortly after finding a place to live, my career took off in a completely different direction, leading me into an area that I hadn't previously realised was my calling. I also met my husband, met my best friend (who is actually more of a sister than a friend), and found my inner strength and a connection to something bigger than me. And I learned to enjoy the ride and trust that, somehow, it'll all work out.

Saved by Grace

By Dawn De'Harmony

How can I be here again? I'm so tired of being here! Terrorizing, consuming thoughts spiraled as I sat alone in the darkness, alternating between body-wracking sobs and silent, surreal numbness. Devastated, I began considering the unfathomable: suicide.

My boyfriend and I had been together for 10 years when he finally asked me to marry him. A year after our wedding, we reluctantly admitted that something was missing – a deep connection that had been eluding us for years. Somewhere along the way, we'd unconsciously agreed that this was okay. Until it wasn't.

Agreeing to let go did not prevent my rooted fears from surfacing to torment me: *What now? How am I gonna do this? I don't want my son to lose another dad! What are people gonna say? I'm so afraid...* Overwhelmed, I envisioned my life falling apart.

Feeling helpless in that dark, desperate space of sorrow and dread, I reached out to my angels and guides to hold me. I saw myself enveloped in white, cleansing light. I did not ask for the pain to go away. I knew, at some level, I was choosing it. Instead, I asked for clarity.

In a way that defies words, I felt the flow of Presence surround me and was comforted by a warm embrace. I felt support for *whatever* my decision would be. And then It spoke: "There is no shame. There is no death, only life on different planes. I have just one question: Have you done what you came to do?"

I echoed the question, "Have I done what I came to do?" As my spine straightened and my vision cleared, I knew beyond any shadow of doubt that I had not yet done what I'd come to do.

Standing up, I took off my wedding ring and bowed my head. Exhausted, yet empowered with a sense of freedom, tears gently flowed as I whispered, "Thank you. Thank you for accompanying me and supporting me toward what I now know is my highest good. I am so grateful."

That's grace.

The Power of Friendship

By Linda Voogd

A couple of years ago, a good friend and I parted ways. We were both changing emotionally. I tried to accept the new her, but she grew more and more distant. She refused to accept the new me, and the friendship ended. Feeling sad and lonely, I reflected on our friendship and what constituted a true friend. In the process, I remembered a dear, old friend named Beth.

Beth and I met while waitressing in college. We'd spend hours talking about relationships, health, happiness, and our life purposes. She had a warmth to her, and I'd never felt so unconditionally accepted by anyone. Three years after we met, Beth's husband was transferred out of state. We kept in contact for a few years, but technology being what it was at the time, we eventually lost touch.

Shortly after losing my friend, I tried looking up Beth online, without result. I found an old card with one of her many inspiring messages. I wondered if she ever thought of me, how her life was going, and what her children were like, when I received an email from her! She had been thinking of me, too, and had somehow found me. Upon talking, we realized that her thoughts of me became intensified as I was going through this very difficult time. I believe she was given the wisdom to find me by the universe, my angels, or my guides.

We made a plan to get together for a weekend, even though we hadn't seen each other in 25 years. We stayed at the Red Lion Inn in the Berkshires because we both loved history and antiques. I arrived a couple of hours after her; and when I got to the room, she was waiting with open arms and an assortment of wine, cheese, and fruit – just like old times. Our friendship hadn't skipped a beat.

That weekend, I realized the power of strong friendships. Beth provided me with renewed faith in myself and in others. For the last three years, we have continued to meet at the Red Lion Inn. We've tried to figure out how she found me, but she cannot remember! It remains a mystery. What I do know, however, is that I am profoundly grateful for her and the synchronicity that brought her back into my life when I truly needed a loving friend.

Surrendering to a Higher Power

By Lupe Ramirez Peterkin

I sat in the doctor's waiting room with my then-husband, feeling that something was very wrong with my baby. My mind flashed back to the party a few weeks earlier, sipping my first beer of the night and feeling euphoric. Before the night was over, however, that euphoria was replaced with tormented thoughts: *Aren't I supposed to stop drinking in my condition? Why can't I stop?* These thoughts continued to plague me every day for weeks afterwards, until I found myself in a doctor's office.

The doctor called us in and said, "You're losing your baby, and we have to do a uterine scrape." My 10-year drinking party had turned into hell.

I don't remember very much after that except sobbing uncontrollably all the way home. I felt spiritless. Of course I lost my baby; I wasn't taking care of myself at all! My poor child didn't have a chance with my constant intoxication. I told myself I deserved this. I spent a few days in bed, all the while thinking that if I had a gun I would use it on my head.

I knew these thoughts were not of God. That night, I implored Him with all my might to help me. I exhaustively surrendered to my higher power. I promised I would take care of myself and be the best mom ever if he helped me stop drinking. The next few days, I felt like I saw blue sky for the first time in my life. I felt calm and peaceful.

I was still sober when I went back to work and subsequently got a job at a recovery program. Eight months later, I became pregnant with my baby, PJ, the light of my life. If you would have known me before I got sober, you would have never thought I'd stop drinking. It was all God's handiwork, I tell you. In May 2016, I celebrated 15 years of being clean and sober, thanks to the grace of God.

Pearls of Divine Grace

By Lisa Rachel Cohen

In July of 2014, my daughter Alia and I traveled to Paris and Barcelona to celebrate her 16ᵗʰ birthday. Upon arrival, Alia deftly activated the Google Maps app on her iPhone, then proceeded to lead. There were tubes to catch, shops to scope, museums to visit, and limited rest for the weary.

One evening while visiting Barcelona, Alia was bent on locating an obscure restaurant. On the way, we spotted an oasis in the dark: a brightly lit bridal salon. We were catapulted into a scene from a nostalgic movie. Within minutes, a friendly tourist joined our window-shopping jaunt. Before leaving our company, Jeri graciously invited us to befriend her on Facebook, which we did.

Then, in January of 2016, I received a last-minute invitation to attend a peace summit hosted by a Beverly Hills philanthropist in Edison, New Jersey. Incredibly, guests from Hollywood were flown cross country to meet in my home state. Magic was in the air.

On the second day, those present were gifted a private tour of Manhattan. Although most of us had just met the day before, many felt as if we had known each other for our entire lives. Soaring upon the wings of angels, we shared music, dreams, and stories and became fast Facebook friends. When Effie, a filmmaker from California, and I friended each other, we unearthed a celestial "message in a bottle": our one and only mutual friend was none other than Jeri!

Serendipitous encounters such as these lovingly remind me that I am not in charge. Each gift of presence affirms my faith, reassuring me that I am never alone. My life is a magical mystery tour seeded with pearls of divine grace. Welcome to the Garden of our Eden.

Living with Everyday Miracles

By Joy T. Barican

"There are two ways to live your life. One is as though nothing is a miracle. The other is as though everything is a miracle."

- Albert Einstein

Seeing the traffic light turn green, Mum and I stepped off the footpath, arms intertwined as we started to cross the street, when out of nowhere, we suddenly felt the heat of the car's engine as it revved past, a mere centimetre away from our bodies. Mum and I froze on the spot. In a split second, a powerful yet calming energy seemed to have pulled us back, with just enough gap to avoid being dragged by the car. Like rag dolls doing a somersault, our small frames would have been no match for the car speeding through the red light. Mum and I were still muttering prayers of thanks as our shaking knees brought us to the other side of the road.

Another grace-filled traffic incident involved Mum and me on the bus. We were happily chatting away in our seats when we simultaneously decided to get up and move to two newly vacated seats, as if summoned to the opposite side of the bus. We resumed chatting, and barely 10 minutes passed when a huge rock was thrown through the window where we had originally been seated. We exchanged glances of gratitude as we removed fragments of glass from our hair, clothes, shoes, and bags. We shivered at the thought that, had it not been for our inexplicable simultaneous decision to change seats, it could have been much worse for both of us.

In both of these instances, I gave thanks for the life-saving grace that was there exactly when and how I needed it. Indeed, when God steps in – or when He sends His angels and saints – miracles happen, mishaps are avoided, prayers are answered, and we are protected as we go about our daily routine. On occasions when I experience a crisis of faith, I draw upon these (and other) miracles that take place every day in numerous ways, reminding me to build and maintain unwavering faith in God and continue to see *everything* as a miracle.

Divine Intervention from the Heavens

By Jennifer "Elemental" Larkin

Years ago, I went on tour for a year with a song-and-dance show that went to 30 states in the USA and 10 countries in Europe. It was designed to be a professional internship and cultural exchange. Cast members were ambassadors for their countries, staying with host families in each town visited. The massive cast of 130 people from 28 countries filled three passenger tour buses and numerous cargo trucks packed full with sets, lights, costumes, and instruments.

Nine months into the tour, having just arrived in Europe, my last pair of contact lenses tore while cleaning them after a show. I was devastated. I would not be able to participate in any remaining shows on the European Tour since wearing glasses on stage was prohibited due to the glare from the lights.

That night, in the pitch black of my host family's loft, I curled up at the foot of my temporary bed, crying and pleading with the universe to show me a way to move through this situation with ease and grace.

A bright flash of light woke me with a start, and I found myself encircled by a bright beacon of light. A skylight (which I had not noticed before) provided a window to the heavens, which shone a spotlight down upon me. A perfect heart-shaped gap in the thick clouds covering the night sky opened to reveal a bright, bold, full moon, filling my soul with love of the purest form. In that instant, I *knew* that divinity and grace were my birthright.

I slept soundly that night and woke to the smells of home cooking and my host family eager to connect with their foreign guest. Tingles surged through my body as I learned over breakfast that one of my gracious hosts was an optometrist. He enthusiastically insisted that replacement contact lenses would be arranged for me at no cost. Without missing a beat, I departed two days later, back on tour with a new pair of contacts and enough awe and wonder in the divine to last a lifetime!

Waking Up in Grace
By Cheryl Hope

As I dragged myself out to my living room, I noticed a newspaper headline saying that methamphetamine use was taking over the Midwest. I read the article, which said that 99% of meth users never recover. *Could I be in the 1% of success stories?* I wondered.

I had just arrived home from a trip to see my niece get married; but instead of attending a wedding, I ended up in jail with an intoxication charge and possession of marijuana and meth. I was so humiliated yet also relieved that my secret was out. That Monday morning, after reading that article, I decided I was willing to do whatever it took to get and *stay* sober.

I had slipped into using every day instead of taking my antidepressant. (Silly thinking, I know now. Yet at the time, it seemed logical to me.) I was living life in the fast lane – working hard every day and going out every night. I had just gotten my first apartment with a good friend, and I was flying fully out of control. My favorite drug was "more" of anything. My friend had no idea what to make of me. I would say one thing and do another – the push-pull of an addict trying to play it off as though *others* are the crazy ones.

Eventually, I realized that I couldn't keep going like this; something needed to change. I tried to quit meth on my own, but the withdrawals were so rough and then my dealer would call at my weakest moment and I would cave. Finally, in October 1997, I cried out to God for help. Three weeks later, my answer came in the red, white, and blue lights of a police car.

That was the last day I ever drank or did drugs, and it was the first day of a new life. What made it stick? Why have I remained in that 1% of people who stay off of meth? No one rescued me or made recovery easy, but I was granted a moment of grace. Grace was able to reach through the fog and show me that I was worth a second chance and that life was worth living sober. It showed me that it was worth relearning how to drive, how to work my trade, how to think; and each day I live without taking a substance is a day I live in grace.

The Moment My Life Made Sense

By Ayeesha S. Kanji

Every day I jumped to check the mail. No, I wasn't expecting a check; I was waiting for the final decision. It was a moment I had long been dreaming of, a moment I had visualized every day. And now, finally, the moment had arrived.

One evening after finishing up with a client, I sat in my car, waiting for it to warm up. I sent my mom a message that I was on my way home and put on some music for the drive. And then I checked my email. At a glimpse, I could see that I had an email from New York University. Without reading the message, I put the phone in my bag and drove straight home.

When I arrived home, I told my mom we had to read the email together. The email reviewed the next steps should I choose to attend a graduate program at NYU. I had been accepted!

At that moment, my life made sense.

Not because of school or because I was choosing to write papers for the next two years, but because my dream – which I had visualized and worked so hard to achieve – had actually materialized in front of my eyes.

I wanted this dream because I wanted to feel whole and alive. I wanted to feel passion for my future and happiness in my present, and now this passionate happiness filled every part of my being.

This was the first time I experienced a moment like this, and I could only say two words: *thank you*. Thank you to this dream come true, thank you to myself for believing in my dream, and thank you to a life that finally made sense.

The Weeping Walls

By Lori Santo

CRACK!!! WHICKSH!!! She sends a thunderous crash across the ceiling, stinging me like a bullwhip. Shards of glass fly all around me as I shrink into my own skin, recoiling from this demon who has invaded my home, my soul, my self. Cowering under the rug, I cry out: "God, where are you?! I beseech you – stop this insanity!"

Instantly, I feel my own God-presence whisper in response: *Open your heart...even wider. Slowly...open your eyes. See just how extraordinary and powerful you really are.*

Slowly, I peel open one eye at a time, and I am overcome with a phenomenon too great for my mind to fathom: The walls in my house are weeping. Wet. Soiled with tears. Every single wall in my house is crying. Tears from Heaven. The dam has broken open; it is gushing all over my life. And the demon is gone.

I am left with peace, but also with questions. In the days to come, I ponder this experience – on my own and with friends (who came to my house and verified the miracle of the weeping walls). While it defies explanation, this is my best attempt: Holding back so many wounds and traumas had been too much for me to manage on my own, so the walls took the pain for me. Every shadow, every abuse that I had commanded to the cellar of my psyche came pouring out to greet me. I had been broken open, and I learned that I am strongest in my broken places. This was my sacred initiation, an offering of this holy message from my soul:

Bravery means turning toward love when it asks you, even when you are trembling like a small, scared child. Courage is falling to your knees and admitting there is a place in your soul that still has a sword in it, and staying present as the blade gets pulled out. It's being willing to step into your own fire, feel the flames envelop you, and trust that you will emerge shining. It's facing yourself down to the core, again and again, facing down your dark, shadowy, uncomfortable, and scary places. You are their source. Only you can release, transform, or replace them, but not before their presence is acknowledged. No bypassing. No gloss. No hiding. No conquering. No running. Bravery is naked, and she's trembling.

The Rise of the Phoenix
By Sheila Sutherland

I was the kid who always had my entire life planned out. From a young age, I knew where I was going and how I was going to get there. I was driven, determined, and stubborn – nothing was going to stop me! Then life happened, and those big plans – the successful career, the happy marriage and family, the security – all failed to materialize.

I struggled to make the best of things, but I could feel myself becoming depressed, angry, and devoid of that spark I'd once had. But I couldn't show that to the world, so I put on my "happy mask" and tried to give the perception that everything was wonderful. I received many signs that I needed to change, each sign trying harder than the last to get my attention, but I continued to ignore them…until I couldn't.

December 28, 2010, was the day that my whole life changed. A fire in the condo above mine destroyed my home and everything in it. I went into shock. My home – my sanctuary, the one place where I felt safe and secure, the only place where I could take off the mask of perfection and truly be me – was now gone. I was lost.

Starting life over at 40 was definitely not part of my plan, but now I had no other choice. Grace had given me what I've come to see as a cosmic kick in the ass. This shocking "kick" flipped a switch inside of me, shedding light on something I'd known for a long time: something had to change, and that "something" was ME!

Through a process of inner reflection, I discovered how the words I say, the thoughts I think, and the programming I received as a child shaped the course of my life. As I looked within, I saw myself in a new light, and the gap between what I felt and what I showed the outside world began to close.

That unplanned fire lit an inner spark, inspiring me to empower myself and others to live our best lives, to move beyond the past, and to free ourselves of the barriers that we create. Just as the phoenix rises from the ashes as a symbol of rebirth, I have been reborn as the ashes of my old self fall away, revealing a stronger, more vibrant version of me. It's time to rise again!

The Miracle Man

By Tiffany Andersen

What does divine intervention mean? For me, it simply means when something happens that seems as if only angels could have orchestrated it. One such example from my own life involved a special man who saved my life after a serious car accident where I was lucky to be alive. Not only that, with the hands of angels, he miraculously gave me back the use of my legs. Divine intervention was certainly at play.

Twenty-five years after this experience, I met with a new client. She shared with me her broken heart as she told me about her husband who had suffered a devastating stroke. As she continued describing the pain in her heart, her struggles reminded me of the hardship I once suffered.

"It's such a tragedy – he can no longer practice his special gift," she told me. His patients loved him. They came from miles away and waited for hours to see him. Now, since the stroke, he can't practice anymore. He feels trapped in his own home, but it's a miracle he can do the things he can do. He is *my miracle man*."

I had no words to offer comfort; I could only relate with a compassionate heart.

"Laura, my heart breaks for you. I truly appreciate a good spinal cord surgeon." I explained that I had my own miracle man who once saved my life.

By graceful coincidence, it turned out that my miracle man was indeed Laura's husband – the man who enabled me to live with quality, free of struggles that surely would have led me to an early grave. Now, he had lost his special gift; yet before doing so, he had given me back my life.

We stood in complete awe and amazement.

The angels reunited us so I could take Dr. Thomas's hand and say, "Thank you. Your work lives on in the lives of everyone you have ever touched."

A Miracle Baby Girl

By Michelle Anne Gould

My heart ached with a longing to have a second baby, a bundle of love to hold in my arms. My son had brought so much unconditional love and wonderful shifts into my life, but I didn't know if I'd ever be able to repeat the miracle of childbirth because I faced so many health issues after he was born.

After numerous gallbladder attacks, I had my gallbladder removed. Between attacks, I delayed my postnatal healing. Trying to reclaim the old me, I started exercising before I was healed and tore my core muscles apart again and experienced other female-related issues. Later, a stillbirth exposed multiple cysts in my ovaries and the likelihood of ovarian cancer. This time was quite dark, but my son remained a beacon of love and light for me.

My specialist quickly booked me for surgery to remove my right ovary, advising me that I could not have any more children. I prayed and wept. I released my wanting to have another baby. I surrendered it all, including my life. My prayers were heard; after the operation, I still had my ovaries, the cysts were gone, and I seemed to be clear of cancer!

Ten months later, another miracle unfolded: I delivered a beautiful baby girl into my own arms who awakened me to the most brilliant life.

I see magnificence and playful mischief in her divine eyes. She is a gift to the world. I love to secretly observe her beauty and silently give thanks to the great blessings I have been given.

Her baby brother (another miracle) joined us two years later.

I feel so honored for us to share, grow, and evolve together. Miracles, magic, magnificence, and grace live in our hearts as we play in the playground of life. Our unity is a brilliant dance with life.

I look forward to creating memories and dreams. I look forward to watching each of my children blossom and fly.

My little Princess: May you always know how loved, wanted, and precious you are. My great wish for you, little one, is to live passionately and become all you are meant to be. I love you… xoxo Mummy xoxo

Grits and Grace

By Aliza Bloom Robinson

While traveling in the south for the first time, I went into a diner for breakfast. When my bacon and eggs arrived there was something extra on my plate. I asked the waitress about it. "What is this? I didn't order it."

She replied, "Oh, honey, that them there is grits. You don't order it, it just shows up. It's like grace, you know."

Grace has shown up in my life in the best of times and in the worst. Grace is said to be God's love in action. It is a free gift that can't be earned. I've experienced grace in the beauty of nature and the face of a newborn baby. Grace is exquisite in those moments.

But the grace that really swept me over, knocked me off my feet, and took my breath away was another experience altogether. It was profound and life changing.

I had moved across the country not once but twice with two young children. Then one day I woke up and everything crashed and crumbled around me. I was suddenly lost and alone, terrified and filled with shame. I was a mess – a big, fat, total, slobbery basket of nerves and tears.

I fell on my knees and prayed: "God, help me. I can't handle my life. Show me the way, and I will follow." And then grace appeared. A sense of peace washed over me and the tears stopped. I was calm and quiet; I felt love in a new way. I heard a small voice from the depths of my being saying, "I've got you. You are loved. I'll show you the way."

In that moment, I began an intimate relationship with grace that has led me every step of my life since. It hasn't always been an easy journey. It's involved some tough decisions, but grace has always prevailed.

Grace brought light and clarity to that moment so many years ago and continues to guide my way today. I went from broken, alone, and scared to living the life of my dreams. Through my experiences, I've been shown that grace is available in any moment. It comes with a deep surrender to the present moment, whatever that may hold.

I now am always on the lookout for grace, knowing that it may appear on the "plate" of my life…just like grits!

Shopping with Grace

By Catherine Walters

I was overweight until my mid-20s, which made me feel embarrassed while shopping for clothes. Fortunately, my mom was a fabulous seamstress. She sewed and also altered my clothes after I lost weight. When she passed, I not only lost a wonderful mom, I also lost my shopping buddy and seamstress.

As that winter approached, I discovered that all my clothes were now several sizes too big and hung on me. Then I received a secret-discount coupon from a clothing store in the mail. Although I dreaded the thought of shopping alone and didn't know my coupon discount (they ranged from 10% to 50% off and couldn't be scratched until checking out), I went to the store the last day of the sale. I found two turtlenecks and a jumper for work and took them to the register. I listened to the squeals of delight or disappointment when the clerks scratched other shoppers' coupons. As a clerk started on my small pile, I found myself telling her about having weight issues and losing my mom. She smiled kindly and said, "Let's hope you're lucky and have 50% off."

I did! It was a miracle – the first time I'd won anything.

Technically, the clerk should have completed my transaction, but instead she said, "Would you like me to help you find a few more items and take advantage of your coupon?"

I nodded, close to tears, sensing my mom and grace watching over me. With the angel clerk's assistance, I soon had a huge pile of gorgeous skirts, sweaters, and pants that coordinated into beautiful outfits. I wore those outfits for several years since they were classic styles and well made – just like mom's!

As I drove home from the store that day, tears of gratitude streamed down my face. I thanked grace for the savings and for the angel clerk who assisted me.

That experience has remained with me over the decades. Even now, every time I go shopping for groceries, shoes, clothes, or anything else, I always ask grace to be with me and help me buy exactly what I need at the best value. Grace always does…and makes it fun, too!

An Angel Ran Me off the Road

By Stacey Hall

I was driving from St. Paul to my home in Minneapolis late one night. Earlier in the day, my car had a full tune-up and oil change.

As I approached an upcoming exit, I would have to merge into the lane on my left in about a mile to avoid exiting the highway. I looked to my left and saw a long, black sedan parallel with my car.

I increased my speed to pull ahead, and the sedan sped up, too. I slowed down to merge in behind the sedan, and it slowed down, too. I was unable to see who was driving the other car. I attempted to get the driver's attention, but nothing I did worked.

I realized I was arriving at the exit and had no choice but to leave the highway. The exit brought me to a stoplight in a deserted part of town. It was pitch black, and I felt uneasy. I could not wait for the light to turn green. Except once the light turned green, my car would not move. There was no one around to ask for help. I lived alone, so no one would be concerned if I did not get home that night.

I prayed to God for help. Within two minutes, a light turned on in a building across the street, and out came five men. I hesitated for a moment, then I trusted that they were the answer to my prayer and yelled to them for help.

I explained what happened, and they said I was lucky that I caught them because there were no homes or businesses still open in the area. They pushed my car into the parking lot of their business, which happened to be an automotive repair shop!

They drove me home, and the next day, one of the men called and said the fan belt had not been put on properly and had slipped off. I was lucky it had happened while I was stopped at a light. If it had happened on the highway, my car would have locked up and I might have been hit by another car.

I was filled with such love for the driver of the black sedan, who I feel was actually my guardian angel watching over me and ensuring my safety by running me off the road and into a band of angels who answered my prayer.

Reasons to Stay

By Colleen Leaney

As I awaken, the memories of a hundred lifetimes of sorrow weigh on my shoulders. Must I remain in this earthly domain? I am ready to return home – where heavenly stars and celestial beings embrace me, where pain has no existence and the ego is left behind. I am ready to leave this foreign place where our souls temporarily reside as a place for learning lessons. I am ready to receive my fullest blessings, to leave the burden of this world behind and return to a realm with no judgments.

I hear a voice softly saying, "Close your eyes and rest your weary soul. Soon you will be free. For now, sleep." I close my eyes and open my heart. I fall back asleep with a smile on my face, trusting that my Creator will soon beckon me with open arms of love.

But instead I receive more visions from the past – of war, of murder, of plundering. I see famine and starvation, torture and captivity. I see chemtrails and devastation, dictators and greed. I see religions and governments failing, animals suffering, and families disassociating. I feel sadness and guilt at my own poor choices, pain at my personal losses, fear of hurting others, and resentment towards my ego. *Why must I be reminded of such tragedies? Stop this nightmare now! No more videos within my brain! I've served my time and learned my lessons. I'm ready to leave; I truly am! Please, let me return home to you!*

I reawaken and it's midmorning, the sun glittering through my window. I see the promise of a blue sky and feel the sun warming my face, melting my brokenness, and filling the cracks with molten gold. I open my eyes and remember all the reasons I'm not yet to leave. My heart fills with such gratitude. There's so much to do. There's so much to see. There are beautiful skies and life-giving seas. Flowers and music. The whisper of the wind as it chimes through my garden. The kiss of a butterfly. The mystical eyes of a dragonfly touching my soul, telling me that all is going to be okay. And I remember my family and friends who have supported me on this journey. I can't wait to return and pay it forward! I am not ready to go home yet. Please, let me stay a while longer! It's time to be present once again.

Angels to the Rescue

By Courtney Long

Angels often come to our rescue in times of great need. Yet they love helping with little things, too, as an experience yesterday gently reminded me.

I panicked when I realized I had forgotten to print handouts for an Angel Class I am teaching in two days. Usually, I upload the handout to a local printing company's website and pick up the copies in-store.

As usual, I consulted my friend, Mr. Google, and found a color-copy coupon code to save money. After entering the coupon code during checkout, my hopeful demeanor deflated. A red error message flashed on the screen saying, "This coupon is inactive."

Interestingly, the website reported that 300 people had successfully used this same coupon code the day before. *It worked for them*, I wondered, *so why isn't it working for me?*

Four more tries with four different coupon codes left me stumped and frustrated.

In my classes, I teach the importance of asking the angels for help. You know that saying that we teach what we need to learn? It's true. Apparently, I needed a dose of my own medicine.

After taking a deep breath, I asked out loud, "Angels, I really need your help. I need these flyers printed. I don't know how you can do this, but I would love for this coupon code to work."

I entered the first coupon code again, even though five minutes earlier it had not worked. I hit the Enter button, and *voila* – almost like magic, it worked! A 25% discount was applied to my order. Smiling, I thanked the angels and quickly finished checking out.

This experience reminded me that the angels want to help us with anything that will make our lives smoother – big or small. Apparently, the angels agreed that saving money would make my life smoother yesterday. And apparently, they appreciate coupons. Now, if you'll excuse me, I'm off to pick up my color copies!

Messages on a Stormy Night

By Maura Smith

It was a dark and stormy night. I was looking forward to driving up north with my husband and daughter. We were going to visit my parents for the weekend at their home near the beach – a place where I'd spent many happy summers – but this time, things didn't go as planned.

The first warning sign about the trip was a casual comment from my friend. When I mentioned our plans, she simply asked why we didn't wait until the morning when the storm would be over. I dismissed her comment, pointing out that we were accustomed to traveling in all kinds of weather.

Then came the phone call from my son, who was staying at his father's place. The fact that he called me was, in and of itself, highly unusual. (He normally didn't communicate by phone.) I remember the conversation clearly: after he said hello, there was a very long pause; then, with tension in his voice, he asked what we were doing. When I told him our plans, his concern was obvious. I reassured him that everything would be fine, then I said goodbye and continued to pack.

Finally, the message came through loud and clear. With everything packed and ready to go, we were on our way out to the car when our daughter turned to look back at the house and made a statement that shook me to the core: "I feel like I'll never see this place again."

That was it. In that moment I realized that the universe was desperately trying to tell me something, something that could have a massive impact on our family and generations to come. I immediately changed my decision, unpacked the car, and stayed at home that night. As I watched the sheets of rain through the window, I felt so grateful for the signals I'd been given and for my ability to listen and respond. Although I'll never really know what might have happened had we gone on the trip that night, I do know that the moment I recognized the message was a moment of grace.

Boy, Oh Boy, Oh Boy

By Erin Miller

If anyone had told me 10 years ago that I would be the mother of three boys, it would have sent me into a spin. I'd always envisioned myself with daughters. Heck, boys were far too noisy, messy, and full of energy for me. Besides, I'm a girlie girl!

But the universe has a funny way of providing what you need, rather than what you expect. So, four weeks ago, I gave birth to (you guessed it) my third beautiful boy…and I wouldn't have it any other way!

I've already got all kinds of superheroes looking out for me on a daily basis, all of whom are willing and able to slay dragons, trap monsters, and catch baddies that might be lurking in the bedrooms or hiding in the cupboards, threatening my safety. I'm never short of hands to help out or fix anything around the house, and every day is a laugh! And if I want an honest opinion on my hair or clothing choice, I'm sure to get one, such as, "You look groovy, Mummy" or "Why are you still wearing your pyjamas, Mummy?!"

Yes, my world is noisy, messy, energetic, and a little crazy at times…and only to get more so – of that I'm certain! But I believe that everything happens for a reason and that the universe delivers what is necessary for your journey. I am yet to fully understand my lesson or gift. In the meantime, however, I am honoured and humbled that I have been graced with three little men who have chosen me to be their Mummy.

Dedicated with love to Nate (5), Jensen (3½) and Sonny (4 weeks)

Following Divine Assistance

By Nikki Ackerman

In 2014, I was struggling each day with maintaining my health, household, and finances. I was working full time in an intense, risky profession while being a part-time business owner. I had been praying for a social-work job that would allow me to grow my holistic practice, but I lacked the time and energy to devote to job hunting.

Then, out of the blue, I received a job proposal from a friend who I hadn't spoken to in months. The position came with excellent benefits and a tremendous increase in pay, and it would allow more time to devote to my holistic practice. Realistically, it made sense to accept the job, but it was a difficult decision because I'm highly respected and relied upon by my colleagues, who are like family.

Because this opportunity came to me – I didn't seek it out – some people would consider this divine intervention. Yet I was hesitant to leave my job. I did some soul searching and heard something within say, "Have faith" – so I did! This opportunity was placed on my path, and I knew I had to follow it. Listening to my inner wisdom and working with my friend enhanced my spiritual growth.

It became obvious that God (or the Universe) guides us, protects us, and provides for us. Within six months, I was financially stable again. The change in jobs allowed me to dedicate more time to my holistic practice, which prospered so much that I was soon able to transition to working at it full time!

Through this experience of faith and divine timing, I have learned that there is more to life than me individually. I reside in the western world where we have dualistic beliefs, but I have witnessed the greater picture of interconnectedness that is veiled with the notion that everything is individualized or separate. Each of us is part of a greater whole! When I shifted my perception and recognized that there is a universal connection between everyone and the divine, my life changed. It brings me peace to know that something beyond me is assisting and sustaining our experiences.

Pink Slip of Grace

By Davalynn Kim

My heart was in my throat. As I stared at the pink slip in my hand, tears blurred my vision. I was among the thousands of Americans affected by the Great Recession of 2008. As a single mother of three, I wondered how I would provide for my children. For a moment, I wallowed in self-pity. Then I realized that I needed to find the message in the mess. Seventeen years in the mortgage business meant finance and money were deeply entrenched in my being. Obviously, it was time for something different.

While I searched for a new position, I also searched my soul. I meditated and prayed. Meditation became my go-to activity. I spent more time with my children, parents, and horses. I got in touch with my spirit. Even though I was losing everything I owned, a glorious peace had taken root. This layoff pushed me to remember that material things have nothing to do with a beautiful life.

After a jobless 3½ months, I secured a position. The pay was more than unemployment, and that was a start! My home was going into foreclosure, and I was evicted from the barn where I boarded my horses. My world, to an outsider, appeared to be falling apart. Yet I was filled with joy. I knew God was at work.

I meditated on a solution. I asked for a home to rent that was no more than five miles from the children's schools and had room for us all, including the dog, cat, and horses. I prayed for affordability and asked to be notified by Him when it was available. I trusted Him completely.

After approximately two weeks of focused meditation, my soul was urged to check the rental listings. My country dream home was divinely delivered. It was perfection, as only God can give.

When I received that pink slip, I had no idea that I would be led to this beautiful life. I surrendered to God's grace and the miracles poured in. When we think we need more than Him, He reminds us: Grace is enough.

Grace Stepped In

By Ginger Gauldin

I saw him begin to fall, and I managed to move the chair aside to keep him from harm. Next thing I knew, a phone was in my hand.

Just as methodically, an inner voice was saying, "Oxygen...he needs oxygen. He is not breathing! Tell them."

I had dialed 911 without thinking. "What is your emergency," the dispatcher said.

Inner Voice said, "Blood needs to get to the brain. Do it...do it for him...now!"

I thought, *Okay, how do I do that? I don't know how.*

The dispatcher said, "Can you do CPR?"

How? I thought. *He's face down. He's so heavy. I have to turn him over.* My head told me I should be freaking out, so I did...for about five seconds while I told the dispatcher what was happening. Then Grace glided in, and the next few minutes became a blur as Grace and I became one. Ego and emotion took a back seat while calm and persistence took over.

"Just do it...all will be made right...they are coming," my Inner Voice reassured me. "TRUST ME. Keep going...listen to the directions...focus. Don't worry that he's turning gray. Gray is only a color; it doesn't mean anything. You can do this."

I'm hesitant to believe that I may have disconnected from my body, yet it's the only way to understand what took place in those moments. I do remember feeling somewhat disoriented as I stood up when the EMTs arrived, thinking, *What's happening?* I answered questions. I felt my throat vibrate...did I make a sound? I was on some kind of auto-pilot. It was like being enclosed in a cocoon...a soft, enveloping calm, an involuntary trust.

I had been semi-present. Something else had taken over, causing me to move – breathing and thrusting, again and again. Amazingly, death never once crossed my mind. Emotions flooded in only much later – feelings of gratitude for the gift of life, second chances, and immeasurable love and devotion. In the absence of fear, Grace had stepped in, holding us all together and providing space for the miracle.

Time Bestowed by God

By Patsy Hillman

Tall, aged oak and maple trees canopied our path as my husband and I drove along the streets of Leamington towards our anniversary date. We arrived at the charming, red-bricked Victorian home, which was now a fine-dining restaurant. As we crossed the front porch, our host greeted us with kindness and led us into a quaint, dimly lit room with a flickering white candle in the centre of our table. Our anniversary dinner was delicious and delightful in every way. The entire experience felt like a mirror reflecting my dreams and desires back to me.

I appreciated this magical evening for so many reasons. Living on a farm with three kids and one income, we had faced hard times; so having such an extravagant outing was a rare occasion for us. We had been married young (over 30 years ago), and we'd never had such a special anniversary dinner. Also, the past few months had been very disturbing, as my father was dying of cancer.

A week earlier, Dad asked where we were planning on going for our anniversary. I told him that we had no plans, but he insisted that we go. "Life is too short," he said. "Go out and enjoy yourselves!" We had no worries about him being left unattended, for his siblings and other family members were helping as caregivers. So the next day I made all the arrangements. I booked our dinner, made a hair appointment, called my aunt for babysitting, and called my husband's boss to get Mike the evening off on our special day, September 24th.

The night after our anniversary dinner, my father passed away in his sleep. That afternoon, my stepmother handed me a gift and apologized for dad passing on our anniversary. I was confused; I thought it was the day after. Puzzling as it was, though, the death paper stated September 24th. Everyone involved with our night out had believed it was the 24th the day before. Somehow, time had changed for us, or we wouldn't have had our magical dinner date.

Dad's final wish was for us to go out and enjoy our anniversary. So, with love and prayer, it was made possible. Now, each year on September 24th, we think about this miracle, giving thanks for the day we were given time bestowed by God, filled with grace.

In loving memory of my dad, Edmund Bastien.

The Grace of Infinite Source

By Faith Freed

Grace gives me the shivers – in a good way! It's like magic, knowing that the universe is conspiring in my favor. To experience grace is to be held in the embrace of the divine, or what I call *Infinite Source*. It's easy to talk about faith, but when it's *felt* – THAT'S grace! (Can you tell I'm a fan?) I welcome grace when it comes, and I notice, appreciate, and celebrate it – from the biggest miracles right down to finding the perfect parking space.

Although grace sometimes arrives unbidden and unexpectedly, I find that it helps to open myself up to grace on a daily basis. Just like I schedule other priorities, I have a go-to time to connect with Infinite Source: at 11:11. I chose this time because it reminds me that everything is lining up as it should. Also, each 1 represents an aspect of my spiritual system: Infinite Source (higher power), Inspired Self (higher self), Incarnate Self (body/mind), and Incarnate Source (nature). So I have a twice-a-day reminder to get grace on the radar.

Of course, 11:11 isn't the only time when grace happens. It can be found in *any* moment of true presence, and it often comes as a delightful surprise! On occasion, grace totally rocks my world, such as when I received a calling to write a spiritual book titled *IS* (short for *Infinite Source* – a pointer to all-that-is). When I got this divine directive, there was nothing to do but surrender, show up, and bring it through. I've done many jobs in my life, but the creation of this book was different. I felt pregnant with the material and guided to get the word out. It really wasn't up to me, and, ironically, that gave me a certainty like I'd never felt before. My co-author was Infinite Source – how could the endeavor be more blessed?

Even when Infinite Source doesn't arrive at exactly 11:11, I feel that creating this regular reminder helps me to open to grace...*all* day, *every* day! I invite Infinite Source to infuse all that comes through me, writing and otherwise. And when I live and act in the space of grace, I'm at the peak of productivity, service, and bliss.

Grace Demonstrated with a Drugstore Bath Set

By Lori Thiessen

I love bath sets. It was just after Christmas 2003, and I stood in the drugstore admiring the shelf full of them. They were on sale, and I wanted to buy one. *What a ridiculous thought*, I told myself. *You have NO room in that little house. There isn't a spot in that bathroom for anything else.*

With five young children, the bathroom was filled with towels, bath toys, and other essentials, including a potty. There was no room for frivolous items like fancy bath sets. Nor was there room in the budget.

Yet I lingered at the display. One set in particular caught my eye. I picked it up. The label read "Pure Indulgence Vanilla Milk," and it came with sponges, soaps, and lotions, all packed in a wicker basket. Beautiful. I held it, standing there for several minutes.

Setting it down, I chided myself for letting my thoughts wander to things luxurious.

Then I heard a voice in my head saying, "Buy it."

The voice startled me, and I picked the set up again, arguing back, "But I can't afford it, and there's no room in the bathroom."

"Buy it. You will have a place for it."

I bought it, took it home, and then, embarrassed by my impulsiveness, left it in the bag and shoved it in the back corner of my closet.

That October, I was unpacking and moving into our new house, when I came across the bath set. I was overcome by emotion as I took it out of the original shopping bag and set it prominently on the ledge of the Jacuzzi tub in the ensuite and remembered the voice saying, "You will have a place for it."

Overwhelmed, I paused to allow my heart to reflect on all the events of the past 10 months that had brought me from that moment in the drugstore, that little house in that small town, to this city and this house.

God's love, care, promises, and provision were demonstrated to me through a moment of grace with a drugstore bath set.

Chapter 9
Grace-Filled Transitions

W e have both lost loved ones, so we know that it is not easy or pleasant. We've experienced intense grief – feeling depressed, desolate, and empty. And, eventually, we've come out the other side, emerging back into the light.

Losing a loved one is among the most difficult experiences most of us will ever go through. Even if you believe with all your heart that they are in a better place, it is still natural to miss their physical presence, to go through the stages of grief, and to need some time to adjust to life without them. In addition to the pain and challenges, however, times of transitions can also bring profound moments of grace – deeper connections, emotional healing, and miracles from beyond.

In this chapter, you'll read about people saying goodbye to loved ones – stories touched by pain and heartbreak, but also filled with miracles, life lessons, and grace. Some of the stories focus on the period leading up to a loved one's passing – sharing special connections (or reconnections), forgiveness, and healing. Other pieces describe miracles at the moment of death – getting a glimpse of someone's soul or even feeling their soul depart as a physical sensation (like an electric charge or a "wind" passing through the body). And many of the pieces describe the lasting legacy left by loved ones after their transition – how their spirit lives on, ways in which they continue to positively impact people's lives, and messages of love that they leave upon our trail (oftentimes filled with their special humor).

We hope that you are as moved by these stories as we were – that you are touched by the lives and loss, the heartbreak and healing, and the legacies of love. And, ultimately, we hope that you are also inspired by the grace-filled reminders that our souls never die.

Gifts from Grief

By Arielle Ford

My sister, Debbie Ford, died in 2013, and I have been truly humbled by this experience. Through the painful parts, I have been inspired to continuously look for the gifts from grief. It is a process, and it is quite imperfect, yet I have learned that it is also rich with new discoveries and opportunities to grow. I am forever altered by Debbie's passing, yet I now see that the gifts from this experience have benefited me in profound ways.

Since her death, I have developed a deeper gratitude for every aspect of my life. I have set aside time to let go of stress and have awakened to the realities of how I have been endangering my emotional and physical health. Recognizing this prompted me to make some huge changes, including taking my first-ever sabbatical from work, where I devoted time to love, healing, resting, and restoration.

Perhaps the most surprising gift, and the one I am most reluctant to even share, is that being in this delicate state has given me the freedom to just say no. I constantly get requests for my time and connections, for endorsements and introductions. I like to say yes – it's fun to assist people and be connected, so I rarely said no. Saying yes always came easily, and because I work at such a fast pace, none of these things seemed to take a lot of my time or energy.

But now, having so little energy to spare, I have found that saying no is essential. I have no extra bandwidth to deal with the demands I once juggled every day. I now love that I can get through a busy work day and know that a restful night where I can plop onto the couch and relax is part of my new routine. Allowing myself to say no has helped me find a new freedom, and I am certainly grateful for that.

So while this process of grief hasn't been an easy one, it did bring along some gifts that continue to give even to this day. Each day gets a little easier and a little better.

Grace in Transition

By Rebekah Bernard

Lucille looked up at me with bright eyes and a smile. She held my hand and whispered, "You kept your promise." She slowly exhaled and comfortably rested, emanating peace. The hair on my arms stood up. I silently expressed gratitude for blessed moments like this one.

Six months earlier, Lucille had decided she was feeling well enough to fly off to Las Vegas. Her hospice team – a nurse, social worker, and myself (the spiritual counselor) – assured Lucille that we would be there if she needed hospice in the future. During the next few months, everyone scattered. Her social worker chose to spend the next six months in Washington, and the nurse was approaching her last day in her current hospice role.

I came into the office and the admission nurse gave me a new patient. I looked at the document and gasped. It was Lucille. Deciding to discontinue dialysis, she had turned again to hospice.

Lucille smiled knowingly as I told her that her social worker had just returned two days ago, her nurse's last day was two days away, and I was able to be completely present. She was convinced that her faith had opened up the possibility of the improbabilities that all three of us would be there for her again.

Lucille was indeed a woman of grace. With spiky, punked hair, Lucille wore heavy-framed black glasses that enhanced her soulful eyes. She was in the professional field of healing, with a strong spiritual foundation that contributed through lasting ways in the community. Lucille role-modeled and taught love to all who knew her. As her time of transition approached, her heart rested in serenity. This woman beamed with transcendental truth. Lucille, both practically and spiritually, arranged her entire end-of-life experience. The harmony felt by those who entered her room was palpable.

In my hospice work as a spiritual counselor, I bear witness to the raw beauty in the psycho-spiritual transformation that occurs at the end of life. These are blessed moments of pure, unconditional love with no filter and an awe-inspiring inner peace. Lucille clearly lived this sacred grace, and I am eternally touched.

The Stain of Grief

By Tanya Levy

It was a hot day in July when I got the call from my father. I was away taking a summer course four hours from home. Dad said, "He died." The world caved in all around me. My son's father had died? How was that possible?

I somehow managed to stumble around the campus until I found my professor. I explained that I had to go home and be with my son to tell him what happened. My professor told me, "Do what you have to do."

I went home and comforted my son, and on the way back to school I got another call. This time my son's grandfather had died. I called my professor. "I have to miss another day of class for another funeral."

For the second time within just a few days, I felt blessed by my professor's response: "Do what you have to do."

I got back to class and picked up a book I needed through interlibrary loan. Without realizing it, my portable teacup stained the book. I soaked the stain, put a fan on it to dry it and even bleached it. Nothing got those stains out. Finally, I had to send it back. I sent it with this note.

Dear Librarian:

I tried everything to clean this book. This summer I lost two people I truly cared about. Just like the stain that I cannot remove from this book, their grief will stain my heart forever. Some stains never leave the heart. Yet those stains make our heart what it is. Our hearts are more beautiful with those wounds, and I hope this book can still be useful with this dried stain. If I need to replace it, let me know.

I never heard a word from the librarian.

I believe she/he heard me from a place of grace, knowing that after my summer of grief, I could not bring myself to replace the book. Somehow that stained book comforted me in my time of loss. It was still serviceable in spite of its stain, and thankfully, so was I. And I got an A+ in my course.

Grace of Mama

By Arwen Lynch

Mama died as we held hands over her body. It wasn't meant to be an endearing moment. I don't think the three of us – my sister, my stepsister, and I – really thought about what we were doing. We just heard her breathing change. As she began her transition from this life to the next, we three girls held onto one another. We made promises over our mother's deathbed. Promises to be friends. Promises to not tear our family apart. Then it was over. My mother was gone. My guiding light went out when I was 41 years old. I thought my world had ended. In a way, it had just begun again.

I moved through the next few days – the funeral, the gatherings of friends and family – as if I were wrapped in a thick, grey blanket. I heard their words. I felt their touches. But it felt as if it were from a great distance. My sister and I went through the house. We split things up. Even though the family was sure we would fight, we didn't. The only argument we had was over one item that I thought Mama wanted my sister to have. My sister thought I should have it. Strange to think of that now since my sister and I tended to fight a lot. I think the loss of our mother brought us closer rather than driving a wedge between us.

I didn't think grace was possible after that loss. I wondered if there was even any point to doing more than drawing breath just to make it through each day. Grace was a foreign concept to me. I couldn't orient myself when my compass was gone. Mama must have known. She came to me in a dream to remind me of a story she'd told me about a sparrow, a pile of manure, and a cat. That message woke me up. I moved back into an attitude of gratitude. I allowed grace back in. In that moment, my mama began to live again.

The Grace and Gift of Deb's Transition

By Karen D. Cote

In August of 2014, my friend, Deb, was hospitalized and placed in the intensive-care unit. Things went rapidly downhill, and her death came very quickly. I viewed her passing through my lens as a hospice volunteer, friend, and shamanic minister of The Circle of the Sacred Earth. I told her we were all okay and she could choose to go whenever she wanted. I encouraged her to look for her deceased family members.

Moments before death, there was movement under her eyelids as if she were seeing someone. The energy of the room changed abruptly, becoming almost electric. I could feel the hair on my arms standing up. The room felt "full," and I intuitively sensed that deceased loved ones were coming forward to welcome her as she was soon transitioning to the other side. I felt a "wind" begin to pass through me from her body as her heart slowed, and then an even bigger "wind" blew through me as she flatlined. As she and the others who had come forward to greet her left this realm of existence, the room once again felt "normal." I smiled and knew it was okay to leave the ICU. Deb had transitioned over and was no longer here.

A few days later, while being driven to her wake, I looked at her photo and said, "Hey, Deb, wait until you see all the people who are coming. What do you think about that?" At that very moment, my phone lit up with a text from someone named Deb. After the wake, I spoke again to my photo of Deb, "They did a great job with your hair and put you in your favorite shirt. What do you think about that?" Once again, my phone lit up with a text message from yet another person named Deb. I chuckled, for I knew that Deb had heard me and was communicating from the other side. This synchronicity was a gift of grace. She let me know that she was okay.

Doorway of the Soul

By Elaine Lockard

For 53 years, my mother endured being confined to a wheelchair due to polio. In her later years, post-polio syndrome set in, and her body slowly weakened until a stroke finally put her in a nursing home. Even though her body was betraying her at every turn, her mind was never affected. It was always sharp and clear.

One day she had a heart attack that sent her to the hospital, which was the final straw in compromising her ability to breathe on her own. She was ready to leave this life, but it took some convincing, by both her and me, for the doctors to know that she was clearly able to make that courageous decision for herself.

As they removed her oxygen, Mom motioned for me to completely lower the head of her bed. Because of her experience with her weak condition, she knew that gravity would work against her being able to breathe and help hasten her transition.

I had never witnessed a passing before. What drew my undivided attention were her eyes. As her time approached, her pupils got extremely large – as if her eyes had turned black – and she stopped blinking. It was like she was seeing something that was so amazing she could not look at it intently enough.

I kept thinking, *What is she seeing?* Suddenly, I remembered that it is said that "the eyes are the windows to the soul." Since I knew that the eyes often stay open when a person passes, it occurred to me that they are also the "doorway of the soul." They allow us to see the truth in someone we meet. However, they also allow a person's truth, their soul, to finally see that pure, white Light of Love, which then welcomes their soul and allows them to pass between the veils.

When I think of that day, I remember my mother's courage and determination, but I don't remember seeing her dying. I only remember seeing her amazing eyes – the doorway of *her* soul!

Heaven Was Sent an Angel

By Marla David

Some people believe in Heaven, and some don't. Auntie believed in Heaven. She had hopes of meeting her mother, father, and other family members who had passed on.

Auntie had a hard life. She was the black sheep of the family. At school, as she was left-handed, she was hit on her wrists and forced to use her right hand. She had to quit school to watch my mom when my grandmother had to work in their store. She was married for six months but slept on the floor until she could pay for their divorce. She worked at the post office sorting mail, standing on her feet, which I suppose is why she ended up with terrible bunions.

Auntie slept at our place on weekends, with me on the pull-out couch in the den. She took me everywhere – to movies, parks, Centre Island, the Exhibition, and to Niagara Falls. What wonderful memories. We were best friends.

Auntie was a pure soul. In Florida, at the hotel where she stayed, she took in a homeless couple. I was taken to see her mentally and physically handicapped acquaintances who lived in the projects. They looked forward to our visits, welcoming us with smiles and serving us tea and cookies, as Auntie would tell stories and ask about their well-being.

During the last month of her life, Auntie told me her family members came through her walls at night, but she was sending them away. As her health deteriorated, she got an infection, which became gangrene. It didn't look good. Before I left her that final time, I told her I loved her and kissed her cheek.

The call came in the wee hours. Auntie had passed away. In the morning, I closed her eyes and sat with her for a while. I wasn't afraid. I knew that last night, when her family came, she went with them. Heaven was sent an angel.

Unimaginable Grace

By Heather Wiest

Within the first week of living with George, he accused me of stealing. My little-girl gut feeling was not good. I had known George as the neighborhood troublemaker since 1977; cops frequented his home for disturbing the peace. My mother, tangled in the chains of depression and addiction, divorced my father and soon married this decorated WWII Veteran. During the five turbulent years they were together, our lives were in perpetual crisis, stemming from substance abuse and domestic violence. In an attempt to escape, I moved out at age 15. This independence offered freedom, safety, and grace upon grace.

Despite our difficulties, George considered me his daughter, and we remained in contact throughout the years. In 2007, his health rapidly declined and he needed support. My husband and I cared for him, determined to extend grace and unconditional love. Our young daughters were innocent rays of light, encouraging us all.

Upon George's death bed, I experienced the most surreal, grace-filled connection with him. I was reading Psalm 23 – sharing about God's love, forgiveness, peace, the afterlife, letting go – and asked if he was ready to receive it all. From a body that had been unresponsive for weeks, he slowly raised his hands, placed them in prayer position, and motioned his lips to utter, "I believe."

In complete awe, I fell on my knees and bowed to the omnipresence of the Divine – one of the most amazing, serene moments of my life! George felt unconditional love. George knew peace. George experienced unimaginable grace. *Thirty years of my life invested into his life mattered.* All the trauma, hurt, and challenges were worth it. Every experience came together for a purpose way beyond my human comprehension.

George passed on Veterans Day in 2007. I have no doubt this, too, was purposed.

Cherish Each Precious Moment

By Hue Anh Nguyen

I had mixed feelings about leaving my family, friends, and second homeland, Australia, to move to a foreign country, but I was following my heart's calling. My world had opened when I traveled in Europe in 1996 and met the man of my dreams. So I traded the warm, sunny weather and wonderful friends and family to be with the one I love in Oregon, USA.

Five months later, while getting comfortable with my new surroundings (despite being cold and wet outside), I found myself missing my home and family. Just then, the phone rang. I was so excited to hear my father's voice, but my heart sank when I heard the news: My 51-year-old mother had been diagnosed with end-stage lung cancer and given just months to live.

I was shaken by the news and felt helpless being so far away. I wanted my mother to still live her dream of visiting the United States, to see the world like I did, to be at our wedding, and to hold my baby. This was a nightmare that I couldn't wake up from.

I had never prayed so hard before that time. On my knees, I begged and pleaded to Quan Am, the compassion deity, bargaining for more time for my mother. Suddenly, it became clear what I needed to do. I gathered myself together, packed up my 25-pound wedding gown, and flew to Australia to spend time with my mother and have the wedding there so she could attend.

I spent the last year of my mother's life learning more about her and her childhood than I had over the 28 years of growing up with her. For that, I am forever grateful. Through this experience, I learned so much about my mother and also about life itself. I learned to appreciate my health. I learned that nothing is permanent and time does not wait for anyone. I learned to love now, to live now, and to cherish each precious moment.

Grandma's Hand

By Karen D. Cote

Grandma was the most important woman in my life. Near the end of her life, she became ill with Alzheimer's and eventually entered a nursing home. Early one morning, I got a call informing me that she was about to die. I knew there was no way I would be able to get to her side in time, so I lay in bed in the semi-darkness of the early morning and prayed to God that she would quickly be released from her years of suffering.

As an intuitive shamanic minister of The Circle of the Sacred Earth, I spoke to Grandma in an altered state of consciousness. I told her that we were all okay and for her to transition to the next realm of existence. I felt her energy reach out and grab my hand. At that instant, I felt as if someone had gently wrapped their arms around my entire chest area, and I was lifted up off the bed. Although my eyes were closed, I saw a light that was brighter than a thousand suns yet did not hurt my eyes. Warmth spread deep through my chest as I rose up towards that bright, loving light.

For a brief moment, I was filled with such love, peace, and grace that went beyond words. Suffice it to say that it was so wonderful that I did not want to leave this amazing place. At that moment, I heard, "It is not yet your time." I felt the energy of Grandma's hand slipping away as she moved forward into God's grace, and I came crashing back into this world and my body on the bed.

I looked at the clock, and it was 6 a.m. Later that day, I received a phone call confirming that Grandma had indeed died at 6 a.m.

This gift of grace motivated me to lead my life in a positive way so that I will someday see that light and feel the touch of my Grandma's hand once again.

The Parting Gift

By Patricia Downing

She's sleeping peacefully. Dad and I are sitting quietly at her bedside, not wanting to pull her away from her journey. My husband, Larry, is sitting nearby. My mind goes back through the day – a visit from my son and his wife, and phone calls from her other grandchildren, my sister-in-law, and my brother. So many sweet moments, words of love and appreciation, gentle closings. The day has brought her a sense of completion.

Mother wanted to leave her body. She never had a fear of death but thought of it as "going home." Recently, she had been longing to take that next step. After several years of diminished functioning, she regretted the loss of the independence that had defined her life. Despite the serious challenges of the last several years, however, she had maintained a mostly positive outlook, and we still laughed a lot and shared a close, loving companionship.

Now, as I wonder at the peace on her face, she opens her eyes, looks right into mine and smiles the most beautiful smile I have ever seen. Her eyes have an inner light that reaches into my soul and brings tears to my eyes. I see joy, even ecstasy on her face. Not a word is spoken, but so much more is communicated in that moment than words could convey. The love flows between us for several seconds – then she moves her eyes to my father at my side and sends him the same silent message. When she closes her eyes, she leaves me reeling from the power of the love and the joy she had shared with us.

What was she seeing that brought her such joy? It's not yet time for me to know, but her very last act was to assure me that she was fine and excited about the next part of her journey. Her gift to me in that moment of grace was too precious for words. I carry it in my heart even now, and it continues to bless me every day.

Healing Is Simple

By Suzanne M. Fortino

Recently, I experienced a loss that has impacted my being more than any other loss before. I have been blessed to assist my loved ones preparing for their journey home many times, but this time was much more enlightening. I walked into this journey with the knowledge of healing. I brought with me the elixirs that I believe – and my mother's doctor believed – dissolved her tumors. And I brought an intense desire for my spirituality to shine brightly for the world to see through this healing. While embracing this journey with courage and conviction, I never allowed fear to enter my being. Throughout the many shared moments of tragedy and grace, I never wavered from my belief that love heals all.

Although this journey did not have the exact outcome I expected, it did help me to realize that the true meaning of healing is simple: It is allowing the light to shine brightly through you for everyone to see…and absorb when they're ready. It is accepting with courage that not everybody's physical being is ready for healing when their spirit is. It is seeing the positive in everything, no matter how tragic, and not giving up. It is being grateful for the ability to share our unconditional gifts of love and light. It is learning every day about how we can make life better by practicing forgiveness of self and others.

Through moments of tragedy and grace, I've been enlightened and have embraced my spirituality again. I believe in myself and my message to the world: Healing is simple. We all get there in different ways, but that is our own journey. On January, 9, 2015, my healing began. Since then, through many moments of grace, I've reminded myself daily to continue to nurture the growth of my spirituality.

More Faith, Less Worry

By Monica Wilcox

Four weeks after my mother's unexpected passing, she came to me in a lucid dream. I dreamt I was sitting in an unknown living room with my father. My mother's oversized picture on the wall came alive, and she began to reassure us that she was happy and safe. Then the image changed to a family picture of my brother and his wife. Two young boys sat at their feet. My sister-in-law had been only few weeks along at the funeral. At the time of my dream, they still hadn't discovered the sex of their first child. Revealing their future family was my mother's way of validating her presence before she gave me her message.

"It's so easy," my mother said. "If I had known how easy living is and how easy dying is, I would have worried less." Of all the wisdom she could have imparted in our first spiritual connection, "stress less" was at the top.

Alan Watts says, "Man suffers only because he takes seriously what the Gods made for fun." From her higher perspective, my mother could see how much of her life energy had been consumed by worry. Being the creator of her own strain had not served her well. Her message – *more faith, less worry* – is one that resonates for the majority of us in this hectic, technological age.

At the time, I didn't tell my brother and his wife about my dream, but I did tell my father. The two of us shared a secretive smile when they told us they were having a boy. Two years later, we finally told them about the dream…after they discovered they were having a second boy!

You Talk the Loudest When You Are Speechless

By Nishani Sakizlis

About two years ago, I was awakened by a long-distance phone call informing me that my father had been admitted to a hospital in Sri Lanka in critical condition. At that time, I could only think that I wanted to be with him in his last hours, but being six months pregnant with my second child and facing a long flight made me wonder if the trip was safe for me.

However, a spiritual prodding convinced me that this trip would be safe. So, the next thing I knew, I found myself on my way to Sri Lanka. It seemed almost instantly that I was at my father's side, holding his hand.

He was still breathing but wasn't able to speak. Despite this, I felt that we were having the longest continual conversation we'd ever had. My logical, engineering mind led me to doubt his ability to converse. But there, all my doubts were cast away by the simple act of my father putting his hand on his chest every time I visited him.

Shortly after I arrived, he passed with very little suffering.

Looking back now, assured that my father is resting in peace, the vision of him lying quietly with his hand on his heart gives spiritual truth to my newfound belief that you talk the loudest when you are speechless.

As a case in point, I have spoken more to my father since his passing two years ago than I had in my entire life. My only real sadness is that he had to pass in order to communicate with me, but the fact that he communicates regularly with me now fills me with the utmost joy.

A Peaceful Transition

By Jeanette St. Germain

I sat beside her hospital bed, our fingers entwined against the rough fabric of cold, gray sheets. There were screens beeping, flashing green and red buttons, and paper printouts of perfectly timed snapshots showcasing her shallow breath. Each passing hour, a nurse would pop in to make sure all of the monitoring was going smoothly, double checking heart rate and coma symptomology.

My great-grandmother looked shrunken, a shell of the vibrant, stubborn woman I knew and loved more than anyone else in the world. It had been a simple broken hip, something that happens when you are 86 years young and are determined to dust the top of your freezer. They had said it was a clean break and should heal nicely, that she would only need a bit of physical therapy, and then she would be good as new. A week later, there were blood clots in both legs, a staph infection, and a myriad of other fallen dominos that no one could fully explain. Her unresponsive, vegetative state was simply a formality to the end we all knew was near.

I squeezed her hand and started talking softly, shifting my voice into a relaxing, meditative tone. I intuitively knew she could hear me and that she needed release. I guided her to imagine her favorite places: a sandy beach, a lush forest, or one of the red bridges she loved when traveling in China. I detailed angels, loved ones, and animals waiting to greet her. The energy in the room lightened, and I sensed her spirit was more relaxed.

I continued, taking her deeper into an otherworldly place of pure love. There was music, dance, and art of all kinds, and my great-grandfather there to help sweep her off her feet. I assured her that we would be fine if she left, that our hearts would mend and that we would celebrate the blessings of her life.

Breathing deeply, I felt a sudden peace descend around us. It was almost as if I could hear angels whispering in our ears. Only a few moments more, and then alarms signaled that she had taken her last breath.

Someone Dies, Someone Lives

By Lori Evans

I called 911 in the early morning. My dad's lungs were hardening, making it nearly impossible for him to breathe, even with oxygen.

The next day, which happened to be my birthday, I was sitting on his hospital bed. He peered over the ventilator keeping him alive and pointed at me. "Forty-eight," he said. Tears flooded our eyes as we nodded. "No Dairy Queen…"

~~~

One day several months earlier, I grabbed a pen and wrote in his antiquated datebook.

"What're you writing?"

I showed him what I'd written on October 3rd: "The Best Day EVER!!!"

"Hmm…" He muttered with pursed lips. "Why's that?"

"It's the best day ever because I was born!"

He thought about it and nodded. And then I told him what I wanted for my birthday: to have ice cream with him at Dairy Queen, our favorite childhood eatery. He smirked.

As time lingered, I'd tenaciously remind him of our special upcoming day. "You ready?" I'd ask.

"Oh, boy, yes!" he'd reply sarcastically. "I've already got my clothes picked out!"

~~~

I was checking in with security when I got a call from an unidentified female telling me my dad was holding on and needed me NOW. Not waiting, I raced to get to him.

Once in his room, the nurse ushered me to his bedside and told me to talk to him. Confused, I took his hand, sobbing, "He's gone."

"No," she assured me, showing me the monitor. "He still has a very faint pulse. The hearing is the last to go. Talk to him."

"Okay…" I began to rub his chest. "I don't know why you chose this date, Dad, but I'm choosing to be honored…I'll be okay…go be with Mom and the others…they're waiting…go on."

I was born October 3, 1967. My dad died October 3, 2015.

The Limits of Heroism

By Jerri Eddington

On October 5, 1986, I woke up to an early phone call from my sister, Rose. She was hysterical because she had no platelets. She had been in the hospital battling leukemia since late August. The doctors changed rotations every month, and the new doctor had not ordered her backup platelets. She wasn't eligible for a bone-marrow transplant, and I was a platelet donor for her. Rose's life expectancy without the transplant was three to five years, and she was nearing her fourth year. I calmed Rose down and told her I would contact the Red Cross so I could donate my platelets.

"I must come in and donate platelets for my sister," I told the receptionist. I was told that donors don't usually call in to make an appointment. "Don't you understand? My sister will die! She has NO platelets," I pleaded. Soon, I was given approval to donate my platelets at the only Red Cross open on Sundays, which was in downtown Columbus.

Normally, I could have gotten there in 30 minutes. As I approached the downtown area on that day, however, I was greeted by a series of roadblocks. An auto race was being held on the streets, and I couldn't get to the Red Cross center! As I navigated the streets, I kept running into roadblocks. Finally, I decided to park my car and walk.

By the time I got to the Red Cross center, I was hyperventilating. I was taken to a chair and asked to breathe into a small brown bag. As my breathing became regular, I was hooked up to a one-armed machine to begin the process. "This is why we don't usually have family members donate platelets; it's too hard," one of the nurses remarked. At that moment, through grace, I realized that I could not continue to try to save my sister's life. It was out of my control.

As it turned out, this was the final time I would donate platelets. Two months later, just one month before her 41st birthday, Rose transitioned. Through the process of my sister's illness, I discovered that there is a Creator...and it's not me. Even heroism has its limits.

An Instrument of Grace

By Cynthia L. Ryals

The morning was crisp and bright, two days before Thanksgiving. Grateful to have a break from school, I was already packed to make the drive home to visit my dad in the hospital. I awakened to the haunting sound of Dan Fogelberg: "The leader of the band is tired, and his eyes are growing old; but his blood runs through my instrument, and his song is in my soul."

This song I loved was suddenly jarring to my soul, as if it had been played especially for me. It was unsettling yet oddly comforting. My dad and I, both frustrated musicians, bonded over our love of music. I instinctively knew he was speaking to my heart.

The leader of the band was gone.

Arriving home to the news, the change in the air was palpable, suffocating; the earth crumbled in slow motion beneath my feet. The remainder of the day was a whirlwind of necessary activity. I was grateful for a quiet moment when my mother sent me to purchase food for visiting mourners.

Standing in line at a crowded take-out restaurant, desperately clasping a $20 bill, I stared blankly at the menu. The task was simple, yet I had no idea what to do. The young man behind the counter looked into my eyes and understood. I was truly seen. He was gentle, kind, and compassionate as he patiently guided me through my order. I could only gesture, unable to speak. There was no judgment, only tenderness and reassurance that I would be alright. In the depth of my unspeakable despair, grace was offered through the kindness of a stranger.

Decades have passed, and I am still deeply moved by that young man who embodied the essence of what my father taught me through his own example – to extend love and compassion to all, for we are all the same. I aspire to be an instrument of this grace.

Grief, Grace, and Eternal Love

By Veronica Mather

My brother's passing when he was 39 and the recent loss of my beloved sheep, Womble, provided me with life-changing lessons about grace. Both times, grief wrapped her fingers around my heart and threw a dark blanket over my world. And both times, grace bestowed me with strength, courage, and resilience.

Womble, my rescue sheep, was unwell for months. Despite all efforts, the day came when I knew the struggle to save him was in vain. I had saved Womble's life, yet here I was about to take it away. The guilt that comes with such a decision is hard to live with. On reflection, my grieving began the day Womble became unwell. Despite glimpses of hope, the fear of losing him was always present.

Womble was a sensitive soul, yet he possessed inner strength, determination, and resilience. His dignified courage during his illness and at the time of his passing was incredibly moving and will stay with me forever.

My brother Carl's passing after a car accident was devastating. While there was a lot of support from friends and within the community, I discovered that, for many people, grief and loss is a taboo subject. Some people ignored my loss. Others made insensitive comments that I'm sure were not intended to hurt me, but they did nonetheless. This made my already dark world a little darker. But it also made me more determined than ever to live my life with grace – grace to accept that life will never be perfect and grace to accept that I cannot control all aspects of my life, including other people's reactions, a loved one's health, or whether they live or die.

Grief and loss have taught me to accept *what is* with grace. And so I thank you, Carl and Womble – two precious souls whose lives here on Earth were fleeting – for your eternal love and all you have taught me about life and grace.

My Father: Fear in Life, Love in Death

By Chantal Vanderhaeghen

Something I have learned is that no matter how much you think you are prepared for a parent's death, you are not. This is particularly true if it is unexpected. We logically understand that our parents are meant to die before us, but nothing prepares us for that loss when it actually happens.

I had been getting visions about my father's death for 18 months before he passed. Still, I was not prepared when he died suddenly. His death rocked my world for so many reasons, principally because we had only started to reconcile six months beforehand.

My memories of childhood had been emotionally, spiritually, and physically violent and void of love and joy. For so many years, I wanted my father to be out of my life. I feared him. Only when he was gone did I realise that my longing to be rid of the fear of him had overshadowed what I really yearned for: to feel his love that was hiding somewhere behind the façade of his own fears. Through my father's transition, he finally showed me the pure love and grace that he was unable to share in his lifetime.

Three weeks before his death, he appeared to me as his French mother, announcing that he would die within a month. And it came to pass. What I found interesting was that he channeled this "visit" to me through the female line of his family. This meant something to me, as my father had been so sexist and demeaning of women in his lifetime. For him to appear through his mother meant that he was embracing his gentle feminine aspect.

It took me a long time to understand and accept that this was his only way of being able to embrace me with his love. I now feel his purity of heart that he had never before shared with me. I have transitioned from anger and hate to love and faith. After years of fearing him, I now absolutely love having my father's spirit in my life.

Sunflower Love
By Malaika Murphy-Sierra

My mom died on October 14, 2014. I learned she had stage-4 colon cancer during my freshman year of college; a few months later, as I started my sophomore year, I learned she only had about a month to live.

I flew home to Virginia to be with her and my family. The last few days as she lay dying at the hospice center were the most intensely terrifying, disheartening, and stressful days of my life. The night before she died, I completely gave up. I asked, "How can we live in a universe where we lose everything we've ever loved?"

But then, late that night, something miraculous happened. I felt as though every cell of my being was slowly being filled with unconditional love. My sense of self felt much larger than solely a 19-year-old girl. I felt no separation from my mom's unconditionally loving spirit. I was the same energy, and because I could keep passing on this love she gave to me, her essence could never die. I understood the larger tapestry of how we are all connected through unconditional love. I felt an absolute lack of fear, complete safety, complete peace.

The next couple of months I journeyed with my dad to Sedona, Arizona, where incredible synchronicities started to occur. I was reading *Conversations with God* by Neale Donald Walsch, which stated, "there are no coincidences in the universe." I wrote this down in a journal, and as soon as I took my pen off the page, I heard the next lyrics of a new song called "#88" by Lo-Fang: "an idea growing quietly from something within spreads quicker than the cancer that destroyed your mother's skin."

Later that month, I asked Mom to show me sunflowers, since that was the flower I placed on her casket. In the next 48 hours, I received five instances of sunflowers from important people on my journey.

Many more synchronicities have occurred to show me there is much more than this physical realm – and that all that really exists is unconditional love, which cannot die.

When Grace Speaks

By Tandy Elisala

Grace comes to us and through us in many forms. It is a quiet whisper, a gentle nudge, a song, a rainbow, a butterfly, or a meaningful coincidence. Grace is God's way of letting us know we are all connected. Sometimes, in the hustle and bustle of daily life, we don't always notice signs of grace, but grace has a way of showing up anyway.

Grace powerfully spoke to me on September 5, 2012. At 9 p.m., I felt a strong yearning to visit my father, who had been in hospice for 36 hours. Just after I left, my spiritual mentor, Tarra, called me with specific instructions. She advised me to visit him immediately (I was already on my way) and share my feelings about having to move the second semester of my senior year in high school. Then she wanted me to tell him how much I loved him. All the way there, I kept rehearsing what I wanted to say.

Just as I was getting off the freeway, the nurse called and told me that my dad was actively dying. I arrived six minutes before he died. I had just enough time to play soothing music and tell him how very much I loved him.

On my way home, I called Tarra and told her that I didn't have time to both yell at him and tenderly tell him I loved him, so I chose love. Tarra opened a fortune cookie in that moment and told me, "Oh my, this is for you, Tandy. The fortune says, 'A woman's thoughts are more powerful than her words.'" She affirmed that my dad DID hear me. As she said that, dragonflies were swarming around her. My dad loved dragonflies. What a beautiful way to end my night, even though it was the night I lost my hero.

River of Grace

By Julie Jones

The patient in Bed 8 of the ICU is a lifeless young girl. This morning, she was vivacious and healthy. That all changed in the moment of her impact with the tree. As her nurse, I wait with her while the tests are completed, watching her ventilator breathing rhythmically – in…out…in…out…until the doctor comes in with the grimmest of news: brain dead…no hope.

The parents are told. They come into the ICU. I stand with the father – a big, strapping man – and answer his questions. So many decisions – funeral home, organ procurement. Then, suddenly, the news hits. He gently bends over, lifts his beautiful daughter, and sobs – not a few tears but gut-wrenching sobs that tear at every ear and heart. My heart is broken. The tears flow. I stand. The family leaves, and I prepare their daughter, gently cleaning her body.

I have witnessed these scenes many times before, but today I am not ready. She was so young, my own children's age. I walk slowly to the bathroom. I feel sick and exhausted. I bend over, unable to stop the tears. I feel a sense of failure.

I take another breath, and with my tears still flowing, I call on the river of grace. Soon, I begin to sense its flow; this is the rhythm of life. I feel the gentle lapping against the edges of my heart. I allow the river to revitalize my spirit, reminding me that I am bound to divine love. I am called to serve as a hope bearer – a bridge between health and disease, life and death.

I do not understand these dark moments. I simply know that, during these difficult times, it is most important for me to step into the river of grace – to be able to extend grace to those who need it most. To stand with another person with compassion and empathy. To be present and bear grace.

I take another deep breath, and then I hear the announcement: a new Level-1 trauma patient is scheduled for Bed 8. Grace received, I am ready once again to be the hope bearer for one more hurting soul.

A Call from Beyond

By Robert D. White

When my uncle called to tell me that my great-grandmother had been hospitalized, I was baffled. *How can this be?* I thought. *I was just talking to her the other day, and she seemed healthier than ever.* As I made my way to the hospital alongside my uncle, all we could talk about was how mystifying this situation was. True, some people might not find it so unexpected for a 91-year-old to become seriously ill, but this was a woman who'd been living independently, had no medical history, and possessed the spirit of a much younger person.

As we sat at her bedside while she lay in a comatose state, our perplexed consternation grew deeper. We considered all the logical explanations for her state, from psychosomatic conditions to the possibility that she'd lived almost a century with an illness festering deep within. After about an hour, however, an intense feeling of peace filled the room. We shifted from feeling perplexed and sad about her possible death to celebrating and commemorating her life. But as strange as this shift was, something even more bizarre was about to happen that caused us to forget the strangeness of her unexplained illness.

As we began to reminisce, we laughed about one of her quirks: she refused to call her great-grandchildren by their names. Instead, she came up with her own set of names that she preferred, such as Sarah and Pete, which had no relevance to our birth names. I mentioned to my uncle that she had already adopted a new name for my nephew, who was only one at the time. For some reason, though, I couldn't remember this name. I thought and thought, but it just wouldn't come to me. Finally, I yelled out, "Gonnie, what is that name you called him?" Suddenly, my uncle's phone rang – presumably a wrong number, because it was a voice he didn't recognize asking for someone he didn't know. All I heard my uncle say was, "Who? There's no *Glenn* here!"

Immediately, I jumped up and hysterically yelled, "That's it! She called him *Glenn*!" Then I smiled at my great-grandmother and said, "Wow! Thank you." A few hours later, she peacefully passed on to the other side.

Love from the Other Side

By Marie Spencer-Rowland

I remember the night my mother died as if it were yesterday.

I had always promised myself that I wanted to be with Mum when she crossed over, but that wasn't to be.

I got a call from her husband. He didn't give me any explanation of why he was calling; all he said was, "Talk to your Mum."

I wasn't sure what I was supposed to say, so I just talked until I cried and told her how much I loved her.

My stepdad got back on the phone and said, "She's still here; keep talking."

I was confused but did as I was told until my stepdad got back on the phone for the final time. "She's gone," is all I remember him saying.

In a daze, I called my aunty, my mum's sister, to let her know that Mum was gone and wasn't in pain any more. As I sat there crying and talking to my aunty, I suddenly felt someone walk into the room. They didn't use the door; they came through the wall. The energy was overpowering. I turned around and looked over my right shoulder. I knew, without a doubt, it was my mum.

I casually said to my aunty, "Mum's here; she's just walked into the room," to which she replied, "Well, give her my love." And with that, I looked Mum straight in the eye and said, "It's okay, Mum, you can go now." The energy left straight back out the way it came in, and I felt at peace.

I will never forget that amazing final moment with her, which left me with no doubt that we live on once our bodies give out. I might not have been able to be there with her during her last moments on Earth, but I know that she is with me always. I know that I can ask for help, and she is there. I know that our souls never die.

A Visit from Uncle John

By Karen D. Cote

In the winter of 2013, my husband and I flew from Connecticut to Florida to attend a 100th birthday celebration for my husband's Uncle John. Uncle John and my husband were the spitting image of each other in both profile and facial features – one just much older than the other. The day after John's wonderful birthday celebration, we flew home and fell right back into the routine of life. Two months passed, I returned to work, and memories of that trip filtered into the recesses of our minds.

One night as I worked with a client in my home office, I needed to go downstairs to make a photocopy. As I passed through the kitchen, I caught in my peripheral field of vision the image of my husband sitting in the semi-darkness reading the newspaper. I thought to myself, *He will hurt his eyes in the low light.* I continued downstairs to the copy machine only to find my husband watching television! I then wondered who it was that I saw upstairs!

As a medium and channel, I often see dead people; yet I did not make the connection to the similarity between the ghostly figure and my husband until the next morning when my husband commented that he had a dream in which Uncle John waved goodbye to him. I turned to my husband and said, "Uncle John died last night." Sure enough, within a few hours, family from Florida called to say that Uncle John indeed did pass away that very night when I "saw" him and my husband dreamt of him. We both smiled and gave many thanks for the gift of grace of having Uncle John visit. It was an affirmation of the transition from one existence to another.

A Loving Message in the Mess

By Kristine Carlson

On December 13, 2006, my husband, Richard, boarded a flight to New York to promote his latest book. He wasn't feeling well but decided to power through his fatigue in response to pressure from his publisher. Sadly, Richard died instantly from a pulmonary embolism during the flight, and my life was forever changed.

Being married to Richard was simply delicious. He was a true gentleman and a delight to be in partnership with for 25 years. Upon his death, my ego went through an annihilation; I felt like I died when he died, yet I had to physically continue to live. Learning to be without him was a very messy process – much like the caterpillar in the cocoon that has to practically die in its own messy goop before breaking out and becoming a freed butterfly.

Slowly, after a period of time, I was able to see that Richard's death breathed new life into me. My identity as his wife began to crumble along with my outdated beliefs and the invisible wall that my ego-mind had formed around my heart, shrouding my deepest ability to experience true passion, meaning, and joy. As my identity shattered, my true essence had a chance to be reborn. Throughout this journey, I began to find the message in the mess: the unexpected gift that comes from the ending of something sweet is the possibility of our next level of greatness.

For me, the gift that came from losing Richard was being able to find myself. My heart broke wide open, and through this loving mess I have been able to start a new chapter where I get to continue Richard's legacy while also honoring my own.

December 13th is a Swedish holiday where they light candles to honor Saint Lucia – the patron saint of love and kindness. Richard had been working on an article called "How to be more loving and kind to yourself" on the flight just before he died. I believe that this was more than just a coincidence; it was an incredibly loving message in the mess. And I will hold that (and Richard) close to my heart forever.

Chapter 10
Graceful Epiphanies

One of the first greeting cards one of us got for the other (on the occasion of Jodi getting a new pair of glasses) featured this quote from Marcel Proust: "The real voyage of discovery consists not in seeking new landscapes but in having new eyes." These words embody the essence of epiphanies: seeing the world through "new eyes" – from a fresh perspective, with new understanding.

Epiphanies are also referred to as insights, realizations, revelations, and a-ha moments. What all of these words have in common is that they refer to something that makes us see the world differently. Epiphanies are moments when, even if nothing changes externally, *a lot* changes internally. The picture shifts into focus. We see things in a different way. We know what direction to take. Life makes sense.

We've experienced epiphanies in many areas of our lives: emotional (realizing the importance of shifting to gratitude), physical (understanding that our bodies are not testing us or punishing us with pain, but lovingly sending us helpful messages), and spiritual (realizing the nature of God and the presence of the Divine within each of us).

This chapter includes epiphanies of all sorts. Some of the authors describe moments when they understood how they define success. Some describe moments in which they got in touch with their emotions…and their power. Some of the stories involve receiving clarity about what direction to take. And all of them deal with a shift in perspective – a time when the way the author viewed the world was dramatically changed…for the better! As you read these pieces, we hope you'll gain insight from the authors' experiences, open yourself to new perspectives, and perhaps experience an epiphany of your own!

The Blue-Butterfly Effect
By Sharon Halliday

It was spring, and I was still buzzing after attending a writers' workshop in Sydney. I'd been lucky enough to rub shoulders with Pam Grout, author of E^2.

This had been my first time away since the birth of my second child. Adding to this momentous occasion, the trip had reignited my dream of becoming a published author. It had, however, turned out to be an emotional time as, on the morning I flew out, I was told that my last remaining grandparent had passed away.

After a whirlwind of a weekend, I tucked into my seat and soaked in the night lights of Sydney as the plane left the runway. I took a deep breath as I opened Pam's book. I couldn't put it down. I was forced to return to reality by the pilot's voice informing us that we were about to descend.

The next morning, as I lounged in my pyjamas in front of the TV with my kids, I described to my mum (who had now been relieved of grandparent duties), the details of my magical weekend. I attempted to convey the ideas I had been trying to wrap my mind around from my new, revolutionary book.

I could feel myself getting more and more enthusiastic as I explained one of the energy experiments. "And so," I announced confidently, "If, for example, I said to myself I'm going to see a blue butterfly today, and then I do, I would know that I had actively manifested that into my experience. And if you can do that, you can do it with anything!" I said emphatically.

Within a few seconds of saying those words, not one, but three butterflies flew into the scene of the children's program we were watching. "Just like that!" I exclaimed pointing at the TV, barely believing what I'd just witnessed.

Now, whenever I'm recounting this manifestation experience to anyone, I refer to it as "The Blue-Butterfly Effect," and it reminds me of our innate ability to create miracles every day.

Firewalk

By Janet Dhaenens

We passed the wood from one person to the next, putting our intentions into each piece: courage, trust, family, home, love, friends, connection. It was a big stack of wood. After the fire was burning, we went into the teepee for the instructions. We talked about our fears. My strongest fear was how self-critical I would be if I didn't walk.

I don't know if I would have had the courage to walk on those hot coals if I hadn't been surrounded by people who were already doing it. But I decided that if they could do it, so could I.

I stepped up to the edge, saw myself on the other side, and walked like I knew where I was going. By the third step I was thinking, *This is easy! I thought I had to do something!* I found out that all I had to do was make the decision and take the action. My body and nature did the rest. My feet were fine!

WOW!!! The high I experienced was amazing! I carried it with me for days. I walked on hot coals and did not get burned! It was an incredible experience! The question I had then, and continue to work with, is: How do I apply that same experience to other parts of my life? How do I overlay the fact that my part of the "doing" is to make the decision and act on it without letting any other thoughts come in to distract me and cause me to doubt?

It has taken lots of practice, but I am often able to hold my focus where I choose now. I think of it as mind training; I ask my mind to hold only the thoughts I want. This patient repetition requires time and effort, but I feel it is worth every minute! Now, I often *feel* the joy of living the life I've dreamed of.

My first firewalk gave me a physical experience of what is possible when I trust completely. My goal now is to trust completely in *all* areas of my life!

The Power of Intent
By Atherton Drenth

My little sister and I were both very excited when we found out we were to spend the summer at a farm. When we arrived, we were told that we could go anywhere and do whatever we wanted, but we were to stay out of the house until meal times. I was four and my sister was three. It was a magical, bohemian summer of running wild and free. There were all manner of farm animals and, much to our joy, lots of cats!

It didn't take long for us to discover that all the cats lived inside a rickety old barn filled with rusty farm implements scattered around a dirt floor. One day, we were chasing a kitten around the barn when my sister stepped onto a plank with a rusty nail sticking out. She screamed in pain as the nail punctured her shoe and went into her foot.

At the local doctor's office, I watched in horror as my sister was given a tetanus shot. I had never seen a needle before. She shrieked in pain as the needle seemed to disappear into her skinny little leg. The next morning, I stomped back to the barn to throw that nasty plank away. But as I entered the barn, I was blinded by a shaft of sunlight coming through a crack in the wall. I lost my bearings and gasped as pain suddenly shot up through my foot as I stepped onto the same plank.

Terrified of getting a needle too, I snuck back into the farmhouse to clean up the blood coming from the hole in my foot. The farmer's wife, furious to find me in the house, promptly sent me to bed without supper. Relieved that I had gotten away with what I had done, I looked at my foot and thought, *This has got to be gone in the morning.*

Imagine my surprise when I awoke the next morning to find my foot completely healed! Overjoyed, I remember thinking, *Oh, I can heal myself.* I have never doubted the power of intent ever since.

Epiphany on the F Train

By Amanda Johnson

After quitting my job and exploring what it was I wanted to do and create and how I wanted to serve others, I was standing on the F train in New York City when it struck me: *What if it's not about doing more or being better; what if it's about being good with being you?*

This became my mantra and, though I didn't know it at the time, my personal and professional mission for the next 365+ days. This was not just a pivotal moment for me; it was a whole new way of looking at the world and at my life.

Ever since I was a little girl, I looked for ways to improve myself, thinking that *if* I shaved the hair off my arms, *then* I would be accepted; *if* I got better grades, *then* I would be enough; *if* I figured out why I am the way I am, *then* I could finally "fix" it and be lovable.

I have always had this knack for self-improvement. I just love to pick up a good self-help book, curl up on the couch, and mull over all the ways I have been doing it wrong. I certainly don't believe that personal growth is a bad thing – after all, change/growth/evolution is the only constant! The thing is, though, I'd spent the past 30-some years forgetting a *crucial* part of this: *grace*. Unmerited favor. Knowing that I am accepted, loved, and enough just the way I am. There is nothing I can do for this to be more or less true.

It's all too easy for me to make things bigger, better, and faster, which is why it was so important for me to consciously set that aside and practice the thing I had neglected my entire life: love and acceptance of who I am, exactly as I am. Without this, any pursuit simply reinforces the false belief that I am not already a masterpiece and am only a never-ending work-in-progress that is not quite yet deserving of love and acceptance.

This new understanding is not the end of the story for me, and I am ready for the next stage in my evolution; but this time I know that it will include a whole lot of self-acceptance, love, and grace.

Grace Is Never Late

By Ginger Gauldin

Please don't pull out in front of me, I thought.

The scooter pulled out anyway. I sighed and thought, *I just can't be late...I don't even know exactly where I'm going.*

I was on my way to a new veterinarian for the second time in as many days, having just been squeezed into their schedule. My puppy was in great pain, due to a kidney stone, and I was stressed and putting a lot of hope on the outcome of this visit. All morning, I'd been running a dialogue in my head of everything I needed to tell them.

Oblivious to my need to be on time, the man on the scooter was driving very carefully, *very slowly*. I'm not usually so impatient, but this was becoming the last straw on the camel's back of worrisome energy I had been carrying around for several days. I needed to pull myself together.

Okay, I thought. *Breathe. Look around. It's a gorgeous day...it's not raining. The scooter really is a pretty shade of blue. And the man on the scooter is, well, rather fit and good looking for someone I had initially thought was quite old.* I had made the assumption that his white hair and beard indicated a decline in ability and perception. I know better than that.

In those few moments, I was able to calm myself and notice that now there were several cars bumper to bumper behind us, swerving in and out, trying to catch a glimpse of the reason for the 30 mph crawl. *He's got every right to be here, just as we do*, I thought. *It's the law.* I backed off to give him even more room. Just then, a loving inner voice came through and clearly said, "You are keeping him safe." I was overcome, as peace and clarity washed over me.

When I had become present, calm, and relaxed enough to see that this man and his scooter were not causing me a problem, I heard and felt the wisdom of grace as it settled into my mind and body. I arrived at our destination with 10 minutes to spare, and my puppy received the care he needed without surgery and recovered completely.

A Mirror-acle of Grace

By Sophie Maya

Growing up in a Catholic home and school, something felt "off." I was taught to "judge not" while witnessing judgments spewed about. A little voice within said, "Show me the love, and I'll buy what you're selling." I left the church at an early age and didn't look back.

As an adult away from the church, however, I still didn't find the nonjudgmental love I desired. After numerous failed relationships, I asked to understand what I was doing wrong. I began meditating and praying daily, which helped me feel more peaceful...until I engaged with judgmental or unkind people, and I'd find myself thrown right back into inner turmoil.

What finally broke this cycle were three simple words suggested by a mystic friend. He said that in order to know myself and find lasting peace, whenever I spoke or even thought of anyone, I should add the words "...just like me." As I took his advice, I began to see the world and everyone in it as a miraculous mirror, which I've come to call a "Mirror-acle of Grace."

Although this mirror was enlightening, it wasn't always flattering! I found that I was, indeed, "just like those" I viewed as judgmental and unkind. So I decided to give others what *I* wanted to receive: honest, vulnerable communication without judgment. When their actions or words offended me, rather than judging or simply dismissing them, I shared my feelings and perceptions, seeking to connect and understand. As the doorway to honest communication opened up, some friendships and relationships fell away and new ones appeared with people who also celebrated the value of authentic connection with a willingness to be wrong...*just like me!*

This process has given me insight about myself and allowed me to connect deeply with others. I now share confession (expressing my truth) and communion with the God in others, and I feel the love that had been missing during my early years. These days, my church is life and my religion is Love. And instead of seeing the world as judgmental or unkind, I see it as a "Mirror-acle of Grace"!

When What You Wish for Comes in Another Package

By Mary Meston

I think we can all relate to opening a highly anticipated package...only to discover that it isn't what you expected – the sense of exhilaration and excitement immediately transitioning to disappointment and sadness.

That's exactly how I felt when, within a week of our wedding, my fiancé said he no longer wanted children. I had waited to marry a bit later than many, so I was eager to start building the picture-perfect family. I even had names picked out for the children, including one based on my long-deceased mother's name, Kay.

I told myself this was okay, that it was meant to be. I believed in the marital oath that you are married for life, through good times and bad, in sickness and in health, till death do you part. So I spent the next decade putting myself into my career, staying involved in volunteering, and keeping myself too busy to wonder what might have been.

Then, a decade into our marriage, my husband surprised me again – telling me (in a note left on the counter) that he no longer wanted to be married. The marriage ended as did my chance at having my own children: suddenly and without my input.

Once again, I poured myself into staying busy and put aside my old dreams of having children. Nonetheless, my desire has been fulfilled, as I've become a two-time stepmom and have created a family, though a bit out of the ordinary. Although she is adopted, my youngest stepdaughter is more like me than many children are like their parents. She is often mistaken as my biological child because of her resemblance and our shared traits. She goes by the nickname "K" – pronounced just like my mother's name!

As I sit here writing this, I now see it was all part of a plan all along. I didn't know I was opening this package, but it is just what I wanted – though not exactly as expected. The universe knew long before I did that I would receive this package with grace.

Spiritual Awakening

By Lisa "The Link" Rizzo

As a child, I realized that I had the gift of being able to connect with loved ones on the other side. Even before I knew the word for it, I was what is often called a "medium." For many years, though, I didn't want to share these experiences with anyone. I was afraid of judgment from those who couldn't understand. It took many years for me to understand it myself…and I'm still learning!

Over time, I became able to control my gift better, and I developed a deeper respect for my visions, my faith, and the gifts my creator gave me. I came to realize that part of my purpose was to overcome my fear (and my doubts and questions about "Why *me?*") and start sharing the messages from the beyond. In my 20s, I knew in my soul that I could no longer keep hiding my gift, so I began to share what I knew. As I did, the gift became stronger and stronger, and I was shown more and more from spirits.

Part of what I have learned and shared is that everything we go through in this life is a lesson. It doesn't matter what our struggles have been; it's the overcoming of those struggles that keeps us on the path of our greater purpose. I have also learned that not everyone and everything that comes into our lives is meant to stay. Sometimes, the best approach is to wish them well and move on to the next lesson. Most of all, my spiritual awakening has shown me how easy our life could be if we didn't live in fear of what *might* happen, instead of knowing that we are the creators of our own destiny!

This journey has been a long but rewarding experience for me, which Spirit tells me to continue – to keep sharing my gift with others so that they may find their true paths and experience their own spiritual awakening.

The Meaning of True Success

By Maryann Candito

As the rain pelted the window of my office, I desperately tried to concentrate. I needed to create a plan for my business, but I couldn't hear beyond the rain. Once it stopped, I thought I was in the clear – but no such luck. What remained was the all-too-familiar noise going on in my head – from coaches, from my peers, and from social media. Everywhere I looked, I would see rules and guidelines on how to be successful in business and in life. But what does success really mean? How does it feel? As I pondered these questions, I connected to my spirit.

Not long after asking, I began to receive. As I looked around my world, I noticed a wave of friends ready to leave the cities and move to the country, smaller towns, and coastal communities. It seemed as though what fulfilled us in the past was not feeding our souls in the present. Simplification, getting back to nature, and living life while connecting to our inner spirit was winning over city life, high-profile careers, and money or ego-driven concerns.

This is what I had been struggling with for so long! At some level, I knew what I needed. That was why a few years ago I moved to the coast. I was drawn to living near the ocean – my soul was speaking, and I was listening! Internally, however, I hadn't completely aligned energetically. I still needed to clear all the internal programs and misguided beliefs that were at the heart of my frustration. It was time to fully align with my version of success, not the "success" I was being fed by my industry. That a-ha moment was my moment of grace.

It feels refreshing to just BE and not worry about what "success" looks like or "should" be. Peace and harmony have now taken the place of any old ideas of what I needed to do or be in order to be successful. It's quite liberating to embrace my free-spirited self and do enjoyable things and meaningful work while releasing all the ego-based pressures.

Through this journey, I've learned that what matters most is that I am living life on my terms and that I can wake up at peace and in alignment with myself each morning. That's *my* meaning of success. Somehow I feel like I've known this all along.

I Am Good Enough the Way I Am

By Janet Dhaenens

My son got home last night from a camping trip with his girlfriend. He was busy cleaning things he had taken on the trip and putting them away. I expected him home today and thought I had this morning to clean up, so things were a mess in the house.

"Do you want to wash dishes with me?" he asked.

"All right." As I walked into the kitchen to help, emotion welled up inside. The feelings were familiar and made me want to hide. But my son is one of my best friends, and I feel safer being myself with him than with most other people, so I went ahead and opened up to him. "I'm feeling really vulnerable and close to tears," I said.

"Okay."

Neither of us needed more words, and in the calm space between us, I realized why I felt vulnerable: I have had a very deeply held pattern of thinking I should be different than I am. I had a clear comparison of how I felt when my son came home, after being in the house by myself for 10 days. It seems like my desire for me to be different is activated as soon as I am with another person – any other person. Or maybe this desire is there all the time, but when I'm alone, it's easy to focus on other things and not notice it as much.

This realization eased how uncomfortable I felt. My son shared things about his trip, and our conversation was easy. Within a short period of time, I did not feel vulnerable at all. What changed? I stopped judging myself and thinking that I should be different, and I accepted myself the way I am. I let it be okay that having a clean house is not high on my priority list most of the time. In fact, washing the dishes together gave me enjoyable time with my son – and *he* certainly wasn't judging me!

One step at a time, I am changing the pattern of seeing myself as not good enough, to valuing myself just the way I am.

A Fork in the Road

By Michelle McDonald Vlastnik

We had been married 20 years. I had been growing spiritually, and my husband had not. Unhappiness fueled my search to feel whole again. Our marriage had gone through a few years of troubled waters, and it came to the point where I filed for a divorce. We were living in the same house but sleeping in separate bedrooms. My husband never gave up on us, though.

One day, I had an overwhelming urge to go to Sedona, Arizona. The feeling was so strong that it could not be ignored. I had been there several times but had never driven myself. I only knew the general direction to head, and I put it in the hands of the Universe to get me there. I needed to go visit one of the vortex locations and was guided to go to the Chapel of the Holy Cross.

I was led to the front of the chapel, where I lit a candle, knelt on the front bench, and prayed. I prayed for direction concerning my happiness, my marriage, and my life. I prayed and prayed and prayed until I felt peace.

In that divine moment of grace, my life changed and I knew what to do: I went back to my car, called my husband, and asked if he wanted to rent a movie and spend the evening together. I am sure he was shocked.

I never finalized the divorce.

Nine years later, during a palm reading, I was told what I had divinely contracted for during this lifetime. My contract hand had shown an interesting point in my life: a fork in the road nine years earlier, at which time I could have chosen either one person or another and lived a happy life.

After 31 years of being married to my life partner, I shared my retrospection with him about my journey. That opt-out clause in my contract may have been an easier path for my soul, but if I had chosen it, I know that I would not be the spiritual teacher I am today.

The Sun of Grace

By Farooq Shah

I've known for a while now that I'm an odd duck. I like – no, I *love* – rain. Soft rain, drenching rain. Light rain, hard rain. Sometimes I think I should have been born a duck instead of a human being. In spite of my rheumatoid arthritis, when it's raining I love nothing more than to be out playing in it, flapping my wings and wagging my bright-yellow tail with uninhibited enjoyment, spraying water everywhere.

But every so often, I encounter a less enjoyable "rain" – the kind that isn't physical. This rain isn't wet or refreshingly cool, and it doesn't tickle my cheeks or make teasingly wide puddles. It's more like a dreary downpour that just won't stop, one that won't allow the clouds to break up or the sun to peek through. The puddles this rain forms are chin-deep and leave my spirits drenched and shivering, crouching beneath its onslaught. It's a soaking, cold greyness of the mind that can affect anyone at any time, for any reason. It's the soul rain: hopelessness.

In the summer of 2011, I felt myself drowning in hopelessness following a near-death experience that left me with a severe neck injury. I could no longer feel anything from the waist down. I could no longer walk. I felt as if I was in a stormy season of my life, and the rain had become a flood of despair. However, that season would not last. Eventually, I would recover; the sun would shine again and let me know that there is peace, joy, love, beauty, happiness, and grace.

We all go through these seasons from time to time. And, just like the patch of soul rain comes rolling in, so does the warmth of grace, always hiding behind the clouds, just waiting for someone to notice its shine. In these times, I've found that when I change my focus from hopelessness to hope, the soul rain does actually let up and, eventually, the sun shines again. At some point, we all have to deal with the soul rain, no matter who we are. But it's good to know that, like any other weather, it will change.

Silver Linings of Grace

By Tara Leduc

Everything changed when my fiancé left. I was devastated. I lost my voice. I lost my peace. In that time of pain, I watched a lump grow where my voice had been.

They say there are no failures, only successes and lessons. Our wise inner voice speaks to us, starting as whispers. If we don't listen, the voice gets louder and louder, until its message becomes undeniable: "Listen to me!"

I could have heard the message the first time the doctor said, "You have cancer." I could have listened the second time. But when he said that my cancer, twice treated and cured, had returned a third time, I finally heard the lessons in this for me.

One lesson is the willingness to listen to my wise inner voice. My silver lining is the ability and desire to be quiet, be still, and listen to what I really want, what I actually need. For this gift of listening and inner wisdom – thank you, heartbreak. Thank you, cancer.

Thank you for the silver lining of finding my silver knight, the man I did marry. Thank you for the lessons of trust, commitment, and unconditional love. Even when we're angry and not speaking, he is my best friend, my solace, and the solid foundation from which I can fly. For this gift of love and faith – thank you, heartbreak. Thank you, cancer.

Thank you for the silver lining of my realisation of my true purpose. I lost my voice and lost my peace. And in hearing "You have cancer" three times, my wise voice told me I HAD to do something differently. I had to find my voice to find my peace. And I had to use my voice to help others find their peace. And in finding their peace, together we'd create world peace. For this gift of joy in my right livelihood, my calling and ability to change the world – thank you, heartbreak. Thank you, cancer.

My wise voice taught me that, even in the midst of hardships and challenges, there is always a silver lining. These silver linings, these lessons, these hardships, this gratitude – each is pure grace. And, for each one, I say *thank you.*

Cleaning Closets

By Margo Kirzinger

"Okay," I told myself, "I'm ready. I'm goin' in!"

This was me psyching myself up to tackle one of the chores I thoroughly dislike: cleaning my bedroom closet. This is one of those jobs I always feel the need to brace myself for because there is SO MUCH STUFF!

Armed with designated donate and garbage bags in hand, I stood in front of my closet, contemplating this lofty endeavor. As I surveyed the vast amount of clothes, shoes, books, and various other items that had been placed there for safe keeping for one reason or another, I felt my spirit and energy dissipate. I was ready to throw in the proverbial towel, and I hadn't even started yet!

I stepped away from the closet and pondered my aversion to this task, and it suddenly became obvious that my inability to part with things goes far deeper than the clothes. I thought about how it's a good practice to clean out our emotional closets every so often as well. But it also became crystal clear that, for me, this is much easier to preach than to practice.

This process raises feelings of fear when I contemplate "junking" not only physical stuff but also old and tired thoughts or ideas, even when I am aware they no longer fulfill me in any way. What really immobilizes me is that once I clear out my (literal or emotional) closets, there will be an emptiness, a void, which creates feelings of discomfort, sadness, and loss. It's these feelings that inevitably keep me from completing this task.

No, I did not finish cleaning my closet that day, but I did arrive at a new perspective and a fresh insight that goes far beyond closets!

The next time I do clean my closets, I will allow myself time to breathe deeply, examine all my "stuff," and, with strength and grace, only keep what I truly love and what makes me happy *now*. I will gently remind myself that empty space is not a bad thing; it is reserved for future treasures of happiness, positivity, and joy.

Cracking the Vault

By Carrie Kondor

For many years, I did not feel my emotions. For the most part, this worked just fine...or so I thought. Yes, there were some rare times when I allowed myself to feel fear or pain rippling though me; but as soon as those moments passed, I continued doing what I believed was right: shoving my feelings aside and putting on a smile. "This is how it's done," I concluded, as I perceived the world around me. "This is how to fit in."

Yet, truth be told, my strategy was not working. It was choking the very breath out of me. The vault I put my feelings in was beginning to crack.

One night, I opened the vault sealed deep within my subconscious mind and experienced the wonder. What was inside this cave? What was behind the walls I put up within myself, against myself?

As I tiptoed into the cave, through meditation and stillness, I felt the loneliness, the pain. I cried the tears. I released the pain and the feelings I had placed in my body. My ego begged me to wonder, "What triggered this?" My ego was desperate for answers so I could avoid experiencing this pain again. My soul whispered, "No need to wonder; just cry," and so I did.

As I opened the vault and felt these tears, I could feel the warmth of my soul ignite.

The next morning, I lay in bed, snuggled in between my pillows, and basked in the warm embrace of the Divine. I felt the pain and the burden of my fears being lifted from me.

That moment became one of grace intermingled with tears. I allowed my tears to fall without wondering why, without judgment, without holding back. Grace held the key to the vault. Grace worked in partnership with my soul to set me free. I am now free to feel.

The Whisper of Grace
By Jenna Kelland

Faced with health challenges, I was convinced that gathering data would provide me with answers. I knew my body was out of balance, and I was sure that, with my education as a holistic nutritionist and the right information, I could find a solution. I began collecting data: I bought blood-pressure and glucose monitors; a fitness tracker to count steps and monitor sleep; a smart scale to measure weight and BMI; and several apps to track food, supplements, mood, and energy levels. I used checklists and alarms on my phone to remind me to do yoga, drink water, and listen to health-related webinars. But, though each night I faced more data, I found no answers. What was I missing? What was I doing wrong?

Then one day I heard a quiet voice within myself whisper, "The answers aren't *out there*. You need to listen *inside*." So I stopped measuring and recording. Instead of aiming for 10,000 steps a day, I asked my body what felt good and right in the moment. I realized that some days I needed yoga, and other days I needed to move and sweat. Some days I needed a smoothie with spinach and kale, while other days I needed nuts, eggs, and salmon.

As I continue to pay more attention to the voice inside, it grows more confident. I'm learning to trust it more and more. Each day, I focus on deep breathing and creating moments of calm inside when I'm about to make a decision. In those moments, I can hear my inner voice tell me what is best for me when faced with choices of what to do, what to eat, and how to be. Now, I'm walking the talk of a holistic nutritionist; I care for myself with grace, rather than with technology and data. And that quiet voice is helping me feel better every day.

The Truth of Letting Go
By Isabella Rose

I recently visited one of my comfort spots: the ocean. I had set the intentions to finish a piece I was working on for this book and to try my hand at a landscape finger painting. I had recently started to experiment with other paint media as well as canvases. For this trip, though, I brought a spiral-bound scrapbook so the pages would not blow away in the wind.

Up until this point, I generally relied on my intuition to create my paintings. But as I prepared to begin this new painting, I remembered my art professor in college teaching me how to paint what I saw during a visit to a local state park. (At that point, even in college, I was still painting lollipop trees.) I decided to start with an easy focal point: I wanted to include the lighthouse and the merging of the ocean and the sky.

I didn't like how the painting was turning out, so I turned to the last page of the notebook, which had come off of the wiring in a few spots. I took out my markers and began to outline what I saw. While doing this, I remembered what a friend of my mine had taught during a free online painting class: "Remember, if you don't like it, you can always go back and fix it." I continued to outline what I wanted to capture for a little while longer.

After a while, my hands became too cold to continue, so I began to clean up. As I did, the wind caught the page I was working on and took it off the binding. It began to blow towards the shore. Not wanting to litter, I began to swiftly walk after it. The wind picked up its speed, and so did I. I chased the paper until I saw it touch the waves. It was then that I knew I had to let it go – along with the old pieces of myself – in order to create a masterpiece.

Honoring Myself

By Janet Dhaenens

I'm one week into a class in which we're exploring our emotions around money. Through this process, I've realized that sometime when I was young, I developed this not particularly helpful set of beliefs: "Money comes from other people. In order to please them so they will give it to me, I have to betray myself. Therefore, it's best to live without money." But trying to live without money in this world is also a way of betraying myself, so these beliefs put me in a situation of dishonoring myself no matter what choices I made.

I also realized that these beliefs had implications in many areas of my life, far beyond the realm of money. This realization arose from a simple conversation with my partner, Celeste. "I'm miserable with this head cold," I told her.

"I will hold you in love today," Celeste said.

Her words brought immediate tears. I cried intensely, suddenly clear about why I was sick and what was going on in connection with this class about money. I realized *I just wanted to be taken care of!*

I learned as a child that it is more important to do what others tell me than what I personally want to do. So, my whole life, I have been taking care of others. On this day, I saw that I've been trying to take care of others in a way I never realized before. When I set aside my own inner knowing of what feels good to me in order to follow someone else's instructions, in essence, I am trying to take care of them.

Money represents freedom of choice. I see that choosing to set aside my own knowing and do things the way others tell me to do them – for money or any other reason – is me setting aside my power of choice.

Today, I give myself permission to take my power back. I'm willing to listen to others and check in with how I feel about it, but never again am I going to disregard how something feels to me in order to follow someone else's instructions. I'm going to trust and honor myself and how I feel inside. I have decided to always make choices based on how they feel for me. In doing this, I give myself the freedom I have always wanted!

In Dying, I Learned to Live

By Russell R. Shippee

I was conceived to become the fourth generation in a family insurance agency.

From an early age, I knew what was expected of me and had no idea that I had any choice. Like so many people, I did what was expected and filled the role given to me.

At the age of 43, after having been sick, I had a vivid dream. In the dream, the preacher was on the pulpit pointing at me lying in the casket, saying, "He was a GREAT insurance agent."

Quickly, still in the dream, I realized there was more to life than being a great insurance agent, and I was meant to do more. I looked over the side of the casket yelling, "Hey, I'm not dead! I'm alive! look at me!" No one heard me. The church was full, but they all thought I was dead.

The next morning, I realized that this dream was a message – a message of death if I did not change. It was also a message that there were other things I was to do rather than be an insurance agent.

For the first time, I realized I was the captain of my life. I was in charge. In the past, I had relinquished control of my life. It was time to take control back. The family opposition was strong, yet I knew what I had to do.

It took me three years to sell the business and another three years before I was able to completely leave. But mentally and physically, I left the morning of the dream.

Now I am living my own life. I am healthy, happy, and productive. I smile and I'm more fun to be with. My poor health, my frustration, and my life of quiet desperation are now just a distant memory that's faded away like a bad dream.

The Umbrella Man

By Murray James

A friend enlisted my help to find some cheerful, nostalgic music to play to her 90-year old mother, who was terminally ill. I thought of "The Umbrella Man," popularized by the performers Flanagan and Allen in 1939. The song was based on a historical figure who plied his trade of mending umbrellas in Victorian London.

The more I engaged with this song, the more I realized that the Umbrella Man was an archetypal figure from my own past. It was calling me back to my creative potential, from a current period of staleness and apathy.

Surprisingly, it took me back to two long-forgotten memories of repertory performances in which I had used an umbrella while tap dancing and singing two songs. The first was as a nine-year old, singing the song "Jiminy Cricket Is My Name" from Walt Disney's *Pinocchio*. The second occurred in my early 20s when I performed "Singing in the Rain" from the musical of the same name.

As I listened to "The Umbrella Man," I reflected on the symbolic aspects of umbrellas – in both rain and sunshine. I thought of how they could be a metaphor for meditation – keeping us safe and centered, even when life seems stormy and stressful. I also realized how the umbrella man is a flexible worker who takes on various tasks. He embodies resilience and optimism. People trust him because he's a good listener and he shows kindness. This reminds me how I need to integrate these qualities into my own life as I give service to others.

My Umbrella Man remains a positive archetype. I find that when I harness his transformative energy, it makes a difference in my life. Somehow, from across the years, he teaches me universal lessons about maintaining hope, positive focus, and finding creative solutions.

We Are Not Separate

By James Kelly

My moment of grace came when I made a deliberate choice to not see my interests as apart from someone else's.

I was at a communication training event and expressing my needs during a one-to-one exercise. Then I had that moment of grace. I deeply realised that connecting with the needs of the other person was my interest in that moment and in every moment. If I was just focused on satisfying my own needs, I was not truly meeting with myself or the other person.

I realised that I cannot think of myself as a separate person and truly meet my needs. It's not about being a saviour for anyone or about being under obligation to meet the needs of another person so that I can feel good about myself. It is about remembering the contract that we all have with each other. We cannot leave each other out of the journey home and remember our shared identity. We travel together or not at all.

In that moment of grace, I experienced that we are all connected, and behaving as if I wasn't could no longer satisfy me again. Many times since, I have acted as if I had forgotten that moment, but in truth, I can never really forget. I'm soon able to recognise that when I'm only thinking about myself, I feel disconnected. Then I choose to have another moment of grace.

Now I know that self-interest in the truest sense includes the interests of others – not just the *needs* of others on the level of surviving in this world, but the interest we all share to remember that we are more – more than the physical, something other than an individual mind.

I believe we can all be in a state of constant grace if we remember that we are love and so is the other person. No matter how the other person is expressing their needs, we can always meet them on the level where we are all joined in love.

A Walk of Grace

By Annie Price

"Never criticize a man until you've walked a mile in his moccasins."
(American Indian Proverb)

I was about 11 when I first read this proverb on a plate my father hung on the wall. I've always liked it. It sounded like the right thing to do. But, oh my goodness, some days, it's another matter altogether to put this into action!

This is especially true for me on those days when I'm feeling I've gotten the "short end of the stick." Maybe it's just being cut off by someone in traffic. Maybe I paid for it, but when I got home, it wasn't in the bag. No matter how irritating these incidents may be, however, they're easier to move through when I can put myself in the other person's shoes. Maybe they're having a bad day or they just made a mistake. It happens to all of us.

But then there are those more challenging situations where the shoes just don't seem to fit. One occasion was my experience with an advertised "master spiritual expert" who offered a special deal. Even though I fulfilled the necessary requirements, this guru chose to back out of her original offering. The lesser replacement was of little value to me. I felt cheated and angry, and I questioned how I could be so gullible.

It's so disappointing when clay feet are exposed! The last thing I wanted to do was put myself in this knucklehead's shoes! But how long I continue to beat myself up or remain smoldering in anger is up to me. I've found that the anger usually lasts until I begin to understand that there's probably a lesson here that was meant to be learned – maybe for both sides. That's when I begin to walk in the other person's shoes and see it from their side, gaining more awareness of the possible whole picture.

While I'm feeling empathy, I only need to take what was mine and not carry what was meant for them. And as I release this (which often takes several attempts), I feel forgiveness – for them and for myself. And I'm humbled to remember that we are *all* only human.

Focus on What Really Matters

By Millen Livis

As part of my self-care routine, I take long walks on the beach every morning. These walks have become my meditation practice. I like to pay attention to and appreciate simple things: birds having a tribe gathering, children playing in the sand, people jogging and walking, and seeing footprints get washed away by the rhythmic movements of the ocean waves.

During one of my walks, my mind zoomed in on the washed footprints on the sand, and I thought: *That is a symbolic image of our lives. We, too, leave a footprint as a proof of our existence on the physical plane. Then one day our "footprint" will be erased in an instant, and we'll return back to our Divine Source.* Suddenly, the brevity of our existence struck my awareness. I realized that all the worries and struggles, fears and pains, physical possessions, and material achievements that we identify with are *not* our identity but simply passing experiences along our journey.

Then what remains? What is lasting? Love, grace, kindness, and joyful memories you share with others are the legacy that you can leave behind one day.

If you are like me – ambitious and constantly driven by new and exciting ideas and projects – you are motivated by the desire to authentically serve others with your talents and skills. In my case, this passion and drive helped me achieve freedom and independence, and I am infinitely grateful for my life. Yet I often push myself and multitask to the point of exhaustion. I get caught up in busyness, which is a self-created illusion, and overlook the real priorities. In the instant that I was watching the footprints get washed away, however, I felt that I truly want to refocus on what *really matters* in life, especially in the midst of busyness. I want to focus on what makes me feel good: love, joy, grace, deep connections, and inner peace.

What a Difference a Word Makes

By Elizabeth R. Kipp

"How is your year so far?" I asked Jo.

Jo replied, "Okay, I guess. But March will be difficult because I don't have the rent money."

I considered Jo's words and noticed something missing.

"March will be difficult because you don't have the rent money...*yet*," I said.

"No I don't," Jo replied. She added, "*Yet!* I like the sound of that. Just hearing that word makes me feel better."

"The word 'yet' can really shift my perspective on something when I include it," I shared. "You state that March will be difficult because you don't have the rent money. This sentence holds the energy of fear. I see that you believe this is how your reality will unfold, but by asserting this statement, you are not allowing possibility to act in your life and grace to enter. You have decided that March will be hard and that you will not have the rent money. You do not have the rent money now. It is true for this moment. Add the word 'yet' and you tell yourself and Source that you are open to your future. This sentence leads us into the energy of empowerment in the future *and* right here, right now – where all possibilities lie open for us. You tap into the pivot power and grace held in the word 'yet.' By adding 'yet' to your sentence, you move from the energy of fear and lack into the energy of manifesting and abundance."

Jo replied, "I feel much better when I add that word 'yet.' What a difference one word makes! March is suddenly looking much brighter! I'm going to go make a list of what I can do to get the rent money I need."

For me, this conversation reinforced that when we are conscious of and precise with our words, we actually define our world. Our thoughts and our words have the power to move us into whatever we bring to the moment. It is up to us to make the choice to fall into the lack that fear brings or step into empowerment.

Finding My Happiness

By Haley Reese

As far back as I can remember, I felt plagued by anxiety, fear, negativity, and hopelessness. My depression worsened and my anxiety attacks became more frequent as I attempted to navigate the already tempestuous waters of high school and college. I tried countless therapists, psychiatrists, and most of the "magic, cure-all" prescriptions in the book, all to no avail. I perpetually believed that something bad was going to happen.

And then the worst did happen: In my second year of college, one of my best friends – the most kind, beautiful, and good-hearted being I'd ever known – took her own life.

I was devastated and felt more hopeless than ever. And yet a teeny-tiny part of me knew I needed to hang on, knew there was a better way. And in my whole body, mind, and soul, I was determined to find it.

Through the grace of my desire and the universe, I slowly but surely began to discover authentic happiness.

It started with my semester abroad when I attended culinary school in Florence, Italy. For the first time in my life, I discovered my passion and knew that I could build my life around it. I became immersed in the world of food, which soon led me to nutrition and the ability to heal my mind and body with the foods I consume.

My spiritual awakening emerged in parallel. It started slowly, then fully engaged one beautiful summer day as I sat in my backyard reading *Science of Mind* magazine. One particular article, about anxiety and our thoughts, beautifully and perfectly connected me with the power I hold in my own mind – revealing the truth that my thoughts have the ability to shape my reality. I jumped out of my chair and beamed up at the sun with arms reaching out towards the sky in pure gratitude. Pure bliss. Pure grace.

In that moment, I not only found my life's purpose in helping others learn and apply these universal laws, I found my happiness.

You Decide

By Suzanne Zupancic

"What if I told you that nothing is a problem until you decide there's a problem?"
- Gurudev Amrit Desai

This a-ha moment came to me as I was sitting in a lecture by Gurudev Amrit Desai in Phoenix, Arizona. I realized that there are essentially two ways we can go through life: resisting or surrendering. We can resist everything that happens, attempt to manipulate the world to the point of exhaustion, and think obsessively about our situation. Or we can surrender to what *is*, to the mystery, and accept each moment as perfect and essential to our evolution.

Option one is predictable and repetitive, and it promises suffering. It supports the illusion that things can be different than the way they are. Option two allows for life to surprise us. It allows this moment to be complete as it is, regardless of our preference. And we get to decide.

I've used this second approach in many areas of my life, from big, personal issues to small, everyday matters. For instance, one time when I was driving around in a hurry, I found myself sitting at a red light, becoming frustrated by the delay. But then I realized that I had a choice! I could continue to resist the situation, or I could simply surrender to it. I could wish for things to be different than they were, or I could accept them as is. "Is there anything I can do about it?" I asked myself. Of course I would have preferred for the light to be green so that I could be on my way. But why does a red light have to be a problem? Instead, I surrendered to the idea that I was, in fact, sitting in my comfortable, temperature-controlled car with dozens of songs to choose from on the radio. Was this really a problem? Not really…unless I insisted on saying that it was. I could almost hear Gurudev saying those words again: "You decide."

This phrase continually brings me peace during challenging situations. A red light may seem trivial, but if we can surrender to what is, maybe we can find that feeling a bit more accessible in other situations – situations where we need an extra hand on the shoulder to say that everything is okay.

December 6

Asking for What I Need

By Janet Dhaenens

I was trying to squeeze more activities into the time I had than would fit. I felt rushed and irritated with myself. I got my granddaughter, Vanessa, into the car; we were going to story time at the library where her mother works.

"Grandma, turn the radio on!"

"The radio doesn't work in this car."

"Sing to me then."

The happy memories I have of my father singing to me and my siblings when we were children prompted me to sing to Vanessa often when we were traveling. We both enjoyed this way of connecting and sharing. But this day, singing seemed like one more job when I already felt overwhelmed with everything I was juggling.

"I will sing, but I've had a tough morning and I need a few minutes of quiet first."

She immediately agreed and was quiet.

Vanessa and my daughter were living with me, and at times her many requests felt like demands. I found myself resentful of her needs when I couldn't even seem to meet my own! I knew she felt my irritation. I felt guilty about the way I felt because I didn't want her thinking her desires were wrong. I was surprised with her response when I asked for some quiet time. *Wow!* I thought. *Even a four-year-old can give me what I need...if I ask for it!*

This was a turning point in our relationship. After that, I began sharing with her how I felt and what I needed. If I was working on a task I needed to get done, I would ask her to occupy herself until I was finished. Her positive responses clearly showed me that she was thrilled to know what she could do that was helpful to me. She also loved the attention I could give her as I joined in her play when I wasn't splitting my attention and feeling irritated. We both felt much better!

I was amazed that sharing my needs and desires with her transformed our relationship. Through this experience, I've learned to share my needs and desires more often, and it has improved *every* relationship I have!

Doing Well by Doing Good

By Mary Meston

As a small-business owner working hard just to break even – let alone earn a profit from all my effort, frustration, and risk – the less-than-ideal financial results were wearing on me. But each time I wanted to raise the white flag of surrender and walk away, a magical, marvelous, heartwarming, and unexpected reminder of the true "why" of my business presented itself.

My initial desire was to "do good while doing well" – or so I thought! Now, running a financially floundering business left me wondering what I'd been thinking! How did I not see this was going to be harder, longer, and more costly than I'd initially imagined? Whatever got into my mind – did I really dislike the corporate lifestyle so much that I didn't perform due diligence before deciding to build a brick-and-mortar school for children? Now I was more stressed and frustrated than in my corporate career and worse off financially. It felt like a double whammy.

I kept trying to understand why I'd gotten myself into this position. Upon deeper reflection, I realized that my intention really had been to *do well* financially by *doing good* in the world. I wanted the lifestyle of a good income and the freedom that my corporate job didn't provide. My desire and focus was on building a lifestyle free of worry and stress – to have a high quality of life without giving up any resources.

And then it hit me: I *was* doing well…because I was *doing good*. The school was helping students learn, grow, and achieve what they'd once only dreamt of. It was building their confidence and self-esteem, and it was winning awards from the business community and gaining positive recognition from the innumerable life-changing stories of the impact on our young students.

What began as a financially focused business choice has become a thriving, heart-centered success. And this is the greatest reward of all.

Asking for 20 Cents...and Receiving Grace

By Chey Bodhi

It was a magical Sunday morning. I was enjoying my coffee on the deck, soaking up the sunshine, and allowing my mind to drift away. Suddenly, a childhood memory popped into my head – one I had recalled many times before, one that always made me feel uncomfortable. It was from a time when my father was working far away and only came home for an hour or so each Sunday to take care of household business with our mother. During these times, because I was the youngest, my older siblings would plead then bully me into running to Dad, hugging and cuddling up to him...and then making sure that he gave us all our 20 cents pocket money.

My siblings were afraid of his violent temper, which they had all endured through his beatings. I could sense their fear, even though I was only three years old. And I knew that if anyone else asked for our allowance, he would tell them to go away and stop bothering him (or worse). However, if I ran to him calling out, "Daddy! Daddy!" he would toss me onto his shoulders and play with me while he went about his business.

Resistance to this responsibility was futile, as my siblings were much older than me. If I had refused, they would have made my life even more of a living hell. This responsibility weighed heavily on my tiny shoulders, and I quickly learned how to manipulate my father's attention to achieve the desired goal. I rarely failed.

All these decades later, as I sat on my deck that Sunday morning, it hit me like a bolt of lightning – I could see how this pattern had played out through my entire life. I had always felt that I had to do what other people wanted me to do to earn an income. I had to meet everyone else's expectations of me and never my own.

This spontaneous moment of grace was a powerful catalyst for me. It changed my world and set me on a path to where I am now – doing what I love!

Nothing to Lose

By Nicole Black

"Why on earth would you ever in a million years run for senior class president at a high school with 2,500 students when you have four friends and you have only gone there for a year?" my friend asked me.

"Well, why not?" I said. "What have I got to lose?"

"But you won't win," said my friend.

"How do you know that I won't win? What if I write the best speech ever and win over the hearts of the student body?"

"It won't matter. It's not like you can promise them that you will make lemonade flow freely from the drinking fountain."

"So what? I'm going to run because I want to understand how government and politics works. Maybe that's what I want to do when I finish school."

"But you don't understand – it's only a popularity contest, and you don't have the numbers. These people don't know you. They won't vote for you. You shouldn't run."

"Well, you make a good case: I have no chance of winning and every chance of losing. I don't know any of these people, so they may think I am weird. Then I think I should *definitely* run. After all, I have nothing to lose!"

It turned out that my friend was right – I lost the election. But *I* was also right, because what I won that day was self-respect and courage to know that even if I am going to fail miserably, at least I will have tried. And I learned this important lesson: Don't ever let someone tell you not to do something because you can't win. The test of a true competitor is when you know you cannot win and choose to go into battle anyway.

Grace Through Seeing

By Karen Hicks

For a couple of my university years, I began and ended each day with an hour-long bus trip through the city. One of the joys of riding the bus was people-watching. I became familiar with the other regular riders, who their travelling companions were, when they got on, and when they got off. I also noticed the infrequent riders.

One of the regular travel groups I looked for each day was a family of four: a mother, father, sister, and brother. They looked so alike! What intrigued me about this family is that both the mom and dad were blind, while their children were sighted. I was fascinated by their interaction. I wondered at the ways in which the children "saw" for their parents.

As I thought about this family, I became more aware of my own thoughts as I watched people come onto the bus. What I suddenly realized was that my thoughts were critical. I was judging clothing, hairstyles, "beauty"…*everything!* I shocked and surprised myself.

At that exact moment, I promised myself that I would notice at least one positive thing about each person who came onto the bus. And I did. Every person. Sometimes it was the shape of an eyebrow, a cheekbone, a hand, a smile, the way someone moved, the scarf someone was wearing.

At first, this new way of seeing took effort; however, it soon became second nature…and fun! I began to notice more how people moved and how much beauty there was in the world. I realized that "ugly" did not exist.

I continue this habit to this very day. Most often, I now find that it's easy, except when I'm experiencing internal conflict. When I don't easily see beauty, I know I need to look inward. And when I do, I often think of that family of four, remembering the graceful flow between the children and their parents. As they were going about their daily business of riding the bus, they didn't know that they were doing much more. They were teaching and helping me see what truly mattered.

Miracles, Grace, and Pinball

By Cathie Bliss

I always have ideas rambling around my head. From practical to hilarious to deeply meaningful, they appear as unrelated as cats and suitcases. But when these distinct, random thoughts come together, uniting into one, that is a fantastic moment of grace!

How does this happen? The merge usually takes a while. The thoughts and concepts need to bounce off each other, as if several pinballs have been released all at once into the pinball machine of my mind. There they linger, needing time without conscious attention, a meditation without meditating.

Here's an example of the process:

Pinball #1: I've always been intrigued by Albert Einstein. I'm drawn in by his philosophical intelligence, our shared birthday, and his crazy hair. I especially love his quote, "There are only two ways to live your life. One is as though nothing is a miracle. The other is as though everything is a miracle."

Pinball #2: Just what *is* a miracle? A miracle is a wonder, an amazing event, often attributed to divine intervention. A shift in perception can also be a miracle, and certainly, miracles are moments of grace.

Pinball #3: Your attitude toward any given moment in life is more important than specific circumstances. Where does attitude come from? It comes from the beliefs you hold. And their source? Whether conscious or subconscious, beliefs are repeated, embedded thoughts that feel like truth.

Initially, these are three individual ideas. Then, after several games of pinball, the thoughts coalesce. My moment of grace, the moment when the pinballs hit a new high score, is when these multiple concepts become one. They have merged, and the strangely familiar result, the blended whole, becomes part of me.

And this moment of grace? If we can change our thoughts and limiting beliefs, and know this shift in perception is a miracle in itself, it confirms an overall philosophy, á la Einstein, that we can truly live our lives as if everything is a miracle. Imagine a world where we live from this perspective: pure grace!

A Reminder to Let Go

By Ellouise Heather

As I wait for my flight home to depart from its gate, I watch the other aeroplanes from my window with awe and appreciation. There's something majestic about these flying machines that I have come to respect, and I watch with wonder as a Boeing descends onto the runway, takes command of its momentum, and comes to a halt.

I smile serenely as I think back to the first time that I flew. It was during a period in my life that I was finding exceptionally stressful. This was largely due to my numerous attempts to fix other people's problems, regardless of the variables beyond my control. Feeling I was in control made me feel safe, and I believed that not being in control meant that the world was an unsafe place to be.

When I embarked upon my first flight, I experienced an unprecedented lightness from within. Goosebumps danced across my arms, and my stomach flipped with excitement as we accelerated along the runway. Instinctively, I was fully embracing the moment and somehow letting go with ease. As the wheels left the runway, I felt a calmness that I couldn't recall ever feeling before. The aircraft continued its ascent, and I peered, through the tears of joy clouding my eyes, at the cumulus formations outside.

Flying stirs paradoxical feelings for me. Soaring across the sky brings a sense of strength, but also a certain fragility. To relinquish control and to just trust is to accept the vulnerability of what it is to be human. And yet, if it weren't for my first experience flying, I might not have discovered how liberating it can be to just trust and let go of the need to be in control. I'm deeply grateful that, every time I've flown since, I've been reminded of this lesson.

My Daughter, My Teacher

By Linda Voogd

A few months ago, I experienced an a-ha moment: My shadow self emerged with a vengeance when a colleague's rude statement triggered my insecurities. Continually challenging my decisions, this colleague forced me to question my abilities as a therapist. She routinely refused to respect my knowledge and experience.

I described this particular moment to my daughter with all the anger and indignation to which I felt entitled, all the while knowing I was stuck experiencing the world from a wounded part of myself. It was a time of crisis, so my reserve was already low, but more than anything, I wanted someone to tell me I was right.

I knew something in me needed healing. Where was my belief in myself? Why had I gotten so rattled? I was a teacher poised to become the student. As so often happens, however, the teacher who shows up is not the one you expect. In this instance, she was my own daughter.

I retold the story, feeling a surge of humiliation and rage. She stopped me and – in a calm, clear, and focused voice – said, "Mom, you know this is *your* stuff, but you can't seem to get past it. Each person acts as a mirror, reflecting back what is already inside of you; so each time you look at this person, why don't you put your face on hers? Literally see your reflection."

I was dumbfounded! What a brilliant idea. What if I *could* see myself in every person? Not just the good parts, but also the parts I didn't like or own. Suddenly, it all made sense. I wondered how my daughter knew this. This idea was magic, and I now use it whenever I struggle. As I see my face on each person, I recognize where I am like them and how I have acted similarly. This has changed my life, and I always consider it a moment of divine intervention. Out of the mouth of babes!

Introducing Myself to Myself

By Christina Araujo

I will never forget the time when I finally introduced myself to myself. It was an early Saturday morning in April 2014. I had just arrived at a workshop that was going to teach us how to become better speakers – or so I thought. Walking in, I had no idea of the overwhelming emotion that would soon run through my whole soul.

Shortly after the workshop began, the instructor had us stand in front a mirror and look at ourselves while we repeated four powerful statements that would forever change my life: *I love you. I am sorry. Please forgive me. Thank you.*

As I stood in front of the mirror, speaking these words, I suddenly realized that I was staring at a stranger. I meditated into my eyes and studied my soul. What I found was amazing! I saw strength, love, power, and a young woman on a mission of inner growth. I also saw the pain from my childhood that was still causing conflict in my adulthood. And then I heard, as clearly and forcefully as if someone were yelling into my mind, "You are a very strong, powerful woman! Heal your wounds!"

As I stared into the mirror, I felt such a rush of emotions and I knew that I had to do something. I had to deal with the wounds that I had been temporarily covering up with a bandage. I had to let go of all the emotions that had been bringing me down and blocking my success and happiness. And I had to release my addictive behaviors, which were no longer serving me.

For a whole week afterwards, I was very emotional as I released my emotional baggage. Many times, I was tempted to not deal with it and continue covering it up with the same bandage I'd been using for the past 25 years. But I knew that if I did this I would stagnate my own growth and wouldn't be able to help others who have gone through similar situations. I knew it was my time to step up and shine, and I was ready!

Grace in Town, in the City, and on the Farm

By Holly Noella Labrecque

Growing up in a variety of settings in Saskatchewan, Canada, was a blessing for me. I was able to experience the various pleasures and also the restrictions (which are often blessings in disguise) of being a town girl, city girl, and farm girl. There was good and grace everywhere, every day, and in every way.

As a town girl, I experienced the safety of living in a small community where everyone knew each other. I enjoyed hours at the skating rink conveniently located across the street from our home. I learned to drive where there were barely any vehicles; hence, no need for parallel parking!

Then, as a city girl, I learned about "strangers" – a foreign word for small-town people. I recall my mother scolding me as a young girl for always waving to everyone. All the while, I was thinking they *must* know me, so *I* must know *them*.

And lastly, as a farm girl, I learned to long for the scent of burning stubble in the fall. I experienced the warmth of freshly laid eggs and the excitement of announcements that our school bus was not starting on cold winter mornings.

Perhaps, as the saying goes, "you had to be there to appreciate it." Therefore, no matter what my age or where I lived, I readily accepted and spiritually connected with these everyday moments of simple yet amazing grace. I learned that grace is contained in small moments yet is also infinite. It is the young girl waving to everyone. It is the brilliant "awe-wakening" to life as a gift and to the magnificent Power and Presence of the Divine that creates harmony within ourselves, with others, and with the Universe.

How Sweet the Sound

By Amy Gage

For my whole life, I've had fears about speaking – especially speaking in public. Writing has allowed me to share my voice with others. But, fear aside, I've always had a deep burning desire to share my soul voice through my physical voice, too.

The opportunity to come face-to-face with my public-speaking fear arrived at a recent event. I was scared to speak, but somewhere in the distance, under the fear, was passionate excitement.

Could my fear be overcome? This one felt so big and tightly woven into me, I couldn't know for certain. But I had to try to find out. I prepared to accept my fate if it went terribly, but promised myself that if it went well, I'd never give up on using my voice or let fear lead me astray again.

I knew nothing short of a miracle would be necessary to find my courage on stage. Yet, in spite of my doubts, a voice in my head kept saying, "It's better to speak with a shaky voice than to not speak at all." I followed that voice.

Onstage that evening, I openly acknowledged my fear as well as my soul. That felt experimental but true to who I am. Then a miracle did happen: I felt the presence of Amazing Grace. I found out some fears need to be shared to be healed.

That event was divinely orchestrated to support me in speaking my truth, which allowed me to support others in speaking theirs. I was humbled by the love from everyone who received my vulnerable voice graciously and for those who shared theirs with me.

Fear starts losing its power when we give our soul more attention by letting it lead us to courage in spite of the fear. Love always has the final say, but we must trust it to experience it. Sometimes uncertainty is part of the mystery of love, and that is where we find our true voice.

We Are All Cells in God's Body

By Karla Joy Huber

I always struggled with the idea that certain spiritual concepts are exclusive to one religion. I'm more of a spiritual free-agent, and much of what I believe contradicts what many people around me consider to be absolute spiritual truths.

Despite this, I have always been blessed with unconditional love from many people of various faiths, people who love me for who I am rather than for my similarities to them. One of these people was my beloved Granddaddy, John Christian Huber. Granddaddy was a devout Moravian Christian, but it never fazed him that I was participating with the Bahá'í community, engaging in Native American spiritual practices, or studying Buddhism. He never argued that I needed to believe his way, and he trusted my judgment and respected that I was walking a good path.

Granddaddy once said something that blew me away: "Maybe we're all cells in God's body." That statement really struck a chord with me, the idea that the Creative Force of the Universe *is* the Universe, and we're all components of it rather than isolated pieces being independently controlled by an external force, such as God or fate.

It made me think that the great spiritual concepts many of us grew up thinking are exclusive to Christianity, such as grace, are available to everyone, because they're already woven into the fabric. It's up to us to be receptive to them, to make the conscious choice to manifest them in our lives.

Whether we're Christian, Jewish, Muslim, Bahá'í, Hindu, Buddhist, traditional Native American, Jain, Sikh, Zoroastrian, or Pagan, we can recast the idea of grace for ourselves and make it part of our way of life. We manifest grace in how we handle things, in the unconditional love we hold for the people who are most important to us, in the courage we muster to face challenges, and in the dignity we maintain when facing failure or persecution.

Whether our spiritual practice is humanistic or God-centered, grace is available to each of us. No one has to confer it upon us, and no one can take it away.

From Overwhelmed to Whelmed

By Elizabeth R. Kipp

For many years, whenever I felt an intense emotion or sensation, my mind would scream at me, "This is too much!" Deeply embedded somewhere inside of me, I heard the message, "It's not safe to feel all of that!" And I trained myself to shut down, avoid, or stuff down all such feelings. What an unhealthy habit this became! I suffered chronic pain for years as a result.

After years of living this way, I began to retrain myself and change my old habits. Now, when I feel a surge of fierce emotion or a powerful sensation, I tell myself, "It is safe to feel. I am not being annihilated. Whatever happens, I am okay."

I turn to my breath and presence myself in the moment. I tell myself this new story: "Of course I am fully capable of handling what I am feeling. This is not 'overwhelming.' This is what it feels like to be 'whelmed.'"

I remind myself that I am nestled firmly and held forever in the safe and loving arms of the Universe. I put my attention on my breath and all that I am feeling. I sit with this. I let this sensation course through me, and I fully feel it. I do not try to dodge, stuff, avoid, smother, medicate, or look outside of myself in any other way to change, dull, or otherwise affect this. I turn into it. I face it. I invite it in. I accept and welcome it. I consciously bring in the breath as my faithful companion as I open to it and allow it to run free throughout me. I dance with it.

Ahhhhhhhhhhh. This is what it means to be me. To be.

Thank you, Universe, for bringing me this assignment and showing me such contentment within the very vibrancy of life. I am here, open, ready to take on whatever you bring me. Thank you for the gift of this remarkable life.

Failing Charm Class, Finding Grace for Life

By Cindy Harpe Hively

As a little girl, I can remember hearing, "Here comes Grace." It was usually my mother saying these words and laughing. My real name is Cindy, and being graceful or full of grace was not, indeed, my forte. I was a mess – dirty or muddy most of the time. As I grew older, I would still get the occasional bruise, grass stain, or bloody knee playing every sport that girls were allowed to play. I was darn good, too!

In 12th grade, a new required class was added at my school: Charm Class. We were taught so many important ways of being graceful and charming. I learned the correct way to walk with a stack of books on my head, where the length of my skirt should be to catch the desired husband, how much makeup to wear, how to hold a teacup, and how to eat a full-course meal. At this time, it was demanded by society – especially in the Baptist school I was attending – that this was the way young ladies were to behave.

It was a hot June afternoon when my report card arrived in the mailbox, revealing the devastating news: I had failed Charm Class. My parents looked at each other, and my dad said, "Charm Class? What's *that*?" My dad, who was an instructor in the Marines, must have had a little chat with the Charm Class teacher because, not long after that, my grade magically changed!

As a teenager, I was humiliated; but now, as a Goddess in her Queendom, I am thankful for the lessons life has taught me about grace and charm. As I've come to see it, these are not actions or qualities that can be taught in school. Grace is an inside job. It is both the conscious and subconscious appreciation of life.

Today, I feel so blessed to share this message with many young girls who have been bullied or abused, and with women of all ages who have lived their lives feeling they were not good enough. If I were teaching a class on grace and charm, this is what I'd say: "Grace is our birthright, and it knows that we are *all* perfect within our own imperfection...no matter how we hold our teacup!"

In the Blueberry Patch

By Janet Dhaenens

During a recent talk with my sweety, Celeste, I wanted to direct our conversation to something that felt good. I'd been listening to Abraham-Hicks often, and I was drawn to the idea of thinking about and appreciating things I already have to immerse myself in the feelings I want to experience more. I suggested we take turns sharing what we want that we already have.

"I appreciate that I drive right by a you-pick blueberry farm on my way to town and can stop often to enjoy eating blueberries!" I said.

"I appreciate that I get to talk with my sweety while she is picking blueberries," Celeste added. "I so appreciate that she is in my life. My life is rich and full because of her!"

"I appreciate that even though we live more than 700 miles from each other, I get to talk daily with my sweetheart and share a deep, meaningful relationship."

"I appreciate I get to help her with things she needs," Celeste said. "I am grateful that I have enough money to help her financially."

As I felt her appreciation, a new understanding dawned in me. Something I felt shame about, wished was different, and spent so much time and effort trying to change (not having much money) was something that brought my partner joy, because it gave her the opportunity to help me and feel good in doing that.

I also saw the flip side: When Celeste was emotional and felt shame, thinking that she shouldn't feel the way she did, her emotion did not bother me. In fact, I always felt closer to her when I knew how she felt! I wanted her to share with me when she felt bad and let me be with her in the experience.

I saw the beauty of a universe arranged in such a way that one person's need becomes another person's joy. I didn't need to feel shame about what is true in my life or work hard trying to change it. Instead, I could choose to trust life, and trust that by being who we are and showing up to share with each other, everyone's needs can be met.

The Music of Touch
By Tamiko S. Knight

When I woke up this morning, I prepared to write my vision of how Reiki and massage relate to health and wellness. As I typed the first keystroke, I heard the Steve Miller Band being played on a nearby radio: "I want to fly like an eagle, let my spirit carry me."

In that moment, my life changed. I realized the connection between words, music, and touch – and how they all have the power to heal.

Words, music, and touch play such an integral role in so many of life's milestones – from birth to death and so many important moments in between. They are part of rituals that carry deep significance. They move energy, and they convey love.

I think of the most meaningful experiences in our lives as the "lyrics" that touch our hearts, and touch as the music that carries them from one person to another. Through Reiki and massage, I use my hands to interact with a person's energy – creating a kind of "music" played upon the instrument of the physical and energetic body.

I find it truly amazing how a loving touch – such as through Reiki or massage – can have such a profound impact on people's lives. When someone is in a moment of hopelessness or doubt, it is often the touch of a friend or family member that can change their life. Touch can build connections between individuals and even help communities to grow.

Touch can also help us tap into an even greater energy – an energy that connects and transcends humanity – the therapeutic touch of love. I am truly grateful to be part of this grand network, and my journey of healing on this path will never stop.

Warrior Within

By Lisa "The Link" Rizzo

I am a warrior. I seek out fears within me in order to overcome them in this lifetime. I knew when I came into this world that I was coming to fight a battle that I did not finish in another lifetime. I also knew that this earthbound world, filled with much darkness, would do its best to break my spirit.

As I walked this world as a child, I learned how to deal with pain. I went without food most of the time, was beaten for no reason, and survived rape as a young teenager. But these things that I went through didn't define me. I knew that, with faith and prayer, someday I was destined to help many and would share my warrior spirit.

As I overcame my fears of this world, I was given a gift from the heavens to be able to speak to spirits. As I put my trust in my spirit guides, I was gifted with even more insight from the other side. And the more I trusted in my own spirit, the more I understood and could see, feel, hear, and touch from the universe.

I'm blessed to be a medium who seeks out answers from the spirit world regarding mind, body, and spirit. I know now, as I look back at my life, that the warrior within me chose not to be a victim of this world. I chose to walk with my head held high, even when I wanted to fall apart. In return, the warrior has been gifted with everything she wanted in this life, including becoming a mother, wife, and businesswoman. And now, I'm blessed to be able to share my journey with you.

Breathe into Life

By Elizabeth R. Kipp

Breath is our direct connection to the Divine and to others. It is our constant companion through life. It supports us through difficult times, centering us in a place of peace. And it helps us appreciate ordinary moments of calm routine. It softens us and shows us that *all* of life is amazing. Even a single breath can open us to grace.

I experienced the power of breath one time while I was having a difficult conversation with a friend. As we talked, I felt fearful about whether I would say the right words. I was frozen, unsure of what to do next, and I noticed that I was holding my breath. So, instead of withdrawing or saying anything out loud in that moment, I consciously released my breath. I allowed myself to be right there where I was – with all the fear and hesitation. I took another full breath – in…and out. I opened more space for myself and asked for help from my Higher Power. As I inhaled again, Grace flooded in. I felt powerfully buoyed by The Divine. I exhaled slowly and felt my fear dissolve into peace, confidence, and compassion for my friend and myself. Blessed with this remarkable shift after just a few breaths, I was able to move forward in the conversation with love.

There are moments when I feel like there is all the space in the world to breathe. And there are other times that simply take my breath away. Through it all, I breathe. I breathe into the difficult. I breathe into the ordinary. I breathe into this amazing, healing, heartbreaking, soul-connecting, breathtaking life…again and again and again. And I repeat as often as needed.

Gracefully Letting Go of Anger

By Victoria L. Mai

One bright summer day, I had a terrible fight with my parents. Afterwards, I felt distraught and angry – the way I typically feel after arguments. Usually, I would have allowed this fight (and my feelings about it) to ruin my whole day – perhaps even more, for as long as I held on to the anger.

But this time was different.

I distinctly remember the moment when I realized I could shift into feeling better...if I made the choice to do so. A part of me wanted to hold on to the anger because I was so used to it, but this time I allowed myself to choose happiness over any emotion that didn't serve me. So I asked for help to let go of this anger and all the accumulated anger with forgiveness. Immediately, I felt a wave of peace wash over me and through me. I felt held and loved.

I felt better.

Since that experience, I've realized how important it is to acknowledge our feelings and then reach out to grace to help us choose a mindset that feels better. Through choice and through grace, we heal and grow. I've also realized that grace is always present. It is always here to support us; we just have to remember to ask for its help.

The more I remember to reach out to grace and connect to its ever-present peace and love, the more I realize that it has always been there, nudging me to smile. Grace reminds me to love myself and others. It reminds me to feel gratitude, which helps me to be at peace within the present moment. And, ultimately, that is what we have: moments in which we connect to the divine and our own divinity.

Fire Kiss

By Janet Dhaenens

When I went to a firewalk the second time, I thought it would be easy. Heck, I'd already done it the year before! But my fear of walking on hot coals felt every bit as strong as the first time. I don't know if I would have been able to do it if I hadn't been surrounded by other people who were walking.

I decided to walk. On the second step, I felt the pain. I got burned! I made it the rest of the way across the coals, and once I was in the cold dirt on the other side, I could tell that the burn was not very bad. It was only in one area, on some toes.

But now I was scared – *really* scared! I also knew I had to walk again. I had to get through my fear. The only question was: Would I be able to get through my fear now, tonight, or would I wait until next year to do it again?

The coals were cooling off, so I knew I had to make the decision quickly or this opportunity would be gone. "I'm going!" I decided. I stepped up and walked, the last person for this night. I did not get burned! I made it through my fear!

Even though I overcame my fear and made it through unscathed the second time, all I could think about was the first time, when I got burned. *Why had this happened? What did I do wrong? Why did I feel like a failure?* I was surprised and confused with what I felt. I didn't tell anyone what happened until the next day, when I called the instructor.

"I got burned," I told her.

"Oh, you got a fire kiss. The fire energy is intelligent, and sometimes it will give you an extra burst of heat to help you move through some challenge in your life."

Her words calmed me. So I hadn't made a mistake after all! I didn't "do it wrong." There was no shame in getting burned. I felt relief!

Now, several years later, I realize my success is determined by how I see any situation. I choose to see myself as successful as I learn from every experience.

December 26

Releasing "Success" and Following Passion

By Robert D. White

I always fancied the idea of being a mental healer. But I also wanted to be a successful businessman because I knew this was the quickest route to fortune. So I completely ignored my impulse toward healing and diligently moved in pursuit of material success.

I enrolled in college and pursued all roads leading to a career in management. I knew this would afford me the opportunity to work for Fortune 500 companies, which would surely put me in a position to attain the level of success I so desperately desired.

This determination even forced me to relocate to an entirely new city where I continued this assiduous chase toward what I thought was "success." With all the promotions, recognition, and money that came with this striving, there followed an even greater number of agonies, antagonisms, and antipathies. All of this adversity served to strengthen my yearning to follow my passion for healing. Nonetheless, even with all signs showing me that *enough is enough*, I still chose to continue down this destructive path.

Then, late one afternoon during the summer of 2014, I received a phone call saying my grandmother, who was like a mother to me, had had a stroke. It was later discovered that she would have to live the remainder of her life with dementia.

My world was crumbling fast! My grandmother was critically ill, I had a job I despised, and my passion was eating me alive from the inside out. In that very moment I realized that the Universe was calling me to follow my heart's desire. And this time, I listened to that call.

As soon as I released my grip on my earlier notion of "success" and began to follow my passion, my life quickly filled with the people, knowledge, and opportunities that put me on a new path to fulfilling my purpose as a mental healer.

Say Yes to the Journey

By Freda Durden

I began my spiritual journey from a dry place. I had been pushed out of my comfort zone by a feeling of lack in my life. I hungered for something more, so I said yes to the spiritual journey and set off in the direction of my soul's calling.

In the beginning, each step I took revealed such beautiful treasures. It was enticing. I was happy. I found joy in everything within me and around me. It was all so new and fresh, yet there was something familiar about this process – like a native language I had somehow forgotten.

As I continued my journey, I remembered more and more and experienced visions so real it was as if they occurred in real time. They spread into my sleep – my dreams were no longer my own. I received even more from the spirit world when, during a Reiki session, I began hearing messages from a deceased relative of someone in the room.

Others became intrigued by my experiences – the clairvoyance, mediumship, and intuitive gifts that were somehow flowing into me. And I was grateful for all of these gifts; however, I missed the beginning of my journey – when I was amazed by the blooming of flowers, when spirituality was simply about being happy. Now, my journey began to feel like a punishment. I wondered if I had gone too far into the light. Was the other side darkness?

It seemed that my journey had led me to a place of darkness deep inside myself. And, as I learned, the shadow of our souls is the most frightening darkness there is, because it is our own – our own pain, our own fear. Even though I had been seeking the answers in the spiritual knowledge all around me, it was the journey within that taught me Who I Am. Sitting in the darkness, grace was unveiled.

I experienced the integration between my inner and outer worlds and realized that the gifts I had received during the journey were tools to produce both the external rewards and the internal abundance of love that I desire. And I learned that you should never worry about where you start or fear where you may end up...as long as you say yes to the journey.

The Borrowed Book

By Sharon Halliday

The book beckoned me. Books can have a funny way of doing that. This particular book didn't belong to me. I was returning it on behalf of someone else to a mutual friend.

It hadn't been on my kitchen counter for more than a few hours when I felt its call. So, that evening, as my husband worked late and after my kids had been fed and bathed, I picked it up. I had a mile-long list of things that I could have chosen to do instead. Thankfully, I acted on that inner nudge. I'd been learning lately that it's one thing to have intuition, another thing entirely to act on it.

I held this book, *Simple Abundance: A Daybook of Comfort and Joy* by Sarah Ban Breathnach, and opened with gusto to a page that spoke to my soul. There on the page before me – in big, black, bold print – were the words: *Reordering Your Priorities.*

Although I'm sure my kids were playing somewhere in the background, I was so mesmerized by the words cascading into my consciousness that I felt as though I were in my own private, silent library. It felt nurturing to honour this time-out for myself. It didn't matter how brief it would be, for the quality would far outweigh the quantity.

One sentence that I read and re-read was, "The more our lives and attention spans are segmented by our children, our careers, our homes, our marriages, and our needs for personal expression, the more we need to identify what is truly important in our lives." Whoa! These words encapsulated my ongoing quandary (and possibly one I shared with mothers around the world). Here I was on the day before New Year's Eve, flooded with 12 months of flashbacks of all the moments I'd spent wrestling with "what is truly important" throughout the year.

Towards the end of these brief yet perceptive paragraphs was a reminder that as we get in touch with the silence within ourselves, everything else will fall into place – exactly the advice I needed! In that moment of grace, I was living the truth of these words as I was reading them!

Living the Dream

By Margo Kirzinger

I've often posed the question to myself: *What is the "dream life," and when am I going to have mine?*

Many of us have been predisposed to think and feel that living our best life, our dream life, can only happen in the future: when we get that promotion, when we retire, when our bank account is at *x* dollars, when we have that luxury car we've always coveted, when our kids are grown and out on their own (successfully, with no chance of their coming back!), when we win the lottery...the list goes on.

I, too, was guilty of this if-and-when type of thinking, spending far too much time on what I thought I still needed in order to have my best life. I was living so far in the future that I had forgotten all the beautiful blessings that I *already* possessed.

As a professional, I spent many years walking out of my own life and into someone else's. I wanted to help and heal – so much so, that I completely shut down on myself. I began to see the harsh reality that while others were receiving something positive from me to assist with their own personal fulfillment, I had become mentally, emotionally, and spiritually bankrupt. I had slipped into a mindset of lack and loss, rather than one of gratitude and abundance. This heartfelt realization is when I knew it was time to re-evaluate.

My saving grace was the epiphany that I was not going to save the world and, more importantly, that I didn't *have* to!

There will always be some disappointments and sadness. These setbacks help us more readily recognize and appreciate the joyous moments of life in all its beauty and mundanity. I now see that, even in the midst of all this, my dream life is in the *here and now*, and I'm going to start living it – every day, always, no apologies, no exceptions.

Meeting Grace

By Sharon Rothstein

I am a teacher and student of spirit. I have the ability to notice what is happening around me. I usually stay in the moment and do not respond unconsciously to stimuli. There are times, however, when I wish that I could become even more conscious of the Grace in my life. I wish that I could consistently meet Grace head-on and stay in that moment where Spirit takes over and my timing is on point. I would like to surrender and be led to a life of opportunity and, more importantly, joy.

I have longed for the place where I thrive and excel. It seems to be happening now, since Grace is swaying the stars in alignment for my highest good. Things are good now in this moment that I meet with Grace. Grace is inside me, amazing, comforting, and enlightening. And Grace is always ahead, waiting for me to notice and ready to make things right. Grace is my sensor of happiness. Grace takes charge and allows me to sail with the wind behind me, steadying my course through right vibration and focus.

When I meet Grace, I feel as if I am wrapped in a cocoon of safety – like a babe in the womb, sheltered from my own self-imposed chaos and nurtured by the Divine. I am fed only positive nutrients of thought under a blanket of understanding. As I meet Grace, I feel what it is like to become enveloped by the purest form of love. In this space, there is no comparison, and my misperceptions about myself and others are corrected. I see with Spirit vision, and my truth is revealed and supported.

I can say that I am now meeting Grace more in my life. How fortunate I am to have found this state of awareness. I am sensing a calm and utterly grateful state. My journey with Grace in my life is becoming effortless, and everything is falling into place.

Unexpected Homecoming

By Christine Callahan-Oke

I've always believed that when we die, it's not the end. But it wasn't until 2004 that I actually knew this to be true. That year, I participated in the Toronto Weekend to End Breast Cancer.

Like many families, mine has seen various types of cancer. My mom had cancer in 1989, and I'm grateful to say she is now happy and healthy. My aunt, on the other hand, unfortunately passed away at age 26 after a heart-wrenching, courageous fight with the disease.

So when I heard radio ads for the 60-kilometre walk, I felt an undeniable inner pull to do it.

Walking for two days alongside dear friends – surrounded by thousands of people committed to making a difference – was inspiring and life-changing. Yet it was emotionally difficult; most of those people had lost a loved one to cancer, so it was a sharp reminder of the widespread impact of the disease.

But there was also lightheartedness on the journey. The checkpoints were run by enthusiastic volunteers in wacky costumes. Those volunteers kept our spirits high, especially when fatigue set in and blisters flared.

At the finish line, hundreds of people cheered us on. The energy was palpable, giving us the boost we needed to take those final steps. I noticed the checkpoint teams in their costumes, grinning from ear to ear.

And then it happened.

Out of the blue, as I looked at the volunteers and the cheering crowd, my drained senses were overtaken by a powerful, indescribable rush of love, and a feeling – a *knowing* – from the depths of my soul: this is what we experience when we die. We're greeted by souls who were part of our life's journey and who transitioned before us. They cheer us on with love and excitement, so happy to welcome us home.

Whether it was déjà vu or a window of insight, it doesn't matter. I now know that we're loved more deeply than we will ever understand. And what an incredible comfort that is.

Conclusion

H ere we are at the end of our journey together (at least for now).
It's our hope that after reading each of these moments of grace,
you've been experiencing and recognizing your own as well. It's our
hope that you've been moved by the pieces and have felt goosebumps
and epiphanies along the way. And it's our hope that this book has
helped you to see that grace can be found anywhere – in the
supernatural miracles and also in our day-to-day routines. It's right there
for us to see – we just have to be open to it.

This book is wonderful for keeping out and referencing from time
to time, especially in those moments when your faith is wavering and
your heart is longing for something more. Flip to a page at random and
trust that your soul will guide you to the exact piece that will help you to
reconnect with the magic that's all around you.

If you enjoyed this book, please be sure to share it with your friends
and family! Helping someone recognize and connect with the grace in
their life is a beautiful gift! We would also be so grateful if you left a
positive review for us on Amazon, which will help it reach even more
people. And we would love for you to join us on our Facebook page,
where you can share some of your favorite pieces, connect with the
authors, and be part of our wonderfully loving and grace-filled
community: www.facebook.com/365momentsofgracebook.

Thank you so much for taking the time to read our book. We hope
that it's been an enlightening and positive experience for you!

Hugs, love, and gratitude,
Jodi and Dan

Contributor Biographies

O ver 250 authors contributed to this book with the hopes that sharing their life-changing moments of grace would open everyone who reads it to recognizing their own moments as well.

Grace knows no boundaries, and this book is a true testament of that. The co-authors come from many different walks of life from many parts of the world. The common thread that links each of us is our desire to share our words and to inspire others by doing so. That's all, and that's everything.

As you read through each author's biography on the pages that follow, you'll find that some are already bestselling authors and others are sharing their words in print for the first time, which is such an exciting moment!

It's our hope that you'll enjoy meeting them through their photos and biographies, and that you'll reach out to those you resonate with and let them know how much their piece moved you. What a gift that will be for them to receive!

About the Editors

Jodi Chapman and Dan Teck are a husband-and-wife team who loves living soulfully and joyfully. Since 2005, they've been living their dream of writing books and creating products that inspire others to connect with their soul and live fully and passionately.

Jodi has a BA in English/Technical Editing and Sociology, and Dan has a BA in Religious Studies and an MFA in Creative Writing. Together, they have over 30 years of experience with editing and publishing and have sold over 35,000 books. They have written 20 books, 10 ecourses, and over 1,000 blog posts/articles.

Jodi is an award-winning blogger at www.jodichapman.com and the creator of Soul Clarity Cards. Dan is the author of the personal-growth blog *Halfway up the Mountain* (www.halfwayupthemountain.com). They are the co-creators of the *Soulful Journals Series* and the *365 Book Series*.

They live on the Oregon coast with their sweet cats. They enjoy hanging out at the beach and working, creating, and playing together.

They feel truly blessed to be able to spend each day together, doing what they love. It's their heart's desire that their books and products bring joy to everyone they reach.

About the Contributors

Nikki Ackerman is a holistic business owner and a Master in Usui/Tibetan Reiki, Karuna® Reiki, and Holy Fire® Reiki. She recognizes the rewards are very beneficial for mind, body, and spirit wellness. Her desire is to provide others with peace and balance through a soulful and holistic approach to self-care and well-being.

Aprile Alexander is an Australian artist, a creativity coach, and an intuitive energy healing practitioner. She helps people and animals clear energy blockages and move forward in life, to more easily express their God-given magnificence. She works with clients from any country in the world by phone. www.TimeForFlourishing.com

Karrol Rikka S. Altarejos is a ritual wisdom keeper, intuitive empath, Reiki Master/Teacher, and certified crystal/vibrational healer. She nurtures empaths to embrace, empower, and embody their gifts by honoring the rituals and everyday spiritual practices that cultivate connection with their higher selves, nature, and Source. www.karrolrikka.com

Tiffany Andersen is a medical aesthetician with 20 years experience, stage-4 cancer survivor, and victim of a major car accident. She turned tragedy into triumph, which is described in her award-winning memoir, *Finding Faith*. On a quest for elements to repair the body, she developed the toxin-free skincare line, Gavée Gold. www.gaveegold.com

Chris Anderson, Gentleheart Therapies LLC Founder, is an international bestselling author, nurse, and educator who helps individuals and families experiencing end-of-life transitions. She provides empowering workshops for caregivers and helps families honor their loved ones with Gentleheart Memorial Cards. www.1gentleheart.com

Christina Araujo has a background in the medical field and has graduated from the University of San Francisco with a degree in Business Management. She hopes to become a spirituality coach and help others connect to their whole being. She enjoys meditating, networking, and living life from the soul and heart.

Carol Ann Arnim's website, www.creatingwhatyoudesire.com, offers life-changing sessions through the tapping modality of FasterEFT. She is a certified FasterEFT Practitioner. She has authored *Crossing My Rainbow Bridge,* stories of her dog-blessed life and a coming sequel, *Tapping on the Wings of Angels.*

Christine Arylo, Spiritual Catalyst, MBA, and Bestselling Author, is the founder of the international movement of self-love and a sought-out advisor on women's leadership, feminine power, and living in alignment with your true soul path. She speaks, teaches, and leads retreats around the world and lives in northern California. www.chooseselflove.com

Joy T. Barican is a life coach who is passionate in assisting you to make meaningful, exciting, and viable choices for yourself based on your individual values, personal strengths, and beliefs. When results matter, contact her via email: jbarican@hotmail.com.

Melissa McHenry Beahm is living her dream: making beautiful music with her adored husband, Larry, and traveling in their RV. A former registered music therapist, she promotes healing and spreads joy, laughter, and love by connecting with and entertaining seniors and boomers across the USA. www.OMTmusic.com

Roxanne Beck is an award-winning writer, voice actor, singer, and dog lover. Her first children's book, *Caterpillarland,* was published in 2015 and is available on Amazon.com and other retail sites. She lives in Los Angeles with her wonderful dog, Truman. Please visit www.RoxanneBeck.com.

Dana Ben-Yehuda, Certified Alexander Technique teacher and Movement Expert, has a BA in Theater/Acting and has acted in film/TV. She is a competitive ballroom dancer, Argentine Tango aficionado, musician, and singer. She helps dancers increase freedom in movement, poise, balance, and alignment. www.alexandertechniquestudio.org

Sarah Berkett is a certified spiritual teacher, Reiki Master, animal intuitive, reflexologist, author, crystal healer, and angelic life coach. www.beamerslight.com

Rebekah Bernard is fulfilled with her work as a spiritual counselor through hospice care. She has a Master's Degree in Counseling Psychology and has been a student of interdisciplinary spirituality for over a decade. She teaches, speaks, counsels, and writes about living a love-centered, thriving existence. www.rebekah-bernard.com

Nicole Black is a certified Rolfer™, massage therapist, and writer. She lives in southern California with her daughter. When she isn't writing, she enjoys Pilates, traveling to distant lands, and chasing butterflies.

Cathie Bliss, MBA, cultivated a career in international business for two decades. When her daughter developed severe special needs in the 1990s, she reoriented to the healing arts, becoming a Certified LifeLine Practitioner and Intuitive Astrologer. Visit www.CathieBliss.com for her heart-centered offerings.

Aeriana Blue is a mystic, artist, and photographer. Her body of work reflects the joy she finds in capturing Essence both through her unique perspective in photographs and in the channeling of Spirit through her abstract paintings. Visit her online portfolio at www.aerianablue.com.

Chey Bodhi is passionate about assisting you to de-stress your mind and body, stimulate your body's own self-healing mechanism, and embrace a calmer you. She specialises in stress solutions, biofeedback, soul regression therapy, quantum healing hypnosis technique, spiritual guidance, and energetic alignment. www.stress-solutions.com.au

Karen Bomm is a lifestyle entrepreneur who realized her "passion before profit" philosophy was more in alignment with Main Street than Wall Street. She is an international bestselling author and the CEO/Founder of aBeansTalkSocial.com, attracting business owners who value integrity, honor, respect, team, grace, and community.

Natasha Botkin is a master intuitive energy healer, writer, teacher, and Sacred Heart High Priestess. With multi-dimensional divine wisdom, she helps to guide and empower others by transforming heart and soul with passion, creative play, and healing energies. www.magicalblessingshealingcenter.com

Bonnie L. Boucek has a passion for assisting women in rediscovering themselves after being diagnosed with a chronic illness. As a fibromyalgia sufferer, she shares a unique understanding of their journey ahead. She is an ordained Reverend, Pure Reiki Healing Master, educator, published author, and mother. www.BonnieBoucek.com

Lisa Miles Brady is a writer, coach, and intuitive artist who believes the greatest gift we give the world is to be unapologetically who we are. She mentors women in accessing their own truth so they can create fully expressed lives. She blogs at www.Lisa-Unmasked.com.

Shannon Leigh Brokaw is a writer, yogi, and Usui Reiki practitioner who loves the outdoors. She is a seeker of anything that makes her laugh in life and puts a smile on her face. *La Dolce Vita!*

Suzanna Broughton is a world-class intuitive financial healer. She supports artists, teachers, healers, authors, and coaches to rewrite their money story and earn a living sharing their beautiful gifts and talents. Her unique approach blends grounded practicality with metaphysics and spirituality. www.HerMoneyHerPurpose.com

Gail Butt is a personal-development and life coach. She helps women connect to their "True You" (who they really are and what drives them), believe in themselves, achieve their goals, and make their dreams come true. www.trueyoucoaching.co.uk

Laurie Cagno, Singer-Songwriter, has colorful, passionate ways of bridging communication through story and song. A professional in the metro area of NYC, she is a crystal-clear voice accompanied by a fun-loving spirit with keen intuition to tune in to the hearts of people worldwide. Find her song "Think of This" at www.cdbaby.com.

Sheila Callaham is an author, motivational speaker, and life coach with a passion for inspiring others. After a career in corporate communications, she resigned to spend more time with her family, write, and coach others to live their dreams. Learn more at www.sheilacallaham.com.

Christine Callahan-Oke is an empowerment coach, mom, inspirational writer, and positive thinker. Through coaching and writing, she offers practical tips and straightforward wisdom to help people achieve their potential, see the beauty in everyday moments, and live authentically. Download her free *5 Keys to Loving Life* guide here: www.YourInspiredLife.ca/free-guide.

Maryann Candito is an author, intuitive healer, and Akashic Records consultant. By healing the past on the subconscious, energetic, and soul levels, we change current paradigms and create new realities. She would love to help you heal, connect, and transform. www.MaryannCandito.com

Kristine Carlson, *New York Times* bestselling author and world-renowned speaker, is passionate about spreading her message of returning from grief and waking up to life with more joy and gratitude – and certainly not taking life too seriously. She is a mentor for people navigating the challenges of "middle age." www.kristinecarlson.com

Cindia Carrere is a certified coach, award-winning author, and Intuitive Art instructor. She understands that success – in business and in life – is about allowing your energy to flow. Using her lifelong intuitive abilities, she helps remove hidden blocks and open your floodgates to intuition, creativity, and abundance. www.healyourgrid.com

Angie Carter is a grieving mother and inspirational writer who began writing as a way to cope with the sudden loss of her 19-month-old daughter, Bella. Her blog, *Stay Strong: Project Life* (www.staystrongprojectlife.com), is dedicated to Bella's memory. Her writing offers perspective and encouragement to parents worldwide.

Marian Cerdeira is an intuitive channel and medium who works with a beloved group of beings known as "The Brotherhood." Her messages from spirit and The Brotherhood are shared on Facebook at "A Slice of Light" and at www.asliceoflight.com.

Robin Chellis is the founder of Light Code Healing™ and Auroric™ Facets serving Lightworkers, healers, and leaders to help with abundance, alignment, and ascension. She incorporates energetic healing work, energetically infused artwork, and other modalities to activate and amplify your true self. www.robinchellis.com

Judith Clements is a perennial teacher/student who is now retired from the kindergarten classroom and continues exploring her passions for language, people, and creativity. An avid reader/writer, she enjoys collaborating in a creative writer's circle. Inspired energy comes from swing dancing, camping, and professional hockey.

Vanessa Codorniu is the founder of Intuitive Leverage™, an eight-week intuition bootcamp that trains people to leverage their sensitivity in life and business! With more than 10,000 intuitive sessions and hundreds of students, she is an acclaimed psychic intuitive, clinical hypnotherapist, and international intuition trainer. www.vanessacodorniu.com

Lisa Rachel Cohen, CEO of InSparkle Media, is on a sacred mission to "embrace the heart and grasp the hand of every woman, child, and man." She coaches, hosts Global InSparkle Compassion Celebrations, and is the author of *Grace is Born* and *My Grace is Born Companion*.

Marva Collins-Bush holds an MA in Psychology and a BA in Metaphysics. She is a Certified Metaphysical Practitioner, ordained metaphysical minister, Certified ARTbundance™ Coach, and author of three books: *Screams from the Heart of a Woman; My Daughter, My Mother, Myself;* and *Dances with Divinity*. www.earthmotherdivinesage.com

Joanne Angel Barry Colon has been blessed with a beautiful daughter; is the business owner of Fitness "R" Us; and is a personal trainer, nutrition coach, Reiki/crystal healer, and speaker. She is the author and publisher of *Healing Within Meditation*. www.fitnessrus.org

Karen D. Cote, BS, RMT, CHT, is the owner of The Well Sanctuary LLC, shamanic minister of The Circle of the Sacred Earth, hypnotherapist, Reiki Master/Teacher, and Shr Jye of T'ai Chi Chuan/Qigong. She is published in *The Door Opener Magazine, Hartford Magazine,* and *365 Days of Angel Prayers* and appeared on *Better Connecticut*. www.thewellct.com

Jodi Cross is an ordained Interfaith Angel Minister and the owner of Faith Therapies. She is the author of *An Introduction to Angels & Angelic Healing* and a contributing author of *Bring the People Back to My Love*. She lives in England and France. Connect with her at www.facebook.com/jodi.cross1.

Amanda Dale is a spiritual empowerment coach, healing energy practitioner, and Master's-level social worker. She combines academic training, over 10 years of professional experience, and spiritually inspired passion to encourage harmonious evolution within the lives of her clients. amandadale888@gmail.com

Marla David, a retired stay-at-home mom, gained experience by raising three daughters and volunteering. She's achieved the following certifications: TESOL, NLP Practitioner, Law of Attraction Basic Practitioner, Ericksonian Hypnosis, Coach in Life Optimization, Master Life Coach, Basic Hypnotic Communicator, and Coach Practitioner.

Dawn De'Harmony, MEd, is a pioneer of the heart who follows her inner truth and gratefully embraces life. She is a passionate middle-school teacher and loves supporting and inspiring others in their journey. In 2015, she published the beautiful *Seasons of Gratitude* journals. www.followyourinnerturth.org

Reverend Scott M. Dehn has 18 years of experience in metaphysics. He has been teaching Reiki, coaching spiritual values, and is currently using his ministry to share New Thought. He has formal training in Science of Mind and professional photography and has a BS in Holistic Nutrition.

Maya Demri is not an illusion; she is the real thing. She has always valued nature and has a deep desire for living in a condition of global peace. She is an author, dancer, actress, and activist who strives to awaken the world with the arts.

Dr. Tanya Destang-Beaubrun, a family physician, certified lifestyle and empowerment expert, wife, mother, and passionate lover of life, has dedicated her career to helping people connect more deeply to themselves and their truth. She is a strong advocate for a holistic approach to health and well-being. Connect with her at www.tanyabeaubrun.com.

Janet Dhaenens is an author, speaker, coach, and circle facilitator. She has learned to follow emotions to uncover the thoughts that cause them, revealing true choice and personal power. She creates safe space in her circles, assisting others in finding their own power and choice. www.EmergingBalance.com

Felicia D'Haiti is an Energy Empowerment and Feng Shui Coach who guides clients in shifting their perspectives and environments to move beyond perfectionism, fear, and self-imposed limitations. She is an author and long-time educator who lives in Maryland with her husband and four children. www.feliciadhaiti.com

Linda Dieffenbach, BSW, is a holistic healer and coach with over 10 years of experience. She works with individuals, couples, and groups, helping her clients to reduce stress and anxiety, overcome barriers and challenges, and heal their relationships. She also provides healing services for animals. www.wellnessinharmony.com

Nathalie Dignard is an intuitive artist and creative guide who uses bright colours and positive mantras as a compass to the heart whispers that connect us to life, dreams, and each other. She inspires women to lead a braver, bolder, and more vibrant life. www.nathaliedignard.com

Ruth Donald is a strategist, coach, and educator. She works with individuals and enterprises from across the world, helping them to connect at the heart. Her number-one priority in life is seeing the love in every situation. www.ruthdonald.com.au

Jody Rentner Doty is a writer, healer, seer, and a bit of a mystic. She is "Jody Doty Soul Reader" to her clients. Her written words are inspired through meditation on the divine. She lives in the Pacific Northwest with her husband, Dave, and three amused cats. www.jodydoty.com

Patricia Downing is a writer with a background in social services, counseling, and mediation. She is founder of Peaceful Caregiving, an online community that provides practical techniques, inspiration, and support to caregivers in creating harmonious, heart-centered relationships with the family members in their care. www.peacefulcaregiving.com

Atherton Drenth is a medical intuitive and author of *Following Body Wisdom* and soon to be released *The Intuitive Dance: Building, Protecting & Clearing Your Energy*. She also appears in the documentary *Voyage to Betterment*. www.athertondrenth.com

Kimberly DuBoise is a poet who loves to inspire with words. When not writing, she is probably reading, cooking, or walking. She lives in the Midwest with her husband. You can find her book and blog at www.kimberlyduboise.com.

Freda Durden is the owner of 813WellBeing LLC, where she uses a mixture of tools for an eclectic and unique healing experience. She is a Holy Fire Karuna Reiki® Master, clairvoyant, medium, shaman, alchemist, and facilitator of new beings. She is leading a renaissance of integrative healers deeper into the art of life.

Jerri Eddington, EdD, is the creator of Energy Connections and the co-creator of Lighten Up and Thrive, which is a sacred vision of sharing our expertise and wisdom as transformational life coaches. She facilitates powerful, transformative programs that help others experience joyful living for mind, body, and soul.

Meilin Ehlke aspires to express her sacred wisdom by celebrating life's beauty in every moment. Playing with her son and two cats are a big part of it. She invites the world's wisdom seekers to walk with her to fully feel their wisdom and unfold their true beauty. www.meilinehlke.com

Tandy R. Elisala, CPSC, is a #1 international bestselling author and coach. She helps women who are going through life transitions to heal, rebuild their identity, and create a success plan so they can live their lives with passion, grace, and ease. Learn more at www.tandyelisala.com.

Gabriele Engstrom's love for holistic health, science, and spirituality has made her a unique healer and energy worker. She supports people who forever search for equilibrium on a physical, emotional, and spiritual level. www.gabrieleengstrom.com.au

Lori Evans is an educational health expert and holds a BA in Education in the fields of English and Health. Over the course of her career, she's taught academically to children, adolescents, and young adults. Her first solo book, *The Teenage Emotional Abyss*, is in development. www.lorievans.biz

Shirlzy Everingham is from HorseGirl Farm, a horse biz in the Northern Rivers of Australia. She was tired of feeling ordinary because she didn't ride horses or create anymore and hadn't found her true north. Join her as she saddles up and helps others sparkle. www.horsegirlfarm.wordpress.com

Sophia Ellen Falke, author of *Never Too Late for Great!* (summer 2016), is a Life Mastery Consultant, coach, and professional speaker. She has worked in leadership positions in education, healthcare, and religious organizations and is an ordained Unity minister. www.EmbracingGreatness.com

Martina E. Faulkner, LMSW, is an author, certified life coach, and Reiki Master Teacher. In addition to her book, *What if..? How to Create the Life You Want Using the Power of Possibility*, she writes *InspireBytes*™ – a weekly blog where she shares inspirational writings. www.martinafaulkner.com

Helen Ferrara, PhD, is passionate about the world we live in, believes that we are all creative, and has experienced that the broadening of one's perspective strengthens personal transformation. She researches creativity and is a mentor who assists the nurturing of self-knowledge and authentic expression. www.creativenurture.com.au

Meredith Fjelsted is a Nationally Certified Health Coach and founder of Dream2bhealthy. She is a professional speaker and healthy-lifestyle expert who loves being outdoors, gardening, dogs, going on mission trips, and living healthy. She lives in Minnesota with her husband, Scott; two stepsons, Colin and Aidan; and three dogs.

Scott Fjelsted has been a Certified Personal Trainer since 1998 and is the author of *ForeverFitU: Making Fitness a Lifestyle that Lasts a Lifetime*. He is committed to the wellness of his clients, community, and home. He lives in Minnesota with his wife, Meredith, and two sons, Colin and Aidan.

Jen Flick is a #1 bestselling author and inspirational speaker. Her essay, "Seek Heal Grow," is featured in Riverhead Books' *Eat Pray Love Made Me Do It*. After surviving a cancer diagnosis, she now lives a healthy, joyful life and supports others who want the same. Learn more at www.jenflick.com.

Arielle Ford is a gifted writer and the author of 10 books, including *Wabi Sabi Love* and the international bestseller, *The Soulmate Secret*. She has been called "The Cupid of Consciousness" and "The Fairy Godmother of Love." She lives in California with her husband/soulmate, Brian Hilliard, and their feline friends. www.soulmatesecret.com

Pamela Forseth is an internationally known spiritual medium who loves connecting and being of service to those all across the globe, including New Zealand, Australia, England, Germany, the United States, and Canada. She is highly regarded for her compassion, truth, honesty, and directness. www.pamelaforseth.ca

Suzanne M. Fortino currently resides in Idaho and is a mother of five and grandmother of two. She often finds herself wandering the Northwest, visiting friends and family. She loves nurturing her soul and spreading love and light to everyone she sees, and she's passionate about seeing the miracles in simplicity to help heal the world.

Beth Frede is an intuitive artist and life/career coach who helps women navigate their life transitions with confidence and ease. She understands feeling "lost" as an adult, and the ecstasy of finding purpose and direction through creative self-discovery and mindfulness. www.creative-revelations.com

Faith Freed, MFT, is passionate about psychology, spirituality, and consciousness. She is the author of *IS: Your Authentic Spirituality Unleashed* (Hay House), which models and celebrates do-it-yourself spirituality. Her psychotherapy practice is located in Burlingame, CA (License #92535). Find out more at www.Faithfreed.com.

Laura Freix from iEmbrace Wellness offers coaching, education, and heart-centered community for individuals interested in becoming empowered in their own healthcare and spiritual development. She is passionate about helping you reach your highest potential so you can fully engage in life and enjoy it! www.iembracewellness.com

Amy Gage is a writer and poet who is passionate about wild authentic expression and spiritual connection. She loves igniting and inspiring others to experience more love, unity, creativity, expansion, healing, magic, and beauty in their lives. She shares her Truth and creative expression at www.moondancemuse.com.

Ginger Gauldin is an intuitive creative artist, soul seeker, and grace expander who enjoys writing, diverse reading, and studying holistic wellness and nutrition. As a multi-passionate entrepreneur, she operates an online business, blogs, and collaborates with heart-centered businesses as they help to raise the vibration of the planet. www.graceinsideout.com

Kaylyn Gelata will never abandon her journal again. She trusts in the practice of opening up, both physically and emotionally, to help her move more thoughtfully through the world. She finds moments of grace through reading, writing, traveling, exercising, laughing, practicing yoga, photography, and creating art.

Dr. Colleen Georges is a Nationally Certified Psychologist, Certified Positive Psychology Coach, educator, and bestselling co-author of *Unleash Your Inner Magnificence*, *The Wisdom of Midlife Women 2*, *Contagious Optimism*, *10 Habits of Truly Optimistic People*, *101 Great Ways to Enhance Your Career*, and *The Book of Success*. www.LifeCoachingNJ.com

Bryce Goebel is an intuitive, visionary, energy healer, and empowerment coach. She's passionate about helping you find your voice and learn to love who you are in this moment, without fear or shame. Get free tools to help you live a fierce, authentic life at www.AReikiPlace.com.

Ana Gordon is a gifted intuitive consultant for entrepreneurs and creatives. She is an energy alchemist and modern mystic, empowering through the Divine Feminine and shifting the legacy of wealth through conscious entrepreneurship. Her motto: "Envision the world you wish to live in, and then take inspired action to create it." www.dakiniswisdom.com

Michelle Anne Gould is a soulpreneur, mother, founder of Abundant Spirit Education, and creator of SoulMagic™. She supports people who are committed to enhancing their lives through personal transformation, unlocking and activating abundance from within. She awakens people to their unique, infinite magic. www.abundantspiritedu.com

Linda Graziano is a life coach, inspired by her personal experience with bipolar disorder. She supports women with depression or bipolar disorder to overcome self-criticism, handle uncomfortable feelings, and connect to their higher selves so they can sustain their wellness and live life fully. www.embracetheinneryou.com

Stacey Hall, LSH, CNTC, CAC, CRTS, is a spiritual healer, success coach, speaker, author of the bestselling *Chi-To-Be! Achieving Your Ultimate B-All*, and co-author of *Attracting Perfect Customers: The Power of Strategic Synchronicity*. Access her *Attraction Tips* to attract the aCHIevement of goals with ease for free at www.chi-to-be.com.

Sharon Halliday is a columnist, Reiki practitioner, angel intuitive, and mother who discovered Louise Hay's book *You Can Heal Your Life* and began learning about all things self-help. She has had her posts liked by Colette Baron-Reid, Denise Linn, and Cheryl Richardson. Her book debuts in 2016. www.messagesfromtheheart.com.au

Jane Hamilton is a busy city professional, wife, and mother of gorgeous Grace, as well as a Reiki and mindfulness practitioner, personal development coach, aspiring author, and lifelong learner. Her greatest wish is to contribute to the betterment of our planet. www.livelovesparkle.biz

Marihet Hammann is an author, teacher, and transformational guide. Creator of Living Life in Full Colour M.A.P., she helps women discover their brilliance in everyday life. She believes people have a S.T.O.R.Y. to share, and she approaches her own life as living, breathing art. www.marihethammann.com

Misty Harding, Angelic Channel and Healer, empowers others by helping them connect with their intuition, God, and the Angels by bringing forth messages and healing from the Angelic Realms. She is creator of the Archangel and Angelic Chakra Oil Blends. www.YourInnerLandscape.com

Charise A. S. Harkin recently returned to college and successfully earned her diploma in Social Work. She is passionate in her charitable endeavors and also enjoys the arts, traveling, and spending time with her family and friends. She lives in Canada with her husband and two sons.

Annalene Hart is an Enchanted Living Life Coach, poet, and visionary artist who creates soul paintings. She has inspired her clients to pursue and realize their dreams. She conducts individualized Magical Child sessions to help activate the participant's innate creativity and imagination. www.mydivineenchantedlife.wordpress.com

Mathew Hart is a sensitive, a channeler, and a Hollywood film producer. His awakening journey and channeled messages from a group soul called "The Guardians" can be found on his website: www.thelifeintended.com. He lives with his wife, Nola, their youngest daughter, Kaylin, and their Mini Golden Doodle, Maggie.

Ellouise Heather is a wellbeing coach and creative writer. She is passionately committed to helping women who are suffering and recovering from illness find joyfully inspired new meaning in life. For helpful tips and insights, be sure to visit her blog: www.ellouiseheather.com.

Colin Hegarty is an associate writer at www.JennyMcKaig.com, creating blogs, articles, and website content. He was also in the editing process for the #1 international bestseller *Empowering Women to Succeed*. Writing has been one of his lifelong passions, alongside hockey, golf, and badminton.

Cynthia Helbig is a spiritual life designer and creator of Empowered Heart. She uses powerful meditation practices plus ceremony, ritual, and other tools to invite your inner greatness to reveal itself. Download her free *The Art of Meditation* ebook and guided meditation to empower your heart at: www.empoweredheart.com.au/free-gift/.

Nukhet Govdeli Hendricks is a proud female leader, Certified Art of Feminine Presence Teacher, leader catalyst, and contributing author to the #1 Amazon bestseller *365 Ways to Connect with Your Soul*. As a nonprofit executive, she leads her life and her organization with the power of grace. www.nukhets.com

Emily Herrick is a private yoga teacher and distributor of positive-aging products who is also studying to be a wedding celebrant. She grew up on the east coast and lives on Vashon Island, Washington, with her husband and two labs. www.emilyherrickyoga.com

Sharon Hickinbotham is an intuitive Tarot/oracle card reader with the ability to communicate with departed loved ones. She is a writer of poems and true stories and loves animals and nature. She is a caring, sensitive empath whose abilities and love for helping others and nature is her life purpose and drive. Facebook: PurpleReign444

Karen Hicks lives in Ontario, Canada, with her partner, daughters, and dog. She is passionate about people discovering their brilliance and assists this journey through her coaching practice. She practices hypnosis, EFT, and NLP, and might even have a soft spot for Crossfit!

Karen Hill received her Bachelor's Degree in Human Services from Union Institute and University in 2009. She has extensive experience working with adults in residential drug and alcohol treatment. She is skilled at working with drug courts, the adult justice system, and the health and human services system.

Patsy Hillman lives in Ontario, Canada. She's been married for 32 years and has three children and grandchildren. She is a Usui Reiki Master, writer, artist, and owner of Spirit Wings Healing Garden. Visit her on Facebook for healing and angel-card readings: Spirit Wings – Whimsical Healing Garden and Spa.

Cindy Harpe Hively is a transformational intuitive and a healing catalyst for women. She's the "Goddess Creatrix" for *In Her Fullness*, an Awakened Living mentor, columnist, and published author. She empowers spiritual women and teaches them how to create an abundant life that they love by strategizing and optimizing each key area of their life.

Gretchen Oehler Hogg is the co-creator of Lighten Up and Thrive (www.LightenUpandThrive.com) and owner of Conscious Health Medical Hypnotherapy. She helps people transform and enrich their lives using hypnotherapy, Soul Coaching®, ThetaHealing®, and aromatherapy. She's also a faculty member at Southwest Institute of Healing Arts.

Cheryl Hope has worked as a hairstylist and a massage therapist for the past 23 years. She is a natural-health advocate and is currently in training as a caretaker with the Chi-To-Be! Coaching program in order to assist others in living healthier and more prosperous lives!

Chrysta Horwedel is a Certified Stepfamily Coach and stepmother of two. Her approach is holistic, supported by certifications as a health and ayurvedic wellness coach and yoga instructor. She enjoys writing, hiking, healthy food, wine, and travel. She lives with her family in Los Angeles. www.instantblendedfamily.com

Alicia Isaacs Howes, International Soul Connection™ Expert, specialises in helping others to align with their brilliance using her Soul Purpose, Passion & Prosperity™ system. Ready to love your life and your business so life can love you right back? Go to www.yoursoulstory.com to learn more!

Karla Joy Huber is a writer, tutor, and artist in Michigan, who has both a conventional day job and a freelance writing gig with a holistic health specialist. She finally found her spiritual home within Nichiren Buddhism and is now looking for a husband to share this home with. www.karlahuberblog.blogspot.com

Mandi Huffhines is a stay-at-home mom. She has three children: a daughter, Jessica; a son, Trey; and an angel baby, Jenna Belle. She co-founded The Jenna Belle Huffhines Foundation for SIDS in 2007. She and her children currently reside in Texas where they love one another and God, and always remember Jenna Belle.

Lacey Dawn Jackson is an author and internationally known psychic. She has been called the "Abundance Babe" because of the impact she has in helping others obtain their dreams and manifest their hearts' desires. You can find her latest book, *Journey of the Groovy Goddess*, at www.LaceyDawnJackson.com.

Murray James, RN, is a Life in Balance coach and an energy intuitive, assisting people to find harmony and peace in their lives. Mindfulness is at the heart of his work. He offers harmony coaching sessions and energy-clearing sessions by phone to people anywhere. www.murrayjamescoaching.com

Amanda Johnson is a writer, speaker, and creator of the Being Good with Being You online class. She inspires recovering perfectionists and over-thinkers to turn their critic into their ally so they can love the life they have. Learn more and get free access to her virtual classroom: www.amandajohnson.tv.

Jack V. Johnson is a transformational author, certified life coach, certified meditation teacher, and Reiki Master Teacher. He would love to help you find and explore your own soulful path and offers resources for your spiritual journey on the Soulful Path website at www.soulfulpath.com.

Tia Johnson is a spiritual mentor, speaker, and bestselling author. She helps people ignite their spirituality and empower their quality of life so they can achieve the life they want to live. She has spoken at the Mind Body Spirit Expo™ and the DivaGirl® Conference.

Julie Jones is a nurse, researcher, aromatherapist, energy practitioner, health and wellness coach, inspirational speaker, and author. Her supportive coaching with small steps inspires and empowers people to move from sick care to health care – restoring balance for wellness. www.restoretobalance.com

Michelle Wangler Joy, MA, MFT, specializes in helping couples have great relationships. Based on the philosophy that "people have their best relationships when they are their best selves," she also offers products and workshops to help individuals live from their highest, truest self. www.MichelleJoyMFT.com

Nancy Merrill Justice is an author and intuitive business mentor for entrepreneurs. She draws on her 25 years of successful entrepreneurship to help her clients master "mindset of success" techniques applicable to any business, so they can achieve their dreams and succeed at their highest potential in their business and personal lives.

Ayeesha S. Kanji is a poet and blogger who has been writing for over 20 years. A recent MA Graduate of New York University's Class of 2015, her background includes human resource consulting, creative writing, and adult learning. In her spare time, she dances and practices yoga, while living it up in "The Big Apple."

Sue Kearney is "Chief Inspiration Officer" at Magnolias West, a coaching and branding spiritual business. Part technology and neuroscience geek, part partially tamed hippie, she is passionate about and dedicated to helping women with heart and soul rock their businesses and share their *awesome* with the world!

Jenna Kelland is a Certified Holistic Nutritionist™ with a PhD in Adult Education. As the owner of Spark Wellness (www.sparkwellness.ca), she helps moms receive nutrition education to have balanced, energized lives. A self-employed mom, she consults her inner voice for insights about her health and business.

James Kelly created the *Miracle Choice® Board Game*. Since its rapid spread to different countries and requests for more material, he developed the *Certified Facilitator Game Training* and other online material about the power of inner choice. He lives with his family and two cats in Scotland. www.miraclechoicegame.com

Afzal Khan is a Health Transformation Coach who helps heart-centred entrepreneurs to put more into their self-care so they get more joy and success out of life. www.thehealthtransformationcoach.co.uk

Katie Kieffer, ThetaHealing® Practitioner and Self-Awareness Master Coach, blends a diversity of roles – including being a homeschool mom, wife, and minister. Her mission is to help others heal so they can pursue their passion to a clear mind, clear heart, and clear path to prosperity! www.awakentheinnerlight.com

Davalynn Kim is a dedicated mother, daughter, sister, and friend. She enjoys reading, writing, painting, and bird watching. She loves dogs, cats, horses, and a beautiful brisk winter day. She believes in love at first sight. She believes in doing things that make the soul sing.

Christine King's soul journey began in 1979 after her husband died. She received a powerful message that her work was to help people on a spiritual path discover their soul's purpose. She has 35 years' experience as a metaphysical teacher and Soul Guidance Practitioner. www.soulsplanforyou.com

Elizabeth R. Kipp, Health Facilitator and Empowerment Coach, helps people grasp the power of their own healing. Founder of www.elizabeth-kipp.com, she is experienced in bringing people together, resolving conflict, and generating communication skills. She empowers people to tap into their healing ability and build effective health-care teams.

Margo Kirzinger is a semi-retired holistic practitioner and Face and Body Reader who utilizes a variety of therapeutic modalities to address core-issue healing. She resides in rural Saskatchewan, Canada, and encourages all readers to visit her at her website: www.margok.ca.

Preston Klik is a lover of sound and meditation. He leads his public Ocean Of Devotion Gong & Bowl Meditations and DreamCatcher Native American Flute Meditations around the Chicago area. His wife, Emily, practices CranioSacral Therapy. Together, they offer private sessions at their home, Temple Synphorium. www.Klik.Love

Tamiko S. Knight is a state-licensed massage therapist (LMT) and aesthetician who has studied and practiced energetic healing since 2004. She is excited about her healing career, one where she has the ability to help others realize the benefits of massage therapy and energetic clearing.

Ingrid Koivukangas is an award-winning environmental artist, designer, and writer. She is a word lover, dog slave, flower farmer, author of the YA fantasy trilogy *Hunters of the Dream*, and creator of the Eco Heart Oracle. www.IngridKoivukangas.com

Carrie Kondor is an author, counselor, and the owner of Caria, LLC. She utilizes sound coding, family constellation, and breathwork in her practice to support clients in unlocking their truest potential. Through her writing, workshops, and private sessions, clients can free their mind of negative distractions. www.cariatherapy.com

Holly Noella Labrecque provides personal trauma therapy, life improvement coaching, and special needs consulting. As a licensed spiritual care professional and trauma recovery practitioner, she is the calm in the storm. She is based in Saskatchewan, Canada, and serves clients worldwide. www.TheYouthGuru.com

Jennifer "Elemental" Larkin leads a global initiative to empower and inspire people into greater freedom and conscious choice. Join her worldwide movement and receive access to a massive vault of content celebrating the power of coaching, training, and mentoring. Join her growing tribe of powerful beings here: www.mentoringvault.com.

Catherine M. Laub is an author, speaker, psychic medium, and spiritual guide. She is a four-time bestselling author and continues her writing in upcoming anthologies. She speaks about mental illness in her campaign, "Brighten Your Day with Turquoise." www.catherinemlaub.com

Monica Laws is a proud Canadian with a Business Degree. Her career in sales and marketing has included publishing a home-décor magazine. She is a mother, coach, volunteer, friend, and lifelong learner. Her passion for travel has and will continue to take her on a journey with countless moments of grace.

Colleen Leaney is a registered nurse who began her search back to spirituality in 2008 after the tragic loss of her husband. She opened her heart to receiving healing for herself from many holistic modalities, and through them, she now pays it forward. www.soullifehealing.com

Tara Leduc is an online entrepreneur, yoga teacher, and stepmom who lives in the suburbs and is passionate about helping you find peace in your life. Why? Because she believes that together we can change the world, peace by peace. Join in at www.TaraLeduc.com.

Nicole Levac is currently working on her first solo book in which she will share her wisdom on connecting to your Soul by connecting with nature. She is presently dedicated to her book. You can watch her past show, "Journey to Soul-Full Connections," and read her *Nature's Wisdom* blog at www.nicolelevac.com.

Tanya Levy is a counselor in a community college and an inspirational photographer. She has worked in the human-services field for 25 years. She is a strong and passionate advocate for the healing power of each individual's own learning journey. www.facebook.com/heartladyinspiration

Millen Livis, MS, MBA, is a bestselling author, Wealth and Freedom Coach, entrepreneur, and possibilities' catalyst. Drawing on her experience as a former Wall Street executive, successful entrepreneur, mother, and wife, she helps women who want to get unstuck and yearn for more clarity, freedom, and abundance. www.daretochangelife.com

Elaine Lockard is The Confidence and Credibility Alchemist and Supreme Resourceress™. She helps her clients break out of their spiritual closet to gain confidence in self and their gifts and get the respect, recognition, and rewards they deserve. Learn more here: www.elainelockard.com.

Courtney Long, MSW, LC, CHt, ATP®, is an angel communicator, life-purpose intuitive, psychic medium, author, and speaker. She inspires adults, teens, and kids to joyfully activate the angels' assistance, open their intuition, and discover their purpose and gifts. www.CourtneyLongAngels.com

Fiona Louise is a writer, student, and natural therapist. When inspiration strikes, she enjoys both fiction and non-fiction blogging. She is a contributor in the bestselling books *My Creative Thoughts* and *365 Ways to Connect with Your Soul*. www.fiona-louise.com

Serena Low is the "Midlife Career Mentor" and author of *The Hero Within: Reinvent Your Life, One New Chapter at a Time*. She educates, empowers, and guides women who are going through a personal and professional transition so that they can make the changes essential to regaining peace, purpose, and clarity. www.SerenaLow.com.au

Susan Mechley Lucci passionately weaves a variety of roles together, including dynamic facilitator, purpose guide, community activist, lifelong learner, and midlife mother. She feels graced by the soulful support of friends and family and is passionate about awakening human potential to create a more equitable, just, and sustainable world for all.

Shelley Lundquist is an international bestselling author, motivational speaker, and Self-Mastery & Success Coach who uses her intuitive gifts and powerful transformational breakthrough processes to empower audiences all over the world in breaking through to the unlimited power of their own potential. www.shelleylundquist.com

Mary Lunnen, creator of Dare to Blossom, supports and encourages through 1:1 life coaching, her *Rediscovery Cards*, workshops, and online classes as you find your way home to yourself. Her writing, photography, and artwork are elements of her creative life. She is based in magical Cornwall. www.daretoblossom.co.uk

Arwen Lynch, Professional Joy Seeker, has been writing since someone told her nouns and verbs went together. Mission? To spread her "Seek joy, y'all" motto. She teaches writing, tarot, and joy seeking to bestselling authors, pre-published writers, and people who need more joy. www.tarotbyarwen.com

Linda Lynch-Johnson is a change expert, author, and speaker. Her Adapter Factor program is focused on facing change with open arms and not fear. She has written two books: *Marcis and the Rainmaker* (a children's book) and *The Adapter Factor*. www.lindalynchjohnson.com

Bianca Lynn is a curious traveler who has spent years exploring different paths. Her goal is to help people connect with their inner light and embrace their wholeness. Through writing and transformational workshops, she supports people to live fully in the wonder of life. www.biancadisalvo.com

Tae Lynne is a former type-A driven, career woman turned author and kindness advocate. Forced to slow down by chronic illness, she discovered her true purpose as the "Kindness Junkie." She is currently working on her solo book featuring acts of kindness and writes about her journey of loss and healing at www.60SecondsToKindness.com.

Joni Advent Maher is a spiritual feminist, mystic, and empowerment coach committed to honoring the Sacred Feminine in each of us. She supports women with awakening, appreciating, and expressing their unique Sacred Feminine Essence in their lives, relationships, and businesses. www.Revolutionaryheart.com

Victoria L. Mai helps women who are tired of living a self-sacrificing lifestyle, who feel trapped and labeled in a box, to connect to their passion, access their purpose, and unlock their potential – ultimately leading them to total soul expression. www.victorialmai.com

TaraLynn Majeska is the author of the book *When Your Heart is Cracked Wide Open: Navigating with Your Heart Through the Challenges of Life.* She is a teacher and a Spiritual Response Therapy Practitioner who helps people create positive transformation in their lives.

Roberta L. Marhefka, CHT, has been miracle mentoring souls to live in alignment with the laws of the universe for over two decades. Her unique abilities and tools guide her clients into life mastery by feeling their connection to the Divine. www.RealLifeMiraclesCoaching.com

Lori Kilgour Martin is an angelic counselor and musical theatre artist from Canada. A co-author of the books *365 Days of Angel Prayers* and *365 Ways to Connect with Your Soul,* she is grateful to be here while working in partnership through service with the Divine Realm. Visit her at: www.diamondheartangel.com.

Veronica Mather is a writer and keen photographer. She is passionate about animal welfare and shares her life with her husband, Dale, four rescued sheep, and two high-spirited dogs, Max and Blaze.

Sophie Maya is a prayer visionary and mind-shift catalyst who yokes peace, one heart at a time. She offers self-love solutions, "Oneness Mirror-acle" coaching, prayer meditation, and cellular-memory energy healing. The healing modalities she uses are: Reiki, Healing Touch, Biodynamic Craniosacral, and Access Consciousness. www.prayervisionary.com

Kristy Carr McAdams shares from her "spiritual tool belt" to show people how to discover their own personal gifts. She's a smile purveyor, angel channeler, psychic/medium, artist, Certified Angel Practitioner (ACP), Reiki/IET Practitioner, sound healing facilitator, mandala/art facilitator, author, and hugger extraordinaire. www.EnergyOfAngels.com

Lisa McDonald is a Canadian author, radio-show host, and inspirational speaker. Her approach to daily life consists of gratitude, love, kindness, and being of service to others. She is a connector and a manifester. Please reach out to her at www.lisamcdonaldauthor.com.

Carolyn McGee empowers women to walk with spirit to enhance and embrace divine guidance in soul and body. She is passionate about helping others release blocks, trust their intuition, and turn on the river of abundance so their life flows with ease and grace. www.carolynmcgee.com

Dr. Kimberly McGeorge, ND, CNH, is an expert in energy and naturopathic medicine as well as a remote viewer. She has 26 years of clinical experience. She is the bestselling author of *The Secret to Everything: Manifesting the Life You Desire NOW*. www.secrettoeverything.com

Michelle Marie McGrath is a self-love mentor who encourages childfree/childless women to write their own self-love story. She's birthed many creations under her Sacred Self brand: alchemical oils, self-love cards, and natural perfumes. She hosts the international award-nominated *Unclassified Woman* podcast. www.michellemariemcgrath.com

Jenny McKaig is the CEO, writer, and coach at JennyMcKaig.com; the international bestselling author and senior editor of *Empowering Women to Succeed*; and a certified Awakening Coach. She is an award-winning writer who empowers with transformational tools. She also loves surfing, yoga, and her husband, Shawn.

Judy A. McNutt, author and founder of *The Soul Created Life*, offers guidance to those who want to find their soul-centered happiness, creative expression, and purpose. With 25 years' experience as an artist, intuitive healer, and consultant, she mentors people to express their soul's desires and to live a fulfilling life. www.judymcnutt.com

Giuliana Melo aspires to inspire. She loves life, God, and her family. She spends her days spreading love and light and helping others heal. She is a cancer survivor who is passionate about medicine, non-traditional healing, and angel therapy. She has been married for 28 years and has one 17-year-old son. www.giulianamelo.com

Mary Meston, CHPC, MA, SHRM-SCP, is an inspiring coach, speaker, and success strategist. As a high-performance expert, her practical, informative, and interactive processes enable her clients to elevate their level of freedom, meaning, joy, and happiness in all areas of their lives. For great content, go to www.2SoarSolutions.com.

Erin Miller is a life coach, NLP Practitioner, healer, and writer from Zest Holistic Coaching who aims to live life with excitement, anticipation, and energy! Her passion and purpose is to guide others to find their true calling and zest for life! www.zestholisticcoaching.com

Susan Mullen is a gifted intuitive and a frequent radio guest on intuitive living. She is a certified intuitive coach and founder of the Pilot Light Intuitive Sessions, where she lovingly guides clients to their next right step. She is a writer and a passionate animal advocate. www.SusanTMullen.com

Malaika Murphy-Sierra is a psychology major and actress at Stanford University and is passionate about connecting with others through improv. She has found meaning through coordinating Camp Kesem, a non-profit camp for children whose parents have been affected by cancer. To find out more or donate, visit www.campkesem.org/stanford.

Viknesvari Piche Muthu is a passionate creator of life with an open and brave heart. She works with men and women who are struggling to find their authentic voices by building creative connections to their "heArts" so that they can love the FULLness of who they really are and live empowered lives. www.heartflow.in

Heather Nardi is a healer, a flower and gemstone essence practitioner, and a holistic coach. After discovering holistic modalities to help her child, her soul's work is to help families who are struggling with mental-health disorders work through the pain using these remedies as well.

Lucy V. Nefstead lives in northern Wisconsin with her dog, Sam. She is a retired English, Speech, and Theatre teacher who is co-chair of an animal rescue, president of retired teachers, on Wisconsin's board of directors, and serves on state committees. Spirituality is an integral part of her life.

Janet G. Nestor, MA, LPC, DCEP (Masters in Mental Health Counseling, Licensed Professional Counselor, Diplomate: Comprehensive Energy Psychology) is a teacher and holistic healing facilitator with over 40 years' experience helping individuals, groups, and veterans. She is known by her peers as a distinguished expert in stress reduction.

Lynne Newman is an occupational therapist, coach, and highly sensitive mother who has found her purpose in supporting families to shift significant challenges and frustrations of everyday life so they feel centered, no matter the situation. www.lynnenewman.com

Hue Anh Nguyen, Master Energy Healer, has pioneered a powerful process for correcting reverse polarity. By detecting blockages and negative energies within the body and energy field, she is able to transform negative energies in order to re-balance her clients' natural positive flow. Receive a free "I am Love" meditation at www.polarity4harmony.com.

Nadean Ollech is a spiritual life coach with a degree in Religion. She is the founder of Healed Daisy Intuitive Guidance, where she helps women connect with themselves, learn to recognize their guidance, and live their best life.

Karen Packwood is a clairvoyant, healer, and #1 bestselling author who loves to work with people who have suffered extreme trauma in life. Her mission is to prove that it is possible to come back to a place of joy no matter how broken someone may have been. karenpackwood@gmail.com

Wendyanne Pakulsky is very passionate about the importance of finding your light within and using that light to guide you towards the Light, no matter what is happening in your own life.

Lisa Anna Palmer launched her business as a career and leadership coach and Certified Passion Test® Facilitator in 2011 and has helped hundreds of people gain greater clarity about what is most important and leap out of their comfort zone.

Tanya Penny, Abundance Catalyst and Freedom Coach, teaches and supports healers, coaches, and women-on-purpose to break through fear and self-doubt, and heal illness and trauma so they can step into self-confidence and create a healthy body and a balanced lifestyle filled with passion and purpose. www.tanyapenny.com

Lupe Ramirez Peterkin remains strong in her recovery from alcoholism. She uses her experiences with God to inspire others. Time spent dancing, writing, and visiting New York keeps her passion alive. She is writing her musician father's autobiography and shares her life's adventures with her husband, children, and grandsons.

Claire Peters' true passion is to serve. Her moments of grace come when she makes a difference in the lives of the women she meets via her books, motivational speaking, life coaching, and Paparazzi Jewelry sales! And all of this at age 76!

Katie Power is an author, spiritual messenger, and intuitive healer who loves channeling Spirit and helping others to connect with the infinite wisdom of their soul. With a BS in Nutrition, she is passionate about leading a healthy and well-balanced life. Visit www.KatiePower.com to learn more.

Annie Price is a spiritual healer who uses heartfelt, intuitive guidance to empower others in their divine purpose and in living the joyful expression of their soul. Her Fearless, Fun & Free™ program assists in permanent weight release. She has a BA in Psychology and loves being Mom to three teenagers. www.SoulSoaring.com

Donna S. Priesmeyer is a media professional who enjoys many creative pursuits, including: gardening; traveling; writing; creating art; and spending time with her husband, family, friends and pets. She is the publisher of a spiritually-based website featuring consciousness-raising, art, music, and literature: www.LightonLife.net.

Saira Priest loves sharing joy through her books. She is the author of *Zen of Hoarding*, for clearing clutter; *Seek Joy*, a reading meditation; and *If We Were...*, a children's book. Find out more at www.sairapriest.com.

Kathy Proctor has been writing short stories and poetry since childhood. She works as a Barbara Brennan energy healer and incorporates her interests in yoga and meditation in her practice. She has a passion for sharing joy and possibility with others.

Sally Pullinger is a deep-trance medium who, along with her family, facilitates spiritual self-development work and holds a safe space for dynamic transformation. She helps people integrate their shadow and make a direct connection with their Higher Self and Spirit Guides. She lives in Glastonbury, England. www.deepsoulconnection.com

Lesley Pyne coaches childless women. She uses her first-hand experience and professional skills to help others own their story, heal what holds them back, and understand the meaning of what they've been through so that they can fully embrace a fulfilling life. www.LesleyPyne.co.uk

Mimi Quick is known as the "Prosperity Muse." She is a psychic business mentor and owner of the Spiritual Business Institute – a spiritual coaching and training company that empowers spirited entrepreneurs to create prosperous, aligned businesses and lives doing what they love. www.MimiQuick.com

Michelle Radomski is a mandala artist, graphic/book designer, and author. For 35 years she's created customized, inspiring designs for purpose-driven individuals and organizations. She helps her clients embrace the power of their voices, become more visible, and make a more meaningful impact in the world. www.OneVoiceCan.com

Lore Raymond founded Women as Visionaries and the Divine Dialogue Writing System™. A Peruvian shaman bestowed her the title of "chacaruna – bridge person," challenging her to help others connect to their authentic power. She serves as a spiritual tour guide, heart-centered visionary, and author. www.LoreRaymond.com

Helen Rebello is a peaceful pathfinder who provides a safe sanctuary space for heart-centred women who've lost themselves a little in serving others. She helps them reconnect to their inner light to find their way back home to themselves and to a wholehearted, aligned life. www.thetranquilpath.co.uk

Twyla Reece brings a dedication to teaching life, light, and the remembering of our divine nature. When we remember who we are, we express love and compassion to self and others. As well as being a Unity minister, she is a HeartMath® Coach and HeartMath® Resiliency Trainer. www.twylareece.com

Haley Reese is a Holistic Health and Happiness Coach who specializes in empowering women who are tired of drowning in depression and are ready to find their happiness so they can live a life filled with passion and freedom! She invites you to connect with her at www.HaleyReese.com.

Alexa Rehrl lives near Seattle, Washington, with her husband and cat. Currently, she spends her time studying for her meditation teacher certification. Her philosophy is "Kindfulness" – engaging and cherishing life in the present moment through compassion, playfulness, and love. www.alexarehrl.com

Brenda Reiss loves coaching women to find their "happy" again in life. Using her wisdom and certifications as a Radical Forgiveness® coach, Soul Journeys® Akashic Records consultant, and Heal Your Money Story coach, she helps them unpack life's baggage that weighs them down to re-create a life they love. www.therecreationcoach.com

Jovon Renee is an Empowerment Coach/Transformation Catalyst who helps women find their personal power through self discovery, overcoming their fears and limitations, and remembering who they truly are in order to create the life of their dreams. She would love to connect with you at www.jovonrenee.com.

Lisa "The Link" Rizzo is a businesswoman, mother, wife, and full-time spiritual medium. She lives in Toronto, Canada, with her wonderful husband and three children. She would love to share her gift with you and can be contacted here: lisathelink@gmail.com.

Rev. Aliza Bloom Robinson is a master spiritual facilitator, speaker, author, ordained Unity Minister, and founder of www.Divine-Awakening.org. She has walked a Spirit-led life through both the valleys and peaks of experience. She facilitates the discovery of peace, purpose, passion, and fulfillment in living a dream-filled life.

Tara L. Robinson is the publisher of *Whole Living Journal*, host of *Waves of a New Age* on WAIF 88.3FM, event producer of Infusion, life coach, workshop leader, and inspirational speaker. Her book *The Ultimate Risk* will be published by Hay House in 2017. www.TaraLRobinson.com

Faye Rogers is an animal communicator, visionary, writer, intuitive healer, and qualified teacher of the Diana Cooper School in Angels and Ascension. She works with animals and people to bring more harmony and awareness. She is passionate about humanity and empowering others. www.animalcommunication-newzealand.com

Isabella Rose is a certified aromatherapist, angel card reader, and angel energy healer. Her passions include holistic healing, helping all beings, and creating art of all kinds. She loves to spend time with those dear to her heart and in the outdoors connecting with nature. She knows dreams really do come true! www.asabovesobelowhh.net

Denise L. Roseland is a business strategist who shows female founders, entrepreneurs, and changemakers how to navigate the space between where their business is now and where they want it to go. www.changemakerconsulting.com

Sharon Rosen is a writer, healer, teacher, and guide for women hungry to find their balance within life's chaos. She's especially passionate about helping those who've experienced a life-altering diagnosis or loss to reclaim their footing and live with presence, hope, and grace. www.heartofselfcare.com

Susan Parker Rosen resides in Delaware with her two dogs, two cats, and her husband of approximately one year. She is a writer and a real estate agent. Her self-published work includes *The Bastard Child* and a new short-story series, the first being *Alone in Rehoboth Beach*.

Dr. Maria T. Rothenburger, PhD, LPC, is a therapist and coach specializing in infertility, adoption, and loss. She's weathered the infertility storm and now lives happily with her husband and three sons (one human, two canines). She sings, hikes, and makes mad dashes through thunderstorms, because…moments are awesome.

Sharon Rothstein is a bestselling author, contributing to the internationally acclaimed *365 Ways to Connect with Your Soul.* She is a Feng Shui Practitioner, having studied under Professor Thomas Lin Yun. She studies, teaches, and writes about Spirit. She may be contacted at SharonRothstein@aol.com.

Farah Joy Rupani is a former HR Professional with over 15 years' experience in corporate America. She is a Certified Professional Life Coach, specializing in Law of Attraction and mind-body healing. Passionate about transforming lives, she powerfully guides clients to release mental resistance and manifest miracles from the inside out. www.farahjoy.com

Cynthia L. Ryals is a bestselling author, coach, speaker, and spiritual messenger who guides you in rediscovering your highest self and life's purpose. She believes that reconnecting to our soul is key to consciously creating a life that feels good, honors our truth and, ultimately, heals the world. www.myevolvedlife.com

Milada Sakic is a transformational teacher, intuitive healer, and expert astrologer. She teaches advanced astrology courses for the Canadian Association for Astrological Education (CAAE) and teaches the Akashic Records through The Soul Journeys® Akashic Records Certification Program. www.miladasakic.com

Nishani Sakizlis is a 39-year-old woman of Sri-Lankan birth who has lived in England for the majority of her life. She holds a PhD in Engineering and is happily married to a Greek man and has two young children.

Teresa Salhi is a success coach and certified Law of Attraction trainer. She is passionate about helping women close the gap from where they are now to where they really want to be. She is the founder of www.EmpowerTheDream.com, providing women life-enhancing resources.

Qatana Samanen has walked the transformative path of imagery for over 30 years. She remains awed by the power of spirit guides to help us create lives of greater peace, joy, and love. She works with people individually, in workshops, and in teleworkshops. Learn more at www.personaltotempole.com.

Marcia Sandels is a former public-school teacher. Her interests include spiritual and inspirational writing, and she is the author of the book *Living Beyond the Veil: How My Mystical Incidences May Help You and/or Your Rainbow or Crystal Children.* She is also a world traveler and fine-arts enthusiast. Find her on Facebook at "Marcia Sandels, Writer."

Lori Santo is an artist, poet, writer, storyteller, dreamweaver, soul-recovery artist, life coach, ancient priestess, highly sensitive being, creativity maven, lover of life, and spirit. She is on a mission to bring light to the darkest caverns of our existence through writing, artistry, and creative soul recovery.

Sylvie A. Savoie has been successfully striving to make this life the best one ever! She enjoys life and retirement alongside her husband and their feline friend in Mont Tremblant, Canada. She is passionate about spreading positivity everywhere. She is the artist behind the internationally known Sylvie Angeline Collection. www.sylvieangelinecollection.com

Susan Elizabeth Schoemmell's journey as a seeker has led her to Czechoslovakia, Italy, Ireland, Scotland, and Hawaii in search of her authentic self. She is grateful for the grace and blessings that have come her way and hopes to be a light on the path for other seekers. Sesangel@simplesite.com

Christine Schwarzer is an awesome human being who is kind and inspires others. She is a coach and a revolutionary leader who guides others via her workshops, retreats, writing, and speaking. To receive her free gift, without having to enter a night train, simply go here: www.christineschwarzer.com/grace.

Farooq Shah is a writer, thought leader, and spiritual teacher. He was born near Chicago and has traveled the world. At age two, he was diagnosed with Juvenile Rheumatoid Arthritis. For the next 30 years, he endured physical and emotional struggles. After a near-death experience, he discovered the healing power of choice and love.

Pooja Shende is an entrepreneur who believes in Mahatma Gandhi's quote: "Be the change you wish to see in the world." Lotus Soul 9 is her initiative where she guides people in increasing their self-awareness, identifying their strengths and weaknesses, and identifying the potential that already exists within them. www.lotussoul9.com

Russell R. Shippee is an author, speaker, and coach who enables, empowers, and inspires people to live the life they envision. He is the author of *Our Journey is Our Work: Creating My Obituary*. Contact Russell at www.russellshippee.com.

Maura Smith is a fulfillment coach who helps people find clarity and live deeply. Through her unique programs, which combine intuitive energy healing, training, and coaching, clients learn to invest their time in what really matters to them and express themselves through a lifestyle that makes them feel truly alive. www.maurasmith.com

Marianne Soucy is a bestselling author, podcast host, and coach. At HealingPetLoss.com, she connects pet owners with their beloved pets in the afterlife. At GiveYourDreamWings.com, she helps healers and spiritual entrepreneurs manifest their dreams while staying grounded and connected to their soul and to spirit.

H. Michelle Spaulding is a visionary whose soul purpose is to lead, teach, create, and inspire others in the manifestation of their dreams, goals, and desires. She is an entrepreneur, certified dream coach, teacher, expressive arts facilitator, and storyteller who expresses her creativity through the textile and fiber arts. www.Craftydivacottage.com

Marie Spencer-Rowland is a Women's Empowerment Coach and creator of the *Live Fearless!* programme. She would love to help you kickstart your journey by giving you this fun guide to get you super excited about your life: www.mariespencerrowland.com.

Jeanette St. Germain is a spiritual alchemist with a passion for empowering others to embrace their own inner radiance. She offers intuitive guidance, energetic healing, and public events that include inspired angelic messages, clarity of life purpose, and deep rejuvenation through all layers of the mind, body, and spirit. www.sophiastouch.com

Rani St. Pucchi is the founder and designer of the world-renowned bridal house, St. Pucchi, and the author of the upcoming memoir, *Unveiled: A Celebrity Fashion Designer's Story*, and two relationship books: *The SoulMate Checklist* and *Seven Types of Men to Avoid*. www.ranistpucchi.com

Cynthia Starborn is an inspirational author, teacher, and soul guide. She offers transformative classes and private consultations, based on the Akashic Records, for adults and children. Fluent in French, Spanish, and English, she loves helping you transcend challenges and tap into the magic of life. www.CynthiaStarborn.com

Lisa A. Stariha, RD, MA ABS, is a body-empowerment coach who is passionate about empowering women to embrace their authentic beauty and care for their bodies with acceptance and love. Her whole-person health approach is designed to care for all facets of the woman: the physical, mental, emotional, and spiritual. www.LisaStariha.com

Star Staubach is a speaker, *Huffington Post* blogger, bestselling author, light reflecter, "BS" excavator, life coach, world traveler, busy mom of three, and madly in love with her husband, Russell. She is on a mission to balance the truth of our mystical world and our physical experience. www.igniteradiance.com

Kim Steadman is a self-care mentor, author, and doodler who helps you say YES to yourself. When your work ethic no longer honors who you are, she prayerfully encourages you to escape the traditional mold of "success" to repurpose and redesign your life. www.KimSteadman.com

Autumne Stirling is a mother, writer, and advocate for mental-health awareness. A survivor of childhood trauma, she lives with complex mental-health issues and is grateful to have received extraordinary treatment. She is currently working at a yoga studio and plans to continue writing and assisting those with PTSD.

Alison M. Stokes is a native of Dublin, Ireland. With her online spiritual practice, www.silversoultherapy.com®, she combines her healing and counselling skills to treat people (and their pets) on a holistic level. Being in nature and with animals is her passion, and she's looking to live by the sea.

Sheila Sutherland is a personal-empowerment coach, podcaster, and founder of Reignite Your Purpose. She aspires to help people reconnect with who they are at their core so they can move beyond their past experiences to ignite their inner superhero and live their lives more vibrantly. www.reigniteyourpurpose.com

Vicki Talvi-Cole is a LightWeaver, energy tracker, intuitive healer, teacher, and channel who navigates others in living their life as an adventure, empowered with their natural Self expression, activated by their Spirit and Soul journey. "Solutions" are offered by phone, in person, or by partnering with the WindHorse Tribal Herd. www.VickiTalvi-Cole.com

Stella Tassone is a loving soul from Australia who loves to love. She is a mother, certified angel-card and Reiki practitioner, and massage practitioner. She currently works with children who have special needs and enjoys assisting people in remembering who they are. www.stellatassone.com

Ambika Talwar is an India-born author, healer, and artist whose ecstatic style makes her poetry a bridge to other worlds. Author of *Creative Resonance: Poetry – Elegant Play, Elegant Change* and *4 Stars & 25 Roses*, she is published in various journals and delivers powerful healings. She lives in Los Angeles. www.creativeinfinities.com

Gabrielle Taylor is a psychotherapist and a transformational specialist. Her passion is to mentor visionary, sensitive women leaders to shine their light brightly and share their gifts with the world. www.gabriellebtaylor.com

Ioana Adriana Terec is a born philosopher. Moving to the United States from Romania on her own at the age of 22, she is a true testament to the power of dreaming. A Master Empowerment Coach with the S.W.A.T. Institute, she is a witty and profound writer and speaker. www.IoanaAdrianaTerec.com

Michelle R. Terry is a dietitian who keeps people healthy through prevention and chronic-disease management. When she's not working or wrangling her two children, she is writing stories and managing an unruly garden. She shares her imperfect life at www.mamamickterry.com.

Lori Thiessen lives in Alberta, Canada, where she works as an architectural tech during the day, moonlights as a writer, and is mom to five almost-grown-up kids. She is a certified NLP Practitioner, Toastmaster, and runner. www.couragefinder.com

Bland Tyree is a transformational educator, spiritual guide, transpersonal psychotherapist, and co-founder of Whole Hearted Living. She is passionate about supporting awakening women to embody the wild wisdom of their feminine soul and live from the limitless love of an awakened heart. www.wholeheartedliving.org

Julia Van Der Sluys has found her way back to Source and is relearning her spiritual skills and knowledge in order to inspire, empower, teach, and help those around her do the same and come back to a place of positivity, love, light, and a higher vibration. www.ariabellarises.wix.com/ariabellarises

Chantal Vanderhaeghen's purpose is to lead women to rediscover their own power in their personal and business lives. She delivers this through her business, Unfold Your Freedom. She is also a philanthropist, meditation and mindfulness teacher, Reiki Master, and owner of the Franc Essential skincare brand. www.unfoldyourfreedom.com.au

Allen Vaysberg is a Life Recalibration Expert and creator of the SEAMLESS method who facilitates people's transition from unfulfilled and stressed to doing what they love and being at peace. He speaks on life purpose, career change, and work-life balance and runs online programs helping people recalibrate their lives. www.allenvaysberg.com

Lexi Gaia Verano is an angel intuitive, holistic practitioner, and the founder of Archangel Wellness Integrated Health. Living in beautiful Vancouver, Canada, she is the proud mom of two sons. Her life passions are family, the outdoors, holistic wellness, and connecting others with their own angels. www.archangelwellness.ca

Michelle McDonald Vlastnik, Mystic Intuitive, Healer, and Certified Personal Trainer, is passionate about helping each of us rediscover our Authentic Self and healing Mother Earth through that vibrational frequency shift. She lives in Arizona with her husband. They have 3 children and 5 grandchildren. www.facebook.com/HighEnergySixSensoryPersonalTraining

Linda Voogd is a holistic therapist, addictions counselor, and adjunct professor. She offers ongoing workshops and life coaching. She helps others create healthy beliefs, attitudes, and thought patterns that propel them toward personal transformation. She has over 30 years of experience and runs a private practice in northern New Jersey.

Catherine Walters, an intuitive lifestyle coach, hypnotherapist, Reiki Master/instructor, and yoga teacher, assists people who are overachievers and over-givers to nurture themselves first and transform low self-worth, stress, overwhelm and inner-child wounds into balance, passion, and joy! www.guidedchange.com

Rozlyn Warren, CHt, ESLC, directly engages your inner guidance in your Akashic Records to reunite your Soul parts, bringing expansion and healing. She is an Akashic Records Intuitive, energy healer, bestselling author, and publisher of *Lean Toward Happy Magazine* on Apple and Android. www.LeanTowardHappy.com

Suzie Welstead experienced a lot of physical abuse from her mother as a child, and she left home at 17 feeling unloved and unwanted. She has made it her mission in life to help women love, forgive, and accept themselves. www.purearts.co.uk/suzie-welstead-mindset-coaching.html

Dr. Robert D. White is a mental-health practitioner who is dedicated to working with children, adolescents, and adults. His passion is to guide people in recognizing and harnessing their inner truths through self-mastery. His research and areas of expertise are in human capital and self-development. www.rdwassoc.com

Simone Wiedenhöft loves to bring more freedom into this world with her intuitive work, writing, speaking, and living. Freeing energies in people and places makes her incredibly happy. It is her way to contribute to peace and joy in this world. You can meet her at www.simonewiedenhoeft.com.

Brenda M. Wiener's mission is to inspire, educate, and equip overwhelmed women to live a life of health, harmony, faith, and prosperity. She is the owner of Pathways To Harmony and is a Christian Licensed Spiritual Healer, Certified Natural Health Professional, Zyto Elite Technician, and Certified Chi-To-Be! Coach. www.PathwaysToHarmony.com

Heather Wiest is beyond blessed to love, serve, and inspire the community as a yoga teacher, Reiki Master, and Licensed Clinical Social Worker. Her therapeutically oriented yoga sessions are engaging and rejuvenating, leaving one feeling balanced and inspired. Restore your body. Renew your mind. Refresh your spirit. www.loveserveinspire.com

Monica Wilcox is the spiritual columnist for *FemCentral.com*. She's a featured blogger for numerous sites and magazines. When her fingers aren't tapping laptop keys, she enjoys exploring dark corners and dank basements. www.twitter.com/Monica_Wilcox

Ty Will grew up in Billings, Montana where she enjoyed camping, fishing, and just having fun! In 2013, she published a military biography, *The Female Veteran*. In 2015, she co-authored *Superwoman Myths: Break the Rules of Silence and Speak UP Your Truth.*

Cat Williford, MCC, has helped thousands of women move from perfectionism and fear into experiencing deep self-love, authenticity, and success on their terms for the past 22 years. Founder of *The Modern Goddess* and *The Authenticity Advantage*, she is a coaching-profession pioneer, speaker, writer, and frequent expert on TV, radio, and print. www.catwilliford.com

Josie Wood is a Licensed HeartMath Coach, Counsellor, and Therapist with over 20 years' experience of helping people transform and live richly happy lives through accessing their own inner healer, wise guide, and best of friends…their heart. www.heartful-living.com

Pami Woodruff believes in empowering others to discover their inner creativity, be who they were meant to be, and fulfill their lifelong dreams. She blogs and creates videos as "Make It With Pam" and teaches long-forgotten self-reliance skills at www.TheSchoolofLostArts.com.

Jody Wootton is an amazing person. She is a wife, mom, daughter, sister, friend, U.S. Armed Forces Veteran, BCBG Max Azria sales associate, speaker, author, philanthropist, and coach. Her motto is that life is more than about you or me; it is about who you will inspire. www.nailswithjody.jamberry.com

Holly Worton is the business mindset coach for women entrepreneurs who want to take their business to the next level. She helps them release their fear of visibility, set aligned prices for their products and services, and take inspired action to grow their business. www.hollyworton.com

Karen L. Wythe, a lifelong Spiritualist, is dedicated to living life with passion, enthusiasm, and zest. As a Life Transformation Coach, she helps others do the same. She is an ordained minister, medium, healer, workshop presenter, writer, and fiber artist who is married to her best friend. www.enrichingliferesources.com

Yiye Zhang, Intuitive and Abundance Guide, was "made in China" and shipped to the UK at 17. She achieved a Physics degree, chartered-accounting qualification, and launched her spiritual business all by 28. She decodes your soul purpose and simplifies your path to abundance. For practical tips, visit www.yourlifexpression.com.

Joan B. Zietlow, BSN, RN, CHHC, AADP, MBA, is a health coach who helps others thrive through health optimization. She inspires and educates while dispelling myths such as "it's hard to be healthy after 40." Her clients enjoy energy, joy, health, confidence, peace, and answers to long-time health concerns. www.vibranthealthandhealing.com

Suzanne Zupancic is a Registered Yoga Teacher/E-RYT200/RYT500 and creator of *Your Empowered Self* workshops and training modules. Her classes focus on alignment, intention, a little humor, and a lot of realism. She offers support and loyalty in the hopes that others may come to realize their own strength. www.unwindyogallc.com

Contributor Index

For your convenience, we have listed each contributor in alphabetical order by last name and have included the page number(s) of their piece(s). We hope that this makes finding your favorite co-authors easy!

Acknowledgments

T his is our second book in this special series, and we honestly weren't sure what to expect. The loving contributors in our first book and the collective experience that we shared set the bar really high. We had no idea if we would be able to match that magic again. Thankfully, we not only matched it with this book, but we surpassed it. And that's because of the wonderful souls who joined us as co-authors and shared their hearts in such a deep way. We want to thank each of you (many who were part of our first book, too!) for believing in our vision to create books that inspire, to give all of us a voice, and to share something loving and soulful with those who are ready to receive it. This book exists because of you, and we love knowing that the friendships we've made throughout this journey will continue to grow. As you know, our coming together goes way beyond this book – our souls are now connected, which is so special.

From Jodi: My life began the moment Dan walked into it in 2001, and everything that I do is an extension of our love. Thank you so much for being my rock, my best friend, my double helix, my everything. It is such a gift that we have created a life where we get to spend all of our time together while living at the beach and creating soulful books such as this. Thank you for being a perfect partner in life and also in business. You are my everything, and I love you infinitely.

I would like to thank my soul for asking me to move to the beach and then staying on me until I did. Everything changed once we got here, and I am so grateful to have found my forever home.

Thank you, as always, to my angels and loved ones on the other side who continue to cheer me on as I put their ideas into motion. This is one of them, and I can feel their excitement now that it's here!

From Dan: Thank you to Jodi for making my entire life a moment of grace…and infinite love. I am so blessed to have you as my partner in love, in life, and in everything (including this book!). You are everything I've ever been searching for…and more! You make everything worthwhile, you are the reason for everything I do and everything I am, and you inspire me each and every day just by being the amazing person you are. You are my soul's home. I love you forever.

I also want to acknowledge and thank all the people and forces (mysterious or otherwise) that have created so many moments of grace throughout my life. These beautiful, miraculous, life-affirming experiences were the inspiration for this book – and they've also made my life a joyous, magical adventure!

And thank you to *everyone* who has shared their moments of grace – in this book or elsewhere. Hearing your stories renews my faith in this awe-inspiring universe and helps to reinforce the message that *Grace Happens!* The more we realize we are surrounded by grace, the more we expect it…and the more we receive it!

Lastly, we would like to thank you, the reader. We know how many books are out there and what a moment of grace it is that you're holding this one in your hands right now. We hope that it has fed your soul, moved you in some way, and helped you feel infinitely connected to all that is. May it continue to bring joy to your heart and grace-filled moments to your life!

Other Books in This Series

This is the second book in our bestselling *365 Book Series*, and we would love to invite you to learn more about the books and join us as a contributing author, a reader, or both!

365 Ways to Connect with Your Soul

In this #1 international bestselling book, over 200 beautiful souls came together to share how they connect with their own souls with the hopes that it will help you connect with yours as well. It's a wonderful addition to your spiritual practice!

365 Life Shifts: Pivotal Moments That Changed Everything

This book will contain 365 personal stories of life-changing moments that inspired, uplifted, shook us to our core, got us back on track (or onto a new track altogether), and led us toward our true selves. Available in February 2017.

You can learn more about our current and upcoming books from this soulful series here: www.365bookseries.com.

Made in the USA
San Bernardino, CA
29 June 2016